THE STRUGGLE TO UNDERSTAND ISAIAH

AS CHRISTIAN SCRIPTURE

The Struggle to Understand Isaiah
as Christian Scripture

Brevard S. Childs

WILLIAM B. EERDMANS PUBLISHING COMPANY
GRAND RAPIDS, MICHIGAN / CAMBRIDGE, U.K.

Regis College Library
15 ST. MARY STREET
TORONTO, ONTARIO, CANADA
M4Y 2R5

WITHDRAWN

BS
1515.52
.C48
2004

© 2004 Wm. B. Eerdmans Publishing Co.
All rights reserved

Wm. B. Eerdmans Publishing Co.
255 Jefferson Ave. S.E., Grand Rapids, Michigan 49503 /
P.O. Box 163, Cambridge CB3 9PU U.K.

Printed in the United States of America

08 07 06 05 04   7 6 5 4 3 2 1

Library of Congress Cataloging-in-Publication Data

Childs, Brevard S.
The struggle to understand Isaiah as Christian scripture /
Brevard S. Childs.
p.   cm.
Includes bibliographical references and index.
ISBN 0-8028-2761-6 (alk. paper)
1. Bible. O.T. Isaiah — Criticism, interpretation, etc. — History
I. Title.

BS1515.52.C48   2004
224′.106′09 — dc22

2004047242

www.eerdmans.com

This volume is dedicated to Ann,
my wife of fifty years and closest friend,
who alone understands the full extent
of the physical struggle involved in writing this book

Contents

Preface

Several factors have been at work in the shaping of this book. First, I have recently finished writing a technical, modern commentary on the book of Isaiah. The task of treating the entire book of sixty-six chapters was enormous, but in addition, the commentary had necessitated restricting the scope of the exposition. This entailed omitting the history of interpretation and relegating many important hermeneutical problems to the periphery of the exegesis. After the commentary had been completed, I was painfully aware that many of the central theological and hermeneutical questions in which I was most interested had not been adequately addressed.

Second, I have continued to reflect on several important, but perplexing theological problems. If one affirms the Christian confession that scripture has been given for the divine guidance of the church, then the nature of this role assigned to the Bible must be pondered. Can one still speak of a divine coercion or pressure exerted by the text upon its readers? Is there any concord between doctrinal claims regarding scripture and its actual effects on the church throughout its history? Many moderns have described the use of the Bible as a "map of misreading." How should one respond to such a challenge? The difficult questions remain in evaluating this history of reception in terms of truth and error. Can one be misled from the outset by posing the problem in terms of the use and abuse of the Bible, as Dennis Nineham once attempted? Unfortunately, there have been surprisingly few books addressing these problems that are of the quality of M. Kähler's *Geschichte der Bibel in ihrer Wirkung auf die Kirche* or J. A. Möhler's *Die Einheit in der Kirche*.

Third, I am concerned to pursue the issue as to whether there is such a thing as the Christian church's exegetical tradition. When one considers the enormous cultural diversity reflected within the church, the radical changes in understanding effected by historical events over the last two millennia, and the powerful influences of the scientific revolutions transforming every aspect of human life, the question appears to many to be either irrelevant or meaningless. Nevertheless, Christians continue to confess in their creeds that the church is a divine creation, guided by the hand of God, and is an actual historical reality of flesh and blood: "I believe in the holy catholic church." How has scripture functioned as a means of divine guidance throughout its history? How does one understand the changes in its interpretations throughout the ages? Has the church been able to learn also from its misuse of scripture?

Fourth, after working for several months on this project, I discovered a major hermeneutical problem that increasingly cried out for attention. One component of exegesis common to all the Church Fathers has been the application of figurative meanings — call it allegory. I became convinced that unless one could gain a new understanding of allegory, the enterprise of recovering a usable exegetical Christian tradition was doomed from the outset. To put it bluntly: for better or worse, allegory is constitutive of patristic interpretation. But how then is one to proceed when standing at the beginning of the twenty-first century?

Fifth, I have been stimulated by reading J. F. A. Sawyer's book, *The Fifth Gospel*. He is an old friend whose acquaintance goes back forty years, to our time as students together in Jerusalem. His book is filled with learning and insight. Nevertheless, I remain basically dissatisfied with his analysis of the history of the interpretation of the book of Isaiah, and I realize just how different is our understanding of this history. What I miss is a serious engagement with the impact of this prophetic book on the shaping of the doctrine, liturgy, and practice of the church, especially as emerged from the exegetical reflections on Isaiah by the greatest theologians of the church. I do not deny that cultural factors were always present in shaping its reception, but Sawyer's emphasis on the misuse of the book seems to drown out its major role as a truthful tradent of the gospel from the period of the New Testament to the present.

Lastly, I am very conscious of the great confusion in the church generated by an endless number of conflicting approaches for reading the Bible. Not only has the subject been heavily politicized both on the right and the left, but the field has become awash with a parade of fads, each promising major advances in personal and communal enlightenment. Unfortunately, the confusion is just as prevalent on the academic level as among the laity. However, in spite of this bleak picture, the Bible continues to stimulate every new generation of serious readers in unexpected ways and in unlikely places. The power to transform lives, to open new vistas of hope, and to offer the gift of divine reconciliation are part of the unexpected surprises inviting its readers to an encounter with a gracious and forgiving God.

My purpose in writing this book is not immediately to offer yet another approach to the Bible. Rather, I have chosen to trace through the centuries the different ways in which great Christian theologians have struggled to understand the book of Isaiah as the church's sacred scripture, that is, as a vehicle for communicating the Christian gospel. This volume does not purport to be just another history of interpretation. Within recent years there have been numerous such learned tomes (e.g., Reventlow, Saebø). Generally, these efforts to be comprehensive in scope have often pushed hermeneutical reflections into the background. I hope in my study that the hermeneutical issues will be understood as primary.

I have chosen to focus on the book of Isaiah for several reasons. First of all, many of Christianity's greatest scholars, from both the East and West, have written commentaries or extensive treatises on Isaiah (Justin, Irenaeus, Jerome, Thomas, Luther, Calvin). Then again, most of the difficult exegetical problems surrounding the relation of the Old and New Testaments have found a focus on Isaiah. Finally, by limiting the scope of the analysis to one book, an interpreter is able to penetrate more deeply into the subject matter and not be forced to retreat into generalities or in drawing only a few broad lines.

I have concentrated my attention on Christian theologians and their struggle with interpreting the Bible largely within the context of the church. Yet everywhere in such a study the presence and contribution of Jewish scholars are evident. Often their innovations were crucial in evoking major shifts in the direction of Christian exegesis (e.g., Rashi). Indeed, the major contributions of Nicholas of Lyra in the fourteenth century was in introducing Jewish exegetical traditions to a largely ignorant Christian audience. Nevertheless, to treat the history of Jewish biblical scholarship would require at least another volume and would demand someone equipped with expertise and knowledge beyond this author's capacity.

I have tried to keep my focus on those critical questions raised in this preface. Is there a "family resemblance" that emerges from this analysis of many generations of Christian biblical study? Are there any parameters that identify exegesis as Christian? How do successive generations of expositors exert critical judgment in rejecting, correcting, and enriching exegetical moves made by their predecessors in order to address different audiences and changing historical conditions?

Only at the conclusion of my history of interpretation will I attempt to offer my own theological reflections on what is to be learned from this historical perspective and what will be helpful for the study of the Bible as Christian scripture by the church in today's world.

Bibliography

Kähler, Martin. *Geschichte der Bibel in ihrer Wirkung auf die Kirche.* In *Aufsätze zur Bibelfrage,* edited by Ernst Kähler, pp. 131-288. Reprint, Munich: Kaiser Verlag, 1967.

Möhler, J. A. *Die Einheit in der Kirche oder das Princip des Katholizismus.* Tübingen: H. Laupp, 1825, reprint, Köln: Jacob Hegner, 1957.

Nineham, D. E. *The Use and Abuse of the Bible: A Study of the Bible in an Age of Rapid Cultural Change.* London: SPCK, 1978.

Reventlow, Henning. *Epochen der Bibelauslegung.* 4 vols. Munich: Beck, 1990-2001.

Saebø, M. ed. *Hebrew Bible/Old Testament: The History of Its Interpretation,* Part 1. Göttingen: Vandenhoeck & Ruprecht, 1996.

Sawyer, J. F. A. *The Fifth Gospel: Isaiah in the History of Christianity.* Cambridge: Cambridge University Press, 1986.

1

The Early Reception of the Hebrew Bible:
The Septuagint and the New Testament

I. The Role of the Septuagint

In his recent book *The Septuagint as Christian Scripture,* Martin Hengel speaks of the Septuagint not only as a "unique linguistic monument . . . , but it also constitutes the first complete and pre-Christian commentary to the Old Testament" (p. xi). Of course, from the very inception of Christianity the dependency of the New Testament upon the Jewish scriptures — later termed the Old Testament — was fully evident. Moreover, even an initial cursory reading of the New Testament reflects the overwhelming usage of the Greek translation of the biblical text. Because the authoritative Hebrew scriptures of Israel were filtered through a collection of Greek translations, it is obvious that one must first deal with the characteristics of the Septuagint before turning to the Christian appropriation of the Jewish scriptures through the medium of translation.

1. The Study of the Septuagint in England during the Nineteenth Century

The first comprehensive attempt at establishing a critical Septuagint was made by Robert Holmes and James Parson in a five-volume edition (1798-1827). However, it was H. B. Swete's three-volume popular edition (1887-94), which generally followed the text of Codex Vaticanus, that greatly stimulated a wider interest in the Septuagint. In this same period scholars also included Field, Thackeray, Ottley, and Hatch. Swete's edition was shortly to be followed by the beginning of the monumental larger Cambridge Septuagint edited by Brooke, McLean, and Thackeray in 1906. Along with these advances of English scholarship came a parallel project in Germany, generally designated as the Göttingen edition, which was initially conceived by P. de Lagarde. In this early period the major interest fell on the textual critical problems of employing the Greek translation for the recovery of the original Hebrew.

2. The Expanding Scope of Modern Septuagintal Studies

Although textual criticism continued to remain on the ongoing scholarly agenda, a variety of new perspectives emerged in the succeeding decades of the twentieth century that effected a tremendous broadening of the critical enterprise. Above all, it was recognized that the Septuagint should be studied as a document in itself and not just as a witness to the Hebrew *Vorlage*. Usually two names are given much credit for stimulating research in new directions: Joseph Ziegler and I. L. Seeligmann.

In his 1934 monograph *Untersuchungen zur Septuaginta des Buches Isaias,* Ziegler began with highly sophisticated reflections on the methods employed by the translator of the Isaiah Septuagint. He sought to penetrate even to the "personality" behind the translation, not in psychological terms, but in respect to his tendencies revealed both in his preference for many special words and phrases as well as when he chose highly literal or free renderings of the text. Ziegler was attentive to the range of choices found in the Greek language for an appropriate Hebrew equivalent, and he sought to gain insight from the effect on the entire biblical passage. He illustrated his method with a detailed analysis of pluses and minuses in the Greek text and in the relation of the Greek Isaiah to other writings in the Old Testament. His final chapter was of particular importance in his broadening of the analysis in describing the Alexandrian-Egyptian background of the Greek translation and in demonstrating the Hellenistic influence in adapting its terminology in areas of agriculture, geography, clothing, and jewelry. He demonstrated that Hellenism was the medium through which the Septuagint was shaped.

In 1948, I. L. Seeligmann built on Ziegler's analysis with his *The Septuagint Version of Isaiah.* He not only refined Ziegler's methodological approach, but he moved in several new directions. He again pursued the Greek translator's techniques in relation to the Hebrew text, frequently emphasizing the freedom and daring of the translator's rendition. Of great interest was Seeligmann's attempt to date the translator's work, and to show how the translator contemporized the Hebrew text by relating it to events of Hellenistic history in the early Maccabean period after the high priest Onias had founded the temple at Leontopolis (c. 160). Finally, he sought to describe the

Greek Isaiah as a document of Jewish-Alexandrian theology. He stressed that the translator's theological *Tendenz* was apparent not only in the choice of divine terminology, but in the shaping of an entire passage. Emanuel Tov, in a recent article ("Die Septuaginta," *Mitte*, pp. 237ff.), further refined Seeligmann's method and exercised even greater caution against focusing primarily on theological matters, which were only one part of the larger picture.

The fresh interest in the critical study of the Septuagint has derived from several crucial factors. The continuing publication of the Göttingen Septuagint by an international team of specialists has provided critically reliable texts for ongoing new research. Certainly generating even more widespread excitement has been the discovery of the Dead Sea Scrolls of Qumran. For the first time a genuine history of the development of both the Hebrew and Greek text can be largely reconstructed. The effect has been an extensive broadening of questions whose answers had been previously unavailable.

A good indication of the new range of critical research on problems relating to the Septuagint can be found in Martin Hengel's *The Septuagint*. He is concerned to pursue the history of the Septuagint's development into a collection of writings increasingly claimed by the church as its authoritative scripture. He closely follows the paralleled development of the Jewish Septuagint and the parting of the ways between Judaism and Christianity, along with the growing suspicion of rabbinic Judaism toward the Septuagint because of its Christian appropriation. He next analyzes Origen's critical role in attempting to address the problem of the tension caused by the divergence of the Greek translations from the Hebrew. The tension was further exacerbated by the reception of the church of a larger canon formed by books outside the Hebrew scriptures. For the church the relation between the original Hebrew and the Greek translations continued to be largely unresolved, since the authority of the Hebrew scriptures was acknowledged by most Christians in spite of the fact that its New Testament was shaped through the filter of Hellenistic Greek translations. The history of the various Greek recensions demonstrates the continuing effort to adjust the Greek to an evolving Hebrew text (cf. Hanhart, Introduction to Hengel, *The Septuagint*, pp. 5ff.). There is also increasing evidence that the Septuagint was influenced also by Jewish Targumic traditions (cf. Chilton, *A Galilean Rabbi*).

3. The Book of Isaiah according to the Septuagint

Although the works of Ziegler and Seeligmann already demonstrated a strong focus on the Septuagint of Isaiah, there has been much new research in the last fifty years on this book. This is hardly surprising in the light of the enormous stimulus evoked by the Isaiah scrolls from Qumran.

Fortunately, the task of briefly summarizing the scope of this modern research on the Septuagint of Isaiah has been greatly facilitated by the essays edited by C. C. Broyles and C. A. Evans entitled *Writing and Reading the Scroll of Isaiah* (vol. 2, 1997). The lead articles of Eugene Ulrich and Peter Flint offer a comprehensive list and succinct description of all the published manuscripts of Isaiah from the Judean desert. There then follows a careful evaluation of the new information provided by these texts in relation to a variety of issues raised by Emanuel Tov. He argues that the great contribution of this collection of scrolls does not lie in supplying many improved textual readings to the Masoretic text, but rather in providing a whole range of information affecting the growth of the Hebrew text from its proto-Masoretic form to the particular scribal practice of the Qumran community. As a result, there is a wide consensus that the divergences between the Masoretic text and the Septuagint do not derive from a vastly different textual *Vorlage*, or from extensive redactional activity. Rather, the divergences lie in the particular and unique readings of the Greek translators, who sought to negotiate a way between respecting the semantic integrity of the Hebrew and employing a *koine* Greek idiom intelligible to a Hellenistic Jewish audience.

There then follow two articles that analyze Isaiah in the Septuagint. Arie van der Kooij (pp. 513ff.) builds directly on the foundation laid by Ziegler and Seeligmann. He first cites Ziegler in emphasizing the influence of the Hellenistic milieu of Egypt made even clearer from the study of papyri. Next he appropriates Seeligmann's insight in seeing the actualization of the Greek text to contemporary events as an attempt to update ancient prophecies, thus confirming prophetic fulfillment. Finally, citing the work of J. Koenig (*L'herméneutique analogique du Judaïsme*, 1982), he traces a form of intertextual interpretation at work both inside and outside of the book of Isaiah.

The succeeding article of S. E. Porter and B. W. R. Pearson, entitled "Isaiah through Greek Eyes" (pp. 531ff.), continues some of the same emphases of van der Kooij, but they make a valuable contribution in outlining the multiple approaches now used in Septuagintal studies. They acknowledge the continuing importance of textual criticism and the insights gained in the meaning of the translation through attention to the changing historical, sociological, and religious milieus. However, even more challenging is their formulation of a critical methodology that would seek to understand how later groups of recipients construed the text. This recognition of the importance of various levels of contextual meaning provides a new potential for extending the reach of modern interpreters in approaching the Septuagint of Isaiah.

II. The New Testament's Usage of Isaiah

The United Bible Society's Greek New Testament estimates that there are more than four hundred quotations, paraphrases, or allusions to the book of Isaiah in the New Testament. C. A. Evans ("From Gospel to Gospel," *Writing and Reading*, vol. 2, p. 651) notes the remarkably even distribution (150 from chapters 1-39; 168 from chapters 40-55; and 89 from chapters 56-66, with only a few chapters missing). The New Testament's usage of Isaiah varies greatly in terms of context, literary technique, and theological function. Certain topics are especially predominant: the fulfillment of God's eschatological promise of salvation; the identity of Jesus as Messiah, savior, and Lord; the suffering servant; the hardening of Israel; the righteousness of God; the inclusion of the Gentiles; divine reconciliation and restoration; and God's final victory. Characteristic elements of continuity and discontinuity in the New Testament's use of the Old can be illustrated in a striking manner from just two examples.

1. The Good News according to Isaiah and the New Testament

There are five passages in Isaiah in which "the good tidings" are found (40:1-11; 41:21-29; 52:7-12; 60:1-7; 61:1-11). This good news is described in terms of the promise of restoration to Israel, the exultation of Zion, a return to the land of Israel, victory over enemies, and the reign of God. The appeal to repentance is also an essential message. A crucial philological link between Isaiah and the New Testament was afforded by the Greek translation that rendered the verbal and nominal forms of the Hebrew root *bs'r* with *euangelizō* and *euangelion*: to proclaim the good tidings, the gospel.

In his excellent essay ("From Gospel to Gospel," pp. 667ff.), Evans lists some twenty passages from the three Synoptic Gospels that announce the proclamation of the good tidings and describe the multiple aspects of its coming. In each case, the New Testament's reference to the kingdom of God is matched with its Isaianic parallels. For example, Luke 6:20 = Matt. 5:3 "Blessed are you poor, for yours is the kingdom of God," cf. Isa. 61:1 "to proclaim good tidings to the poor." Matt. 11:4-5 = Luke 17:18-23: "The blind receive their sight, the lame walk, lepers are cleansed — the poor have good tidings proclaimed to them," cf. Isa. 35:5-6: "Then the eyes of the blind shall be opened, the ears of the deaf unstopped." Matt. 16:19: "I will give you the keys of the kingdom of heaven, and whatever you bind on earth shall be bound in heaven, and whatever you loose on earth shall be loosed in heaven," cf. Isa. 22:2: "I will place on his shoulder the keys of the house of David; he shall open and none shall shut; he shall shut and none shall open." "In short," Evans writes, "Jesus' gospel is essentially Isaiah's gospel" (p. 671).

Yet there is also an all-pervading element of discontinuity between the two sets of biblical texts. The New Testament's exegetical coherence with Isaiah ultimately highlights a fundamental difference: at the heart of the New Testament's application of the Isaianic prophecy is the conviction that the coming of the kingdom is not simply a promise, but a divine reality experienced in the person of Jesus Christ. Jesus does not merely proclaim the good news of the coming of the kingdom of God; he has realized it through his life and death (Mark 10:45; Isa. 53:11-12). As a result, the same Old Testament texts have been heard in different ways.

2. The Hardening of Israel in the Context of Isaiah and the New Testament

In contrast to the above illustration of New Testament texts making use of a great range of Isaianic passages by means of which to describe a rich and coherent picture of the eschatological kingdom of God, the use of a single passage, Isa. 6:9-10, by the four Gospels and Acts, illustrates in a different manner the complex relationship between the book of Isaiah and its New Testament interpreters. (My analysis is dependent especially on the monographs of Joachim Gnilka and C. A. Evans.)

The Isaianic passage in the Hebrew Bible appears in the context of the prophet's commissioning to deliver a divine message of harshest judgment on Judah. The Greek translation retains the same historical context, but renders several significant changes in its meaning:

1) The Isaiah Septuagint translates the strong imperatives of the Hebrew ("keep hearing . . . keep seeing") with future finite verbs: "You will hear . . . you will see." Accordingly, the prophet is not enjoining the people to become hardened, but predicting that they will remain obdurate.

2) The usage of the passive by the Greek "has grown dull" alters the causative sense of the Hebrew "make fat." It is not the preaching of the prophet that causes the heart to become dull; rather, the prophet preaches because the heart is already fat.

In sum, in both instances the Septuagint has toned down the divine initiative in evoking the people's hardening.

In the New Testament's usage, the context to which the Isaianic word is applied is very different from the original prophetic context: it is now used by the Synoptics to explain why Jesus teaches in parables. Because John's Gospel does not speak of parables, but of signs, the same text is used here in reference to signs.

Mark 4:12 offers a paraphrase of Isa. 6:9-10. In general, Mark follows the Septuagint, but in several instances the Gospel departs from the Greek text by changing the sequence of the clauses. However, the most significant alteration is that Mark retains the telic force of the Hebrew text with its use of the conjunction *hina* ("in order that"). The effect is that Jesus speaks in parables so that the secret of the kingdom is only given to his disciples, but "those outside" cannot perceive or understand. The difficulty of interpreting Mark's use of the Isaianic hardening motif in relation to the parables of Jesus remains a continuing crux, but appears to be an integral component in Mark's much-debated secrecy theme.

When one next turns to Matthew's use of Isaiah 6 in 13:13 and 15, it becomes clear that the Greek translation has taken on a life of its own, as Matthew's paraphrase offers a reading different from both the Hebrew and the Greek. His literary setting, like Mark's, concerns Jesus' use of parables. However, Matthew substitutes the conjunction *hoti* ("because") for Mark's *hina* ("in order that"). The result is that for Matthew, Jesus does not speak in parables *in order* that the disciples may not understand, but *because* they do not understand.

This paraphrase of Isa. 6:9-10 in Matthew 13:13 is followed in vv. 14-15 by a direct quotation of vv. 9-10 according to the Septuagint's reading. The effect is that, for Matthew, the Marcan contrast between the "insiders and outsiders" has been replaced with the contrast between the disciples, who know the secrets of the kingdom, and the rest, who do not. More significant is that the use of the fulfillment formula recognizes that the evangelists' application of Isaiah 6 to Jesus' parables was not just an *ad hoc* analogy; rather, there was a theological substance respecting the nature of obduracy that joins the original text with Jesus' fresh application of it.

Isa. 6:9-10 is cited in Luke 8:10b, the briefest use of these Old Testament verses among the four Gospels. The Marcan form is abridged and somewhat softened in Luke. At times he agrees with Matthew against Mark, speaking of "knowing the secrets" rather than using the singular noun. At other times, he departs from Matthew in retaining the controversial *hina* of Mark.

The most significant change in Luke is that the question of the disciples respecting Jesus' use of parables has been contextualized to only one parable, that of the sower. The move is fully reasonable, since Jesus immediately offers an interpretation of this parable. Luke, like Matthew, does not understand Jesus' parable as designed to prevent forgiveness; for him, the devil comes to prevent repentance (8:12). It also seems quite significant that the Lucan author of Acts ends his second volume by citing Isa. 6:9-10 according to the Septuagint in full as a summary of Israel's obduracy (Acts 28:26-27).

Finally, when turning to John's use of Isaiah 6, one discovers an application very different from that of the Synoptics. The issue now turns on the unbelief of the Pharisees toward the signs performed by Jesus. Two passages relate to the subject of seeing and not seeing. Verse 9:39 appears as an allusion to Isa. 6:9, whereas John 12:40 cites the verse with an introduction formula "that the word of the prophet Isaiah may be fulfilled." Chapter 9 is the story of Jesus' healing of the man born blind and the resulting conflict with the Pharisees. The narrative subtly contrasts the blind man who sees and the Pharisees who are deemed blind, unable in unbelief to see the miraculous sign performed by Jesus. Then in John 12 the evangelist combines a citation of Isa. 53:1 and Isa. 6:10 by means of a verbal linkage in order to draw an analogy between the obduracy to Isaiah's preaching and the obduracy Jesus faced. The analogy is formulated in terms of prophecy and fulfillment: Isaiah had foretold that Jesus' signs would not be believed.

In both these two different examples of the New Testament's use of Isaiah, one can observe that the New Testament's appeal to specific Isaianic texts shows not only a high level of continuity between the two testaments, but also a remarkable discontinuity in the New Testament's application of the Old. The New Testament cites Isaiah through the filter of the Septuagint. Everywhere a coherence of subject matter is assumed that was buttressed with the authority of Israel's sacred scriptures. Yet equally striking is the range of discontinuity reflected in the intertextual appeals. The same Old Testament text can be used to make different theological points. Above all, there is a freedom in shaping the prooftexts by means of omissions, combinations, or alterations to the Greek text. However, before turning directly to an exploration of the crucial hermeneutical questions involved in this exegetical endeavor, it seems useful to analyze in a more systematic fashion some of the exegetical practices employed by the New Testament's usage of the Old Testament, especially of Isaiah. In order to do justice to the diversity and range of interpretive techniques, we shall deal with illustrative passages from the four Gospels and from Paul's letters.

III. Exegetical Techniques of Individual New Testament Authors

1. Matthew 1:23

One of the most characteristic features by which Matthew develops his Christology is his use of the Old Testament, especially his application of "formula quotations." The term designates a series of citations unique to Matthew that contain the phrase (or the like): "then was fulfilled what was spoken by the prophet . . ." The following passages are usually included: 1:22-23; 2:15, 17-18, 23; 4:14-16; 8:17; 12:18-21; 13:35; 21:4-5; and 27:9.

There are a host of exegetical problems arising from a critical study of these quotations. These are thoroughly covered by Ulrich Luz (*Matthew 1–7*, pp. 156-64). Our concern will focus more narrowly on the ruling question concerning the exegetical techniques in the New Testament's appropriation of Isaiah. Still, this endeavor calls for an assessment of certain preliminary matters in establishing a context.

a) It is generally agreed that Matthew is the author of this scheme of formula quotations, although he stood within a prior stream of tradition. The form used is consistent and distinguished from other citations of the Old Testament common to the other Gospels. Although the formula quotations generally follow the Septuagint, there is occasional evidence of a knowledge of the Hebrew text. Most striking is the freedom used in altering the text by means of additions and subtractions. Moreover, these changes reflect an authorial intention and are not accidental (cf. the three textual alterations of Micah 5:1 in Matt. 2:6).

b) The most intensive problem, causing the long history of debate, turns on trying to understand the author's intention and the techniques employed for achieving it. For many scholars the conclusion is largely negative. C. F. D. Moule's assessment is widely accepted concerning Matthew's use of the Old Testament: "to our critical eyes, manifestly forced and artificial and unconvincing" (*The Origin of Christology*, p. 129). Or to cite the title of S. V. McCasland's well-known article: "Matthew Twists the Scriptures" (*Journal of Biblical Literature* 80, 1961).

c) A more promising approach has been to seek ancient Jewish-Hellenistic exegetical techniques on which Matthew was dependent to explain his peculiar usage. The initial attempt to designate Matthew's exegesis as rabbinic midrash was largely unsuccessful, since the dynamics and goals are dissimilar (cf. Soares-Prabhu, *The Formula Quotations*, pp. 15-16). More illuminating initially was Krister Stendahl's appeal to the *pesher* exegesis of

Qumran, but again the comparison breaks down. Matthew's citations do not take their lead from Old Testament texts, but rather they serve as commentary on the meaning of events that constitute the gospel (cf. Ulrich Luz, *Matthew 1–7*, p. 158). Similarly, Barnabas Lindars's argument that an apologetic concern to legitimate previously held ideologies was the primary force at work in Matthew cannot be sustained.

Probably the most serious theological interpretation has recently been mounted by Rudolf Pesch ("'He Will Be Called a Nazorean,'" pp. 129-78). He finds the key for understanding Matthew in what he designates as "messianic exegesis." The community of which Matthew speaks understands itself as the new messianic people, saved through Jesus the Messiah. It sees the fulfillment of the prophetic texts recurring in its own history and thus construes the cited biblical texts as confirming their own existential experience of a community of faith ruled by God. Although I do not doubt that Matthew's gospel includes an ecclesiological element, in my opinion it is a secondary component, subservient to the primary Christological concerns of the author. The fulfillment formula quotations are directed, above all, to establishing the identity of Jesus as Messiah and Lord in relation to the Old Testament prophecy and only secondarily to extending the implications of his commission to his disciples (28:16-20).

It is clear that the formula quotations establish a historical framework for the Gospel of Matthew that extends from the birth and naming of the Messiah, to his flight to Egypt and settlement in Nazareth, to his healing ministry, rejection, death, and resurrection. The citations provide a theological context within the divine economy of God with Israel. The entire Old Testament is understood as a prophetic revelation of God's purposes directed to the future that has now been fulfilled in Jesus Christ, the promised Messiah. A typology is assumed between the history of Israel, viewed prophetically, and the life and ministry of Christ.

There is a dialectical understanding of the history reflected in the choice and shaping of the citation. On the one hand, Matthew reads the Old Testament from the perspective of the gospel, and testifies to the unity of the plan of God within the scheme of prophecy and fulfillment. On the other hand, the very meaning of the gospel to which it bears witness receives its definition from the Old Testament. The citations function on two different levels, as R. T. France has convincingly shown ("The Formula-Quotations," pp. 233-51). There is a "surface meaning" that the uninstructed reader can grasp from the received biblical text. However, there is also a deeper meaning that reverberates from the constellation of prophetic texts linked by the history of tradition (cf. below to Isa. 7:14). Finally, the citations serve as a means of actualizing the presence of the promised Messiah, who is now experienced by the believing community as the resurrected and exalted *kyrios* (cf. Pesch, pp. 129ff.). Thus, when Matthew calls to mind the servant figure of Isaiah 42 by a citation in 12:17-21, he bears witness to the post-resurrection church of the present reality of Christ's healing ministry (God-with-us) within the community of faith.

Theological reflection on Isa. 7:14 cited in Matt. 1:23 offers a highly controversial example by which to illustrate Matthew's exegetical method. At the outset, it is necessary to caution the interpreter not to blur the issue with assumptions derived from modern historical critical analysis. For example, Luz (*Matthew 1–7*, p. 124) proposes at the start that the modern interpreter can no longer speak of the fulfillment of Old Testament prophecies in this text, since the traditional Christian interpretation of the Messiah Jesus as an exegesis of Isa. 7:14 is obviously untenable. Rather, the Isaianic text refers to Hezekiah, as the synagogue correctly argued, and refers only to a contemporary historical figure.

Such a historically reconstructed interpretation fails to reckon with the messianic shaping of the larger Isaianic narrative context, specifically by the function of Immanuel in chapter 9, and the larger narrative of chapters 7–11 within an eschatological framework (cf. Childs, *Isaiah*, pp. 62-106). Of course, this canonical shaping of the Hebrew text has been greatly expanded by the subsequent history of interpretation, starting with the Targumic traditions and culminating in the New Testament's usage.

The Septuagint's translation of '*almāh* with *parthenos* (virgin) shifts the focus from a maiden sexually ripe for marriage to virginity as such, but the mystery of the passage, the vague and indeterminate tone that pervades the entire chapter, cannot be resolved by limiting its reference solely to a contemporary historical personage. Not only does the interpretation of Immanuel's role in Isaiah 8 point to a continuing eschatological role of Immanuel; the linking of Micah 5:1-3 and 2 Sam. 7:12-16 also points to the expectation of a future David. Thus, the "prince of peace" forms a messianic texture joining Isa. 9:5-6 and the shoot of Isaiah 11 (cf. H. Gese, "Natus ex virgine," pp. 73-89).

Obviously Matthew's Jewish-Hellenistic rendering of Isa. 7:14 goes far beyond the original eighth-century context of the Hebrew prophet, but his is a Christian reading that stands in continuity with a wider theological tradition of biblical prophecy. Pesch speaks of the "unusual history of the nation of God." Only a view through the eyes of faith, only a theological and historiographic interpretation can do justice to the text of Matthew. Why is this so? Because this New Testament witness is presented by the evangelist as a testimony to the special history of God and has thus become an inspired document within Israel's tradition.

2. Mark 1:2-3

Mark begins his narrative by setting forth the beginning of his story and describing its context: "the gospel of Jesus Christ." His approach differs from the other evangelists by neither presenting a genealogy of Jesus nor recounting his birth and family history.

The beginning is the proclamation of the good news of Jesus Christ. It does not begin with John the Baptist, or with the prophecy of Isaiah, but with the announcement of the inbreaking of God's kingly rule. Nevertheless, this message of the advent of God's kingdom has been planned, prophesied, and announced from long ago. Its coming has been confirmed by what is written in Isaiah, whose words are then quoted preceded by a formula: "as it is written in Isaiah the prophet."

Several points are of particular interest concerning the manner in which he sets forth his account.

a) Verse 1:1 speaks of the gospel, the *euangelion*. The noun in the Septuagint occurs infrequently, twice with the meaning "reward for bringing good news"; however, the verb occurs often. It is usually represented in the Septuagint by the middle tense of *euangelizō*, and translates the pi'el of the Hebrew verb *bs'r* "to bear good tidings." In the Old Testament the verb appears especially in Isaiah, chapters 40-55, and speaks in eschatological terms of the entrance of God's promised divine rule. However, the term also has Hellenistic roots associated with the emperor cult of Rome, which also promised a new world order (cf. Walter Bauer, *A Greek-English Lexicon*, English Translation, 4th ed., 1952, p. 318, for a bibliography of the classical background).

b) The confirmation of the gospel is found written in the prophecy of Isaiah. The formula for the prooftext is common in the Septuagint, the Apocrypha and Pseudepigrapha, as well as in the rest of the Old Testament. It serves a transitional role between a previously mentioned fact or event and the biblical citation.

c) The form of the quotation is not solely from Isaiah, but is from a catena formed with a conflation of three passages: Exod. 23:20, Mal. 3:1, and Isa. 40:3. As Stendahl pointed out (*The School of St. Matthew*, 1954, pp. 47ff.), such conflations of Old Testament texts within a catena with catchword links were familiar in postbiblical Judaism, and especially in the Dead Sea Scrolls. There is a wide consensus that, although the basic texts are from the Septuagint, several factors point to the evangelist's knowledge of Hebrew. Both Malachi 3 and Isaiah 40 use the phrase "prepare the way," which is not evident in the Greek. The choice of texts appears traditional as possibly stemming from an anthology.

d) Mark's use of the Old Testament serves not just as a formal prologue, but as a key for understanding his entire witness to the identity of Jesus Christ. He presents the story of Jesus as gospel, the coming triumphant rule of God. He thereby introduces his work from a theological perspective not shared by Jesus' disciples, who are repeatedly described as blind to his identity. Only by their being led in the way of the cross is the eschatological triumph of the Son revealed.

Mark's use of the Old Testament shares fully the exegetical techniques of its Jewish-Hellenistic background. His texts derive largely from the Septuagint, yet the shaping influence of the Hebrew original remains. He uses the Old Testament as a conceptual, theological framework that renders his story as gospel. To what extent the evangelist was conscious of the connotations of the term stemming from the Roman emperor cult is unclear, but it is hard to believe that at least some of his audience would not have sensed the competing agendas.

3. Luke 4:16-30

The concern to illustrate different exegetical techniques in the New Testament's interpretation of Isaiah finds an excellent example in Luke's Gospel. Luke 4:16-30 departs from the Marcan sequence in depicting Jesus' visit to his hometown Nazareth as the beginning of his public ministry. He enters the synagogue on the Sabbath as was his custom, and is offered the honor of reading from the scriptures as part of the traditional Jewish liturgy. He chooses a text from Isaiah to read and, when finished, sits down to interpret it.

The Jewish-Hellenistic milieu of first-century Palestine is everywhere evident. Luke's description accords well with the traditional Sabbath service. Every male Jew had the right to read scripture in the liturgy that Jesus accepted. One can assume that the Torah reading from a prescribed text had already occurred. However, the reading from the prophets (Haftorah) was not yet fixed at this period. Thus, Jesus intentionally chose a familiar text from Isaiah 61, read the passage when standing, and then took his seat in order to interpret it for his audience.

The Lucan form of the text read was actually a conflation of Isa. 61:1, 58:6, and 61:2. Two phrases from the Septuagint version are missing: "to heal the broken-hearted" and "the day of the vengeance of our God." The latter appears to be an intentional omission of the negative aspect of the Isaianic text. In general, the text cited by Luke is that of the Septuagint, however, with the substitution of the verb "to proclaim" for "to call for." The Greek verb "to preach the good news" *(euangelizesthai)* renders the Hebrew idiom of Deutero-Isaiah. Only later would it acquire the full Christian meaning of proclaiming the gospel. Luke's point is that what Isaiah announced, Jesus is now seen doing (Fitzmyer, *Luke,* vol. 1, p. 532).

The crucial question is how to interpret this New Testament passage with its Jewish-Hellenistic form of Luke's portrayal. In a learned and provocative essay, J. A. Sanders ("From Isaiah 61 to Luke 4," *Luke and Scripture,* pp. 46-69) has found the key to the passage to be in midrashic exegesis that developed in a trajectory from the Septuagint, Targum, Qumran, and rabbinic tradition through to the New Testament. Sanders argues that this study of comparative midrash enables one to understand Jesus as debating midrashically with his Jewish audience at Nazareth. Jesus offered an interpretation of Isaiah 61 using material from Elijah and Elisha that would direct the blessings of God's favor not to an "in group," but in true prophetic style, to the poor, captive, blind, and oppressed. His audience, anticipating a positive word from Jesus' winsome style, expected an interpretation favorable to them, but became outraged at his speech, which destroyed their privileged status before God. Thus they sought to destroy him. According to Sanders, the central issue of the passage lay in the controversy over who were the poor, captive, and oppressed of the Isaianic text. Thus, the key to its interpretation lies in decoding the midrashic signals offered by the Lucan text.

In my opinion, in spite of some genuine exegetical insights, Sanders's defense of a midrashic reading remains unconvincing. Its methodological problems evoke the same criticism as Stendahl's use of rabbinic and Qumran material. Sanders assumes that the setting of the rabbinic synagogue or the "school of Qumran" provides a close analogy to the early Christian community, and thus he claims a common midrashic practice. Particularly in Luke 4, I would argue that the issue is not conflicting midrashic exegesis, but rather the claims of Jesus of bringing to fulfillment the prophetic promise of God's eschatological salvation by his very presence. In a word, the heart of the controversy lay in Jesus' proclaiming the good news of the gospel: "today" God's kingdom had arrived. The offense to his unbelieving Jewish audience arose from this claim. In that moment, the identity of the carpenter's son announcing his divine anointing by the Spirit was at stake. It was not an exegetical debate. Jesus' provocative messianic proclamation pointing to a present fulfillment was the new teaching with authority.

Since the discovery of the Qumran material, some commentators have made a point of sharply distinguishing the so-called *pesher* exegesis from traditional rabbinic midrash. Certainly the concern to interpret prophecy as predictions being fulfilled literally in the present life of the community offered an exegetical analogy close to Luke's resounding "today." The end has arrived! However, the analogy is only superficially persuasive. The force derived from *pesher* exegesis stems from the conviction that a biblical text serves to predict events taking place in the community's own time that can be exactly correlated by the scholarly study of scripture. The conflict portrayed in Luke 4 is of a different order: it centers on the claims of Jesus the Messiah to fulfill the Isaianic promise. Although the Lucan text shares many formal features with its Jewish-Hellenistic milieu, the fact of its totally different substantive context revealed in Jesus Christ calls for the greatest caution in identifying the preaching of the gospel with midrashic exegesis.

4. John 12:41

John's Gospel is structured into two main sections, 1:19–12:50 and 13:1–20:29. In the first section, witnesses testify to the true nature of Jesus. These witnesses are not only the contemporaries of Jesus (1:32-34; 1:46-51; 4:27-30, 39-42), but are also the crucial figures of the Old Testament: Abraham, Moses, and Isaiah.

In chapter 12, two Isaianic quotations, 53:1 and 6:10, are introduced with the formula "that the word spoken by the prophet Isaiah might be fulfilled." Both serve as prooftexts of the hardening of Israel brought about by the mysterious will of God (v. 39). Then in v. 41 the evangelist offers a commentary explaining Isaiah's purpose: "Isaiah said this because he saw his glory and spoke of him." The sequence of the passage makes it clear that John is speaking of the glory of Jesus.

Because it was common in Jewish interpretation to understand earthly visions of God as visions of his glory (Targum on Isa. 6:1 and 6:5), at first it might appear that the same exegetical tradition was intended. Yet quite clearly the evangelist is speaking of the vision by the prophet of the pre-existent Son. His *logos* Christology was already introduced in 1:1 with the Word being with God at the beginning, the Word that became flesh (v. 14). In his earthly life this divine *logos* revealed the glory that had always been his (1:4). Abraham rejoiced to see his day (8:56), and Moses is portrayed as refuting the Jews from their own scriptures (5:45). Following Christ's resurrection, the disciples remembered a saying of Jesus, and their faith was grounded both in the scriptures and in the words of Christ (2:22).

John's exegetical technique revealed in this passage is unique among the other evangelists, and has only a distant parallel in Paul (1 Cor. 10:4). It should not be dismissed as traditional allegory, since this is not a secondary spiritual meaning distinct from its literal sense. Rather, it is an approach that adumbrated the church's later trinitarian theology when it spoke of an "immanent trinity." Although it is true that some elements parallel to John are found in Philo's *logos* doctrine and in various forms of Hellenistic wisdom speculation, once again the content of John's Christology cannot be adequately interpreted by an appeal to general concepts within the broad spectrum of Hellenistic mystical philosophy.

5. Romans 4:24-25

The great importance of the book of Isaiah for the Apostle Paul has long been recognized, but recently new and detailed attention has focused on a deeper probe into its significance. Critical analysis has concentrated on a host of issues: Paul's Greek text of the book of Isaiah, his exegetical techniques in citation, their literary and theological functions, and the range of topics emerging from his use of Isaiah citations. Two monographs stand out as especially illuminating: Dietrich-Alex Koch's *Die Schrift als Zeuge* (1986) and Florian Wilk's *Die Bedeutung des Jesajabuches für Paulus* (1998). Of course, the strengths of these books derive from their comprehensive attention to the work of a century of critical scholarship on Paul and the Old Testament.

The exact number of citations by Paul of Isaiah varies slightly depending on how one counts duplicate and mixed citations and how allusions are defined. Koch lists twenty-five cited texts and twenty-eight allusions; Wilk lists nineteen citations and twenty-eight allusions. Paul uses the Greek text of the Septuagint, but often in a later recensional form that strives to be closer to the Hebrew text. Because of this recension, determining whether Paul's variations from the Septuagint are inherited or from Paul himself is more complicated (cf. Koch, pp. 48ff.). A much-debated question is whether Paul's exegesis of the Old Testament stands in continuity primarily with Jewish and midrashic traditions or within the Greek Hellenism of the diaspora. Koch's analysis (pp. 230ff.) has gone a long way in blurring these sharp distinctions. Paul's exegesis shares features with the Hellenistic synagogue of the diaspora such as the use of allegory, but not in a highly developed form akin to Philo. Then again, Paul's exegesis lacks the characteristic forms of rabbinic midrash, and his use of rules traditionally associated with Hillel is very limited. Finally, only rarely is there a close parallel to the *pesher* approach of Qumran (e.g., Rom. 10:6-8). In sum, he shares throughout features from his Jewish-Hellenistic milieu, but his exegesis cannot be easily fitted into one pattern. It is the unique way he employs his tools toward his theological goals that is most characteristic.

What is crucial in any evaluation of Paul's use of Isaiah is his overt attempt to develop, describe, and defend his theology by means of biblical interpretation. However, strange as it may seem to modern critical sensibilities, Paul clearly intends his use of scripture to provide the grounds on which he argues his case. It is precisely here that the greatest problems arise. In a word, how is one to interpret the enormous freedom that Paul displays over against Old Testament texts, specifically that of Isaiah?

Koch has highlighted characteristic modes of Paul's handling of citations from Old Testament texts (pp. 103ff.). Paul's alterations of Isaianic quotations include

1. change in the sequence of the words: Isa. 52:5/Rom. 2:24; Isa. 45:23/Rom. 14:11.
2. change in persons, number, and gender: Isa. 52:7/Rom. 10:15; Isa. 29:10/Rom. 11:8.
3. omissions: Isa. 40:13/1 Cor. 2:16; Isa. 59:7f./Rom. 3:15-17; Isa. 28:11f./1 Cor. 14:21.
4. additions: Isa. 28:16/Rom. 10:11; Isa. 10:23/Rom. 9:28.
5. change of words: Isa. 29:14/1 Cor. 1:19.
6. combination of texts: Isa. 28:16 + 8:14/Rom 9:33; Isa. 10:22 + Hos. 2:1/Rom. 9:27; Isa. 45:23 + 49:18/Rom. 14:11.

Some of these alterations are simply stylistic changes. Others derive from Paul's attempt to ease the bridge from an Old Testament context to his new application. Yet often there is a conscious effort to reinterpret the meaning of the Old Testament to create a new and different sense. In a summarizing paragraph Koch notes (p. 186) that of ninety-seven Old Testament texts cited by Paul, fifty-two were altered from the Septuagint's reading, while thirty-seven remained intact. Moreover, the changes appear frequently content-oriented and not motivated by a mere stylistic alteration. There are several classic Pauline passages beyond his use of Isaiah that show that he was aware of the Jewish interpretation and altered the text to derive a radically different reading (cf. Deut. 30:12-14 in Rom. 10:6-8; Exod. 34:29ff. in 2 Cor 3:7-18).

A final example of Paul's exegesis of Isaiah should be noted. In a recent article D. A. Sapp (*Jesus and the Suffering Servant*, pp. 170ff.) has pointed out the two different textual traditions of Isaiah 53: the Hebrew (Masoretic) and the Greek. (The Qumran texts are close to the Hebrew and diverge from the Greek.) The crucial difference lies in the rendering of Isa. 53:10b. In the

Masoretic text it reads, "the righteous one, my servant, will justify the many." In the Septuagint it reads, "the Lord desires to vindicate the righteous one who serves the many well." Again, in 53:9 there is a divergence. The Masoretic text has "he (the servant) will make his grave with the wicked and with the rich in his death, although he had done no wrong and no deceit was in his mouth." According to the Septuagint, the verse reads, "I (the Lord) will give the wicked instead of his (the servant's) grave and the rich instead of his (the servant's) death because he did no wrong."

Sapp draws the conclusion that Paul's interpretation of Isa. 53 in Rom. 4:25 and 9:15, 19 serves as a warrant for his doctrine of the atonement through Jesus' sacrificial death and resurrection. He derives it from the Hebrew textual tradition rather than from the Greek Septuagint. Whether Paul's choice of the Hebrew tradition derives from his own exegesis of the Hebrew or is an adoption of an earlier Christian tradition can still be debated. However, the important hermeneutical implication to be drawn is the freedom of Paul to tap the resources of the Hebrew, thus departing from the Greek, when the subject matter of the atonement was at stake.

As a result of this evidence of Paul's freedom, many modern biblical scholars have reached a very negative evaluation of his use of the Old Testament. It is dismissed as his simply reading his own theological ideas back into the Old Testament: Paul's approach is *eisegesis,* not *exegesis!* Others draw the implication that because Paul's reading derived completely from the side of the New Testament, the sense of the Old Testament as originally intended never belonged to the Christian canon at all (Haenchen, "Das Alte"). Similarly, Ernst Käsemann (*Romans,* pp. 285ff.) finds a warrant in Paul's freedom for "discerning the spirits" and rejecting whatever is not gospel in the Old Testament as the dead letter *(gramma)* of the law.

I would caution against such hasty appraisals and urge, above all, putting Paul's exegesis within his larger hermeneutic of interpretation. We should at least be aware of Paul's radically new starting point in approaching scripture. Jesus Christ has become the center, rather than Torah. Paul's point of departure for interpreting Isaiah derived from his Christian conviction that the divine prophecies of the Jewish scriptures had been and were being fulfilled through God's new eschatological action of salvation through Christ for the sake of Israel and the nations. Whereas for the modern biblical critic it is axiomatic that genuine exegesis depends on recovering a text's original historical context, for Paul genuine interpretation depends on its bearing witness to its true subject matter, who is Jesus Christ. There is now a new revelation, a new context, a new divine message. Paul does not relate the past to the present in terms of historical sequence, but rather scripture has a voice that speaks. It is a living word that confronts its hearers now. It is written "for our sake" (Rom. 4:24; 1 Cor. 9:10).

In spite of the fully time-conditioned form of the Pauline letters — Jewish, Hellenistic, polemical — the church received these writings as apostolic and gave them a privileged status as authoritative scripture in the Christian canon. In our final chapter we shall return to explore some of the theological and hermeneutical implications of this understanding of the Christian faith.

IV. The Hermeneutical Problem of the New Testament's Use of the Old

1. The Tension between the Hebrew Text and the Greek Septuagint in the Early Church

Given the increasing role that the Septuagint played as the authoritative scriptures of the Christian church (cf. Hengel, *The Septuagint as Christian Scripture*), there soon arose a heightened awareness of the discrepancies between the Hebrew and Greek texts. Origen's enterprise of seeking to stabilize the fluidity between the Masoretic text and the Greek translations stemmed ultimately from his concern that Christian exegetical debates with Jews needed to rest on a careful, critical assessment of the textual relationship.

However, the actual hermeneutical debate within the church surfaced with a vengeance in the wake of Jerome's appeal to the Hebrew as the truthful and authoritative text of the Old Testament. In contrast, Augustine wanted to affirm the authority of the church's traditional text, the Septuagint. Reacting to the philological force of Jerome's recovery of the Hebrew, Augustine sought to effect a hermeneutical compromise to resolve the differences between the Hebrew and the Greek. Because the same Holy Spirit was at work in the Septuagint as in the Hebrew, the Septuagint could often offer new and additional revelation. Moreover, the Greek translator could express the same meaning as that of the Hebrew, but by means of a different literary formulation. Augustine provided an example of his compromise. In Jonah 3:4 Nineveh's period of contrition prior to the threatened divine judgment lasted three days according to the Septuagint, but according to the Hebrew text it was forty days. Augustine preferred the Hebrew as more historically likely, but he reckoned that the three-day period of the Septuagint also had its legitimate meaning as adumbrating Christ's three days in the grave.

In his treatise *On Christian Doctrine* Augustine developed at length his hermeneutical theory for handling the different levels within scripture. The goal of all of scripture was to engender the love of God and of one's neighbor (3.9.14). Therefore, if a passage, when taken literally, did not refer to this purity of life and soundness of teaching, it had to be understood figuratively. The rationale for legitimating different levels of meaning within scripture was extended far beyond resolving textual discrepancies, but it became the church's accepted hermeneutic in appealing to the legitimate role of allegorical interpretation.

2. Modern Attempts to Resolve the Problem of the New Testament's Use of the Old

The historical-critical study of the Bible that emerged in the late seventeenth century through the Enlightenment raised the problem of interpreting the New Testament's use of the Old to a new intensity. Certainly the most provocative challenge to the church's dogmatic tradition was launched by Anthony Collins in 1724 *(A Discourse on the Grounds and Reasons)*. The first part contained the subtitle "Some Considerations on the Quotations Made from the Old in the New Testament, and particularly on the Prophecies cited from the former and said to be fulfill'd in the latter." Collins sought to demonstrate that the New Testament's usage was tendentious, misinformed, and lacking all rational defense.

The effect of Collins's work was greatly to polarize the ensuing debate. Two diametrically opposed positions emerged. On the one hand, there was a host of attempts at harmonizing the New Testament's usage with the original intent of the Old. Usually the defense of the New Testament's usage tried to maintain its integrity by arguing that the sense of a given text remained the same between both testaments, but differed only in application or in an extension to a *sensus plenior*. Still today such a position continues to be represented in some conservative circles (cf. W. C. Kaiser, *The Uses of the Old Testament in the New),* and has been buttressed by the hermeneutical theories of E. D. Hirsch *(The Validity of Interpretation).* However, it has become a minority position even among Evangelicals.

On the other hand, the critical questions of Collins have been continually expanded, and history-of-religions categories have largely replaced the traditional theological categories of the early church. The aim of this research is no longer to compare authoritative, canonical texts, but rather to trace descriptively the historical development of all of the relevant texts in the broadest context possible within the ancient Near Eastern world and Jewish-Hellenism without privileging any of them. With respect to the translation of the evolving Hebrew text into Greek, the full effect of cultural filtering within the milieu of Jewish-Hellenism has only begun to emerge. As a result, for many modern biblical scholars the theological problems of the past have been rendered largely irrelevant in light of the new, critical agenda.

Nevertheless, it would be a serious misjudgment to assume that the hermeneutical interest in the relationship between the two testaments has completely died with the onset of modernity. Rather, many modern biblical scholars, after having become convinced of the legitimacy, indeed necessity, of the critical enterprise, have returned to the older theological concerns of the church and synagogue, but now with fresh perspectives and newer formulations. It is not my concern at this time to outline the range of newer proposals or to offer an assessment. Rather, my intention is to present a history of the church's major interpreters of the book of Isaiah, and to focus primarily on the hermeneutical issues at stake in each of the various stages of interpretation. Only after this history has been traced will it be possible to return to the larger hermeneutical problems raised by this chapter on the early reception of the Hebrew Bible.

Bibliography of The Early Reception of the Hebrew Bible

I. The Role of the Septuagint

Barrera, J. Trebolle. "The Greek Septuagint Version." In *The Jewish and the Christian Bible*, pp. 301-323. Leiden: Brill, 1998.

Barthélemy, D. *Études d'histoire du text de l'Ancien Testament*. Freiburg and Göttingen: Vandenhoeck & Ruprecht, 1978.

Brooke, A. E., N. McLean, and H. St. J. Thackeray, eds. *The Old Testament in Greek*, vol. 1. Cambridge: Cambridge University Press, 1906.

Brooke, G. J., and B. Lindars, eds. *Septuagint, Scrolls and Cognate Writings*. Atlanta: Scholars Press, 1992.

Broyles, C. C., and C. A. Evans, eds. *Writing and Reading the Scroll of Isaiah*, vol 2. Leiden: Brill, 1997.

Chilton, B. D. "Two in One: Renderings of the Book of Isaiah in Targum Jonathan." *Writing and Reading the Scroll of Isaiah*, vol. 2, ed. C. C. Broyles and C. A. Evans, pp. 547-62. Leiden: Brill, 1997.

Cross, F. M. "The History of the Biblical Text in the Light of Discoveries in the Judaean Desert." *Harvard Theological Review* 57 (1964): 281-99.

Emerton, J. A. "The Purpose of the Second Column of the Hexapla." *Journal of Theological Studies* 7 (1956): 79-87.

Evans, C. A. "The Dead Sea Scrolls and the Canon of Scripture in the Time of Jesus." In *The Bible at Qumran,* edited by P. W. Flint, pp. 67-79. Grand Rapids: Eerdmans, 2001.

Flint, P. W. "The Septuagint Version of Isaiah 23:1-14 and the Masoretic Text." *Bulletin of the International Organization for Septuagint and Cognate Studies* 21 (1988): 35-57.

———. "The Isaiah Scrolls from the Judean Desert." In *Writing and Reading the Scroll of Isaiah,* vol. 2, edited by C. C. Broyles and C. A. Evans, pp. 481-89. Leiden: Brill, 1997.

Hanhart, R. "Die Bedeutung der Septuaginta in neutestamentlicher Zeit." *Zeitschrift für Theologie und Kirche* 81 (1984): 395-416.

———. "Die Septuaginta als Interpretation und Actualisierung. Jesaja 9.1(8:23)-7(6)." In *Memorial Volume Isac Leo Seeligmann,* vol. 3, pp. 331-46. Jerusalem: Rubinstein Publishing House, 1983.

———. "Introduction: Problems in the History of the LXX Text from Its Beginnings to Origen." In M. Hengel, *The Septuagint as Christian Scripture,* pp. 1-17. Edinburgh: T. & T. Clark, 2002.

Harl, M., Dorival, G., and O. Munnich, *La Bible Grecque des Septante.* Paris: Editions du Cerf, 1988.

Hengel, M. *The Septuagint as Christian Scripture: The Prehistory and the Problem of Its Canon.* Edinburgh: T. & T. Clark, 2002.

Holmes, R., and J. Parson. *Vetus Testamentum Graecum cum variis lectionibus.* 5 vols. Oxford, 1798-1827.

Jobes, K. H., and M. Silva. *Invitation to the Septuagint.* Grand Rapids: Baker, 2000.

Koenig, J. *L'herméneutique analogique du Judaïsme antique d'après les témoins textuels d'Isaïe.* Leiden: Brill, 1982.

Kooij, A. van der. *Die Alten Textzeugen des Jesajabuches.* Göttingen: Vandenhoeck & Ruprecht, 1981.

———. "The Septuagint of Isaiah: Translation and Interpretation." In *The Book of Isaiah,* edited by J. Vermeylen, pp. 127-33. Leuven: Peeters and Leuven University Press, 1989.

———. "The Old Greek of Isaiah in Relation to the Qumran Texts of Isaiah: Some General Comments." In *Septuagint, Scrolls and Cognate Writings,* edited by G. J. Brooke and B. Lindars, pp. 195-213. Atlanta: Scholars Press, 1992.

———. "Isaiah in the Septuagint." In *Writing and Reading the Scroll of Isaiah,* vol. 2, edited by C. C. Broyles and C. A. Evans, pp. 513-29. Leiden: Brill, 1997.

Lagarde, P. *Librorum Veteris Testamenti canonicorum.* Göttingen, 1883.

Lamarche, P. de. "The Septuagint: Bible of the Earliest Christians." In *The Bible in Greek Christian Antiquity,* edited by P. M. Blowers, pp. 15-33. Notre Dame: University of Notre Dame Press, 1997.

Marcos, F. *The Septuagint in Context: An Introduction to the Greek Versions of the Bible.* Leiden: Brill, 2000.

Orlinsky, H. M. "The Septuagint as Holy Writ and the Philosophy of the Translators." *Hebrew Union College Annual* 46 (1975): 89-114.

Ottley, R. R. *The Book of Isaiah According to the Septuagint.* 2 vols. Cambridge: Cambridge University Press, 1904, 1906.

Porter, S. E., and B. W. R. Pearson. "Isaiah through Greek Eyes: The Septuagint of Isaiah." In *Writing and Reading the Scroll of Isaiah,* vol. 2, edited by C. C. Broyles and C. A. Evans, pp. 531-46. Leiden: Brill, 1997.

Seeligmann, I. L. *The Septuagint Version of Isaiah.* Leiden: Brill, 1948.

Sundberg, A. C. *The Old Testament in the Early Church.* Cambridge, Mass.: Harvard University Press, 1964.

Swete, H. B. *The Old Testament in Greek According to the Septuagint.* 3 vols. Cambridge: Cambridge University Press, 1887-94.

―――. *An Introduction to the Old Testament in Greek.* Cambridge: Cambridge University Press, 1902.

Tov, E. "Die Septuaginta in ihrem theologischen und traditionsgeschichtlichen Verhältnis zur hebräischen Bibel." In *Mitte der Schrift?* edited by M. Klopfenstein, pp. 237-68. Bern: Lang Verlag, 1987.

―――. "The Text of Isaiah at Qumran." In *Writing and Reading the Scroll of Isaiah,* vol. 2, edited by C. C. Broyles and C. A. Evans, pp. 491-511. Leiden: Brill, 1997.

―――. *The Text-Critical Use of the Septuagint in Biblical Research.* 2nd edition. Jerusalem: Sinor, 1997.

Ulrich, E. "An Index to the Contents of the Isaiah Manuscripts from the Judean Desert." In *Writing and Reading the Scroll of Isaiah,* vol. 2, edited by C. C. Broyles and C. A. Evans, pp. 477-80. Leiden: Brill, 1997.

Wevers, J. W. "The Interpretative Character and Significance of the Septuagint Version." In *Hebrew Bible/Old Testament: The History of Its Interpretation,* vol. 1, edited by M. Saebø, pp. 84-107. Göttingen: Vandenhoeck & Ruprecht, 1996.

Ziegler, J. *Untersuchungen zur Septuaginta des Buches Isaias.* Münster: Aschendorf, 1934.

―――. *Septuaginta. Vetus Testamentum Graecum. Isaias.* 2nd edition. Göttingen: Vandenhoeck & Ruprecht, 1967.

II. The New Testament's Use of Isaiah

Baker, D. L. "Typology and the Christian Use of the Old Testament." *Scottish Journal of Theology* 29 (1976): 137-57.

Barrett, C. K. "The Interpretation of the Old Testament in the New." In *The Cambridge History of the Bible*, vol. 1, edited by P. R. Ackroyd and C. F. Evans, pp. 377-411. Cambridge: Cambridge University Press, 1970.

Beale, G. K., ed. *The Right Doctrine from the Wrong Texts?* Grand Rapids: Baker, 1994.

Carson, D. A., and H. G. M. Williamson. *It Is Written: Scripture Citing Scripture.* Cambridge: Cambridge University Press, 1988.

Casey, M. "Christology and the Legitimating Use of the Old Testament in the New Testament." In *The Old Testament in the New Testament: Essays in Honour of J. L. North*, edited by S. Moyise, pp. 42-64. Sheffield: Sheffield Academic Press, 2000.

Chilton, B. D. *A Galilean Rabbi and His Bible: Jesus' Own Interpretation of Isaiah.* London: SPCK, 1984.

Collins, Anthony. *A Discourse on the Grounds and Reasons of the Christian Religion.* London, 1724.

Dittmar, W. *Vetus Testamentum in Novo.* Göttingen: Vandenhoeck & Ruprecht, 1903.

Dodd, C. H. "The Old Testament in the New." In *The Right Doctrine from the Wrong Texts?* edited by G. K. Beale, pp. 167-87. Grand Rapids: Baker, 1994.

Efird, J. M., ed. *The Use of the Old Testament in the New.* Durham: Duke University Press, 1972.

Evans, C. A. *To See and Not Perceive: Isaiah 6.9-11 in Early Jewish and Christian Interpretation.* Sheffield: Sheffield Academic Press, 1989.

―――. "From Gospel to Gospel: The Function of Isaiah in the New Testament." In *Writing and Reading the Scroll of Isaiah*, vol. 2, edited by C. C. Broyles and C. A. Evans, pp. 651-91. Leiden: Brill, 1997.

Evans, C. A., and W. R. Stegner, eds. *The Gospels and the Scriptures of Israel.* Sheffield: Sheffield Academic Press, 1994.

Fishbane, M. *Biblical Interpretation in Ancient Israel.* Oxford: Oxford University Press, 1985.

Fitzmyer, J. A. "The Use of Explicit Old Testament Quotations in Qumran Literature and in the New Testament." *New Testament Studies* 7 (1961): 297-333.

France, R. T. *Jesus and the Old Testament.* London: Tyndale Press, 1982.

Gnilka, J. *Die Verstockung Israels: Isaias 6,9-10 in der Theologie der Synoptiker.* Munich: Kösel 1961.

Goppelt, L. *Typos: The Typological Interpretation of the Old Testament.* Grand Rapids: Eerdmans, 1982.

Hanson, A. T. *Jesus Christ in the Old Testament.* London: SPCK, 1965.

Harris, J. Rendel. *Testimonies.* 2 vols. Cambridge: Cambridge University Press, 1916, 1920.

Hirsch, E. D. *The Validity of Interpretation.* New Haven: Yale University Press, 1957.

————. *The Aims of Interpretation.* Chicago: University of Chicago Press, 1976.

Juel, D. *Messianic Exegesis.* Philadelphia: Fortress, 1988.

Kaiser, W. C. *The Uses of the Old Testament in the New.* Chicago: Moody, 1985.

Koch, D.-A. *Die Schrift als Zeugnis des Evangeliums.* Tübingen: Mohr Siebeck, 1986.

Kugel, J. L., and R. A. Greer. *Early Biblical Interpretation.* Philadelphia: Westminster, 1986.

Lindars, B. *New Testament Apologetic.* London: SCM Press, 1961.

Longenecker, R. N. *Biblical Exegesis in the Apostolic Period.* Grand Rapids: Eerdmans, 1975.

Moule, C. F. D. "Fulfilment-Words in the New Testament: Use and Abuse." *New Testament Studies* 14 (1967-8): 293-320.

Moyise, S., ed. *The Old Testament in the New Testament.* Sheffield: Sheffield Academic Press, 2000.

————, *The Old Testament in the New: An Introduction.* London and New York: Continuum, 2001.

Silva, M. "The New Testament Use of the Old Testament: Text Form and Authority." In *Scripture and Truth,* edited by D. A. Carson and J. D. Woodbridge, pp. 147-65. Grand Rapids: Zondervan, 1983.

Smith, D. M. "The Uses of the Old Testament in the New Testament." In *The Use of the Old Testament in the New and Other Essays: Studies in Honor of Wm. Franklin Stinespring,* edited by J. M. Efird, pp. 3-65. Durham: Duke University Press, 1972.

Snodgrass, K. R. "Streams of Tradition Emerging from Isaiah 40:1-5 and Their Adaptation in the New Testament." *Journal for the Study of the New Testament* 8 (1980): 21-45.

————. "The Use of the Old Testament in the New." In *The Right Doctrine from the Wrong Texts?* edited by G. K. Beale, pp. 29-51. Grand Rapids: Baker, 1994.

III. Exegetical Techniques of Individual New Testament Authors

Matthew

Childs, B. S. *Isaiah.* Louisville: Westminster John Knox, 2001.

Ellis, E. E. "Midrash, Targum and New Testament Quotations." In *Neotestamen-*

tica et Semitica: Studies in Honour of Matthew Black, edited by E. Earle Ellis and Max Wilcox, pp. 199-219. Edinburgh: T. & T. Clark, 1969.

France, R. T. "The Formula-Quotations of Matthew 2 and the Problem of Communication." *New Testament Studies* 27 (1981): 233-51.

Gese, H. "Natus ex virgine." In *Probleme biblischer Theologie. Festschrift G. von Rad,* edited by H. W. Wolff, pp. 73-89. Munich: Kaiser Verlag, 1971.

Gundry, R. H. *The Use of the Old Testament in St. Matthew's Gospel.* Leiden: Brill, 1967.

Hartmann, L. "Scriptural Exegesis in the Gospel of Matthew and the Problem of Communication." In *L'évangile selon Matthieu: Rédaction et Théologie,* edited by M. Didier, pp. 132-52. Gembloux: Duculot, 1972.

Kamesar, A. "The Virgin of Isaiah 7:14: The Philological Argument from the Second to the Fifth Century." *Journal of Theological Studies,* n.s., 49 (1990): 51-75.

Leske, A. M. "Isaiah and Matthew: The Prophetic Influence in the First Gospel." In *Jesus and the Suffering Servant,* edited by W. H. Bellinger and W. R. Farmer, pp. 152-69. Harrisburg: Trinity Press, 1998.

Lindars, B. *New Testament Apologetic.* London: SCM, 1961.

Luz, U. "Excursus: The Formula Quotations." In *Matthew 1–7,* pp. 156-64. Minneapolis: Augsburg, 1985.

McCasland, S. V. "Matthew Twists the Scriptures." *Journal of Biblical Literature* 80 (1961): 143-48.

Menken, M. J. J. "The Quotation from Jeremiah 31(38).15 in Matthew 2.18: A Study of Matthew's Scriptural Text." In *The Old Testament in the New Testament: Essays in Honour of J. L. North,* edited by S. Moyise, pp. 106-25. Sheffield: Sheffield Academic Press, 2000.

Moule, C. F. D. *The Origin of Christology.* Cambridge: Cambridge University Press, 1977.

Moyise, S. "The Old Testament in Matthew." In *The Old Testament in the New: An Introduction,* pp. 34-44. London: Continuum, 2001.

Pesch, R. "'He Will Be Called a Nazorean': Messianic Exegesis in Matthew 1–2." In *The Gospels and the Scriptures of Israel,* edited by C. A. Evans and W. R. Stegner, pp. 129-78. Sheffield: Sheffield Academic Press, 1994.

Porter, S. E. "The Use of the Old Testament in the New Testament: A Brief Comment of Method and Terminology." In *Early Christian Interpretation of the Scriptures of Israel,* edited by C. A. Evans and J. A. Sanders, pp. 79-96. Sheffield: Sheffield Academic Press, 1997.

Rothfuchs, W. *Die Erfüllungszitate des Matthäus-Evangeliums.* Stuttgart: Kohlhammer, 1969.

Soares-Prabhu, G. M. *The Formula Quotations in the Infancy Narrative of Matthew.* Rome: Biblical Institute Press, 1976.

Stendahl, K. *The School of St. Matthew and Its Use of the Old Testament.* Lund: C. W. K. Gleerup, 1954.

————. "'Quis et Unde?' An Analysis of Mt. 1–2." In *Judentum, Urchristentum, Kirche. Festschrift J. Jeremias,* pp. 94-105. Berlin: de Gruyter, 1960.

Strecker, G. *Der Weg der Gerechtigkeit. Untersuchung zur Theologie des Matthäus.* Göttingen: Vandenhoeck & Ruprecht, 1962.

Mark

France, R. T. "The Formula-Quotations of Matthew 2 and the Problem of Communication." *New Testament Studies* 27 (1981): 233-51.

Hooker, M. D. "Mark." In *It Is Written: Scripture Citing Scripture. Essays in Honour of Barnabas Lindars,* edited by D. A. Carson and H. G. M. Williamson, pp. 220-30. Cambridge: Cambridge University Press, 1988.

Marcus, Joel. *The Way of the Lord: Christological Exegesis of the Old Testament in the Gospel of Mark.* Louisville: Westminster/John Knox, 1992.

Moo, D. J. *The Old Testament in the Gospel Passion Narratives.* Sheffield: Almond Press, 1983.

Moyise, S. "The Old Testament in Mark." In *The Old Testament in the New: An Introduction,* pp. 21-33. London and New York: Continuum, 2001.

Schneck, R. *Isaiah in the Gospel of Mark I–VIII.* Berkeley: University of California Press, 1994.

Watts, R. E. "Jesus' Death, Isaiah 53, and Mark 10:45: A Crux Revisited." In *Jesus and the Suffering Servant,* edited by W. H. Bellinger and W. R. Farmer, pp. 125-51. Harrisburg: Trinity Press, 1998.

Luke

Albertz, R. "Die 'Antrittspredigt' Jesu im Lukasevangelium auf ihrem alttestamentlichen Hintergrund." *Zeitschrift für neutestamentliche Wissenschaft* 74 (1983): 192-206.

Bock, D. L. *Proclamation from Prophecy and Pattern: Lucan Old Testament Christology.* Sheffield: Sheffield Academic Press, 1987.

Evans, C. A., and J. A. Sanders, eds. *Luke and Scripture: The Function of Sacred Tradition in Luke-Acts.* Philadelphia: Fortress, 1993.

Fitzmyer, J. A. *The Gospel according to Luke.* 2 vols. New York: Doubleday, 1981-85.

Kimball, C. A. *Jesus' Exposition of the Old Testament in Luke's Gospel.* Sheffield: Sheffield Academic Press, 1994.

Sanders, J. A. "From Isaiah 61 to Luke 4." In *Luke and Scripture,* edited by C. A. Evans and J. A. Sanders, pp. 46-69. Philadelphia: Fortress, 1993.

————. "Isaiah in Luke." In *Luke and Scripture,* edited by C. A. Evans and J. A. Sanders, pp. 14-25. Philadelphia: Fortress, 1993.

Seccombe, D. "Luke and Isaiah." *New Testament Studies* 27 (1981): 252-59.

Strauss, M. L. *The Davidic Messiah in Luke-Acts.* Sheffield: Sheffield Academic Press, 1995.

John

Barrett, C. K. "The Old Testament in the Fourth Gospel." *Journal of Theological Studies* 48 (1947): 155-69.

Evans, C. A. "On the Quotation Formulas in the Fourth Gospel." *Biblische Zeitschrift* 26 (1982): 79-83.

Freed, E. D. *Old Testament Quotations in the Gospel of John.* Leiden: Brill, 1965.

Hanson, A. T. *The Prophetic Gospel: A Study of John and the Old Testament.* Edinburgh: T. & T. Clark, 1991.

Hengel, M. "The Old Testament in the Fourth Gospel." In *The Gospels and the Scriptures of Israel,* edited by C. A. Evans and W. R. Stegner, pp. 380-95. Sheffield: Sheffield Academic Press, 1994.

Menken, M. J. J. *Old Testament Quotations in the Fourth Gospel.* Kampen: Kok, 1996.

Painter, J. "The Quotation of Scripture and Unbelief in John 12.36b-43." In *The Gospels and the Scriptures of Israel,* edited by C. A. Evans and W. R. Stegner, pp. 429-58. Sheffield: Sheffield Academic Press, 1994.

Reim, G. *Studien zum alttestamentlichen Hintergrund des Johannesevangeliums.* Cambridge: Cambridge University Press, 1974.

Schuchard, B. G. *Scripture within Scripture: The Interrelationship of Form and Function in the Explicit Old Testament Citations in the Gospel of John.* Atlanta: Scholars Press, 1992.

Westcott, B. F. *The Gospel of St. John.* London: John Murray, 1880.

Young, F. W. "A Study of the Relation of Isaiah to the Fourth Gospel." *Zeitschrift für die neutestamentliche Wissenschaft* 46 (1955): 215-33.

Paul

Barrett, C. K. "The Allegory of Abraham, Sarah, and Hagar in the Argument of Galatians." In *Rechtfertigung. Festschrift E. Käsemann,* edited by J. Friedrich et al., pp. 1-16. Tübingen: Mohr Siebeck, 1976.

Dahl, N. A. "Contradictions in Scripture." In *Studies in Paul,* pp. 159-77. Minneapolis: Augsburg Press, 1977.

Dietzfelbinger, C. *Paulus und das Alte Testament.* Munich: Kaiser, 1961.

Dittmar, W. *Vetus Testamentum in Novo.* Göttingen: Vandenhoeck & Ruprecht, 1903.

Dodd, C. H. *According to the Scriptures: The Sub-structure of New Testament Theology.* London: Nisbet, 1952.

Ellis, E. E. *Paul's Use of the Old Testament.* Edinburgh: Oliver & Boyd, 1957.

Evans, C. A., and J. A. Sanders, eds. *Paul and the Scriptures of Israel.* Sheffield: Sheffield Academic Press, 1999.

Fitzmyer, J. A. "The Use of Explicit Old Testament Quotations in Qumran Literature and in the New Testament." *New Testament Studies* 7 (1960-61): 297-333.

Goppelt, L. *Typos: The Typological Interpretation of the Old Testament.* Grand Rapids: Eerdmans, 1982.

Haenchen, E. "Das Alte 'Neue Testament' und das Neue 'Alte Testament.'" In *Die Bibel und Wir,* pp. 13-27. Tübingen: Mohr Siebeck, 1968.

Hanson, A. T. *Studies on Paul's Technique and Theology.* Grand Rapids: Eerdmans, 1974.

———. *The Living Utterances of God: The New Testament Exegesis of the Old.* London: Darton, 1983.

Hays, R. B. *Echoes of Scripture in the Letters of Paul.* New Haven: Yale University Press, 1989.

Hübner, H. *Biblische Theologie des Neuen Testaments,* vol. 2: *Die Theologie des Paulus und ihre neutestamentliche Wirkungsgeschichte.* Göttingen: Vandenhoeck & Ruprecht, 1993.

Käsemann, E. *Commentary on Romans.* Grand Rapids: Eerdmans, 1980.

Katz, P. *Philo's Bible: The Aberrant Text of Bible Quotations in Some Philonic Writings and Its Place in the Textual History of the Greek Bible.* Cambridge: Cambridge University Press, 1950.

Koch, D.-A. "Beobachtungen zum christologischen Schriftgebrauch in den vorpaulinischen Gemeinden." *Zeitschrift für die neutestamentliche Wissenschaft* 71 (1980): 174-91.

———. *Das Schrift als Zeuge des Evangeliums. Untersuchungen zur Verwendung und zum Verständnis der Schrift bei Paulus.* Tübingen: Mohr Siebeck, 1986.

Luz, U. *Das Geschichtsverständnis bei Paulus.* Munich: Kaiser, 1968.

Michel, O. *Paulus und seine Bibel.* Gütersloh: Bertelsmann, 1929.

Oss, D. A. "The Interpretation of the 'Stone' Passages by Peter and Paul: A Comparative Study." *Journal of the Evangelical Theological Society* 32 (1989): 181-200.

Sapp, D. A. "The LXX, 1QIsa, and MT Versions of Isaiah 53 and the Christian Doctrine of Atonement." In *Jesus and the Suffering Servant: Isaiah 53 and Christian Origins,* edited by W. H. Bellinger and W. R. Farmer, pp. 170-92. Harrisburg: Trinity Press, 1998.

Schulz, S. "Die Decke des Moses. Untersuchungen zu einer vorpaulinischen Überlieferung in II Cor 3, 7-18." *Zeitschrift für die neutestamentliche Wissenschaft* 49 (1958): 1-30.

Silva, M. "Old Testament in Paul." In *Dictionary of Paul and His Letters,* edited by G. F. Hawthorne, R. P. Martin, and D. G. Reid, pp. 630-42. Downers Grove, Ill.: InterVarsity, 1993.

Smith, D. M. "The Pauline Literature." *It Is Written: Scripture Citing Scripture. Essays in Honour of Barnabas Lindars,* edited by D. A. Carson and H. G. M. Williamson, pp. 265-91. Cambridge: Cambridge University Press, 1988.

Stanley, C. D. *Paul and the Language of Scripture: Citation Techniques in the Pauline Epistles and Contemporary Literature.* Cambridge: Cambridge University Press, 1993.

Vielhauer, P. "Paulus und das Alte Testament." In *Oikodome. Aufsätze zum Neuen Testament,* vol. 2, pp. 196-228. Munich: Kaiser, 1979.

Vollmer, H. *Die alttestamentlichen Citate bei Paulus textkritisch und biblisch-theologisch gewürdigt neben einem Anhang über das Verhältnis des Apostels zu Philo.* Freiburg/Leipzig: Mohr, 1895.

Wagner, J. R. "The Herald of Isaiah and the Mission of Paul: An Investigation of Paul's Use of Isaiah 51-55 in Romans." In *Jesus and the Suffering Servant,* edited by W. H. Bellinger and W. R. Farmer, pp. 193-222. Harrisburg: Trinity, 1998.

Wilk, F. *Die Bedeutung des Jesajabuches für Paulus.* Göttingen: Vandenhoeck & Ruprecht, 1998.

IV. The Hermeneutical Problem
of the New Testament's Use of the Old

Barrera, J. T. *The Jewish Bible and the Christian Bible.* Grand Rapids: Eerdmans, 1998.

Beale, G. K., ed. *The Right Doctrine from the Wrong Texts? Essays on the Use of the Old Testament in the New.* Grand Rapids: Baker, 1994.

Bellinger, W. H., and W. R. Farmer, eds. *Jesus and the Suffering Servant.* Harrisburg: Trinity, 1998.

Collins, Anthony. *A Discourse on the Grounds and Reasons of the Christian Religion.* London, 1724.

Goppelt, L. *Typos: The Typological Interpretation of the Old Testament.* Grand Rapids: Eerdmans, 1982.

Hengel, M. *The Septuagint as Christian Scripture.* Edinburgh: T. & T. Clark, 2002.

Hirsch, E. D. *The Validity of Interpretation*. New Haven: Yale University Press, 1957.

————. *The Aims of Interpretation*. Chicago: University of Chicago Press, 1976.

Kaiser, W. C. *The Uses of the Old Testament in the New*. Chicago: Moody, 1985.

Longenecker, R. N. "Can We Reproduce the Exegesis of the New Testament?" *Tyndale Bulletin* 21 (1970): 3-38.

Nineham, D. *The Use and Abuse of the Bible: A Study of the Bible in an Age of Rapid Cultural Change*. London: SPCK, 1957.

Stuhlmacher, P. *Biblische Theologie des Neuen Testaments*, vol. 2. Göttingen: Vandenhoeck & Ruprecht, 1999.

2

Justin Martyr

The importance of Justin Martyr is immediately clear when one considers that his *Dialogue with Trypho* is the first lengthy example of Christian exegesis of the Old Testament since the New Testament apart from a few Gnostic fragments, an occasional sermon (Melito), and scattered references from the Apostolic Fathers (e.g., Barnabas). Justin's *Dialogue* addresses a great variety of theological subjects that continued to surface throughout the entire history of Christian interpretation. His extensive use of the book of Isaiah makes his work crucial for the present study.

I. Life and Works

Justin is the most important of the Greek apologists of the second century. He was born in Palestine of pagan parents about the year 100 and died in 165 A.D. In the *Dialogue* he relates his conversion to Christianity, having first experimented with various Greek philosophies: Stoic, Peripatetic, and Pythagorean. As a Christian, he continued to travel about as an itinerant teacher, devoted to the defense of Christianity. He arrived in Rome and opened a school there. He was denounced by his enemies and martyred along with six companions in 165.

Although Justin was a prolific writer, only three of his works have survived. These are his two *Apologies* against the pagans and his *Dialogue* with the Jew, Trypho. The latter is the oldest apologetic against the Jews and was composed after the two *Apologies*. Unfortunately, the introduction to a portion of it has been lost.

II. Recent Research of Justin's Exegesis

The modern scholarly study of Justin's works initially focused on his Greek text as a witness to the early historical development of the Septuagint within the church. More recent attention has broadened the scope to describe his Judeo-Christian setting and to determine the various forces influencing his theology. However, the importance of Justin's biblical exegesis has generally been downplayed as something quite primitive and completely overshadowed by later writers like Irenaeus and Tertullian.

Fortunately, the impressive study of Oskar Skarsaune (1987) has done much to illuminate Justin's prooftext tradition, and to shed much light on complex textual problems, the provenance of his writings, and his theological profile. Of greatest importance for this study has been Skarsaune's evidence that Justin's exegesis was shaped by the conviction of his transmitting a received apostolic tradition from his predecessors.

Skarsaune's careful text-critical analysis has demonstrated that Justin's biblical texts have been transmitted in two versions. On the one hand, his citations represent a Greek Septuagintal text tradition that reflects an early Jewish recension that sought to bring the Greek text into line with a developing normative Hebrew text. On the other hand, there is a non-Septuagintal text, derived most probably from early Christian circles and reflecting some form of a written collection or testimony. Although there are signs of subsequent Christian reworking of portions of the *Dialogue*, it is most significant that Justin's exegesis reflects a strong continuity with earlier streams of Christian tradition within a missionary setting and is not just a later ecclesiastical construct. Although it lies beyond the scope of this study to pursue these various levels of pre-Justin and post-Justin growth, the importance of this evidence provided by Skarsaune cannot be overlooked, especially when seeking to gain a picture of Justin's Old Testament interpretation as a crucial witness from the middle of the second century.

For the purpose of this study, I will bypass two other problems that have arisen from the modern research in Justin. I will not pursue in detail the debate over discerning the structural coherence (or lack of it) of the *Dialogue*, which usually has involved reconstructing various alleged divergencies and expansions. The attempts of Bousset (1891), von Ungern-Sternberg (1919), and Skarsaune (1987) share much in common regarding the structure, but a complete consensus has not yet been reached. Nor will I explore the issue of Justin's knowledge of post-biblical Judaism in any detail, since the evidence remains largely indirect and the experts in this field continue to disagree. Justin knew no Hebrew and thus could not enter the technical debates between representative Jewish rabbis. A. Lukyn Williams (*Justin Martyr*, p. xxxiii) is probably very generous when concluding, "We must grant that Justin had at least a good working knowledge of post-biblical Judaism, a knowledge superior to that of most polemical writers against the Jews."

However, what does remain of continuing importance for this study is Skarsaune's summarizing description of the content of Justin's exegesis as reflecting two different voices (pp. 371ff.). First, there is a Jewish-Christian voice addressed to fellow Jews shortly after the Bar Kokhba revolt, in which various traditional Christian themes were developed in an effort to bring Jews to repentance and conversion. Second, there is the voice of triumphant Gentile Christianity, still in contact with rabbinical exegesis, but which has absorbed the Judeo-Christian tradition, and in so doing has greatly modified the concept of the people of God. By laying sole claim to election for the church, especially in its use of Isaiah, it has fostered a line of anti-Jewish application that issued subsequently in a tragic history of supersessionism (cf. below).

In sum, my own concerns with Justin are highly selective and determined by the overarching purpose of this study, namely, to investigate the church's reception of the Old Testament scriptures when seen especially through the lens of the interpretation of the book of Isaiah.

III. Justin's Exegesis of Isaiah

The explicit citations and implicit allusions to Isaiah in the *Dialogue* far exceed the use of any other Old Testament book. Skarsaune offers in his second appendix analytic tables of Justin's Old Testament quotations (pp. 45ff.). His particular interests cause him to include together both direct citations and allusions, and to distinguish between Septuagint and non-Septuagint quotations. Because it is often difficult to avoid subjectivity when determining allusions, I have tried initially to focus on direct citations. I find seventy-six direct quotations, thirty-nine of which are introduced by the formulae "Isaiah says," or "Isaiah cries," or "the Holy Spirit cries through Isaiah."

In terms of the frequency of Old Testament citations, Isaiah ranks ahead of the Psalter and of Genesis. Justin has not simply followed the New Testament's choice of prooftexts; rather, his citations appear to be derived from an independent Christian tradition as well as from his own creative application of the Old Testament. Of some interest is the large number of Old Testament citations held in common with the book of Romans (cf. Skarsaune's tables, pp. 93ff.). His use of Pauline material derives largely from Romans 2–4 and 10:6–11:4, and is joined within two blocks of the *Dialogue*. Equally significant are Justin's omissions of Pauline citations when addressing topics incompatible with Justin's theology (e.g., Rom. 9:6-24).

IV. The *Dialogue with Trypho*

The *Dialogue* is presented by Justin as representing a genuinely historical encounter with Trypho, the Jew, whose identity remains elusive. To what extent the context is actually only a literary device for Christian apologetics continues to be debated. Many modern Jewish scholars regard the *Dialogue* as only a Christian monologue. Yet in spite of the obvious Christian reworking of the material, it is not unreasonable to accept that some elements stem from a real debate from the middle of the second century. The issues addressed are not abstractions from a later theological age, but focus on highly existential questions rooted in the growing religious tension between Jews and Christians.

The reader of the *Dialogue* is immediately impressed with the seriousness with which the Jewish scriptures are taken by both the participants of the debate. There is a constant concern expressed by both Justin and Trypho to remain close to the biblical text, whose divine authority is assumed. Justin speaks of being "compelled" by the text and mounts a series of rational arguments to clarify his proof from scripture. The basic assumption that underlines all of Justin's exegesis is that he is following apostolic exposition that stems directly from Christ (*Dial.* 76.6). Justin has been given "the grace to understand" (*Dial.* 100.2f.). Skarsaune's interpretation of this technical phrase in Justin is convincing: the "grace to understand" is the apostolic proof from the scriptures taught by Christ to the apostles and transmitted to all Christians (p. 12). No one can understand the scriptures before Christ reveals the meaning of the prophecies.

Justin simply takes for granted that the Jewish scriptures and the apostolic tradition together constitute God's authoritative revelation. However, to speak of the latter as a New Testament is anachronistic before Irenaeus. For Justin, the Jewish scriptures, that is the Old Testament, were simply the revelation of Jesus Christ, and Isaiah was interpreted as a fifth Gospel. The piety of the Old Testament was Christian piety and, when its mysteries were properly understood, it stood in no need of any Christian correction. As one would expect, certain passages from Isaiah were cited from early Christian testimonies, most probably in written form. Chapters 7, 9, and 11 of Isaiah were assumed to be prooftexts of Jesus as Messiah, and chapter 53 spoke of Christ's passion, death, and resurrection. Isaiah 7:14 was a direct prediction of the virgin birth.

What is characteristic of Justin's exegetical approach is the extensive use of larger sections of Isaiah to mount his prooftext arguments. Obviously, Justin was not attempting to establish a historical context according to the modern rules of critical exegesis, but he did make use of the broader narrative context of the book of Isaiah to provide his warrant. Thus, in section 13, when Justin is arguing for Christian baptism as the "laver of salvation" for the Gentiles in the place of Jewish circumcision, he feels constrained to begin his prooftexts with Isa. 52:10, to include all of chapter 53, and to conclude with Isa. 54:6.

Similarly, when citing scripture's promise to the nations, he brings forth as a prooftext the whole of chapters 54 and 55 (*Dial.* 11-12). When arguing for a new dispensation (covenant), he is not content to quote the familiar New Testament warrants from Jer. 31:31-34, but cites a large portion of Isa. 55 (*Dial.* 12.1). Then again, he is not satisfied to follow Matthew's simple quotation of Isa. 7:14 as proof for the virgin birth, but returns again and again to the subject and in *Dialogue* 76 uses the entire chapter 8 of Isaiah to refute the Jewish claim that Hezekiah was the subject of the promise.

One is also somewhat amazed by the sheer scope of theological topics covered by Justin in his appeals to the Old Testament, and especially to Isaiah, as if it brought an essential part to every catena. For example,

1. Christ is Israel's everlasting king, 85.1 (Isa. 43:15)
2. God, the Creator, honors the Son, 65.3 (Isa. 42:5-13)
3. The disobedience of the Jews, 16.5 (Isa. 57:1-4); 17.2 (Isa. 5:2-5)
4. The rejection of Israel by God, 135.6 (Isa. 2:5-6)
5. The law of Moses is antiquated, 11.2 (Isa. 51:4f.)
6. Jewish sacrifices given because of Israel's sin, 20.11 (Isa. 66:1)
7. The promise of salvation to the nations, 13.8 (Isa. 52:10–54:17); 14.7 (Isa. 55:3-13)
8. The coming Messiah of divine origin, 76.3 (Isa. 53:8)
9. The mystery of Christ's birth declared in prophecy, 43.3 (Isa. 53:8); 63.5 (Isa. 7:14)
10. Christ's death and burial foretold, 97.2 (Isa. 65:2; 53:9)
11. The church, not Israel, is God's holy people, 26.3 (Isa. 62:10–63:6)
12. The promise of a new covenant, 11.3 (Isa. 51:4-5); 122.5 (Isa. 49:8)
13. The new birth in Christ, 85.7 (Isa. 65:5-11)
14. Christ will reign one thousand years in the new Jerusalem, 81.1-4 (Isa. 65:17-25).

V. Justin's Exegetical Methods

The dominant feature characterizing Justin's exegetical approach to scripture is its unreflective quality. Nowhere does one find any discussion of hermeneutical rules or any theoretical defense of his assumptions. This feature tends to strike the modern reader as curious, especially since Trypho repeatedly asks for further explanations of proofs he judges, at best, to be ambiguous, artificial, and highly selective (cf. 51.1; 27.1; 35.1; 48.1; 79.1). It is, of course, obvious that Justin assumed the validity of the exegetical approaches found in the apostolic tradition that later became the New Testament. Moreover, he continued the exegetical traditions of his other Christian sources without comment even when developing his own exegesis in new and creative ways.

The one overarching exegetical approach of Justin is that of proof-from-prophecy. The argument turns upon a demonstration that a former word of Old Testament prophecy matches its subsequent Christian fulfillment. Such an approach was common to all of the four Gospels, but was developed in different ways by each evangelist. Matthew's fulfillment formula simply announces a New Testament fulfillment by citing an Old Testament passage, apart from any further rational explanation (cf. 2:15; 2:17; etc.). In contrast, the author of Luke/Acts establishes a correspondence according to a rational two-stage development, more closely akin to that used by Justin. Indeed, Justin goes far beyond the New Testament in offering a variety of arguments based on rational demonstration (cf. N. Dahl, "The Purpose," pp. 87-97). Whereas some recent commentators have seen an inherent contradiction in Justin between his appeal to special revelation of the truth and his use of rationality, Skarsaune rejects this distinction as being incomprehensible for Justin (pp. 12-13). We shall return to this issue later in the chapter.

At times the confirmation of a proof-from-prophecy stemmed from a literal reading of the biblical text. Justin drew his evidence from "the scripture and the facts" (28.2). The birth of Jesus from a virgin as a fulfillment of Isa. 7:14 was evident because no one else has been born of a virgin (66.2). Similarly, John the Baptist's appearance was considered a fulfillment of the prophecy of Elijah's return and was deemed conclusive because he alone appeared after prophecy had ceased (51.1-3). The prophecy of Isa. 8:4 that the power of Damascus and Syria would be broken by the king of Assyria was literally fulfilled in Matt. 2:1 since the wise men came from Arabia — that is, from Damascus — after seeing Herod who was called king of Assyria (Hos. 10:6). In this case, the literal correspondence simply needed a rational clarification (77.2-4).

However, frequently the proof-from-prophecy finds its warrant in a typological interpretation. There is no indication that Justin drew any sharp distinction between the literal and the figurative, because he intertwined the two approaches without any specific hermeneutical reflection. At times a proof-from-prophecy could function both on the literal level (66.1-2) and also on a typological level (68.6). Isaiah 53 is interpreted as a literal prediction of Christ's suffering and death, but also as a type of the passover lamb (111.2).

Certain sections such as 40–42 have often been regarded as a literary parenthesis and abound in traditional typologies. Christ is a type of the passover (40.1-3) and of the day of atonement. The offering for lepers (41.1-3) represents the Eucharist. The bells on the robe of the high priest are a type of the apostles (42.1). Or again, Justin engages in fanciful speculation in seeing the cross in the shape of the horns of the unicorn (109.2) or the shed blood of Christ in the symbol of the scarlet cord in the book of Joshua (111.4).

There is another exegetical approach that runs through the *Dialogue* and is frequently used in a highly polemical context. Justin speaks of God's accommodating himself to Israel (19.6). He gave Israel ceremonies (27.2ff.), rituals such as circumcision, and Sabbath observances as a sign (21.1). However, these concessions had no positive theological dimension, such as an initial step toward a fuller divine purpose. Justin has no concept of a *Heilsgeschichte;* rather, the concessions arose because of Israel's sinfulness and disobedience (22.1; 19.2). These commands were unnecessary for attaining God's salvation, and the rite of circumcision, like the old dispensation, was rendered worthless in the light of Jesus Christ. The fact that Adam was created uncircumcised is offered as evidence that God never desired circumcision (19.2). Justin does develop the concept of two separate advents (111.6; 49.7), but this scheme functions within a special context to explain the Messiah's suffering and humiliation as well as final victory.

Finally, Justin resorts to an interpretation of the Old Testament theophanies as an evidence of Christ's pre-existence before his incarnation, which became a basic component of all future Christian interpretation. Whereas in the New Testament the appeal to Jesus' active presence within Israel's history is infrequent and serves as part of John's catalogue of witnesses (8:56; 12:41), in Justin such interpretations are expansive and form an approach distinctive from simple typology. Accordingly, Christ encountered Abraham at Mamre (56), wrestled with Jacob at the Jabbok (58.6), and spoke with Moses at the burning bush (59.1ff.). The discussion of "another God" (50.1) falls largely in chapters 56–60, 75, and 126-29 in the *Dialogue* (cf. Skarsaune, pp. 409ff.). Only later in the subsequent history of interpretation did the full problematic of this approach emerge as a threat to Christology and trinitarian theology.

When Skarsaune (pp. 380ff.) speaks of the "recapitulation idea," he is describing Justin's pattern of the pre-existent Messiah who as the new Adam conquers the devil and thus reverses the defeat of the first Adam. However, this use of an overarching analogy between the Old and the New has a strong mythological flavor in Justin, and is a typology foreign to a genuine historical sequence developing within the divine economy.

VI. An Evaluation of Justin's Exegesis

1. Strengths

Often in the history of interpretation there has been a tendency to denigrate Justin as an example of primitive exegetical misunderstanding that has largely served as a liability to the Christian church ever since (cf. F. W. Farrar and R. P. C. Hanson). Yet I would argue that this evaluation fails to reckon with Justin's positive contributions. It is imperative to understand how Justin received an exegetical tradition and applied it to the issues of his age, indeed both for better and for worse.

1. First, it is crucial to understand that for Justin, as for the authors of the New Testament, the Jewish scriptures were the sacred writings of the church. This means that, in striking contrast to a later period, the Old Testament was not considered to be a theological problem, but was simply received as divine revelation. The difficulty lay with its interpretation. For Justin the primary challenge to the church's understanding was posed by the strongly divergent reading of the sacred writings held by the Jews. In his *Dialogue* Justin addresses a series of burning issues with the purpose of making the case for the truth of the Christian faith in terms of biblical exegesis. He does not distance himself from the Jewish scriptures or consciously filter them through extra-biblical Gnostic speculations, but focuses his full attention on finding evidence for his faith from the Jewish scriptures he holds in common with Trypho. The wide range of his citations from the entire biblical corpus is also characteristic of his approach.

Justin thus stands in close continuity with what became the New Testament and the received apostolic tradition he inherited. He interprets the Jewish scriptures, now in Greek translation, from the perspective of the gospel, but conversely he shapes his interpretation of the gospel from a careful study of the Jewish scriptures. In contrast to many later Christian interpreters, he does not merely replace the Old Testament voice with that of the New, but seriously wrestles with the Old Testament text as a true vehicle of the evangelical witness.

2. Justin's approach to the Jewish scriptures in his defense of the Christian faith is an attempt to describe it from within the structure of the confessing church. Within this context he then tries to articulate and affirm the theological coherence of his faith. His basic assumption is that he is standing within a received apostolic tradition that issues directly from the risen Christ. Although there are clearly elements of his theology that later Church Fathers and Schoolmen could only regard as idiosyncratic and inadequate for the orthodox faith of the church, many modern readers will react with a favorable impression of how well Justin has grasped the central elements of the faith in spite of some obvious lapses. Justin identifies completely with the Jewish understanding of God as the benevolent creator of the world who has willed the salvation of his people in divine mercy through a promised Messiah, and who demands of his chosen a life of righteousness and obedience.

Justin's contribution is in his great effort to find the Jewish scriptures bearing witness to the divine eternality of Jesus the Messiah. Enormous energy is expended in proving from scripture the mystery of Jesus' miraculous birth and the prophecy of his suffering and death through which salvation for a faithful new people was accomplished. He attempts to show at every point that the pattern of the old and the new dispensation, of sin and forgiveness, of a faithful and rejected response, extends throughout the Old Testament. Moreover, in contrast to many of the early Fathers, Justin has a serious grasp of some elements of Pauline theology: the righteousness of God and the Christological grounds of Abraham's faith. It is also of interest to observe how Justin continues to develop in a creative manner a theological interpretation of the two advents of Christ in order to deal with the diversity of the Old Testament's description of the coming Messiah (14.8; 110.1-6).

3. Along with his explicit confessional stance, Justin also strives to mount a rational defense of his position in an effort to persuade Trypho of its cogency. He treats Trypho with both respect and seriousness. He attempts to argue his case from rational evidence, seeking common ground with his Jewish antagonist. At times he is somewhat effective in showing why the traditional Jewish exegesis that sees Hezekiah or Solomon as the intended referent of the Isaianic promises is exegetically unlikely (43.5; 33.1-2; 35.3-6). Although Justin knows no Hebrew, he is aware of the linguistic problems involved in interpreting Isa. 7:14 (67.1). Occasionally he makes a significant stylistic observation regarding the biblical text when explaining how a past verbal tense can function grammatically as a future (114.1). Moreover, he attempts at least to

blunt the force of mythological parallels when he views them as a challenge to the uniqueness of the Christian faith (69–70).

2. Weaknesses

1. Certainly the most troublesome aspect of Justin's exegesis arises immediately from his serious misunderstanding of Judaism. The distortion lies on many levels and serves to promote a legacy of lasting hostility and alienation between Jews and Christians ever since.

Throughout the *Dialogue* Justin applies all the prophetic attacks on ancient Israel for its disobedience toward God directly to all Jews everywhere, past and present. Thus, in Isa. 3:9-11 and 5:18-20, when Isaiah attacks the rulers of eighth-century Israel for their transgressions, Justin transfers these accusations directly to the Jews of his own day (17.1). He accuses all Jews of having crucified Jesus, God's righteous One. Moreover, he radically politicizes the issue by shifting the context of the Hebrew prophet's attack on his own people to one that sets Jew against Gentile (Christian).

He then develops a most extreme form of Christian supersessionism: God has rejected Israel as his chosen people and replaced it with the Christian church (119.1-5). Since God has now "dismissed his people," Jew and Christian have been totally separated into "two seeds of Judah, and two races and two houses of Jacob, the one born of flesh and blood, the other of faith and spirit" (135.6). The tragic implications of this politicizing of a theological issue became clear very shortly when Christian authorities exerted their political hegemony within the Roman Empire to oppress the Jews as the enemies of God.

2. Second, the theological effect of Justin's approach to Judaism resulted in his widespread Christianizing of the Old Testament. He could find nothing of value in Israel's religious life, its laws, rites, and piety, unless they were interpreted Christologically as pointing to the promise of the new covenant. Accordingly, circumcision, sabbaths, and festivals arose from Israel's "hardness of heart" (18.2). Needless to say, Justin's rendering of the Old Testament severely affected his understanding of the New Testament, not only in his failure to understand Jesus as a faithful Jew, but also in not grasping Paul's hope of the restoration of Israel as the climax of God's eschatological purpose (Romans 9–11).

3. Third, Justin's misunderstanding of the relation of prophecy and fulfillment, which he conceives of as a narrow matching of ancient prediction with an objective, factual event, greatly distorts this biblical category. The very indeterminate and mysterious relation between promise and Christo-

logical fulfillment within the New Testament should serve as a caution against the highly rationalistic formulation of Justin. Skarsaune (pp. 12f.) has argued that there is no contradiction in Justin between his claim of special revelation as the key to correct interpretation and his constant appeal to rational proofs of common human reason. Skarsaune is certainly right in concluding that Justin saw no conflict. However, the theological problem at issue of "revelation and reason," or "foundationalism and fideism," continues to plague Christian theology and cannot be easily dismissed.

4. Finally, Justin received an ecclesiastical tradition of exegesis going back to the New Testament and beyond that saw no real difficulty in interpreting scripture on a variety of different levels. Part of Justin's strength was his ability to enrich his interpretation by appeals to a figurative sense, albeit in an unreflective, uncontrolled manner. But it is clear that Christian theologians would soon have to address seriously the exegetical issues of the text's multiple senses, lest the biblical message be atomized into an incoherent fragment without a clear profile.

To summarize, scholars have often evaluated Justin's contribution by outlining his various theological concepts, such as his doctrines of God, Christ, and the church (cf. Quasten, *Patrology*, pp. 196ff.). The result has been that Justin's positive contributions have emerged as quite minimal and his deficiencies have been emphasized.

In contrast to such an approach, it seems to me crucial in attempting to understand the role of the history of Christian biblical interpretation to focus the investigation not only on the time-conditioned attempts of individual expositors, but also to set their work within a larger ongoing process — both historical and theological — in which exegetical traditions were received, transmitted, and corrected in the light of a continuing response to the coercion of the text itself. When so viewed, Justin's role, in all its frailty and imperfection, forms a crucial stage in the church's struggle with its scripture toward a more faithful growth in the knowledge of God.

Bibliography of Justin

Primary Sources

Justini philosophi et martyris opera, edited by J. C. T. Otto. Vols. 1-3. Jena, 1857, reprinted 1968.

Justin Martyr: The Dialogue with Trypho, edited by A. Lukyn Williams. London: SPCK, 1930.

Justin Martyr. Ante-Nicene Christian Library, vol. 2, edited by A. Roberts and J. Donaldson. Edinburgh: T. & T. Clark, 1887; reprint, Grand Rapids: Eerdmans, 1976.

The First Apology of Justin, the Martyr, edited by E. R. Hardy, pp. 242-89. Philadelphia: Westminster, 1953.

Justin, edited by T. B. Falls. Fathers of the Church, 6. Washington: Catholic University of America, 1948.

Secondary Sources

Aune, D. E. "Justin Martyr's Use of the Old Testament." *Bulletin of the Evangelical Theological Society* 9 (1966): 179-97.

Bardy, G. "Justin." In *Dictionnaire de Théologie Catholique,* 8 (1925): 2228-77.

Barnard, L. W. "The Old Testament and Judaism in the Writings of Justin Martyr." *Vetus Testamentum* 14 (1964): 395-406.

———. *Justin Martyr, His Life and Thought.* Cambridge: Cambridge University Press, 1967.

Bokser, B. Z. "Justin Martyr and the Jews." *Jewish Quarterly Review,* n.s., 64 (1973/74): 97-122; 204-11.

Brox, N. "Zum literarischen Verhältnis zwischen Justin und Irenaeus." *Zeitschrift für die neutestamentliche Wissenschaft* 58 (1967): 121-28.

Chadwick, H. "Justin Martyr's Defense of Christianity." *Bulletin of the John Rylands University Library* 47 (1965): 275-97.

Cosgrove, C. H. "Justin Martyr and the Emerging Christian Canon: Observations on the Purpose and Destination of the Dialogue with Trypho." *Vigiliae Christianae* 36 (1982): 209-32.

Dahl, N. A. "The Purpose of Luke-Acts." In *Jesus in the Memory of the Early Church,* pp. 87-98. Minneapolis: Augsburg Press, 1976.

Farrar, F. W. *The History of Interpretation.* London: Dutton, 1886; reprint, Grand Rapids: Baker, 1961.

Frend, W. H. C. "The Old Testament in the Age of the Greek Apologists." *Scottish Journal of Theology* 26 (1973): 129-150.

Goodenough, E. R. *The Theology of Justin Martyr.* Jena: Frommanische Buchhandlung, 1923; reprinted 1968.

Greer, R. A., with J. L. Kugel. *Early Biblical Interpretation,* pp. 146-57. Philadelphia: Westminster, 1986.

Hanson, R. P. C. "Biblical Exegesis in the Early Church." In *Cambridge History of the Bible,* vol. 1, edited by P. R. Ackroyd, pp. 412-54. Cambridge: Cambridge University Press, 1970.

Hengel, M. "Die Septuaginta als von den Christen beanspruchte Schrift-sammlung bei Justin und den Vätern vor Origenes." In *Jews and Christians: The Parting of the Ways A.D. 70 to 135,* edited by J. D. G. Dunn, pp. 39-84. Tübingen: Mohr Siebeck, 1992.

Higgins, A. J. B. "Jewish Messianic Belief in Justin Martyr's Dialogue with Trypho." *Novum Testamentum* 9 (1969): 298-305.

Horbury, W. "Jewish-Christian Relations in Barnabas and Justin Martyr." In *Jews and Christians,* edited by J. D. G. Dunn, pp. 315-45. Tübingen: Mohr Siebeck, 1992.

Kurz, W. S. "The Function of Christological Proof from Prophecy for Luke and Justin." Yale University dissertation, 1976.

Osborn, E. F. *Justin Martyr.* Tübingen: Mohr Siebeck, 1973.

Prigent, P. *Justin et l'Ancien Testament.* Paris: J. Gabalda, 1964.

Quasten, J. *Patrology,* vol. 1, pp. 196-219. Westminster, Md.: Newman Press, 1950.

Sawyer, J. F. A. "Combating Prejudices about the Bible and Judaism." *Theology* 94 (1991): 269-78.

Shotwell, W. H. *The Biblical Exegesis of Justin Martyr.* London: SPCK, 1965.

Skarsaune, O. *The Proof from Prophecy. A Study in Justin Martyr's Proof-Text Tra-dition: Text-Type, Provenance, Theological Profile.* Leiden: Brill, 1987.

Watson, F. *Text and Truth,* pp. 317-29. Edinburgh: T. & T. Clark, 1997.

3

Irenaeus

The Christian church's struggle with interpreting its scriptures can be most clearly seen when one moves from Justin to Irenaeus. Justin's work was known and cited by Irenaeus. Indeed, much of the inherited exegetical tradition found in Justin continues in Irenaeus, which is evident when one compares the list of his biblical citations in the *Demonstration of Apostolic Preaching* with the *Dialogue*. However, the development of an interpretive method by Irenaeus over and above that of Justin is of critical importance. As a result it is not an exaggeration to say with Quasten (*Patrology,* vol. 1, p. 207), "Irenaeus of Lyon is by far the most important of the theologians of the second century."

I. Life and Work (c. 130-200)

Little is known of the life of Irenaeus. It is thought that he was a native of Smyrna, but the reason why he left Asia Minor and went to Gaul is uncertain. He studied in Rome and later became bishop of Lyon. The tradition that he heard Polycarp as a child rests on fairly good evidence. It further buttresses his connection with the earliest apostolic tradition, and enhances his pivotal role as a link between the Eastern and Western churches. Whether he died as a martyr remains uncertain.

His great work against Gnosticism, *Adversus Haereses (Against Heresies,* or *AH),* is only partially extant in Greek, but fortunately the whole is preserved in Latin. Only in modern times was a second work discovered in an Armenian translation, *The Demonstration of the Apostolic Preaching.* It is an apologetic work, but of unusual importance in its wide use of the Old Testament.

II. Irenaeus as a Biblical Theologian

The concern of this chapter is obviously not to explore the full range of Irenaeus's thought, but rather to focus on his use of the book of Isaiah as an avenue into his larger biblical interpretation. In the late 1940s, John Lawson wrote a book that had a considerable impact on the English-speaking world. From its title, *The Biblical Theology of Saint Irenaeus,* one can discern that it grew out of the renewed interest in biblical theology during the immediate post–World War II period. Lawson used his study of Irenaeus to address a wide variety of hermeneutical problems that were being addressed at that time under the rubric of biblical theology.

My initial interest in Lawson's book arose from his very correct observation that the book of Isaiah played a central role in Irenaeus's theology, and thus it provides a good point of entrance into the heart of Irenaeus's exegesis of the Bible. Lawson offers a list of the chief citations from Isaiah by Irenaeus, and then provides various categories by which to arrange the material. However, very shortly it became painfully clear that Lawson's discussion of Irenaeus's interpretation of Isaiah was flawed and served as a warning for critically trained biblical scholars on how *not* to read Irenaeus.

Lawson's major error is in evaluating Irenaeus's contributions always by the critical norms of late nineteenth-century biblical scholarship. Thus, at the outset he describes Irenaeus's interpretation as hardly scientific or historical. He had no interest in determining the biblical authors' original intentions. Rather, Irenaeus had his own theological agenda, which he imposed on the Old Testament prophet in a heavy-handed manner. Although he does praise "Second Isaiah's" universalistic perspective respecting the nations, and comments positively on Irenaeus's principle of progressive revelation, Lawson is repelled by Irenaeus's allegorical method, in which every detail of the Old Testament is referred to Christ. Lawson concludes by evaluating Irenaeus's exegesis "as fanciful" and far removed from the concerns of the original authors (p. 62).

With much regret, I am forced to conclude that Lawson has not succeeded in doing justice to Irenaeus. His assumption that the nineteenth-century historical-critical approach provides the sole criteria for proper biblical exegesis has virtually blocked his access to any serious understanding of Irenaeus as a biblical expositor. Clearly another tack is needed, one that requires both critical reflection and empathy.

III. Irenaeus's Use of the *regula fidei* as a Framework

The shifting historical context of the Christian church in the middle of the second century is immediately evident in the writings of Irenaeus, and its influence on him should not be underestimated. For Irenaeus, the major focus has moved from controversy with Judaism to an intense controversy with Gnosticism in its various forms. Then again, in contrast to Justin's dependence on evangelical tradition from which to interpret the Jewish scriptures, Irenaeus for the first time speaks of a written New Testament corpus consisting at least of four Gospels, the Acts, and apostolic letters, especially of Paul, which Irenaeus cites in written form as authoritative scripture along with the Old Testament. Finally, the organizational nature of the early church had continued to develop and the appeal to the Great Church with its perpetual succession of presbyters forms the only legitimate source for pure apostolic doctrine (*AH* 1.3.4).

R. A. Greer's illuminating description of Irenaeus's hermeneutical contribution (*Early Biblical Interpretation,* pp. 155-213) correctly focuses on Irenaeus's central innovations, both in clarifying the identity of Christ and in formulating a framework for interpreting the whole of Christian scripture. He extended the hermeneutical issues far beyond Justin and established an interpretive stance that influenced all subsequent Christian theology.

The most succinct formulation of Irenaeus's approach is found in his appeal to a "rule of faith" (*regula fidei*). In the nineteenth century this formula was generally identified with an early baptismal creed, but more recently the term has taken on a sharper profile (cf. Hägglund, "Die Bedeutung," pp. 1ff.). In Irenaeus, the rule of faith was a summary of the apostolic faith that was held as central to the church's confession. It provided the grounds of the church's faith and worship over against deviant Gnostic speculation. The rule was not identical with scripture, but was that sacred apostolic tradition, both in oral and written form, that comprised the church's story. In *Against Heresies* 1.8.1, Irenaeus depicts the beautiful mosaic of a king constructed out of precious jewels, which the Gnostics rearrange to form the miserable likeness of a dog or fox. In contrast to such distortions, the rule of faith was a holistic rendering of the apostolic faith according to its proper order (*Dem.* 52; *AH* 1.9.4; 2.27.1). In other places within Irenaeus's writings it is clear that they adumbrated the Apostles' Creed. In one famous passage (*AH* 1.10.1) Irenaeus sets forth what the church believes:

> in one God, the Father Almighty, Maker of heaven and earth, and the sea
> . . . and in one Jesus Christ, the Son of God, who became incarnate for our
> salvation; and in the Holy Spirit.

Careful attention to this overarching framework provides the key to discerning the hermeneutical contribution of Irenaeus. Although it remains difficult to determine with exact precision how much of Irenaeus's formulation was inherited from his predecessors, it would be surely a mistake to underestimate his individual stamp. Many of the individual parts of his argument are common to Barnabas, Justin, and Clement, but the hermeneutical coherence and depth of theological reflection arise to a different level of understanding in Irenaeus.

IV. Isaiah in the *Demonstration of Apostolic Preaching*

It seems pedagogically advantageous to begin an analysis of Irenaeus's use of the book of Isaiah by turning first to his *Demonstration of Apostolic Preaching*, even though this book was written after *Against Heresies*. (The recent debate over the dating of certain concluding chapters in the *Demonstration* is peripheral to the present study. Cf. the bibliography in J. Behr's translation, pp. 119-21.) In principle, the two works of Irenaeus share the same hermeneutical approach, but in his larger work concern with the description and refutation of the Gnostics often overshadows the clarity and coherence of his biblical exegesis.

The structure of the *Demonstration* is fully clear in offering an exposition of apostolic preaching. In the first paragraphs Irenaeus appeals to the rule of faith *(kanōn)* as keeping the faith firm. Then in 3b-16, after summarizing the three articles of the faith — God the Father, creator; Jesus Christ, Word of God, Son of God; Holy Spirit, instructor of the prophets and renewer of the world — he describes the truth about God and the creation. Next in 17-30, he describes the history of God's preparing the world for salvation by the Son by tracing the Old Testament stories after the fall from Adam to Moses. Paragraphs 31-40a treat of the salvation achieved by the Son by setting up a typology between the first and second Adam, between Eve and Mary, and the tree of disobedience and the cross of Christ. He then concludes by recounting Christ's fulfillment of the promise to Abraham and David, and the calling of the Gentiles.

The second major part of the *Demonstration* offers Irenaeus's proof of the truth of the Christian faith by means of scripture: "All these things . . . were foretold by the Spirit of God through the prophets . . . for our salvation" (42b). A rehearsal of this structure is helpful in showing the great variety of exegetical techniques used within the overarching framework of the rule of faith. The important function of the book of Isaiah also becomes apparent.

48

As we have seen, the introduction of the *Demonstration* (1-3a) set forth Irenaeus's intention to transmit the apostolic faith truthfully by means of the rule of faith. The same concern is exhibited in more detail in *Against Heresies* (3.4.1), namely: "there is one God, the Father, who by the Son, the Word, established the heaven and by the Spirit arranges and shapes it." When Irenaeus in 3b-16 of the *Demonstration* discusses God and God's relation to humanity, his biblical references are mainly to Genesis. However, the framework of his description is interspersed in crucial places with a New Testament formulation: "One God, the Father, who is above all, and through all and in us all" (Eph. 1:10; *Dem.* 5).

When Irenaeus turns to the preparation for salvation by tracing the Old Testament history from Adam and Eve, through the patriarchal stories, Moses, the exodus, and the conquest, several themes appear (*AH* 3.23.1-7; *Dem.* 17-30). First, the Old Testament's narratives are rendered almost entirely according to a literal reading that follows the biblical sequence. Only when his account reaches the prophets is the Christian theology of God's eternal purpose made explicit (*Dem.* 30). Second, the nature of the depiction is of a *Heilsgeschichte,* that is, the purpose of God for his creation unfolds in successive revelations directed toward the eschatological close of the age. Israel's history forms an indissoluble theological unity with that of the church and is not viewed as simply a background for the real event of Christ's incarnation.

In chapters 31-40 of the *Demonstration,* the author describes the salvation accomplished by the Son. The approach here is largely typologically structured (*AH* 3.21.10; 5.19.1; etc.). The biblical references are interspersed from the Old Testament and the New Testament. The first Adam is contrasted with the second, Eve with Mary, and the tree of disobedience with that of the cross. The typology is developed in terms of God's reestablishing in Christ what had earlier been lost through sin and disobedience. The theology is further developed as establishing "our participation in incorruptibility" (*Dem.* 31), that "mortality might be swallowed up in immortality." Isa. 50:5-6 is cited ("I placed my back to the scourging") as a description of Christ's obedience unto death. *Demonstration* 35 ends with an invitation to the dispersed, using an allusion to Isa. 11:12 and John 11:52.

The purpose of regaining what was lost leads directly to the fulfillment of Old Testament promises to Abraham and David (*Dem.* 35ff.). The argument of proof from prophecy is made almost entirely from New Testament citations. The approach is somewhat different from Justin's, although the basic content is the same, and largely conventional. The fulfillment is simply assumed and announced by means of a New Testament citation. There is no effort made to establish an exact historical correspondence. Still, the element of rational proof is not entirely missing. In a series of rhetorical questions, he asks, How can one accept Christ's resurrection from the dead without accepting his birth from a virgin? Can one even speak of the resurrection of one who is not begotten? (*Dem.* 37). The element of proclamation is everywhere dominant in Irenaeus's linking of his biblical exegesis to his Christian audience: "by this communion with God we receive participation in incorruptibility" (*Dem.* 40).

When Irenaeus addresses the eternal existence of Christ in paragraphs 43-52, he returns to an earlier exegetical tradition used by Barnabas, Clement, and Justin. Using conventional texts, Irenaeus is at pains to demonstrate from Old Testament theophanies that the Son of God was actually present and active in Israel's history, and thus he existed before his incarnation. The texts used are familiar, also occurring in *Against Heresies* (4.10.1-2): Abraham is visited by three men (Gen. 18:1-3); Jacob sees him standing upon a ladder (tree) (Gen. 28:10-15); he speaks to Moses at the burning bush (Exod. 3:4).

This inherited exegetical approach cannot be identified immediately as allegory, if understood in its later medieval form. Usually a larger Old Testament narrative text is examined and a proof is sought exegetically that the theophanic appearance can only be understood if interpreted Christologically. The approach is not dependent upon any specific New Testament citation and clearly was developed before the evangelical traditions took the written form of a New Testament. It is noteworthy to observe that this section that deals largely with the Old Testament theophanies is concluded by two citations from Isaiah (45:1; 49:5ff.). In both cases the first person address is construed as the voice of Christ, which is used further to confirm his preexistence. In the case of Isa. 45:1, Irenaeus follows Justin in reading "Lord" *(kyrio)* instead of "Cyrus" *(kyro)*. Scholars differ as to whether this change resulted from an accidental textual error or from an intentional repointing of the Hebrew as occurred in Jewish midrash and in Paul.

Paragraphs 53-66 address the human birth of Jesus, and paragraphs 67-85 follow with a description of his miracles, passion, and glorification. Several things are of interest at the outset of those sections. Instead of focusing on Old Testament theophanies found largely in a narrative context, the major prooftexts are now prophetic. Citations from the Psalms also occur, but these are also explicitly interpreted as prophecy (*Dem.* 72). This hermeneutical move to proof-from-prophecy had already been made in the conclusion of the former section (*Dem.* 48-52). The human birth of Christ is demonstrated, above all, from the book of Isaiah in paragraphs 53-57, 59-61, and 65. Although there are scattered references to New Testament passages, the major attention falls on prophetic texts, which are cited in larger sections, much like Justin.

Yet Irenaeus's appeal to proof-from-prophecy differs from Justin in several respects. The attempt to relate a unified story in sequence is much stronger in Irenaeus, reflecting more clearly the framework of his rule of faith. Then again, the appeal to a demonstrable historical correspondence as the major element of the proof has been somewhat modified. Now the theological issue at stake forms a center into which various texts are interpreted. Larger issues such as the nature of the incarnation, the letter and the Spirit, and the new covenant give an impressive coherence to the string of prophetic texts cited. Finally, Irenaeus offers careful exegesis of the Old Testament prophecies in order to ground the truth of the apostolic faith on the theological substance of the biblical witness.

When dealing with the virgin birth in Isa. 7:14-16 (*Dem.* 53), Irenaeus pursues not only the miraculous elements but also the theological implications of Christ's being truly a man, who ate food, who was called a child and given a name. When interpreting Isa. 9:5-7, he draws from the text that the Son of God was "begotten" and "an eternal king," an issue greatly elaborated on in *Against Heresies* (3.16.1ff.; 3.19.1ff.). He also attempts to demonstrate from the Greek text of Isaiah 9 that there is the hope of salvation for the faithful Israelites living before Christ's manifestation. Although the framework of a history of salvation dominates, the ontological dimension of Christ's work in reference to the Old Testament is already present, though not always fully developed.

Within the larger framework of proof-from-prophecy, an explicit allegorical element appears in both *Against Heresies* and *Demonstration,* albeit in a rather minor role. In paragraph 56 of the *Demonstration* he interprets the phrase "whose government is upon his shoulders" as referring "allegorically" (in a figure) to the cross, upon which his shoulders were nailed. Or again, in *Dem.* 57, he makes use of the traditional allegory that "the blood of the grape" in Gen. 49:11 is the blood of Christ. Finally, in *Dem.* 61, the concord among the animals in Isa. 11:6-7 is interpreted figuratively as referring to "men of different races gathered peacefully by the name of Christ." However a modern reader understands the role of allegory, it is a constant and constitutive element in all the exegesis of the early church that has to be seriously addressed.

As one would expect, the treatment of Christ's passion and glorification, which is the subject matter of paragraphs 67-85, is dominated by a careful interpretation of Isa. 52:13–53:12. The exegesis continually probes into the theological significance of Christ's abasement. Irenaeus sees the judgment affecting salvation for some and destruction for others. He enriches his interpretation of chapter 53 with references to other familiar prophecies (Zech. 13:7; Hos. 10:6), but especially from Psalms 2, 22, and 118 (cf. *AH* 4.32.12).

Matthew's account of the passion fills the picture of his betrayal by Judas and the burial. A citation of Acts 1 concludes the description of Christ's ascension into heaven and his sitting on the right hand of the Father according to Psalm 110.

The final major section of the *Demonstration* (86-97) focuses on the calling of the Gentiles and the formation of a new people of God. Several features are significant in Irenaeus's exegetical approach here. First, in contrast to the earlier paragraphs, the citations of scripture reflect a close intertwining of passages from both testaments. Moreover, there are no larger biblical sections cited, with the exception of Jer. 31:31-34, which of course has its parallel in Heb. 8:8-12. Again, the audience is now the Christian believers, who are addressed homiletically not to return to the old ways of the Mosaic law (*Dem.* 89), but instead to live in the newness of the Spirit. The new people is defined as the church in contrast to the synagogue (*Dem.* 94). Significantly, the eschatological portrayal of the new age is made with continual appeal to Isaiah, especially to chapters 2, 43, 50, 63, 65, and 66. The old things are no longer to be remembered, but the Gentiles are to inherit the promises of the old covenant.

The most characteristic feature of this final section is that the meaning of life derived from God's calling of a new people is depicted from the imperatives of the whole Christian Bible. Because of what God in Christ has done, the Christian is called upon to do what is pleasing to God (*Dem.* 86). The commandments of God are still in force: "You shall love the Lord your God with all your heart and strength." Then Irenaeus notes that Paul writes, "Love is the fulfillment of the law" (Rom. 10:18). The proclamation of the prophets is continued in the apostolic faith that announces the good tidings of the gospel. The letter of the old has been replaced by the newness of the Spirit (*Dem.* 90).

V. Irenaeus's Hermeneutical Contribution

Irenaeus begins his *Demonstration* by appealing to a rule of faith as a summary of the apostolic faith and sure guide for interpreting scripture. Within this overarching framework he employs various exegetical techniques, many of which vary greatly but are closely akin in effect and flow into each other. One approach focuses on Israel's history as the revelation of God's one purpose leading toward Christ's salvation for the world. Another offers a typological pattern matching features of the Old and New Testaments. Then again, Irenaeus employs a form of Christian allegory inherited from earlier apologists in which the actual presence of Christ is drawn from an Old Testament passage without any appeal to the New Testament in order to offer further proof for the pre-existence of the Son at work in the world with the Father and Holy Spirit. This focus predominantly on the Old Testament as evidence for the truth of the apostolic faith continues in a proof-from-prophecy technique inherited from Justin. However, with Irenaeus the Christological reading of the Old Testament focuses on establishing exegetically the theological substance of the faith in which both the unity and coherence of the entire biblical story emerges with great force. Finally, Irenaeus's concern to make the Christian witness from a single vision of both testaments succeeded in joining tradition and scripture into one unified source of revelation for the instruction of the universal people of God throughout all ages and for all creation.

Clearly the contribution of Irenaeus was enormous. Yet major hermeneutical and theological problems remained that were shortly to erupt. This analysis of Irenaeus's biblical approach has sought to show that he attempted to recover a holistic reading of the Bible that united both testaments within a history of salvation. He recognized the unfolding character of the salvific events. Although the Old Testament remained crucial in every way to his thinking, modern scholars have often criticized him as having simply Christianized the Old Testament. They have argued that he used as his context for interpretation not the original historical context of the stories, but a theological one informed by his understanding of God's unified redemptive purpose in Christ, God's eternal Word. There is some truth in the accusation. However, I would argue that the concept of his "transforming the Old Testament" (R. A. Greer's expression) is a more precise description than that of christianizing it. Without denigrating the Old Testament's witness, he sought to extend its message to embrace the overwhelming sense of the newness of the gospel.

Irenaeus's assumption of a pattern of prophecy and fulfillment meant that he followed the New Testament's lead in seeing a typological relation between the Old and the New that moved along an eschatological trajectory toward its final consummation. Yet the very fact that Irenaeus also employed allegory in depicting a symbolic relation between the literal and the figurative dimension of the text, between the earthly and the heavenly, shows that the hermeneutical problem of the text's multivalent character had emerged without careful scrutiny or critical reflection. It was only in the next generation, in the interpretation of Clement and especially Origen, that the full dimensions of the developing Christian exegetical tradition surfaced as a massive challenge.

Bibliography of Irenaeus

Primary Sources

Patrologia Graeco-Latina, edited by J.-P. Migne, 7-7, 2 vols.

Sancti Irenaei Episcopi Lugdunensis. Libros quinque adversus haereses, vols. 1-2, edited by W. W. Harvey. Cambridge: Cambridge University Press, 1857.

Contre les Hérésies, edited by A. Rousseau et al., 5 vols. Sources Chrétiennes. Paris: Editions du Cerf, 1969-82.

Irenaeus, St. Ante-Nicene Christian Library, vols. 5 and 9, edited by A. Roberts and J. Donaldson. Edinburgh: T. & T. Clark, 1868-69; reprint, Grand Rapids: Eerdmans, 1976.

The Demonstration of Apostolic Preaching, edited by J. A. Robinson. London: SPCK, 1920.

St. Irenaeus: Proof of the Apostolic Preaching, edited by J. P. Smith. New York: Newman Press, 1952.

St. Irenaeus of Lyon. On the Apostolic Preaching, edited by J. Behr. Crestwood, N.Y.: St. Vladimir's Seminary Press, 1997.

Secondary Sources

Benoit, A. *Saint Irénée: Introduction à l'étude de sa théologie*. Paris: Presses Universitaires, 1960.

Blanchard, Y.-M. *Aux sources du canon: Le témoignage d'Irénée*. Paris: Editions du Cerf, 1993.

Daniélou, J. "Saint Irénée et les origines de la théologie de l'histoire." *Recherches de science religieuse* 34 (1947): 227-31.

Farkasfaly, D. "Theology of Scripture in St. Irenaeus." *Revue Bénédictine* 78 (1968): 319-33.

Grant, R. M. "The Apologists and Irenaeus." In *The Letter and the Spirit*, pp. 75-84. New York: Macmillan Co., 1957.

Greer, R. A. (with J. Kugel). *Early Biblical Interpretation*, pp. 107-213. Philadelphia: Westminster, 1986.

Hägglund, B. "Die Bedeutung der 'regula fidei' als Grundlage theologischer Aussagen." *Studia Theologica* 12 (1958): 1-44.

Hanson, R. P. C. "Biblical Exegesis in the Early Church." In *Cambridge History of the Bible*, vol. 1, edited by P. R. Ackroyd, pp. 412-54. Cambridge: Cambridge University Press, 1970.

Hefner, P. "Theological Methodology in St. Irenaeus." *Journal of Religion* 44 (1964): 249-309.

Herrera, S. *Saint Irénée de Lyon exégète.* Paris, 1920.

Jourjon, M. "Irenaeus's Reading of the Bible." In *The Bible in Greek Christian Antiquity,* edited by P. M. Blowers, pp. 105-41. Notre Dame: University of Notre Dame Press, 1997.

Lawson, J. *The Biblical Theology of Saint Irenaeus.* London: Epworth, 1948.

Margerie, B. de. *An Introduction to the History of Exegesis,* vol. 1, pp. 64-94. Petersham, Mass.: St. Bede's Publications, 1993.

Quasten, J. *Patrology,* vol. 1, pp. 287-313. Westminster, Md.: Newman Press, 1950.

Reventlow, Henning. "Harmonie der Testamente: Irenäus von Lyon." In *Epochen der Bibelauslegung,* vol. 1, pp. 150-70. Munich: Beck, 1990.

Skarsaune, O. "Irenaeus." In *Hebrew Bible/Old Testament: The History of Its Interpretation,* vol. 1, edited by M. Saebø, pp. 422-29. Göttingen: Vandenhoeck & Ruprecht, 1996.

Torrance, T. F. "Kerygmatic Proclamation of the Gospel: Irenaeus, *The Demonstration of Apostolic Preaching.*" In *Divine Meaning: Studies in Patristic Hermeneutics,* pp. 56-74. Edinburgh: T. & T. Clark, 1995.

Vogt, J. "Die Geltung des Alten Testament bei Irenäus." *Theologische Quartalschrift* 60 (1980): 17-28.

Wingren, G. *Man and the Incarnation: A Study in the Biblical Theology of Irenaeus.* Philadelphia: Fortress, 1959.

Young, F. *The Art of Performance,* pp. 45-65. London: Darton, Longman and Todd, 1990.

4

Clement of Alexandria

As stated in the preface, the purpose of this study has been to trace the understanding and use of the book of Isaiah in the history of the Christian church both from a historical and a hermeneutical perspective. Yet in the period after Irenaeus, in the late second century and especially in the third, major difficulties arose that challenge my project. First, clearly something very different from that represented in the biblical interpretation of Justin and Irenaeus emerged, which at first is closely associated with the city of Alexandria. The initial difficulty is that the history of early Christianity in Alexandria remains obscure, and the historian is forced to project a development from later sources.

The second obstacle to be overcome is that although Clement of Alexandria emerged as a pivotal figure through whom Hellenistic Judaism entered fully into the stream of Christian tradition, he wrote very little indeed on the book of Isaiah. Nevertheless, his philosophical contribution in seeking to relate the moral symbolism of Greek pagan traditions with that of the Bible had major implications for early Christian theology and will, of necessity, have to be at least briefly addressed.

I. Life and Works

Little is known with certainty of Clement's life. He was born about the year 150 and died before 215. He was a son of pagan parents and probably received his first training in Athens. He became a student, assistant, and finally successor of Pantaenus, the first rector of the school of Alexandria. It is also known that he traveled extensively in order to learn from other Christian leaders, but no specific details have survived.

His most famous extant works form a kind of trilogy: *Protrepticus (Exhortation)*, *Paedagogus (Tutor)*, and *Stromateis (Carpets* or *Miscellaneous)*. The first two are largely apologetic attempts to justify the Christian faith to his pagan Hellenistic world as being intelligent and rational. In *Tutor* his concern is overwhelmingly pastoral and, addressing the church, he sets out a detailed portrait of Christian behavior within a Hellenistic setting by outlining proper conduct in the details of eating, drinking, attending the baths, and the like. Of greatest significance is the manner in which he reinterprets pagan symbolism into biblical imagery while at the same time continuing to reflect the world of sophisticated Greek culture. His major aim was to show that faith and philosophy are not rivals, but belong together, as secular knowledge is made truly to serve theology.

Very little of Clement's specific biblical interpretation remains extant. His commentary on the Old and New Testament entitled *Hypotyposeis (Outlines)* has been lost. Two extant fragments, *Excerpta ex Theodoto* and the *Eclogue Propheticae,* contain a constant appeal to the Bible but offer limited help in offering a clear example of Clement's exegesis. The *Excerpta* are chiefly concerned with his debate with Valentinian Gnosticism. This writing is significant in showing Clement's criticisms of Gnosticism, but it also reveals his adaptation of Gnostic and Stoic elements. The *Eclogue Propheticae* demonstrates his use of Judeo-Christian apocalyptic themes. His infrequent citations from the book of Isaiah (cf. Isa. 40:6 in 25–26, Isa. 19:20 in 16.2, Isa. 44:6 and 45:5-6 in 38.1, and Isa. 2:3 in 58) are largely conventional usages of earlier Christian tradition.

II. The Hermeneutic Approach of His Biblical Interpretation

In an illuminating essay by T. F. Torrance on the hermeneutics of Clement (*Divine Meaning*, pp. 130-78), the author makes the interesting observation that Clement repeatedly appeals to a verse from the book of Isaiah: "If you will not believe, you will not understand" (7:9), from which he develops his understanding of faith (*Stromateis* 1.1.8.2; 2.2.8.2; 4.17.4; 4.21.134.4). Faith is not a blind submission to authority, but a basic form of understanding. In faith the Christian believer gains a power of rational judgment that needs to be cultivated in order to reach clarity of understanding. It is essential in probing into divine revelation and in attaining a scientific knowledge of truth and the nature of things. What Clement calls *gnosis* is the scientific knowledge of reality in itself; faith is the means toward this goal. Faith is the recognition of the truth forced upon us from objective reality, a position akin to that of Aristotle.

Torrance is at pains to demonstrate that Clement took over from Greek philosophy its method but not its content. He adapts elements of scientific method to the scriptures with the goal of penetrating to the divine realities. Faith is the needed mode of letting the mind respond to the self-evidence of the real through a rational approach. It is at this point that he takes his lead from Isa. 7:9.

Yet in the end, the distinction made between Clement's adaptation of a method and his rejection of its content remains very fluid and not easy always to maintain. In spite of his stance within an inherited Christian tradition, the historical meaning of the biblical text was often rendered as a symbolic reflection of the realities of a timeless world. This surrender to the Philonic tradition of interpretation increasingly blurred his exegetical vision.

It is thus fully clear that Clement derived both his moral and physical symbols largely from Philo. Jean Daniélou (*Theology of Jewish Christianity,* pp. 240ff.) offers several striking examples. In the Genesis story of Abimelech seeing Isaac "sporting" with Rebecca (Gen. 26:8), Philo offers an allegorical interpretation that Clement adapts but transforms into a Christological interpretation. Isaac represents the little children in Christ. Rebecca is a type of the church, and Abimelech symbolizes the Word looking through the window, that is, the flesh of Christ, which he assumed at his incarnation (*Paedagogus* 1.5.22-23; *Stromateis* 1.5.31.3). Clement follows Philo's moral allegorism in seeing the patriarchs as symbols of virtue. He also assumes the symbolisms of Jewish Hellenism in pursuing the exegetical elaborations of the golden candlesticks, the bells attached to the high priest's robe, and the golden headdress. In these cases, it is clear that Clement also incorporates elements from Gnostic tradition (Daniélou, pp. 245ff.).

One popular homily of Clement has remained extant whose authenticity has never been seriously questioned. It offers a popular exposition of Mark 19:17-31 under the title "Who is the Rich Man That Is Being Saved?" The concern of the sermon, addressed to a Christian audience, is stated at the outset: to remove the Christian community from any despair derived from the biblical text and to show its divine, mystical wisdom, not in a "fleshly sense," but according to its hidden meaning. Actually the sermon offers a typical Christian homily, appealing to a variety of parallel texts to show that what is meant is the complete love of God and a call to banish from the Christian soul all concerns for wealth. Although emphasizing that the believer has a special capacity for understanding, the sermon makes no appeal to a unique allegorical interpretation. The reader can sense the overwhelmingly pastoral concerns of Clement in using the Bible for Christian instruction.

Although it is evident that Clement shared much of the content of his

Christian faith with that of Justin and Irenaeus, his approach to scripture moved in a very different direction indeed. This is not to say that he held scripture in less respect. For Clement the Bible was the central focus of his theological reflection, and he cited it continually. Yet he was in no sense a biblical scholar; he had no interest in the text for itself. Indeed, it is the Word of God, but then nothing directly can be said of God, and therefore the biblical language is symbolic by necessity. Its content is concealed and only available to those able to penetrate the symbolism. Although much of his biblical interpretation is grounded on philosophical assumptions, at times he can use the literal sense in arguing the case for Christianity or deriving an ethical teaching. At other times his use of figurative language can resemble that of Justin, but it is also vulnerable to other forces, such as Gnostic speculation and Philonic exegesis, that lack the Christian doctrinal restraints basic to his predecessors.

III. Clement's Exegetical Contribution

Although in his allegorical rendering of scripture Clement moved in a Jewish-Hellenistic milieu distant from Justin and Irenaeus, nevertheless there are many examples to show that Clement still shared much exegetical typology with these predecessors. He speaks of two covenants, of a divine plan growing in clarity. The Old Testament functions in preparation for the New, and the two testaments are joined in a prescribed sequence (*Strom.* 6.18:166,4–167,1). Daniélou (p. 252) summarizes well the main features of Clement's use of figurative language. First, it conceals from the uninitiated those things that are incapable of being understood. Second, it stimulates the search for truth hidden under a veil by those who are knowledgeable.

In sum, Clement's exegetical contribution lies in his struggle to adapt elements from Gnostic interpretation present in Greek allegory in order to illuminate the mystery of Christian revelation, and to develop a cosmic and moral interpretation with philosophical roots that was still firmly tied to a historical incarnation.

Bibliography of Clement of Alexandria

Primary Sources

Clemens Alexandrinus. edited by O. Stählin. Die Griechischen Christlichen Schriftsteller. Leipzig: 12, 1905; 15, 1906; 17, 1909; 39, 1936.

Sources Chrétiennes. Paris: 2, 1949; 30, 1951; 38, 1954; 70, 1960; 108, 1965; 158, 1970; 278-79, 1981.

Clement of Alexandria, Ante-Nicene Christian Library, vol. 2, edited by A. Roberts and J. Donaldson. Edinburgh: T. & T. Clark, 1869; reprint, Grand Rapids: Eerdmans, 1976.

Who Is the Rich Man That Is Being Saved? edited by P. Mordaunt Barnard. London: SPCK, 1901.

The Excerpta ex Theodoto of Clement of Alexandria, edited by R. P. Casey. London: Christophers, 1934.

Eclogue Propheticae, edited by O. Stählin. Die Griechischen Christlichen Schriftsteller, 17. Lepizig, 1909.

Secondary Sources

Chadwick, H. Early Christian Thought and the Classical Tradition, pp. 31-65. Oxford: Clarendon, 1966.

Chadwick, H., and J. E. L. Oulton, eds. Alexandrian Christianity. London and Philadelphia: SCM and Westminster, 1954.

Daniélou, J. "Typologie et allégorie chez Clément d'Alexandrie." Studia Patristica, vol. 4, pp. 50-57. Berlin: Akademie Verlag, 1961.

―――. Theology of Jewish Christianity, vol. 2, pp. 237-53. London and Philadelphia: SCM and Westminster, 1973.

Dawson, D. Allegorical Readers and Cultural Revision in Ancient Alexandria. Berkeley: University of California Press, 1992.

Ferguson, J. Clement of Alexandria. New York: Twayne, 1974.

Horn, H. J. "Zur Motivation der allegorischen Schriftexegese bei Clemens Alexandrinus." Hermes 97 (1969): 436-96.

Lilla, R. R. C. Clement of Alexandria: A Study in Christian Platonism and Gnosticism. London: Oxford University Press, 1971.

Margerie, B. de. An Introduction to the History of Exegesis, vol. 1, pp. 79-94. Petersham, Mass.: Saint Bede's Publications, 1993.

Méhat, A. "Clément d'Alexandrie et les sens de l'Ecriture" In Epektasis. Mélanges J. Daniélou, pp. 355-65. Paris: Beauchesne, 1972.

Mondésert, C. *Clement d'Alexandrie. Introduction à l'étude de sa pensée religieuses à partir de l'Ecriture.* Paris: Aubier, 1944.

Mortley, R. *Connaissance religieuse et herméneutique chez Clément d'Alexandrie.* Leiden: Brill, 1973.

Osborn, E. "The Bible and Christian Morality in Clement of Alexandria." In *The Bible in Greek Christian Antiquity,* edited by P. M. Blowers, pp. 112-30. Notre Dame: University of Notre Dame Press, 1997.

Paget, J. N. B. Carleton. "The Christian Exegesis of the Old Testament in the Alexandrian Tradition." In *The Hebrew Bible/Old Testament: The History of Its Interpretation,* vol. 1, edited by M. Saebø, pp. 478-99. Göttingen: Vandenhoeck & Ruprecht, 1996.

Quasten, J. *Patrology,* vol. 2, pp. 5-36. Westminster, Md.: Newman Press, 1960.

Simonetti, M. *Biblical Interpretation in the Early Church,* pp. 130-78. Edinburgh: T. & T. Clark, 1994.

Torrance, T. F. *Divine Meaning: Studies in Patristic Hermeneutics,* pp. 130-78. Edinburgh: T. & T. Clark, 1995.

5

Origen

The importance of Origen as a biblical scholar can hardly be overestimated. He was the first major Christian exegete to attempt to interpret the Bible as a whole. In contrast to Clement, Origen was first and foremost a biblical scholar. His genius, industry, and learning were without rival and, in the opinion of many patristic scholars, his achievements surpassed even those of Jerome. Yet he was a highly controversial figure and was condemned as a heretic in the sixth century. In spite of this shadow, his influence remained enormous and his works were widely used even by his opponents.

I. Life and Works (c. 185-254)

Little is known regarding most of Origen's life beyond the broad lines of his illustrious career. He was born of Christian parents, probably in Alexandria, and educated in Greek literature and philosophy. He studied under a leading Platonist, Ammonius Saccas. His early life was soon clouded by Roman persecutions, in which his father was martyred. He survived as a teacher of grammar and later was appointed to give catechetical instruction. During this period he made several journeys to Palestine. Ecclesiastical frictions arose after his ordination, and he left Alexandria to take up residence at Caesarea. There he established a school and continued his biblical writings, especially commentaries. Because of his great learning and sermons, his fame spread. During the persecution of the church by Decius in 250, he was imprisoned, tortured, and survived in broken health for only a few remaining years.

Origen's range of literary publications was enormous. Already Jerome felt the need to compile a catalogue of his writings. His most famous work was his *Hexapla,* which he began even before starting on his commentaries. Over a lifetime he wrote commentaries and homilies on almost all of the books of the Bible. Unfortunately, the great majority have been lost or survive in scattered fragments. Fortunately, sizeable portions are extant of his commentaries on Matthew and John, with considerable sections in Greek from Romans and Exodus. In addition, he composed a variety of theological works, the most important being *On First Principles* and the *Philocalia.*

The scope of my treatment in this chapter will necessarily be restricted because of the loss of his Isaiah commentary. First, I will attempt to outline some of the major features of his hermeneutical approach derived from his larger extant corpus. Fortunately, many of the truly great scholars of the church have done extensive study on the subject. Second, I shall attempt to trace the influence of Origen on succeeding generations of Christian scholars who have been most indebted to him. Eusebius, Jerome, and Cyril wrote commentaries on the book of Isaiah and specifically cite from Origen's lost commentary. My concern will focus on the hermeneutical issues of how Origen's writings were received, modified, and extended within the development of the Christian exegetical tradition.

II. Origen and the Alexandrian School

Although Origen was neither the founder of the so-called Alexandrian school nor the first to employ allegory as an exegetical tool, he has always been regarded as its most notable practitioner. Recent study of the Alexandrian tradition has discovered that many of its roots spring from Jewish sources from the period up to the death of Philo. In spite of the lack of information regarding the Jewish community in Alexandria during the late second century, it does seem certain that Christian interpretation owes much to Jewish exegesis of the earlier period. This insight calls into question an earlier theory that considered the major influence on Origen to be Gnostic speculation.

Few specifics are known of the origins of the Alexandrian Christian community. The name of Pantaenus remains an illusive figure and at most was influential before the arrival of Clement. J. N. B. Carleton Paget ("The Christian Exegesis of the Old Testament in the Alexandrian Tradition," pp. 482ff.) sets forth some characteristic features of the Jewish community shortly shared by Christians. It consisted more as a loose body of scholars than a school, which only later under Origen had an official status. Its exegesis was an effort to relate biblical revelation with Greek philosophy. Allegory was the tool by which a synthesis was achieved. Finally, like Philo, most exegesis focused on individual words that were interpreted by constant reference to parallel passages within scripture.

Within the Christian community of Alexandria there was a wide range of approaches in interpreting the Old Testament. Although Clement and Origen are now the two scholars primarily associated with the origins of the Alexandrian tradition, it is highly probable that within this Jewish-Hellenistic milieu other theories of biblical interpretation were also present, which one can project from later Gnostic writings. However, ultimately the Christian understanding of Christ as the center of biblical revelation and not the Torah led to the creation of a uniquely Christian application of the allegorical method.

III. The Controversy Evoked by Origen's Use of Allegory

In spite of widespread agreement on the importance of Origen, controversy has reigned over his approach from the earliest centuries (cf. Paget, "The Christian Exegesis," pp. 534ff. on Origenism). K. J. Torjesen (*Hermeneutical Procedure*, pp. 1ff.) has succinctly outlined the history of the criticism of Origen since the Reformation. Luther's attack on Origen's use of allegory *(de Servo Arbitrio)* became decisive not only for the Reformers in general, but for much of Protestantism ever since. Luther argued that the simple, natural sense of the biblical text contained its divine meaning. The power of the Word derived from its grammatical sense without the need for allegory. Of course, in actual practice various forms of figurative interpretation continued to be practiced by the Reformers (e.g., homiletical, liturgical, and typological) even when they stressed the primacy of the literal sense.

In the period following the Reformation, already in the early seventeenth century and especially through the impact of the Enlightenment, the rejection of the allegorical method increased dramatically. It arose from the accusation that allegory denigrated history and figurative senses sacrificed the factual sense of the biblical text, which was increasingly identified with the original sense of the author. Later allegory was accused of being totally arbitrary without any rational pretense of being scientific. Some began to argue that allegory was a philosophical importation from outside the Christian tradition that had been falsely introduced.

However, beginning with the period immediately following World War II, a very different approach to Origen and to allegory developed that dominated the modern discussion for half a century. Jean Daniélou, followed by a host of other scholars, proposed a sharp distinction between typology and allegory. Typology was a legitimate interpretative technique from within the Christian tradition that sought to show that earlier events or persons were understood as prophetically adumbrating later, often New Testament, events. Allegory, in contrast, was a form of uncontrolled speculation whose roots lay outside of Christian tradition, and stemmed from Jewish, Philonic, and Gnostic circles. Daniélou's analysis was favorably greeted by theologians, especially in the 1950s, because it presented a way of retaining typology as compatible with a modern critical evaluation of the centrality of biblical history, while rejecting allegory as illegitimate (cf. the classic formulation of Lampe and Woollcombe, *Essays on Typology*).

R. P. C. Hanson pushed the distinction even further in his book *Allegory and Event*, which became the standard treatment on Origen for several decades. According to Hanson, Origen was a major source in leading the church astray because he had no historical sense. Rather, he allowed the genuinely historical character of the Bible to be dissipated into timeless, arbitrary speculations derived from Hellenism but fully inappropriate for biblical exegesis.

In Roman Catholic biblical circles, especially after the encyclical of 1943, exegetical stress fell on recovering the literal sense of the biblical text, which approach found its warrant in Thomas's hermeneutics. Yet at the same time various appeals to figurative senses continued. Raymond Brown's thesis on *sensus plenior* in the early 1950s was the last serious attempt at a defense of the figurative senses in North America from the Catholic side, and Brown himself retreated from his earlier position. In modern Protestantism the term "allegory" continued to arouse largely negative emotions, but appeals to typology, such as that of Patrick Fairbairn's two-volume tome, continued as a form of homiletics. However, with the growing hegemony of the historical-critical method in the early twentieth century, typology, allegory, and other figurative senses became increasingly suspect. Even in Anglican circles, the famous volume of Archbishop Trench on the parables became a "whipping boy" and was used to illustrate how *not* to interpret scripture.

IV. The Recent Attempt to Rehabilitate Allegory

In the light of the history of the rejection of the figurative senses of scripture, and much to the surprise of many moderns, within recent times there has been a fresh appraisal of Origen along with a major reevaluation of the nature of allegory, both in its literary and theological functions. One of the first genuine advances was the recognition that the sharp distinction between allegory and typology could not be sustained. James Barr rejected the distinction as an apologetic move that stemmed from an erroneous modern construct of history. His was an important insight. However, the positive advances toward understanding allegory were made by patristic scholars (Henri de Lubac, Andrew Louth, Frances Young, etc.) who showed that the distinction had no deep roots in antiquity and that the ancient church's wide use of figurative interpretation encompassed aspects of both allegory and typology.

Much modern literary attention began to focus on analyzing the various functions of allegory. First, a very precise philological treatment of Greek exegetical terminology, which included *allegoria* and *typologia,* was offered by R. M. Grant (*The Letter and the Spirit,* 1957). This research was followed by Jon Whitman's monograph (*Allegory: The Dynamics of an Ancient and Medieval Technique*) which greatly expanded the research on the history of the term "allegory." Whitman traces the various literary roles of this trope in antiquity as an oblique way of writing. In the tradition formation, "allegory says one thing, and means another" (p. 2).

However, it was the patristic theologians that pursued the new insights into allegory to impinge directly on biblical interpretation. Andrew Louth (*Discerning the Mystery,* 1983) addressed the larger hermeneutical problem associated with the issue of allegory. He rejects the sharp distinction between allegory and typology of Daniélou and Hanson, appealing rather to the more precise distinction of de Lubac between two different types (or styles) of allegory: *allegoria facti* and *allegoria verbi* (Louth, p. 119). Louth argues that allegory was not a technique for resolving exegetical difficulties of the text, which was a widely accepted critical assumption. Rather, "allegory is firmly related to the mystery of Christ. It is a way of relating the whole of Scripture to that mystery, a way of making a synthetic vision out of the images and events of the Biblical narrator" (p. 121). In sum, allegory is not a contrived technique by which to bend the literal sense of the text into a form suitable to a secular sensibility outside of faith.

In this context attention invariably turns to Origen, who was the first theologian to attempt to address specifically the hermeneutical issue of the multiple senses of scripture. In the past the focus has immediately fallen on Origen's formulation in his treatise *On First Principles* (*Peri Archon,* 4.1-3). In these paragraphs he expresses his approach to exegesis by an analogy of human psychology. Just as a person is constituted of body, soul, and spirit, so there is also in scripture a threefold meaning: the literal, the moral, and the spiritual. The difficulty, however, is that this classification appears to be only one among others suggested by Origen, and its appearance in his actual exegesis is quite rare. Usually his emphasis lies in pursuing the twofold meaning of scripture, namely, its literal and spiritual meanings. In addition, other schemata are used, and the distinction between the anagogic, tropologic, and mystic senses is often fluid. De Lubac (*Histoire et Esprit*, pp. 178ff.) goes so far as to suggest that the later medieval classification of a fourfold division (literal, allegorical, moral, and anagogic) ultimately derives from Origen.

A much more crucial issue turns on understanding Origen's distinction between the literal and the spiritual. The problem is far more complex than often thought (cf. Paget, "The Christian Exegesis," pp. 521ff.). In the past, scholars have been led astray by seizing on Origen's remark in *On First Principles* 4.2 that there are certain passages in which there is no "bodily" (literal) sense at all, and the interpreter must seek only the spiritual. The implication has been drawn that Origen has denigrated in principle the literal or historical sense, seeing it at best as unnecessary and peripheral to his real task. However, both de Lubac (*Histoire*, pp. 92ff.) and Henri Crouzel (*Origen*, pp. 61ff.) have gone to great lengths in pursuing the subtlety of Origen's understanding of the literal sense. The initial difficulty arises from the fact that the literal or bodily sense is not defined the same by Origen and his modern critics. Origen means by it the raw material of the text before any interpretation is made. The result is that the *literal* sense for moderns is often the *spiritual* sense for Origen.

Moreover, as de Lubac is at pains to point out, the denial of a literal sense is in no way a rejection of a passage's historicity. Nor can the literal sense be identified with the so-called original sense of the human author. One of the confusions that has arisen in the works of R. P. C. Hanson and others is the problem of explaining the enormous energy expended by Origen on the narrative details of a passage — textual, geographic, historical — if they were systematically denigrated as unimportant. Rather, de Lubac has gone a long way in showing the organic harmony between the literal and the spiritual in Origen's exegesis, and how the spiritual sense would have been considered disembodied without its abiding relationship to the literal sense. Often when Origen speaks negatively of the literal sense, it is in the context of a debate with Jewish interpretations that would limit a passage's meaning to its alleged plain sense, thus explicitly rejecting its spiritual rendering (cf. de Lubac, *Histoire*, p. 119).

According to Hanson, Origen's pursuit of allegory was in error because he had imposed an alien, quasi-Gnostic system on the biblical text in utter disregard of its historical meaning. Origen would have vehemently rejected this allegation. Rather, Origen justified his procedure by an appeal to the Apostle Paul's usage, frequently referring to several particular texts: Rom. 7:14; 1 Cor. 2:2, 10, 12, 16; 9:9-10; 10:11; 2 Cor. 3:6, 15-16; and Gal. 4:24. He found in Paul his warrant for pressing beyond the letter to the spiritual realities to which it pointed. In fact, the difficulties within the biblical text served precisely to alert the reader to the necessity of probing deeper. Frances Young (*Biblical Exegesis,* p. 3) draws the larger hermeneutical point: "Without a form of allegory that at least allows for analogy, the biblical text can only be an object of archaeological interest."

Young has made a strong case (*Biblical Exegesis,* pp. 119ff.) that the frequent, critical contrast between a literal and an allegorical reading of scripture is far too simplistic to provide insight to the basic hermeneutical issues at stake. Because language and reality have become dissociated in modern thought, it has become difficult to understand that meaning lies in that to which it refers. Thus, in Origen the difference between the literal and the allegorical was not absolute, but lay within a spectrum. Allegory was a figure of speech among others and was symbolic in nature. The crucial question turned on the nature of the reference.

Origen was committed to an understanding shared by the New Testament, the Church Fathers, and the church tradition that preceded him that the sacred biblical text was the vehicle for God's continual revelation. The text, in all its multidimensional shape, both literal and spiritual, pointed beyond itself to its substance, which was a spiritual reality. Young emphasizes (*Biblical Exegesis,* p. 137) that the multiple meanings in Origen are really multiple referents. As a result, Origen's exegetical practice is understood not by contrasting literal and figurative senses, but in his application of cross-referencing within scripture.

One of the most recent contributions to the study of Origen's exegesis has been provided by K. J. Torjesen *(Hermeneutical Procedure and Theological Method).* She is concerned to relate Origen's actual exegetical practice to the theological foundations that inform his interpretation. Torjesen is dissatisfied with the usual analysis of Origen's exegesis that begins with his literal interpretation and then shifts to his allegorical rendering. The problem with this procedure is that the theological dynamic of his exegetical method is missing. Rather, by focusing on some of his most important texts (Psalms, Jeremiah, Song of Songs, and Luke), she is able to demonstrate a basic consistency in his approach even when spanning the different genres of scholia, homily, and commentary.

Origen begins by allowing the situation of the hearer to determine the context of Psalm 37, but shortly the movement is reversed when the actual exegesis of the biblical text in turn illuminates the setting of the hearer. This is to say, the context of even the literal sense of the text is understood theologically as concerned with "the cure of souls." This theological rendering thus stands in immediate continuity with the fuller development of the subject matter by means of its figurative extension. Origen assumes that all of scrip-

ture is about the presence of the Logos that defines its content. This manifested form of the Logos determines the pedagogical function of the divine
presence as the goal of all exegesis.

Origen follows a consistent order in tracing the pedagogical movement
of the Logos. He begins with the grammatical sense of the text, focusing on
the literal, historical reality among the people of God. Then he moves to examine the concrete teaching of the Logos in its fuller spiritual dimension, and
concludes with the application of this larger spirituality to the present hearer.

Because already the literal sense is understood as an essential historical
part of the pedagogical goal of the Logos, the very concrete quality of the narrative demands its spiritual interpretation. The two reflect a different form,
but they share the selfsame spiritual reality on the substantive level. Obviously, what Origen understands by "historical" is not the same as its modern
sense, since for him history is the concrete encounter with the Logos. It is a
symbolic form of truth present universally in the Incarnation. It is the theological reality behind the text and not the naked text that reflects the Logos
engaged in a unified pedagogical activity. The move from the literal to the
spiritual is not an alien transference to bridge a double meaning, but rather a
generalization to a universal scope of the historical particularity, because the
literal sense has already opened up the one spiritual reality.

Origen's final exegetical step after moving the literal sense upward to its
true spiritual meaning is to apply the spiritual matter to its "usefulness" for
the hearer. Exegesis thus outlines a movement directed by the inspiration of
the Spirit to the pedagogy of the Logos in an ongoing movement of salvation
for the reader, who is thus continually instructed through a progress of the
soul to divine truth.

V. Origen's Exegesis of Isaiah

In spite of the loss of Origen's commentary on Isaiah, and the great majority
of his homilies on this book, one gets at least some impression of his interpretation of Isaiah from the nine homilies Jerome translated into Latin (Migne,
PL 24, pp. 901-36). Even though these homilies focus primarily on chapters 6-
11 of Isaiah, certain characteristic features of Origen's exegesis clearly emerge.

First, Origen usually begins his homilies by establishing a context for
pursuing the literal sense, but the pattern employed clearly follows that described by Torjesen — that is, the context either stems from that of the reader
or is closely related to it. Thus, Homily 1 does not focus on fixing an absolute
dating of King Uzziah's death, but rather on the fact that Isaiah only saw the

Lord after the death of sinful Uzziah. Immediately the theological point is made that only the righteous can see God's glory. Then the homily turns its full attention to addressing the Christian audience to pursue a life of holiness in order also to be capable of perceiving God's majesty. Similarly, in Homily 8, Origen begins by speaking of the divine judgment on those who constructed idols in Jerusalem and Samaria, but then moves immediately to interpret the idols of the heart. He applies the imagery of the arrogant claims of the proud in Jerusalem to the great pride of his own audience, who also claim to do great things. Origen often employs the initial reader context to illuminate the historical context of the biblical text.

Second, Origen shows great skill in establishing the significance of his theological context by means of careful intertextual appeal. The sinfulness of Uzziah stems from the history reported by the book of Chronicles (2 Chron. 26:16-21), which provides the key for relating Uzziah's death to Isaiah's theophany. As one would expect, the cross-referencing covers the entire Old Testament corpus and also moves quickly into the New Testament. Origen's attention to the details of textual variants becomes a means for rich homiletical interpretation. Thus, in Homily 2 he notices that the Old Testament text of Isaiah reads *"vocabis"* ("you will call"), whereas the New Testament has *"vocabitur"* ("it will be called"). Origen does not rule out the possibility of textual corruption, but in this case he finds a clear intentionality at work. He notes that King Ahaz is not being addressed, but rather the house of David, which from a New Testament context means the church. Therefore, he concludes the New Testament is prophesying that in the future there will be the faithful community of believers who will confess Immanuel as "God with *us*."

Third, it is significant to see the care with which Origen pursues the biblical imagery of the text. In Homily 1 he develops his theology of the rule of God in contrasting the image of God seated high and elevated with one not seated, but showing his rule in images of action. In Homily 6 he moves to the spiritual level when interpreting the enigmatic phrase "they shall hear but not understand." Israel failed to understand because they were caught by the corporeal sense and, following only the letter, failed to see its higher sense. Jesus Christ was the sign offered to Ahaz, who was blinded by not responding to the promise.

In sum, in all these extant homilies on Isaiah, Origen's dominant concern is to apply the prophetic texts to his present hearers. Although he uses various techniques in moving from the literal to the spiritual, in every case he strives to pass through the literal sense to a higher spiritual level. Nevertheless, his approach is not to denigrate the literal, which from the start is always shaped toward its theological subject matter. Thus, it provides a basic continuity to his exposition of the true substance of the biblical word. Origen's homilies are marked by careful attention to the details of the biblical text, but these particularities are never an end in themselves, but rather a flexible vehicle for confronting the living presence of God manifested in the Logos.

VI. Origen's Enduring Exegetical Contributions

A final word is called for in these preliminary evaluations of the theological contributions of Origen's biblical interpretation. Recent scholarship has greatly sharpened our understanding of his approach and cleared away many of the crude characterizations of his work. Yet in the end, few moderns would be prepared to embrace Andrew Louth's brilliant chapter on "Return to Allegory" (*Discerning the Mystery,* pp. 96-131).

The reasons for the hesitancy are immediately apparent. For the heirs of the Enlightenment, Origen's allegorical approach is rejected as arbitrary, subjective, and basically inadequate in dealing with the original biblical author's intention. For the heirs of the Reformation, Origen's approach is judged to be theologically misconstrued in his blurring of the plain sense of the divine Word. Both of these objections are of genuine importance and need to be rigorously and continually addressed. However, I will postpone this debate to my final chapter in an effort to see how the history of Christian exegesis responded to these criticisms, and to see what insights can be culled from a historical perspective to aid in responding to a crucial hermeneutical problem.

However, I would stress along with Louth some of the important issues in the study of the scriptures of the church that emerged with Origen and entered into the Alexandrian tradition. First, he raised the basic theological issue of the function of scripture to be a living and continuing vehicle of the Spirit for divine revelation to the church. Because for Origen scripture was fully inspired by the Spirit, it contained all the truth necessary for salvation. In contrast to the Enlightenment, the biblical text was assumed by Origen to transcend its single historical context and through ongoing divine action speak to its hearers a contemporary Word of the presence of God.

Second, Origen struggled to do justice both to the particularity of the literal, plain sense of the text and also to its fuller theological function as a divine pedagogy in bearing testimony to the salvific work of Jesus Christ to the church and world. He raised the question of the faithful role of the interpreter in the exercise of creative imagination in receiving and transmitting the truth of the sacred scriptures to a community of faith (cf. Young, *The Art of Performance,* pp. 160-86).

Third, by posing the issue of allegory with such continual force, Origen strove to show that the extension of the figurative sense was not simply a horizontal typology, but was vertical as well. Scripture provides a keyboard for each new hearer to play and receive new variations of the one story of God in Christ, now rendered in liturgy, music, and art. In a real sense, is not the African American spiritual an allegory of the Christian life expressing the need, hope, and faith of a particular part of God's people struggling for many centuries in faithful praise amid deep sorrow and despair?

The fact that all these basic hermeneutical questions are still with us offers a further reason for taking Origen seriously as offering a powerful exegetical model which, for better and for worse, shaped the Christian church.

Bibliography of Origen

Primary Sources

Origen's extant writings, along with the various series of their publications, are conveniently listed in J. Quasten, *Patrology*, vol. 2, pp. 37-100, and in H. Crouzel, *Origen*, "Bibliographical Note," pp. xiii-xvi.

Opera, Patrologia Latina (PL), edited by J. Migne. Parisiis, 1844-64.

Commentary on John and Matthew, Ante-Nicene Christian Library, edited by A. Roberts and J. Donaldson, additional volume. Edinburgh: T & T. Clark, 1897.

On First Principles, edited by G. W. Butterworth. London: SPCK, 1936.

French translations of his commentaries and homilies are available in Sources Chrétiennes: Genesis, Exodus, Leviticus, Joshua, Song of Songs, Jeremiah, Luke.

Secondary Sources

Baker, J. A. "The Permanent Significance of the Fathers of the Second and Third Centuries." In J. Daniélou, *A History of Early Christian Doctrine Before the Council of Nicaea*, vol. 2, pp. 501-6. Philadelphia: Westminster, 1973.

Bammel, C. P. H. "Die Hexapla des Origenes: Die *hebraica veritas* im Streit der Meinungen." *Augustinianum* 28 (1988): 125-49.

Bardy, G. "Aux Origenes de l'Ecole d'Alexandrie." *Recherches de Science Religieuse* 27 (1937): 65-90.

————. "Les Traditions juives dans l'oeuvre d'Origène." *Revue Biblique* 24 (1925): 217-52.

Barr, James. "Typology and Allegory." In *Old and New in Interpretation,* pp. 103-48. London: SCM, 1966.

Bigg, C. *The Christian Platonists of Alexandria.* Oxford: Clarendon, 1886.

Brown, R. E. *The Sensus Plenior of Sacred Scripture.* Baltimore: St. Mary's University, 1955.

Chadwick, H. *Origen: Contra Celsum.* 2nd edition. Cambridge: Cambridge University Press, 1965.

Crouzel, H. *Origen.* Edinburgh: T. & T. Clark, 1989.

Dale, A. W. W. "Origenistic Controversy." In *Dictionary of Christian Biography,* edited by H. Wace, pp. 142-56. London: John Murray, 1886.

Daniélou, J. "L'unité des deux Testaments dans l'oeuvre d'Origène." *Revue de sciences religieuses* 22 (1948): 27-56.

————. *Origen.* New York: Sheed and Ward, 1955.

————. *From Shadows to Reality: Studies in the Biblical Typology of the Fathers.* Westminster, Md.: Newman Press, 1961.

————. "Origen's Exegetical Method." In *A History of Early Christian Doctrine Before the Council of Nicaea,* vol. 2, pp. 273-88. Philadelphia: Westminster, 1973.

Fairbairn, P. *The Typology of Scripture.* 2 vols. Edinburgh: T. & T. Clark, 1847.

Grant, R. M. *The Letter and the Spirit.* New York: Macmillan, 1957.

Grant, R. M., and D. Tracy. *A Short History of the Interpretation of the Bible.* 2nd edition. Philadelphia: Fortress Press, 1983.

Greer, R. A. (with J. L. Kugel). *Early Biblical Interpretation.* Philadelphia: Westminster, 1986.

Hanson, R. P. C. *Allegory and Event: A Study of the Sources and Significance of Origen's Interpretation of Scripture.* London: SCM; Richmond: John Knox, 1959.

Harl, M. *Origène et la function révélatrice du verbe incarné.* Paris: Editions du Seuil, 1958.

Heine, R. "Reading the Bible with Origen." In *The Bible in Greek Christian Antiquity,* edited by Paul M. Blowers, pp. 131-48. Notre Dame: University of Notre Dame Press, 1997.

Lampe, G. W. H., and K. J. Woollcombe. *Essays on Typology.* London: SCM, 1957.

Lange, N. R. M. de. *Origen and the Jews.* Cambridge: Cambridge University Press, 1976.

Louth, A. *Discerning the Mystery.* Oxford: Clarendon, 1983.

Lubac, H. de. *Histoire et Esprit. L'Intelligence de l'Écriture d'après d'Origène.* Paris: Aubier, 1950.

————. "'Typologie' et 'Allégorisme.'" *Recherches de science religieuse* 34 (1947): 180-226.

————. "Sens Spirituel." *Recherches de science religieuse* 36 (1949): 542-76.

Margerie, B. de. "Origen: His Greatness — Typology, His Weakness — Allegorizing." In *An Introduction to the History of Exegesis*, vol. 1, pp. 95-116. Petersham, Mass.: Saint Bede's Publications, 1993.

Paget, J. N. B. Carleton. "The Christian Exegesis of the Old Testament in the Alexandrian Tradition." In *Hebrew Bible/Old Testament: The History of Its Interpretation*, vol. 1, edited by M. Sæbø, pp. 478-542. Göttingen: Vandenhoeck & Ruprecht, 1996.

Procopé, J. F. "Greek Philosophy, Hermeneutics and Alexandrian Understanding of the Old Testament." In *Hebrew Bible/Old Testament*, vol. 1, edited by M. Saebø, pp. 451-77. Leiden: Brill, 1996.

Quasten, J. "Origen." *Patrology*, Vol. 2, pp. 37-101. Westminster, Md.: Newman Press, 1960.

Torjesen, K. J. *Hermeneutical Procedure and Theological Method in Origen's Exegesis*. Berlin: de Gruyter, 1986.

Trench, R. C. *Notes on the Parables of our Lord*. London: Macmillan, 1841.

Trigg, J. W. *Origen: The Bible and Philosophy in the Third Century*. London: SCM, 1985.

Westcott, B. F. "Origenes." In *Dictionary of Christian Biography*, vol. 4, edited by H. Wace, pp. 96-142. London: John Murray, 1887.

Whitman, J. *Allegory: The Dynamics of an Ancient and Medieval Technique*. Oxford: Clarendon, 1987.

Wilde, R. *The Treatment of the Jews in the Greek Christian Fathers of the First Three Centuries*. Washington: Catholic University of America, 1949.

Wiles, M. "Origen as Biblical Scholar." In *Cambridge History of the Bible*, vol. 1, edited by P. R. Ackroyd, pp. 454-89. Cambridge: Cambridge University Press, 1970.

Wood, S. K. *Spiritual Exegesis and the Church in the Theology of Henri de Lubac*. Edinburgh: T. & T. Clark, 1998.

Young, Frances. "The Rhetorical Schools and Their Influence on Patristic Exegesis." In *The Making of Orthodoxy: Essays in Honour of Henry Chadwick*, pp. 182-99. Cambridge: Cambridge University Press, 1989.

————. *The Art of Performance*. London: Darton, Longman and Todd, 1990.

————. "Allegory and the Ethics of Reading." In *The Open Text*, edited by F. Watson, pp. 103-20. London: SCM, 1993.

————. "Typology." In *Crossing the Boundaries: Essays in Biblical Interpretation in Honour of M. D. Goulder*, pp. 29-48. Leiden: Brill, 1994.

————. *Biblical Exegesis and the Formation of Christian Culture*. Cambridge: Cambridge University Press, 1997.

————. "Alexandrian School." In *Dictionary of Biblical Interpretation*, vol. 1, edited by J. H. Hayes, pp. 25-26. Nashville: Abingdon, 1999.

6

Eusebius of Caesarea
(c. 260–c. 340)

Traditionally, scholarship on Eusebius of Caesarea has largely concentrated on his pivotal role as the first real historian of early Christianity. The overwhelming interest has focused on his *Ecclesiastical History* as well as his other historical works (e.g., *Chronicle, Martyrs of Palestine, Life of Constantine*). Of course, his apologetic defenses of Christianity *(Eclogae Propheticae, Praeparatio Evangelica, Demonstratio Evangelica)* have been closely studied, but mainly from philosophical and history of religions perspectives. Similarly, his *Onomasticon* has been often exploited as an important repository of geographical and historical information. Theological interest in Eusebius has tended to pursue his role before and after the Council of Nicea and his political activity in the period after the establishment of Constantine's sole rule.

Until quite recently what has been missing is adequate scholarly attention on Eusebius as a biblical scholar. Fortunately, within the last few decades there has been a new interest in this subject. It was first evoked in the transmission and redaction of biblical textual tradition (cf. J. Ziegler's introduction to *Isaias Septuaginta*). This interest led to the remarkable discovery of an almost complete commentary on Isaiah, long thought lost (cf. R. Devresse, *Revue biblique*, 1933; A. Möhle, *Zeitschrift für die neutestamentliche Wissenschaft*, 1934) and the eventual publication of a superb critical edition of the commentary on Isaiah by Ziegler in 1975. While some excellent historical and theological research has emerged on Eusebius as a biblical interpreter (cf. Wallace-Hadrill, des Places, and T. D. Barnes), the specific subject of Eusebius's *Commentary on Isaiah* has been thoroughly examined by M. J. Hollerich (1999), and for the first time he has been able to provide a penetrating analysis of Eusebius as a biblical scholar with a wide interest in the history of Christian interpretation.

I. Life and Background of Eusebius

Eusebius was born about 260 A.D. His parentage and place of birth are unknown. He was a pupil of Pamphilus, the scholar and martyr, who had collected a large library at Caesarea. Little is known of Eusebius's early life and of his ecclesiastical status. He was imprisoned during the persecution of 309, and later appointed bishop of Caesarea about 315. He attended the Council of Nicea in 325 and emerged as the leader of the moderate party in the Arian controversy. In spite of his involvement in both ecclesial and secular politics in the Constantine era, Eusebius's great contribution lay in his role as a scholar, and through his writings he served as the major caretaker of the Christian history and tradition for his age. Although clearly Eusebius's most celebrated contribution was his *Ecclesiastical History,* his biblical works, while lacking the brilliance of Origen's contributions, performed an indispensable function in preserving the church's exegetical traditions.

Recently attention has focused on determining Eusebius's role within the history of biblical interpretation. An initial comparison with Justin and Irenaeus shows the extent to which Eusebius built on a core of inherited interpretation. He shared the traditional Christian understanding of prophecy and fulfillment and used similar prooftexting and arguments in his anti-Jewish apologetics. However, Hollerich (*Eusebius of Caesarea's Commentary,* pp. 42ff.) makes an important point in noting some important differences between, say, Justin and Eusebius that reflect the changing historical context in which he was writing. For Justin the Old Testament prophets spoke simply and unambiguously. In contrast, Eusebius was far more aware of the need for serious interpretation in penetrating the biblical metaphors. Of course, it was the influence of Origen, above all, that raised the level of Eusebius's scholarly competence and caused him to pay attention to the problems of textual variants and multiple Greek translations. Equally important was his increased hermeneutical sophistication in pursuing the different levels of meaning within a single passage. However, as a study of Eusebius's hermeneutics will show, he developed a very different understanding of the role of history from that of Origen while still remaining firmly within the Alexandrian tradition.

II. Eusebius's Exegetical Goals and Hermeneutical Approach

In order fully to understand Eusebius's mode of interpretation, particularly of the Old Testament prophets, it is important to discern at the outset his overriding apologetic concerns. Two themes continue to emerge especially in his interpretation of Isaiah. First, he is at pains to demonstrate by means of an appeal to various forms of prophecy and fulfillment the church's claim to be the legitimate heir of the sacred scriptures of the Jews. Second, he focuses his attention, above all, on showing that the message of the Old Testament was consistent in its promise of God's blessing to the nations who form God's new people into a godly polity. Although Eusebius represents the early Christian successionist position regarding Judaism, he did modify it to the extent that he acknowledged a faithful remnant of Jews in the pre-Christian era who constituted a part of the one people of God.

Although Jerome quite harshly accused Eusebius of lapsing into Origenist allegory (preface, *Commentary on Isaiah*), the actual hermeneutical terminology used by Eusebius differs markedly from that of Origen. As Hollerich describes it (*Eusebius,* p. 68), Eusebius ignores much of the conventional allegorical terminology, and his hermeneutical vocabulary consists mostly of stock expressions and phrases rather than strictly defined terms. Technical words like *allegoria, tropos, theoria,* and *anagoge* appear rarely, if at all. Rather, the most common contrast appearing is between the literal sense *(lexis, historia)* and the spiritual *(dianoia).*

In the preface to his Isaiah commentary according to Ziegler's text, in a section missing in Migne's text edited by Montfaucon, Eusebius sets forth very clearly his position. Usually the prophet spoke plainly, so there was no need for the techniques of allegory. However, at times he used symbols of other realities that suggest another meaning *(dianoian).* The explanation that then follows indicates that the relation between the literal and the spiritual was integral and often joined. Because it was a fluid relationship, the two avenues into the meaning of the one text were often intertwined. Moreover, from the examples used by Eusebius to illustrate the point, it would appear that the spiritual was often a metaphorical extension of the literal.

When Eusebius spoke of the literal or historical, the phrase conveyed the plain, normal, customary meaning of a word. It referred both to historical events and to the historical fulfillment of prophecy. To establish the literal sense, Eusebius drew on his training in ancient grammar and the disciplines of chronology, ethnography, and geography. Especially frequent was Eusebius's appeal to etymology in an effort to discern a word's root meaning. However, Hollerich (pp. 71-72) is quick to add that Eusebius did not use etymology in order to discover hidden, spiritual meanings, but to understand the literal sense. His concern to recover the literal sense was also the reason for his careful attention to the different Greek translations that he used to complement his primary focus on the Septuagint. He virtually identified Aquila's translation with the original Hebrew, but he used much freedom in his use of Symmachus and Theodotion as well. His choice was largely dictated by which rendering seemed to bring forth the most coherent and intelligible meaning rather than by a prior dogmatic preference.

When Eusebius spoke of a spiritual sense *(kata dianoian)*, he did not envision this sense as a timeless, independent layer of meaning, but rather as an extension of the text "to uncover the inner, religious and supernatural dimensions of historical events" (Hollerich, p. 87). The spiritual interpretations of a prophetic text revealed the meaning of a historical event in the overall design of God's salvific plan. One can discern in this understanding a certain family resemblance to aspects of the modern concept of *Heilsgeschichte* that sees biblical events as distinct and inseparable, but not identical with "secular" historical events.

The relation between the literal and spiritual meaning of events emerges clearly in Eusebius's use of the prophecy-fulfillment pattern of events. Eusebius is initially concerned to demonstrate the literal fulfillment of prophecy in terms of facts available for all to see. This focus remains overriding in all of his apologetic treatises, especially when directed against the Jews. Then the spiritual fulfillment refers to the religious meaning of the events. Thus, the defeat of the Babylonians by Cyrus is established incontrovertibly as a historical fact, but its spiritual fulfillment lies in the defeat of idolatry and victory over the devil's power.

The sequence of prophecy and fulfillment according to both the literal and spiritual dimensions could encompass events internal to the Old Testament, or those of the New Testament and the early church. It was an important theme of Eusebius to see in the Roman peace after the Constantinian settlement a literal fulfillment of the biblical prophecy. Similarly, Eusebius found the ecclesiastical offices and social structures of his day exactly predicted in the scriptures.

There are, of course, continuing elements in Eusebius's exegesis that reflect clearly the Alexandrian exegetical tradition. At times Eusebius resorts to purely allegorical interpretation. Whenever there is a reference to animals (e.g., Isa. 11:6-7), Eusebius assigns them an allegorical significance, as if by reflex. Similarly water is invariably interpreted symbolically in relation to the Holy Spirit or baptism. Yet there are some clear examples of Eusebius's offering a historical interpretation of a text that Origen allegorized (Hollerich, p. 54). In sum, one could conclude with good reason that Origen's form of allegory, while still present in Eusebius, has often been moved to the periphery to function as a sort of ornament.

It is certain that Eusebius read Old Testament prophecy consistently from a Christological perspective. Much of his interpretation did not arise from allegorizing specific features, but in bringing to the passage as a whole a Christian perspective. Then by means of intertextual referencing he uses the Old Testament as a sounding board from which to orchestrate Christian themes. If one were to employ modern hermeneutical terminology, Eusebius offers a holistic Christian reading, making no sharp distinctions between the two testaments, in order to focus fully on the unity of the evangelical witness in all of scripture. As a result, in spite of his often sophisticated use of literary observations, in the end it is the subject matter that exerts the dominant exegetical force.

It has frequently been observed that Eusebius makes no explicit mention of the Arian controversy, nor do the Christological issues of Nicea come into play. Yet there is a continuing emphasis on an incarnational theology (cf. Isa. 61:1-2) that shows a robust dogmatic interest throughout, even when restrained, especially when compared, say, with Theodoret. One of Hollerich's lasting contributions in his recent research into Eusebius's theology is in pointing out a shift in Eusebius's position in his late post-Constantine period, at the time of the writing of his Isaiah commentary. He distanced himself from an earlier eschatological perspective to focus more on describing the Christian church as the godly polity. The reference to Christ's second coming still occurred infrequently, but it would almost appear as if the force of the new political era had pushed his thinking toward a "realized eschatology," to speak anachronistically: "The one (sc. *politeuma*) established of old among the Jews had fallen away, whereas now it has been awakened . . . throughout the whole world by the Church of God" (Hollerich, p. 165).

Finally, much recent work has focused on an attempt to establish Eusebius's position as a biblical scholar within the exegetical traditions of the church. Perhaps the contrast between the Alexandrian and Antiochene schools has been overdrawn; regardless, Eusebius is important in showing the extent to which already in the early fourth century important elements of both traditions had been brought together. Eusebius developed a historical sense unknown to Origen, but he fully shared the Alexandrian concern that the full spiritual and theological dimensions of the text be developed. The very fact that the literal and the figurative senses stood in an integral relationship within the unity of Christian scripture served to check the excesses of Origen without falling into the critical reductionism of Theodore.

III. Eusebius's Interpretation of Isaiah

There are three major works that comprise most of Eusebius's Isaianic interpretation: The *Eclogae Propheticae (Prophetic Selections)*, the *Demonstratio*

Evangelica *(The Proof of the Gospel)*, and *Eis Esaian* (*Commentary on Isaiah*, ed. J. Ziegler). The *Prophetic Selections* were written during the great persecution (303-306/7). *The Proof of the Gospel* was composed after the Edict of Milan, but before Constantine became sole ruler (c. 318-323). Finally, the Isaiah commentary was written not long after the defeat of Licinius. Hollerich sets its composition between the first and second sessions of Nicea (325-327).

These three works represent different literary genres. The *Selections* is a catechetical work introducing Christian doctrine. The *Proof* is an apologetic treatise designed to demonstrate the truth of Christianity from Old Testament prophecy, while the Isaiah commentary is a technical work of exegesis following a line-by-line procedure practiced by Origen. Often one can see much overlap in approach and content because of the overarching dependency on inherited exegetical tradition. Nevertheless, the differences in style and purpose call for caution in attempting to chart any simple developmental system in Eusebius's exegesis.

1. The Prophetic Selections (Eclogae)

In the preface of Book Four, which is devoted entirely to evidence from the book of Isaiah, Eusebius sets forth his reasons for writing this treatise. He wants to show the prophecies of the Jewish scriptures are indeed worthy to be revered as sacred and the source of true wisdom. In spite of attacks against them as being crude and unlearned, he seeks to demonstrate that they are of divine origin. Moreover, he intends to show that biblical prophecies spoken years before in ancient times confirm by their fulfillment the claims of Jesus Christ to be the goal of Israel's past and present history.

It is clear that in this early treatise Eusebius is very much a disciple of Origen. He characterizes Origen as that "wonderful, holy man" (4.4f.), "the most painstaking interpreter of Scripture" (3.6). Eusebius stands fully in the Alexandrian tradition when he asserts that Moses and the prophets foretold every detail of Jesus' life (1.15). Nevertheless, Wallace-Hadrill (*Eusebius of Caesarea*, p. 81) has drawn the wrong implication from this statement when he suggests that because Eusebius's interpretation is subsumed within Christological categories, Eusebius is only concerned with the spiritual sense of the text. Moreover, as it has been already pointed out, Eusebius's understanding of the relation between the literal and spiritual senses is not identical with that of Origen. Indeed, in the *Prophetic Selections* Eusebius is much concerned to defend the historical validity of Isaiah's prophecies, which is an endeavor understood to be an essential and inseparable part of the larger spiritual interpretation.

The choice of passages from the book of Isaiah is highly significant. Of course, many of the passages are traditional prooftexts and used by Justin in the conventional defense of Jesus' messianic claims. However, the manner in which Eusebius mounts his case is not just a repetition of the tradition; one can discern a new sophistication in his attempt to respond to both Jews and pagans in his careful attention to textual variants, grammatical and stylistic observations, and historical specificity.

The passages chosen are in the following sequence in Book Four:

2:1-4	9:5-7	28:14-17a	41:2-7	50:1-11	61:1-3
3:1-10	10:33–11:10	30:27	42:1-7	52:5-7	61:10-11
3:12	16:5	31:9b	43:10	52:10–53:12	62:10–63:3a
7:10-16	19:1-4	35:1-7	45:12-16	55:2-5	63:11
8:1-4	19:19-21	40:3-5	48:12-16	57:1-4	64:10–65:2
8:18-20	26:16-19	40:9-11	49:1-11	59:19-21	

Following an initial preface to Book Four in which Eusebius states his purpose to confirm that the Isaianic prophecies manifestly find their fulfillment in Jesus Christ, Eusebius turns directly to 2:1-4, which describes the assembly of the nations for the new law of Zion. For the Christian believer the explanation is clear: this prophetic event points to the incarnation of Christ and the revelation of the divine Word through whom the Gentiles are called. When the passage is interpreted literally *(kata lexin)*, it points to the nations who have been converted from a warlike disposition and seek the new law of the Savior. Spiritually the fulfillment is of the church of God elevated to the highest peak. Then the divine judgments prophesied against Jerusalem in chapter 1 are applied to the devastation of the Jews and joined in chapter 3 with the Jewish rejection of Christ caused by satanic blindness.

Somewhat surprisingly, Eusebius next skips over chapters 4, 5, and 6 to focus attention on the sign of Immanuel offered to Ahaz. It is immediately clear that Eusebius is consciously entering into a long running battle over this text's interpretation. He is aware that the Jews deny that the Greek word *parthenos* means virgin according to the Hebrew. He therefore rehearses the traditional Christian arguments for the defense of the Septuagint's translation. He begins by affirming that the translators of the Septuagint were the first and therefore also the most reliable. Again, he argues that a normal birth could hardly function as a sign. Then, citing Deut. 22:27, he contends that the translation of *neanis* (young woman) could also be used of a virgin in that context. Finally, he rejects the Jewish interpretation of the sign of Immanuel as a reference to Hezekiah for chronological reasons, since Hezekiah would have already been sixteen years old when Ahaz began to reign. These arguments are largely the stock Christian responses, but later references to Isa. 7:14 by Eusebius reveal that he continued to strengthen his apologetic efforts.

Eusebius's interpretation of Isaiah 8 is a traditional but highly strained allegorical reading. "I went into the prophetess and she conceived . . . " is considered shameful for a prophetic activity if interpreted literally, and thus could only be understood as a divine action described in the New Testament in reference to Mary. The entire passage is thus read allegorically as offering a parallel to chapter 7, the birth of Immanuel. Chapters 9, 10, and 11 are also interpreted messianically and are so obvious as to be so interpreted even by the Jews. However, in Jesus Christ the root of Jesse grows miraculously to transform universal humanity including all the nations.

Chapter 19, the oracle concerning Egypt, is dealt with at considerable length. The description of "the Lord riding on a swift cloud" and coming to Egypt is held to be strong evidence of the defeat of its idols and the establishment of the victorious church that offers true worship to God. Not surprisingly, Eusebius uses the tested stone passage (28:16) in accord with its New Testament application (Rom. 9:33; 10:11) in order to establish Jesus Christ as the foundation on which the church is built and that receives the blessing of God.

Isa. 40:3 calls on the Gentiles to rejoice in preparing Christ's way. The servant passage of chapter 42 points prophetically to the Savior who comes as a "light of the nations." Again, the heavenly Jerusalem is described and interpreted with a catena of New Testament citations. Then again, the passion of Christ is identified as the referent in 50:1-11, and the entire pericope of the suffering servant of 52:13–53:12 is cited. It is assumed that the passage is only intelligible as a prophecy of Christ's bearing the sins of the world. Finally, there is a strong eschatological emphasis in the final choice of passages from chapters 62–66, which look forward to the second coming and final judgment of those opposing Christ's rule as confirmed by Psalm 2.

2. The Proof of the Gospel (Demonstratio Evangelica)

When one turns to examine Eusebius's use of the book of Isaiah in the *Proof of the Gospel,* one is first struck by the very different structure of the treatise. Although many of the same apologetic concerns are everywhere evident, the texts cited of Isaiah are no longer set out in a continuous sequence. Rather,

the arguments in a greatly expanded form have been developed topically under the rubric of various doctrinal points. Instead of having a catena of traditional prophetic texts joined together with minor theological glossing,
doctrines are first announced and then established with texts from both Old
and New Testaments. These are interwoven with logical, theological reflection to provide an inner coherence. In modern terminology, prooftexting
has been considerably relativized by dogmatic categories into a sort of "biblical theology."

For example, in chapter 5 of the *Proof of the Gospel,* the argument focuses on establishing the doctrine of the Father and Son by using a wide
range of texts from the Pentateuch, Psalms, and prophets. These in turn are
linked intertextually with a full range of New Testament texts. In the past,
scholarly attention has usually focused on discerning signs of a pre-Nicene
theology in Eusebius when he distinguishes between one Almighty God and a
"Second Being" coming after him (6.257). In chapter 6 the topic of the treatise
shifts to prophecies describing God's ascent and descent to earth. Beginning
with texts from the Psalter, Eusebius attempts to show the pre-existence and
origin of the One who was to come forth from Bethlehem. Particularly in his
exegesis of Zechariah 14, Eusebius argues that the coming of Jesus was predicted literally and spiritually 500 years before the fulfillment of the judgment
on the Jews by Nero, Titus, and Vespasian. Only toward the end of chapter 6
does Eusebius turn to the familiar texts of 19:1-4; 35:1-7; 48:12, 16; and 16:14, 19.

In chapter 7 Eusebius fixes his attention on the question of how God
came to earth to live among humans. In his preface he sets forth two signs of
his presence: the calling of the nations and the desolation of the Jews. Then,
in order to demonstrate how this divine entry into humanity took place, he
turns to develop his argument almost exclusively from Isaianic texts. However, in contrast with the catena selection of the *Prophetic Selections,* Eusebius
chooses to concentrate on chapters 6, 7, 8, and 9, which he immediately sets
within the context of John's prologue in chapter 1, and he continues to weave
his Isaiah texts with New Testament citations to produce a sort of "biblical
theology" of the Incarnation.

Eusebius begins his interpretation of Isaiah's vision of God in chapter 6
by taking his lead from John 12:41: "Isaiah saw his glory and bore witness to
him." Led by the Holy Spirit, Isaiah was able to describe the Savior's birth
from a virgin and to perceive in the song of the seraphim praise to the kingship of God. Eusebius ends by interpreting the prophetic commission of
hardening as a direct reference to the continuing opposition of the Jews to
Christ.

Next the sign of Immanuel given to Ahaz is introduced by a lengthy interpretation of the entry of death into the world according to Romans 5, from which, however, the incarnate Savior remained holy and immortal, uncorrupted by sin. Eusebius's interpretation of Isaiah 7 covers much of the same ground as in the *Prophetic Selections,* but now with more detail and theological reflection. He develops the hardening thesis by drawing the implication that understanding the prophecy requires both faith and intellect. New to the debate over the unbelief of the Jews is Eusebius's appeal to an argument from history. Since there is no longer a kingdom either of Damascus or of Judea, this part of the Immanuel prophecy could be demonstrated to have been literally fulfilled. Therefore if this part was proved, it stands to reason that the prophecy of a virgin's conceiving should also have taken place as recounted in Matt. 1:18-23. He thus draws the conclusion that only after the birth of Christ did the prophecy receive its complete fulfillment through the Roman Empire. Eusebius also observes that the reason the prophetic writings abstained from naming the Romans was to prevent any offense being taken by the rulers of the empire. Only on the periphery of his interpretation, when explaining the reference "to those left in the land rearing a heifer or two sheep," does he identify this as a symbol of three orders in each church. More characteristic of Eusebius is his appeal to a compelling morphological fit between an Old Testament prophecy and the actual ministry of Jesus — for example, between Isaiah 35 and Jesus' healing.

In chapter 8 Eusebius continues the same allegorical interpretation given in the *Prophetic Selections* and considers the conceiving of a son by the prophetess to be understood as the divine birth of Jesus through the Holy Spirit as formulated in the first chapter of Luke's Gospel. Most of the remaining interpretation is directed to the prophecy's spiritual fulfillment, with the waters of Siloam being rendered figuratively. Finally, chapters 9 and 11 are interpreted in the traditional manner as referring literally to the coming of Christ as Messiah from heaven and his birth in Bethlehem, which Eusebius further supports by appeals to Micah 5 and Psalm 132.

3. Eusebius's Commentary on Isaiah

As was pointed out earlier in this chapter, the recovery of Eusebius's preface to his Isaiah commentary, which had been missing from the catena fragments, filled an important lacuna in understanding Eusebius's exegetical approach. It also set the tone for the ensuing commentary that provided the best example of his mature biblical exposition. Although Origen wrote the first Christian commentary on the book of Isaiah, it is Eusebius's commentary that forms the earliest extant commentary, and for that reason alone it has major significance. The line-by-line exposition came to dominate the model from that time forward, thus replacing the genre of the *Prophetic Selections* and the *Proof of the Gospel* as the major tradent of Christian exegetical tradition up to the present. Our task will be to make a representative reading from this lengthy commentary.

After reviewing God's controversy with Judah and Jerusalem in chapter 1, Eusebius strikes one of his most characteristic themes in interpreting Isa. 2:2-4. The flow of the nations to Mount Zion in search of the law of Christ sounds the book's preeminent note: the revelation of a universal salvation culminating in the ingathering of all nations (cf. Isa. 66:18-23). When the Jews did not call upon his name, the prophet saw a clear prediction of the calling of the Gentiles to form a new godly polity. The law of Christ now replaced the law of Moses, and the literal fulfillment of the prophecy was demonstrated in the reign of peace among the once-warring nations. The portrayal of the final judgment, when Christ sits on his glorious throne (Matt. 25:31), marks the final consummation in Isaianic terms.

In chapter 7 of his commentary, one can see that Eusebius has continued to refine his interpretation of the sign of Immanuel over against his earlier efforts. He attempts to address with more precision how the promise of Immanuel as Savior relates both to Ahaz in the eighth century and to the New Testament, as well as to his present audience. He raises the problem of how the child prophesied by Isaiah was named Immanuel and not Jesus. He uses this issue to draw a distinction and thus to offer a subtle theological reflection. The name Immanuel is a pledge of salvation, God-with-us, and whenever this name is evoked, God is indeed present. He will save faithful Israel at that historical moment. Thus, when his name was called in chapter 7, the promise of deliverance from the two kings of Syria and Ephraim was fulfilled in that moment. It would seem that Eusebius sees in Immanuel a foretaste of Jesus, as if constituting an ontological relationship. He supports this thesis by observing a textual variant. According to the Old Testament prophecy, Isaiah speaks in the singular: "thou shalt call his name Immanuel" *(kalesouseis)*, whereas Matt. 2:23 reads the prophecy in the plural: "they will call his name" *(kalesousin)*. Eusebius interprets this difference between the testaments to mean that the prophecy in the Old Testament, given in the singular, was directed only to the house of David, whereas the plural of Matthew (according to the Byzantine textual form) indicated that Jesus is to be the Savior for all of humanity. It would also seem that Eusebius was acquainted with Origen's interpretation, which is unfortunately only known in his Latin homily.

The traditional messianic interpretation is given in chapters 9 and 11, but there are additional features that emerge as characteristic of Eusebius's approach. He carefully pursues the geographical link between Naphtali and Galilee in the New Testament. He then develops the significance of Galilee being prophesied as the first area to participate in the joy of Jesus' preaching of the good news. The imagery of the joy at the harvest, of dividing the spoil, and of relieving oppression is interpreted in terms of Christ's feeding of the five thousand, his breaking the power of the devil, and his establishing the leaders of the church to be sent out into the world. Again, it is not a simple allegorical reading, but one that develops an analogy of content.

Eusebius interprets the stump of chapter 11 as the destination of the race of David according to the flesh, and the root of Jesse as the promise of the new reign of righteousness. The shoot is from the root of Jesse, who is portrayed as poor and humble, a quality that then leads into the description of the Messiah equipped by the Spirit of the Lord to reign with wisdom, understanding, and might. The animals in the restored paradise are interpreted allegorically with various stock phrases.

The passages in Isaiah against the nations (chapters 13–23) are interpreted largely according to a straightforward historical reading. The judgment against the king of Babylon (14:3-21) is identified with Babylon's monarch and only subsequently used in a figurative sense as a struggle on a higher sphere against pride and arrogance. The fulfillment occurs on both a literal and spiritual sense and relates to the present situation of the Christian church as well.

The prophecy concerning Egypt in 19:1-4 was a favorite of Eusebius. He deals with it once in the *Prophetic Selections* (4.10) and three times in the *Proof* (6.29,2ff.; 8.5,1ff.; 9.2,1ff.), but then again at length in his commentary. All of his treatments share a strong Christological context centering on Christ's victory over idolatry. However, there is much more attention to detail in the commentary. He notes that the superscription is not "against Egypt," but "concerning Egypt," and includes a positive element as well in the gift of the Savior. "The Lord's coming to Egypt riding on a swift cloud" is rendered by Eusebius according to its "historical sense" *(pros Estorian)* as the body that he received when formed through the Holy Spirit by the blessed virgin. The divine Word was everywhere present by an incorporeal and divine power that encompassed all. His coming on a cloud shows that his coming will be both individual and corporate, and for Egypt's benefit as well. However, in an even profounder sense it served to destroy the superstition and idolatry that plagued Egypt. The prophecy in verse 4 of Egypt being given into the hand of a "hard master" was literally fulfilled with the change of government when, at the end of the Ptolemaic rule, Egypt was conquered by the Romans.

In the *Proof* (9.13) Eusebius interpreted Isa. 35:1-7 as a typology of what the Gospels say Jesus did in healing the deaf, blind, and lame, but in the commentary the focus falls on the activity of the church and the role of baptism as the bath of regeneration in transforming the land. The church made up of the nations continues in its liturgical life the redeeming acts of Jesus and brings glory to its Savior even up to the present age.

Hollerich (pp. 137-38) has made the important observation that Eusebius is the first Christian writer (apart from a few scattered references in Origen) to have treated the passage on Cyrus (Isa. 44:21–45:23) largely in a historical manner. Instead of following the Septuagint's reading of 45:1, "The Lord God says to my anointed Cyrus" *(toi christoi mou kyroi),* the early Christian tradition (e.g., Barnabas, Irenaeus, Tertullian, etc.) reads "to Christ my Lord" *(toi christoi mou kyrioi).* Eusebius insists on following the Septuagint, which is also an accurate translation of the Hebrew, but mentions that the Hebrews called the king "an anointed one." Hence Cyrus was God's anointed king. The calling of Cyrus as God's servant was an example of the prophet's encouraging of Cyrus. Further, Eusebius argues that the Hebrew prophet foresaw Cyrus's career and even predicted the strategy of Cyrus in capturing Babylon by drying up the rivers. Eusebius even repeats the legend of Josephus that Cyrus knew the prophecy of Isaiah when he was shown it by the Jews *(Ant.* 11.1-7).

Finally, one can see again and again in his commentary Eusebius's continuing theological interest in Christ's incarnation. For example, the reading of Isa. 61:1-4 in the commentary turns the interpretation in a different direction from that of the *Prophetic Selections* (4.31) and from that of the *Proof* (9.10,1; 4.17,13). By joining 61:1 with the preceding verse in 60:22b, Eusebius is able to discern two different voices, namely, that of the Lord and that of the recipient of the divine Spirit. He is then able to draw the Christological implication that Christ is both God and man (Ziegler, pp. 378-79). He then follows the lead from Luke's citation of Isa. 61 in 4:16ff. to see the literal fulfillment of Isaiah's prophecy in the divine anointing of Jesus by the Spirit "today."

As a biblical scholar and exegete, Eusebius emerged in the post-Constantine era as the caretaker of the heritage of Origen. He continued to develop his own exegetical techniques such as textual criticism and historical precision. Yet he moved in a new direction as a political theologian in focusing his attention on the institutional church and developing the theme of the church as the godly polity. He found the ecclesiastical structure already adumbrated in the prophecies of Isaiah. Although he spoke of a godly seed in Israel, his interpretation emerged as a classic expression of Christianity's supplanting of Judaism as it became the religion of all humanity, whose universalism was thought manifest in the Constantinian settlement.

Bibliography of Eusebius

Primary Sources

Eclogae propheticae, edited by T. Gaisford. Patrologia Graeca, edited by J.-P. Migne, 22:1021-62. Oxford, 1842.

The Ecclesiastical History, edited by K. Lake and J. E. L. Oulton. 2 vols. Cambridge, Mass.: Harvard University Press, 1972.

Die Demonstratio Evangelica, edited by I. A. Heikel, vol. 6 of *Eusebius' Werke.* Griechischen Christlichen Schriftsteller. Leipzig: J. C. Hinrichs, 1913.

The Proof of the Gospel, edited and translated by W. J. Ferrar. 2 vols. London, 1920; reprint, Grand Rapids: Baker, 1981.

Preparation for the Gospel, edited and translated by E. H. Gifford. Oxford: Clarendon Press, 1903; reprinted Grand Rapids: Baker, 1981.

Der Jesajakommentar, edited by J. Ziegler, vol. 9 of *Eusebius' Werke.* Griechischen Christlichen Schriftsteller. Berlin: Akademie, 1975.

Secondary Sources

Attridge, H., and Gohei Hata, eds. *Eusebius, Christianity, and Judaism.* Detroit: Wayne State University Press, 1992.

Barnes, T. D. *Constantine and Eusebius.* Cambridge, Mass.: Harvard University Press, 1981.

Crouzel, H. "La distinction de la 'typologie' et 'd'allégorie.'" *Bulletin de la littérature ecclésiastique* 65 (1964): 161-74.

Devreesse, R. "L'Édition du commentaire d'Eusèbe de Césarée sur Isaïe: Interpolations et omissions." *Revue Biblique* 42 (1933): 540-55.

Grant, R. M. *Eusebius as Church Historian.* Oxford: Clarendon, 1980.

Hollerich, M. J. *Eusebius of Caesarea's Commentary on Isaiah.* Oxford: Clarendon, 1999.

Lightfoot, J. B. "Eusebius of Caesarea." In *Dictionary of Christian Biography,* vol. 2, pp. 308-48. London: John Murray, 1880.

Lubac, H. de. "'Typologie' et 'Allegorisme.'" *Recherches de science religieuse* 34 (1947): 180-226.

———. "Sens spirituel." *Recherches de science religieuse* 36 (1949): 542-76.

Möhle, A. "Der Jesaia-kommentar des Eusebius von Kaisareia fast vollständig wieder aufgefunden." *Zeitschrift für die neutestamentliche Wissenschaft* 33 (1934): 87-89.

Opitz, H.-G. "Euseb von Caesarea als Theolog." *Zeitschrift für die neutestamentliche Wissenschaft* 34 (1935): 1-19.

Places, E. des. *Eusèbe de Césarée commentateur: Platonisme et écriture sainte.* Paris: Editions Beauchesne, 1982.

Quasten, J. "Eusebius of Caesarea." *Patrology,* vol. 2, pp. 309-46. Westminster, Md.: Newman Press, 1960.

Simonetti, M. *Biblical Interpretation in the Early Church,* pp. 55ff. Edinburgh: T. & T. Clark, 1994.

Ungern-Sternberg, A. von. *Der traditionelle alttestamentlichen Schriftbeweis.* Halle: M. Niemeyer, 1913.

Wallace-Hadrill, D. S. *Eusebius of Caesarea.* London: A. R. Mowbray, 1960.

Williams, A. L. *Adversus Judaeos.* Cambridge: Cambridge University Press, 1935.

Young, F. "Eusebius of Caesarea." In *From Nicaea to Chalcedon,* pp. 1-23. London: SCM Press, 1983.

7

Jerome
(c. 345–420)

The enormity of Jerome's contribution to biblical studies is uncontested. He was the most learned scholar of the early church, equipped with vast erudition, the father of biblical studies. His knowledge of Hebrew and Greek in the Western church was unparalleled, and only remotely rivaled by Origen. His most enduring contribution was his translation of the Old Testament from Hebrew into Latin, the so-called Vulgate, the influence of which in the West would be hard to exaggerate. It provided the language of scripture to the Western church for the next thousand years and beyond.

My concern in this chapter is not to review his many accomplishments or to pursue his multifaceted legacy (cf. the standard works of Grützmacher, Cavallera, and Kelly). Rather, my treatment will again focus on Jerome's exegesis of the prophet Isaiah, especially viewed from a hermeneutical perspective. How does Jerome's particular construal of exegesis in his commentary relate to the issue of the authority of the biblical text within a defined Christian tradition?

I. Introductory Matters

1. The Chronology of Jerome's Work on Isaiah

Jerome's earliest exegetical work on the Old Testament, which is no longer extant, was an early allegorical interpretation on Habakkuk, which Jerome described in a letter of 395 (Patrologia Latina 25, p. 1097) as having been written thirty years before he understood the historical sources of the book. During his stay in Constantinople (380-81), he translated nine homilies on

Isaiah of Origen (Patrologia Latina 24, pp. 901-36). Shortly thereafter, not satisfied with Origen's explanation of Isaiah's vision in chapter 6, he published his own treatise. In his epistle 84, written in 399-400, he spoke of this composition as written twenty years earlier. This is his earliest biblical work on Isaiah, apart from his translations. It shows his dependence on Origen and is based on the Septuagint. His translation of the Vulgate occurred between 391 and 404 and was based primarily on the Hebrew. Finally, during the last period of his life, after having finished a commentary on the books of the Twelve Prophets, he turned to the four major prophets. He wrote Isaiah between 408 and 410. Jerome died in 420 before he could complete his Jeremiah commentary.

2. The Development of His Exegetical Method

Jerome's growth and development in biblical interpretation has been much studied, and it has long been obvious that his approach could be characterized initially as eclectic, in the best sense of the term. This observation is hardly surprising when one considers the various influences at work in his training (cf. especially L. N. Hartmann, "St. Jerome as an Exegete," pp. 47ff.). Not only was he trained as a youth by the best of Roman classicists (including Donatus) in Latin philology, style, and rhetoric, but he studied with the most outstanding representatives of both the Alexandrian school (Didymus) and the Antiochene school (Apollinaris and the Cappadocian Fathers). He was also acquainted with rabbinical traditions, and continued to be instructed by learned Jewish scholars, especially when he was translating the Vulgate.

However, the major influence on Jerome was Origen. Jerome's relation to Origen's works remains highly controversial. He began as a devoted disciple, but over the course of his life he began regarding Origen's exegesis with much hostility. Clearly Jerome's exegesis developed as he immersed himself in Hebrew and the search for the *Hebraica veritas,* but there were also dogmatic and political controversies with the Origenists that greatly clouded the issues. Most modern scholars agree that it was not to Jerome's credit that he attacked Origen with such vehemence while continuing to use his works, often without acknowledging his great dependency on Origen and his school.

The various stages of Jerome's exegetical development can best be traced in his translations. During his sojourn in Rome (382-385) Pope Damasus asked him to revise the Old Latin Version of the New Testament, which he did from the best Greek manuscripts available. His first attempt on the Old Latin Psalter following the same approach is usually called the "Roman Psalter," but it never gained wide popularity apart from Rome. His second attempt at the Psalter, "the Gallican Psalter," also used a Greek text. Then in 389, in his commentary on Ecclesiastes, he began to correct the Old Latin according to the Hebrew text. Shortly thereafter he published his *Liber Hebraicorum Quaestionum in Genesim,* which served as a preparation for translating directly from the Hebrew. From 391-406 Jerome completed his new translation of the Old Testament from the Hebrew text, an approach he continued to employ in his succeeding commentaries on the prophets along with shorter treatises.

3. Purpose, Approach, and Structure of the Isaiah Commentary

In the preface to his translation, Jerome characterizes the book of Isaiah as *non tam propheta, quam evangelista.* Then in the prologue to his commentary he develops his reasons for special attention to Isaiah, which turned out to be his longest commentary. He repeats widespread Christian tradition when he describes the prophecies as containing "all the mysteries" of the faith: the promise of Immanuel, his virgin birth, miracles, passion, death, and resurrection. He also emphasizes to Eustochium that one cannot know Jesus Christ without knowing the scriptures. He envisions his commentary as having the practical goal of instructing his readers in the faith, rather than as a scholarly exercise. He argues that the prophets were the inspired vehicles of divine wisdom and provided the foundation of the Christian faith. He also speaks of the need for both a historical and spiritual sense, based primarily on the Hebrew text.

Jerome divided his commentary into eighteen books. With the exception of the first book, he provided each successive new book with a brief introduction. Often addressing Eustochium, he summarizes succinctly the former book and then anticipates the contents of the new. He occasionally uses the metaphor of a fragile ship trying to escape the many dangers of the sea with his task of interpreting scripture (books 3 and 13), or requests the prayers of his readers. At times he apologizes for the length of his treatment and yet expresses his hesitancy to abbreviate (book 10). Then again, he can focus on specific problems such as the relation of the Hebrew text to the Greek (book 15), or why he cited earlier writers in his Daniel commentary but not in Isaiah (book 11).

In his introduction to book 5, he mentions that he had written a commentary on chapters 13–23 many years earlier at the request of Bishop Amabilus. He has decided to use this earlier commentary, which pursued largely the historical sense of the text, but he will offer in books 6 and 7 the spiritual sense of these same chapters. These brief introductions are of interest in showing the piety and intensity of Jerome's struggle with the biblical text and his single-mindedness in completing the commentary even though he is aware of its deficiencies and the criticism it faces.

4. Jerome's Hermeneutical Approach to Interpretation

It seems in order first to describe in general some of the features that are characteristic of Jerome's hermeneutical understanding of the exegetical task of biblical interpretation before turning to specific examples of his approach from the commentary on Isaiah.

Jerome never tired of emphasizing that the central task of interpretation lies in offering a historical understanding of the text *(juxta historiam)*. By this he meant that the interpreter employs the tools of historical study, geographical knowledge, literary analysis, and above all philological examination to determine what the text means. Because the prophet is the inspired vehicle of the divine mysteries, his words must be heard in all their historical particularity. In his interpretation of the oracles against the nations (chapters 13–23), one can see his enormous concern to establish the historical background, whether Assyrian, Babylonian, or Persian.

Yet even in his largely historical sections of Isaiah, one can see his strong Christian orientation in the manner in which he construes the historical context. Old Testament prophecy in its literal sense is seen as foretelling the content of the New Testament. Almost invariably there is an organic connection made as Old Testament sections are directly linked to parallels in the New. However, Jerome is very critical of Christian commentators (e.g., Clement) and the millenarians who neglect a passage's historical moorings and project a heavenly scene of the last days, as in chapter 1.

Equally important to Jerome's exegetical method is his insistence that the historical interpretation be followed by its spiritual meaning (*Unde post historiae veritatem, spiritualiter accipienda sunt omnia,* in the prologue to Isaiah). Jerome does not make careful distinctions among the spiritual senses, but employs a great variety of terminology: mystical, anagogic, tropological, allegorical. Usually he attempts to make some sort of organic link between the literal and the figurative, but occasionally he admits that none can be found. Often for the modern interpreter his move to the spiritual appears arbitrary and dictated by conventional Christian reflexes. However, Jerome was not completely unaware of the hermeneutical problems and continued to struggle with them. He remained, above all, a biblical scholar and did not have the philosophical ability or interest of either Origen or Augustine to provide sophisticated hermeneutical reflection. The well-known exchange of letters between Jerome and Augustine on the interpretation of Galatians 2, reveals with great clarity the different strengths of the two great Church Fathers (cf. J. Schmid's convenient edition of the debate, *SS. Eusebii Hieronymi et Aurelii Augustini epistulae mutuae*).

II. The Isaiah Commentary of Jerome

We turn now to specific examples from his Isaiah commentary to illustrate his exegetical approach.

1. *Textual Issues*

Jerome's commentary on a passage usually begins by offering a translation of the Hebrew. This is then followed by his rendering of the Septuagint, often expanded by citations from Aquila, Symmachus, and Theodotion. Occasionally he discusses variant readings of the Hebrew (e.g., Isa. 15:9, Dibon/ Dimon), but most frequently textual observations occur when there is a difference in the translation between the Hebrew and the Greek (e.g., Isa. 7:11). Jerome frequently states that in principle he prefers the Hebrew to the Greek; nevertheless, he always holds the Greek in high regard, and his careful attention to the nuances of meaning in the various Greek versions is of great interest and value. By his close analysis of the "two editions," as he calls them, he often makes structural observations as well. In Isa. 32:1 the Septuagint connects chapter 32 to chapter 31, whereas the Masoretic text separates the two chapters. In his discussion of the hardening formula (Isa. 6:9), he notes that the Greek uses an indicative mood foretelling the people's future rejection of God's invitation: "you will hear indeed, but you will not understand," whereas in the Hebrew the hardening is given in the imperative mood to signal God's command as the cause of the disobedient response. Jerome's solution is of interest in that he does not offer an easy harmonization; rather, he reflects theologically on the integrity of both interpretations and points out that the New Testament Gospels share the same tension when citing the Isaianic text. Although Jerome is often harsh in his repudiation of Jewish interpretations, he does not accept the widespread Christian allegation that the Jews intentionally distorted the Hebrew text in order to deny a Christian appeal to fulfillment.

2. Grammatical and Philological Problems

Jerome brought a new precision to the Old Testament commentaries by his close attention to the philological side of biblical exegesis. His concern for the exact grammatical sense of the Hebrew shows his familiarity with Jewish exegesis, and he frequently refers to the readings of a Jewish teacher (*Hebraeus*, cf. chapter 22), whom he continued to employ long after he had finished translating the Vulgate. Increasingly the search for the *Hebraica veritas* reflected his concern to recover the original documents of the inspired prophet, which contained the very words of God and effected a change in the authority attributed to the Septuagint. Jerome was not averse to offering different translations of a Hebrew phrase. Thus, in Isa. 6:6 he attributes to Hebrew grammar an ambiguity of whether the seraphim covered God's face and feet or their own with their wings. In Isa. 16:1 he allows the ambiguity to remain as to whether the phrase should be translated "ruling lamb" or "lamb of the ruler."

However, a classic example of Jerome's use of Hebrew philology is reflected in his lengthy discussion of Isaiah 7:14. He is embarrassed that earlier Christian interpreters have been up to now incapable of refuting the Jewish objections to their Christological interpretation, and he sets out to remedy this situation. He begins by reviewing the parallel occurrences of the word *almah* in the Old Testament. He notes that the Jewish commentators and the Greek versions — the Septuagint is an exception — all translate the term as "young woman." The Jews argue that in Hebrew only *betulah* means virgin and that this term is not used in the passage. Jerome sets out to demonstrate, even referring to the Punic cognate, that *almah* does not mean in Hebrew simply young woman, or even merely virgin, but "hidden-away virgin" *(virgin abscondida)*, of marriage age. It is interesting to note that Jerome did recognize that the word has a double sense of both marriageable *(nubilis)* and concealed. He opts for the latter sense of concealed and seeks to support his choice with parallel passages. (Modern scholars, using the tools of comparative Semitics, describe the dual sense in terms of a verbal homonym, but Jerome had no access to this insight.)

3. Historical Realia

One of Jerome's greatest strengths as a commentator lay in his tremendous interest in the historical, cultural, and physical details of the biblical text. This native interest in historical particularity was, of course, greatly enhanced by the knowledge acquired in his early travels, but especially during his lifetime in the Near East. For example, his commentary excels through the vast knowledge of ancient history, which he exploits when interpreting the often obscure references in the oracles to the nations (Isaiah 13–23). He struggles with great intensity to sort out the various historical epochs of the Assyrians, Babylonians, Persians, and Greeks, and he explores to the fullest all the parallel passages in Kings and Chronicles in an attempt to reconstruct a chronology. The same interest in historical reality is abundantly demonstrated in his other famous writings (*onomastica, de viris illustribus,* etc.) and accounts for his careful attention to place names and geographical features throughout his commentary.

Jerome shows much interest in tracing various aspects of Palestinian agriculture (chapters 1, 5, 28), and he brings to bear his own empirical observation on planting, sowing, and harvesting of grain, on how vineyards were tended and fruit trees cared for (cf. Abel, "Le Commentaire," pp. 220-25, on his use of local color). One can see his use of Jewish sources in his comments on the particular kind of tongs the seraph must have used to bring the burning coal from the altar (Isa. 6:6). Jerome also speculates on what kind of material formed the burning coal. He rejects the common view that it was charcoal, or coal, but speaks of an igneous rock *(carbunculium lapidem)* because of the flame it produced.

4. Establishing a Historical Context

As suggested above, Jerome was much concerned to establish a concrete historical context for interpreting a biblical passage. He contested the interpretation of some of the earlier Fathers (Clement, Origen) who, he claims, at times lose sight of real history in their zeal to discover spiritual truths through allegorical interpretation. Yet it is also important to recognize that Jerome's understanding of proper context was strongly shaped by his Christian assumptions.

At the outset Jerome takes for granted that the theological context of his exegesis is the Christian scriptures of both the Old and New Testaments. Although he insists on first focusing on the historical background of the Old Testament when dealing with a prophetic text, he assumes, as if by reflex, that the full context is only recognized when the New Testament is included. Hebrew prophecy always flows in some fashion, directly or indirectly, into New Testament fulfillment. Thus chapter 3 of Isaiah is clearly the divine judgment against Jerusalem manifested in a future captivity. Jerome notes that some commentators consider the executor to be the Babylonians, others the Romans. Without a pause, Jerome concludes that the agent is the latter, because only after the passion of Jesus Christ did the full anger of God's judgment fall on the Jews. The fulfillment of chapter 3 is then further evidenced by his citing corresponding descriptions from the New Testament. In Isaiah 6 the "unclean lips" of Isaiah's people are extended to those calling "Crucify, crucify him!" Isaiah 40 is immediately identified with John the Baptist, and the "servant passages" (49:1ff.; 53:1ff.) with the passion of Christ.

Increasingly, when dealing with prophetic passages in the Old Testament, including above all Isaiah, one notices the effect of historical rationalism. Thus, the terrifying message to Isaiah of apocalyptic proportions (Isa. 6:11-13) is interpreted by Jerome as foretelling the destruction of Vespasian or Titus, followed fifty years later by Hadrian. In sum, in spite of his vast historical knowledge, Jerome may have had far too narrow a view of biblical history, which was lost in his simple correspondence theory of prophecy and fulfillment.

5. Jerome's Hermeneutical Approach

Right from the outset, in his prologue, Jerome describes his exegetical approach to Christian tradition as involving two different hermeneutical levels, the historical *(juxta historiam)* and the spiritual. However, it shortly becomes evident that he deals with the latter under a whole variety of different terminology, as mentioned above: mystic, anagogic, tropological, allegorical. Jerome has often been described as an eclectic interpreter influenced by both the Alexandrian and Antiochene schools, which in a formal sense is undoubtedly true. Still, this description does not go to the heart of Jerome's method. On the one hand, from a hermeneutical perspective he did not have the theoretical sophistication found in the best of both schools. On the other hand, he was unique in seeing a whole range of practical and technical problems arising from the Hebrew and Greek.

Under the rubric of the spiritual sense, Jerome's approach includes a variety of different moves. Often without great reflection, he draws a simple analogy between the Isaianic prophecy and the New Testament. Israel's enemies are identified with the heretics; the new sprout of Isa. 11:1 was the new people of God, the church. Then again, the spiritual sense is a form of homiletical, moral appeal. Indeed, his search for a tropological sense was the most frequent usage of a spiritual sense for him. It was only after the death of sinful King Uzziah (Isaiah 6:1) that Israel was able to receive a revelation of

God's salvation. Again, very frequently when using the prophecy-fulfillment pattern, the New Testament fulfillment provides the spiritual sense for the Old Testament's historical meaning. When the Jews failed to acknowledge the correspondence, their rival interpretation was deemed "carnal," without a spiritual sense. In fact, the "hardening of Israel" (Isaiah 6:9-10) is cited as the theological grounds for Israel's inability to transcend the historical sense of the text. Finally, it is quite common for Jerome to use a typological appeal, in which an event or object fits a common pattern. The request for a sign (Isaiah 7) immediately calls to mind a host of other New Testament signs with some common ideological features.

In most of his commentary Jerome tries to keep a certain organic unity between the historical and figurative senses within a passage, but in spite of his valiant effort, the linkage often appears arbitrary. In book 5, when he is treating chapters 13–23, he informs his readers that he is reusing an earlier exegesis that is confined to discerning only the historical sense of this section of Isaiah's prophecies. For that reason, in the following two books he returns to this same material to offer his spiritual interpretation. However, the effect is often quite different even when the historical sense is presupposed. For example, when Jerome interprets chapter 15, the oracle against Moab, his interpretation in book 5 is largely historical. But when he returns to the chapter in book 6, the spiritual interpretation has turned into pure allegory. (He calls it *secundum anagogen.*) The key words are given an allegorical meaning completely divorced from the literary context. Thus, Nebo means "prophecy," Medeba "forest," Heshbon "knowledge," Elealeh "ascension," and Luhith "cheeks." Because he judges the passage to be fragmented, he resorts to an extreme form of allegory to render a unified meaning without any attempt to link the figurative sense with the historical.

Even in these books (5-8) Jerome is not fully consistent. When he treats Moab in Isa. 16, he gives an equally allegorical interpretation in book 5 as in book 6. In the former, Moab's consolation is the coming of the immaculate Lamb who will remove the sins of the world. The "rock of the desert" *(de petra deserti)* is interpreted as Ruth, whose marriage with Boaz produced Obed, the forefather of David and of Jesus. At times Jerome seems aware of the tension between the literal and the figurative. In treating chapter 19 (book 7) he admits that in this chapter it is not possible to reconcile the historical to the figurative, where one has to search for a higher level of understanding.

6. Jerome's Theological Reflections

In spite of the contrast between Jerome's philosophical talents and those of Augustine, Jerome never doubted that he was responsible for a theological handling of the biblical text as the sacred scriptures of the church. The reader often sees his concern to offer serious theological reflection, particularly in response to opinions that he deemed erroneous or even heretical.

In Isaiah 6 Jerome raises the question of how it is possible for Isaiah to see the Lord, especially since both the Old Testament and the New affirm that no one can see God and live (Exod. 33:20; John 1:20). He responds by saying that flesh cannot view the divinity of the Father, nor of the Son or Spirit, because there is not just one and the same nature within the Trinity. Rather, it is a question of the eyes of the soul *(oculos mentes),* of which Jesus said, "Blessed are those pure of heart, for they shall see God" (Matt. 5:8). Then Jerome cites those theophanic passages in the Old Testament that report the patriarchs seeing God (Gen. 22:30), and he concludes that a mere mortal cannot behold God, but that God does reveal himself in whatever form he pleases.

Earlier we noted that Jerome was fully aware of the striking difference between the Hebrew and Greek rendering of the hardening of Israel in Isaiah 6. The Septuagint uses the future indicative form of the verb, while the Hebrew employs the imperative to link the cause directly to the intentional will of God. Jerome does not attempt to blur the distinction, but to exploit the problem theologically. He notes that the New Testament citations of the Isaianic passage continue to reflect the same tension (cf. Matt. 13:14; John 12:40; Acts 28:26-27) by using both the Hebrew and the Greek formulations. Jerome thus concludes that this is a theological mystery, and that the same Lord who judges is the one who decrees to save his people as a mother chicken gathers her brood.

Finally, Jerome addresses the theological problem associated with the sign of Immanuel, "God with us" (Isa. 7:14). How could the promise of a coming Savior serve as a sign to King Ahaz, who is facing imminent defeat before the invading armies of Syria and Northern Israel? For Jerome, the sign of Immanuel can only be interpreted as the coming of God's son, Jesus Christ, miraculously born of a virgin. Yet the revelation of the name of Immanuel carries with it the power, when invoked, to save Israel not only in the distant future, but also in the present as well. The fact that the child will eat butter and honey is seen as further evidence that this promise is not an empty fantasy, but an event of a genuinely historical reality entering into human affairs. Jerome continues to argue ontologically when he identifies the promise of Immanuel with the same Savior encountered by Abraham, Moses, and the

Magi. Jerome does not pursue the issue further, but subsumes the prophecy under the category of mystery.

III. An Evaluation of Jerome's Hermeneutics

It is important to be fully aware of the difference between Jerome's era and our times. It is a sign of modernity within biblical studies to take for granted the priority of the historical and only subsequently, whether in an aggressive or timid fashion, to search for a spiritual or non-literal dimension. In Jerome's era, Christian tradition almost universally assigned priority to the spiritual or figurative levels. Jerome's lasting contribution lay in reversing this trend, giving priority to the historical and grammatical sense before the interpreter was permitted to talk of a spiritual meaning (*sed quod spiritualis interpretatio sequi debeat ordinem historiae,* on Isa. 13:19).

Jerome saw in the written text of scripture the very Word of God. Only by rigorously pursuing the author's intentions was there access to the divine revelation. Increasingly he emphasized the *Hebraica veritas* as providing an unfiltered and direct avenue to divine speech, and thus he established once and for all the abiding role of philological study of the biblical text. Clearly his focus on history and language matched his own personal talents, but his zeal was always grounded in his theological conviction.

Despite his vast erudition, Jerome's exegesis can be characterized above all as practical in orientation. His brief introductions to the various diversions within the book of Isaiah constantly support his deeply practical and theological motivation. He always remained unswervingly Christological in his interpretation and continued to stand consciously within the broad stream of early Christian orthodox tradition. The ferocity of some of his polemics against those he considered heretical arose from the intensity of his own Christian faith. In those places where he allowed two or three different interpretations to remain as options, the subject matter involved was never anything that substantially touched on doctrinal matters.

Jerome often speaks of his dependency upon his Jewish assistants, and his exegesis of Isaiah shows a wide acquaintance with Jewish exegetical tradition. When working on problems within the Old Testament he is often defensive regarding the serious lack of knowledge within the Christian church when debating with Jews. Yet for all his apparent closeness to Jewish scholars, his own exegesis, generally speaking, is largely negative respecting rabbinic interpretation. He frequently dismisses it as "carnal" and unable to rise above the plain sense to a spiritual dimension. Israel has been hardened and cannot any longer perceive the truth. Even more troubling is that Jerome very rarely recognizes in the Jews of the Old Testament signs of genuine faith (Isa. 53:1f.: *"raritatem credentium significat ex Judaeis"*).

Usually, the evidence for a faithful response from Israel is interpreted as a foreshadowing of the new (e.g., Jesse's root), or of a remnant adumbrating the church, or a future promise awaiting its fulfillment. For this reason, in spite of Jerome's rendering the Hebrew scriptures accessible to the church, his great achievement did not have the effect of recovering the theological reality of the "old covenant" as a faithful witness to God in its own right, but only as a foreshadowing of the New Testament's salvation in Jesus Christ.

Up to now, I have stressed Jerome's deep concern to combine the historical sense of the biblical text with its spiritual. I noted that Jerome never sought carefully to define the various traditional categories, but intermingled references to the various figurative senses. Yet in spite of his great efforts in supplementing the historical sense with the spiritual, Jerome never adequately resolved the problem of the relation between the two levels. His formulations of the spiritual often appear arbitrary and conventional. At no place do we find in Jerome a theoretical hermeneutical tractate such as appears in the work of Origen (*De Principiis,* Book 4) or in Augustine *(De doctrina christiana)*. The concern to find a genuinely organic, hermeneutical linkage like the one Augustine provided most brilliantly is simply lacking.

Finally, I would venture the theory that the hermeneutical deficiencies in Jerome's biblical exegesis in large part stem from a lack of theological understanding of the uniqueness of biblical history. Jerome showed little sophistication in formulating a concept of history as a dialectic between events that shaped the world of human affairs and the unique and mysterious ways of God in accomplishing salvific purposes in creation and redemption. In contrast with Justin, Irenaeus, and Augustine, Jerome appeared to have little grasp of biblical eschatology. He certainly perceived the theological problems arising from the crude millenarianism that was prevalent in the early church. However, without a multifaceted understanding of the intersection of the divine and the human within an unfolding divine drama, he was left with a flat, empirical history as a form of chronicle, and a non-historical realm of spiritual truths that floated above the "real" history of the world. For example, when handling the eschatological portrayal of the return of paradise in Isa. 11:6-9, Jerome begins by rejecting the "carnal" literalism of the Jews who demand to see the literal evidence of peace among the animals. He then interprets the eschatological description of the prophet in moralistic, spiritual terms as depicting the life of the Christian church where the rich and poor, the powerful and humble live in harmony. Similarly in his rendering of the great apocalyptic passages culminating in the entrance of the new aeon (Isa. 35, 65, 66), Jerome envisions the new as an improvement and restoration of virtue and morality, which he contrasts with the righteous judgment against the enemies of God.

And yet this criticism bears modification. In Jerome's handling of Isaiah 65 (the new heavens and earth), he reflects a much more powerful eschatological vision than earlier. Two reasons seem to have exerted a particular force. First, he felt constrained when treating the imagery of paradise to combat the literalism of Jewish commentators, whom he dismissed as carnal in glorifying an earthly form of the future life. Second, his very strong intertextual use of the Apostle Paul and the book of Revelation constrained him to interpret the imagery in a much more radical fashion as a genuine transformation by the new rather than as merely a refurbishing of the old.

To conclude, Jerome can hardly be faulted for continuing to search for a spiritual sense of scripture, but he did so in such a way that the historical and the figurative were increasingly fragmented, thus weakening the unity of the whole witness encompassing both testaments.

Bibliography of Jerome

Primary Sources

Opera, Patrologia Latina, edited by J.-P. Migne, pp. 22-30. Parisiis, 1844-64.

Commentarium in Esaiam, books 1-18, edited by M. Adriaen. Vols. 73, 73A, Corpus Christianorum, Series Latina. Turnhout, 1963.

Commentaires du Jérôme sur le prophète Isaïe, edited by R. Gryson et al. 5 vols. Freiburg: Herder, 1993-99.

St. Jerome: Letters and Selected Works, edited by W. H. Freemantle. Nicene and Post-Nicene Fathers, second series, vol. 7. Edinburgh: T. & T. Clark, 1893.

Secondary Sources

Abel, F. M. "Le Commentaire de Saint Jérôme sur Isaïe." *Revue Biblique* 25 (1916): 200-225.

Antin, P. "Introduction," *Saint Jérôme. Sur Jonas.* Sources Chrétiennes, 43. Paris: Éditions du Cerf, 1956.

Auvray, P. "Saint Jérôme et Saint Augustin: La controverse au sujet de l'incident d'Antioch." *Recherches de science religieuse* 29 (1939): 594-610.

Bardy, G. "S. Jérôme et ses mâitres hébreux." *Revue bénedictine* 46 (1934): 145-61.

Braverman, J. *Jerome's Commentary on Daniel: A Study of Comparative Jewish and Christian Interpretation of the Hebrew Bible.* Washington: Catholic Biblical Association, 1978.

Brown, D. *Vir trilinguis: A Study of the Biblical Exegesis of Saint Jerome.* Kampen: Kok, 1992.

Cavallera, F. *Saint Jérôme. Sa vie et son oeuvre.* 2 vols. Louvain, Paris: Bureaux, Champion, 1922.

Clark, E. A. *The Origenist Controversy: The Cultural Construction of an Early Christian Debate.* Princeton: Princeton University Press, 1992.

Ginzberg. L. "Der Kommentar des Hieronymus zu Jesaja." In *Jewish Studies in Memory of G. A. Kohut,* edited by S. W. Baron and A. Marx, pp. 279-314. New York: Jewish Theological Seminary, 1935.

Gozza, S. "De S. Hieronyme commentario in Isaiae librum." *Antonianum* 35 (1960): 49-80, 169-214.

Grützmacher, G. *Hieronymus: Eine biographische Studie zur alten Kirchengeschichte.* 3 vols. Leipzig/Berlin: Dietrich's Verlag, 1901-1908.

Hartmann, L. N. "St. Jerome as an Exegete." In *A Monument to St. Jerome,* edited by F. X. Murphy, pp. 37-81. New York: Sheed and Ward, 1952.

Jay, P. *L'Exégèse de saint Jérôme d'après son Commentaire sur Isaïe.* Paris: Études Augustiniennes, 1985.

Kamesar, A. *Jerome, the Hebrew Bible, and Greek Scholarship.* Oxford: Clarendon, 1993.

Kelly, J. N. D. *Jerome: His Life, Writings, and Controversies.* London: Duckworth, 1976.

Loewe, R. "The Medieval History of the Latin Vulgate." In *The Cambridge History of the Bible,* vol. 2, pp. 102-54. Cambridge: Cambridge University Press, 1969.

Murphy, F. X., ed. *A Monument to Saint Jerome.* New York: Sheed and Ward, 1952.

Quasten, J. *Patrology,* vol. 4, pp. 212-46. Westminster, Md.: Newman, 1991.

Schmid, J. "Prolegomena." In *S. S. Eusebii Hieronymi et Aurelii Augustini epistulae mutuae,* pp. 1-24. Bonn: Peter Hanstein, 1930.

Sparks, W. F. D. "Jerome as a Biblical Scholar." In *The Cambridge History of the Bible,* vol. 2, pp. 510-41. Cambridge: Cambridge University Press, 1969.

Vessey, M. "Jerome's Origen: The Making of a Christian Literary Persona." *Studia Patristica* 28 (1993a): 135-45.

8

John Chrysostom
(c. 349–407)

I. Life and Works

From an initial reflection, one would expect to find a rich source for biblical interpretation of the Old Testament in the writings of John Chrysostom. He ranks among the four great fathers of the Eastern church. He wrote commentaries and homilies on most of the books of the Bible, and exerted a far greater influence in the shaping of the church than the other Antiochenes, such as Theodore or Theodoret. Yet unfortunately very little of his interpretation of the book of Isaiah remains extant.

Six homilies on Isaiah 6 have survived in Greek (Patrologia Graeco-Latina 56, pp. 97-142). These homilies demonstrate Chrysostom's rhetorical power as well as his ability to address an audience regarding the practical, moral challenges of the Christian life with great skill and profundity. Yet these six homilies — homily 4 is probably inauthentic (cf. *Homélies sur Ozias*, pp. 13ff.) — do not add much in understanding Chrysostom's understanding of Isaiah. The homilies are structured topically and focus on a general theme such as divine condescension (homily 2) or on the diabolical nature of sin (homily 3). As a result, they hang very loosely on the Isaianic text. In their dating these homilies followed the earlier commentary of Chrysostom and are largely dependent on the earlier exegesis for their Isaianic content.

A small portion of his larger commentary in Greek has been preserved on Isa. 1:1–8:10 (Patrologia Graeco-Latina 56, pp. 11-94). A study of these chapters does reveal some interesting insights into his hermeneutical and theological understanding of the prophet. Our major concern in analyzing these chapters will be to understand how he moved from the Old Testament text to the Christian sermon, since the commentary is oriented to a homiletical application. But there is another methodological obstacle for the modern interpreter. Quasten (*Patrology,* vol. 3, pp. 435f.) shares a view held by many that these extant parts of Chrysostom's commentary have been editorially reshaped. That is to say, the present text "is probably nothing but an excerpt from homilies which the compiler stripped of their oratorical garb" (p. 436). Nevertheless, in spite of this problem, the preserved text remains useful when seeking to explore Chrysostom's hermeneutics.

Finally, an Armenian version of a complete copy of Chrysostom's commentary on Isaiah from a twelfth-century manuscript was published by the Mechitarists in 1880, which was then followed in 1887 with a Latin translation. Controversy continues as to whether the commentary is authentic, particularly because Chrysostom's name has been attached to inauthentic writings more often than any other of the Church Fathers throughout the centuries. Opinion regarding its authenticity remains divided. Several French scholars support its authenticity, and Quasten has accepted their judgment as probably true. In contrast, Ziegler (*Isaias,* vol. 4, Septuaginta, p. 13) remains doubtful of its authenticity. The issue thus remains undecided and will need a critical edition of the Armenian text to stimulate further research by the experts in the field. (I have been unable even to secure a copy of the Latin translation in the United States or Britain.)

Chrysostom's life has traditionally been divided into five periods: early education; ascetic period; deacon, priest, and presbyter at Antioch (381-98); bishop of Constantinople (398-404); and exile (404-407). His most famous homilies fell in the period at Antioch ("On the Statues") but continued during his tumultuous period in Constantinople. Chrysostom's homilies are extant on parts of Genesis as well as on certain psalms from the Old Testament; in the New Testament his most influential homilies are on Matthew, John, Romans, and 1-2 Corinthians. Some of these are carefully crafted, while others show signs of haste.

II. Chrysostom's Commentary on Isaiah 1–8

A few formal features of his commentary should be noted. The literary style is straightforward and largely unembellished. This characteristic of the commentary is in some contrast with the style of the homily on Isa. 6, which is generally elevated and highly rhetorical. This difference is one feature that caused scholars such as Quasten to conjecture that the commentary has been editorially redacted by simplifying the text. However, the style of the commentary is in no sense flat or pedestrian. It is filled with succinct turns of phrase: "There is no equal to virtue — made of good deeds" (Garrett, p. 50). He is also very effective in offering paraphrases to assist his audience. Moreover, he is keenly aware of the importance of correctly interpreting the metaphors of the prophetic text; to take every phrase literally would be to render meaning impossible.

Chrysostom's commentary on Isaiah is based on the Septuagint, but often according to its Lucian recension. Chrysostom had little interest in textual matters; never does his Isaiah commentary cite differing Greek translations. (In his Psalms commentary there are a few references to "other" translations.) Chrysostom also makes no reference to earlier commentators by name, although at times the parallels with others show some acquaintance with a broader Christian exegetical tradition (cf. Isa. 6 and Uzziah's sin). Only rarely does he refer to literary critical problems of the kind that have occupied modern scholars. However, he does note that the oracles of Isaiah were spoken at different times to different audiences and only subsequently joined together to form a complete book. Chrysostom had no firsthand knowledge of Hebrew. When occasionally he makes reference to Hebrew, it most likely stems from a secondhand source and frequently introduces confusion. Any reference to classic Greek literature is exceedingly rare and foreign to his style.

When one turns to the hermeneutical guidelines that shaped his exegesis, one finds, by and large, the traditional view of all the Fathers concerning the Bible. The scriptures are the divine oracles in which each word has sacred meaning. When Isaiah speaks of receiving a vision, Chrysostom affirms that no prophet or apostle expresses his own private opinion. Yet he does not ignore the human elements of scripture; the natural human powers are awakened and strengthened by divine inspiration. Still, Chrysostom makes a distinction between divine grace and human wisdom. Divine grace is represented by Elisha, human wisdom by Solomon, but both are employed in service to God.

Throughout his Isaiah commentary one can perceive clearly that Chrysostom belongs to the Antiochene school of exegesis and follows the lead of Diodore of Tarsus. Interpretation must not be strained or based on overly nice distinctions (ch. 2). When interpreting the Song of the Vineyard (ch. 5), Chrysostom expands his exegesis by addressing the issue of allegorization. His reflections are simple but sophisticated. He does not categorically rule out allegory, as has often been suggested, but rather he provides rules for proper restraint: "We ourselves are not the lords over the rules of interpretation, but must pursue scripture's understanding of itself, and in that may make use of the allegorical method." "This is everywhere a rule in Scripture: when it wants to allegorize, it tells the interpreters of the allegory, so that the passage will not be interpreted superficially" (Garrett, p. 110). For Chrysostom a proper use of allegory is to recognize the figurative dimension implied by the text itself.

Chrysostom in his Isaiah commentary does not frequently make use of the technical hermeneutical terms usually associated with the Antiochenes, yet his approach reflects exegetical techniques without the terminology. The one technical term he does use often is *sunkatastasis* (condescension). The use of this term dominates his interpretation of Isa. 6, with the prophet's seeing a vision of God seated on a throne considered an act of sheer divine condescension, in which God graciously adapts his revelation of himself to match human capacities.

Chrysostom also shares with the Antiochenes his understanding of history. Biblical prophecy derives from a divine disclosure that becomes more and more clear. Its meaning increases in specificity. Then again, the relation between prophecy and fulfillment is not a mechanical process. In ch. 2 he speaks of many things that are prophesied and spoken in one way, but fulfilled in another. In ch. 6 he describes a "double sense." The prophetic oracle has a discrete meaning for the present, but at the same time it possesses a subsequent, eschatological sense. This traditional device, usually called typology by modern interpreters, allows Chrysostom along with the other Antiochenes both to retain a historical sense of a prophetic passage and also to see a continuity with a future eschatological referent in the New Testament. Chrysostom also uses this understanding of prophecy to explain theologically how Old Testament laws are later rendered inoperative within the New Testament because of the coming of Christ. What is said of the Son in the Old Testament is spoken of him behind the mask of an ordinary name (Garrett, p. 62).

Finally, any appraisal of Chrysostom's commentary that does not address his unique homiletical skills is inadequate. It was not by chance that he was called "Golden Mouth." It may well be that the commentary on Isaiah has lost some of its original rhetorical embellishments through the editorial process, but in its present form his literary powers and homiletical skills are everywhere apparent.

Chrysostom's great strength as a preacher derived in part from the moral seriousness of his interpretation and his application of the biblical texts to the everyday issues of his Christian congregation. His preaching wrought tremendous opposition when he relentlessly exposed the corruption and superficiality of the people and their rulers (cf. Kelly, pp. 83ff.). He frequently showed his contempt of the luxury of the wealthy and passionately identified with the poor and helpless. Often in his Isaiah commentary his preaching shows enormous sensitivity to ordinary human nature. He could paint verbal pictures that immediately resonated with experiences common to all. When he expands on the prophet's attack on the rich women of Jerusalem, he does not fall into a flat moralism, but probes to the heart of their flirtatious behavior: "For everything a woman does — her eyes, her clothes, her feet, her gait — will indicate either modesty or wantonness. Just as artists mix colors for the pictures they wish to draw, so the movements of the body's limbs project pictures of the soul" (ch. 3, Garrett, p. 94).

Since much of Isaiah's message was condemnatory of Israel's covenantal responsibilities, Chrysostom found it appropriate in this context to expand on the same vices among his people: bribery, ignorance, and oppressive rule. His homily concludes by urging his hearers, "You have to be vigilant!" Again, he writes, "widowhood and orphanhood are themselves unbearable, but when the victims are abused by other people, the personal calamity is doubled" (Garrett, p. 52).

In sum, Chrysostom did not engage in lengthy theological discussions on the authority of scripture, nor did he break new hermeneutical ground in his exegesis. However, he did what he did with homiletical excellence matched only by Augustine among the Fathers. He used scripture in such a way as to confront his audience with a power and clarity commensurate with scripture's claim to be the direct voice of God. As such, his work as a preacher of the gospel remains a model for every successive generation in rendering the scriptures faithfully and with inspired imagination.

Bibliography of Chrysostom

Primary Sources

Patrologia Graeco-Latina (MPG), edited by J.-P. Migne, 47-63.

St. John Chrysostom, Nicene and Post-Nicene Fathers, first series, vols. 10-14, edited by P. Schaff. Edinburgh: T. & T. Clark, 1886-1888.

Homélies sur Ozias, edited by J. Dumortier. Sources Chrétiennes, 277. Paris: Éditions du Cerf, 1981. (Migne, Patrologia Graeco-Latina 56, pp. 97-142.)

Commentaire sur Isaïe, edited by J. Dumortier. Sources Chrétiennes, 304. Paris: Éditions du Cerf, 1983. (Migne, Patrologia Graeco-Latina 56, pp. 11-94.)

Commentarius ad Isaiam. An Armenian version was published by the Mechitarists from a twelfth-century manuscript: Venice, 1880; Latin translation, 1887.

Secondary Sources

Bardy, G. "Interpretation chez les pères." Dictionnaire Biblique, Suppl. 4, pp. 569-91. Paris, 1949.

Baur, C. *John Chrysostom and His Time*. 2 vols. Westminster, Md.: Newman Press, 1959.

————. "Der Kanon des Johannes Chrysostomus." *Theologische Quartalschrift* 105 (1924): 258-71.

Chase, F. H. *Chrysostom: A Study in the History of Biblical Interpretation*. Cambridge: Deighton Bell, 1887.

Dieu, L. "Le commentaire arménien de S. Jean Chrysostome sur Isaïe ch. VIII–LXIV: est-il authentique?" *Revue d'Histoire Ecclésiastique* 17 (1921): 7-30.

Dumortier, J. "La version arménienne du commentaire sur Isaïe de Jean Chrysostome." In *Studia Patristica*, vol. 17, pp. 1158-62. Oxford, 1982.

Garrett, D. A. *An Analysis of the Hermeneutics of John Chrysostom's Commentary on Isaiah 1–8 with an English Translation*. Studies in Bible and Early Christianity, vol. 12. Lewiston, N.Y.: Edwin Mellen, 1992.

Hill, Robert. "John Chrysostom's Teaching on Inspiration in 'Six Homilies on Isaiah.'" *Vigiliae Christianae* 22 (1968): 19-37.

————. "Akribeia: A Principle of Chrysostom's Exegesis." *Colloquium* 14 (1981): 32-36.

Kelly, J. N. D. *Golden Mouth: The Story of John Chrysostom*. Ithaca: Cornell University Press, 1995.

Krupp, R. A. *Saint John Chrysostom: A Scripture Index*. New York: University Press of America, 1984.

Margerie, B. de. "Saint John Chrysostom, Doctor of Biblical 'Condescension.'" In *An Introduction to the History of Exegesis*, vol. 1, pp. 189-212. Petersham, Mass.: St. Bede's Publication, 1993.

Old, H. O. *The Reading and Preaching of the Scriptures*, vol. 2, pp. 171-222. Grand Rapids: Eerdmans, 1998.

Quasten, J. *Patrology*, vol. 3, pp. 424-82. Westminster, Md.: Newman Press, 1960.

Nassif, B. "Antiochene Theōria in John Chrysostom's Exegesis." Ph.D. dissertation, Fordham University, 1991.

Venables, E. "Chrysostom, John." In *Dictionary of Christian Biography*, edited by W. Smith and H. Wace, vol. 1, pp. 517-35. London: John Murray, 1877.

Wilken, R. L. *John Chrysostom and the Jews*. Berkeley: University of California Press, 1983.

Woollcombe, K. J. "The Biblical Origins and Patristic Development of Typology." In *Essays on Typology*, edited by G. W. H. Lampe and K. J. Woollcombe, pp. 39-75. London: SCM, 1957.

Young, F. "John Chrysostom." In *From Nicaea to Chalcedon*, pp. 143-59. London: SCM, 1983.

9

Cyril of Alexandria

I. His Life and Background

The date of Cyril's birth is uncertain, but the modern reconstruction of his life usually sets it at 378. His death occurred in 444. Little is known of his early life, including his education. Egyptian traditions recount that he was born in Alexandria and received a good education there. His writings attest that he was acquainted with the classics, though he probably cited them from secondhand sources. His education was undoubtedly overseen by his uncle, Theophilus, who was elected Patriarch in 385 and succeeded by Cyril in 412. A decisive turning point in Cyril's life came in about 430, when he entered into heated conflict with Nestorius.

Cyril is mostly remembered in the history of the church for his role as leader of the anti-Nestorian party and for his running doctrinal battles with the Antiochenes, including Theodoret. As a brilliant and extremely aggressive representative of the Alexandrian tradition he was highly influential in shaping the classical Greek doctrines of the Trinity and Christology. He has often been disparaged because of the vigor and even harshness of his polemics, but his contribution to the doctrinal development of the church is undisputed.

II. His Writings

Usually Cyril's writings are classified according to the two major periods in his life, namely, before and after 423. In his earlier period he cultivated a wide range of writings in both theology and biblical exegesis, including *De adoratione in spiritu et veritate,* the *Thesaurus,* and the Easter encyclicals. It was in this earlier period that he also did his major biblical work, writing commentaries on the Minor Prophets, Isaiah, and John's Gospel. The exact date of his Isaiah commentary is unknown and can only be inferred as subsequent to *De adoratione* and before 423. After this date he devoted himself unswervingly to polemical treatises for the rest of his life, first against the Arians and later against Nestorius and his defenders.

III. Cyril as a Biblical Scholar

This chapter focuses on Cyril's role as a biblical scholar within the history of exegesis. Although his biblical interpretation forms the largest part of his writing, only rather recently has serious attention been paid to this body of his work. Rather, throughout the nineteenth century and the first half of the twentieth, scholars have treated Cyril as one of the greatest of the Greek Fathers and the great defender of orthodoxy while dismissing his exegesis as of less value. (The obvious exception is the critical editions of certain of his commentaries by P. E. Pusey.)

The most serious attempt to right this situation has been Alexander Kerrigan's dissertation, "St. Cyril of Alexandria, Interpreter of the Old Testament," published in 1952. Through years of meticulous study he has placed all subsequent students of Cyril's exegesis in his debt. Of greatest interest is his decision to place at the center of his analysis the hermeneutical issue of the literal and the spiritual senses of scripture in Cyril's exegesis. His thorough study of the terminology provides a solid foundation for all subsequent work. In addition, he deals with the usual technical questions: the form of the text used by Cyril, his historical sources, his geographical knowledge, and the like. In his conclusion he raises broader theological issues of the theological and historical significance of Cyril within the church's exegetical tradition. However, specifically in relation to this last section, I will suggest that so much has changed during the last fifty years in respect to the modern hermeneutical debate that other perspectives need to be considered.

IV. The Literal and Spiritual Senses
of Scripture according to Cyril

1. The Literal Sense

Cyril makes the same distinction between the literal and spiritual senses shared by all the previous Church Fathers. Yet precisely what he means by the literal sense and its relation to the spiritual is not immediately obvious. The problem arises because nowhere does Cyril offer a simple and fully consistent interpretation of his understanding of the literal sense. The issue is further complicated by the very large and diverse terminology that Cyril employs to delineate the literal sense. Kerrigan (pp. 35ff.) lists some twenty different expressions, including *to gramma, ho nous tōn eirēmenōn* (the sense of that spoken), and *ho procheiros logos* (the obvious word). The most frequent term is *historia*. Kerrigan offers a number of subdivisions in an attempt to bring further clarity, speaking of expressions that are exclusively exegetical and others only indirectly related to exegesis. Kerrigan insists that what determines the literal or spiritual sense for Cyril is the object being referred to rather than the manner of its signification, though the relation between the object and its signification is not rigidly fixed. At times Cyril fuses the two, thus blurring the distinction. Still, Kerrigan insists that reference to different objects determines the level of signification.

What then are the objects of the literal sense? Generally speaking, the objects of the literal sense are things or events perceived by the senses and exposed to human perception. Accordingly, they are identified as *ta aisthēta* (that perceived by the senses) or *ta en aisthēsei keimena* (that evoking sense perception). They can include events in the past, legal enactments (like Deut. 23:1ff.), or material prosperity promised by a prophetic oracle. The objects are ordinary things of the earth — animals, plants, food — which are frequently designated as "coarse." They are the source of knowledge acquired by the senses and thus distinct from the *nous,* which is superior.

Bertrand de Margerie ("Introduction," pp. 244-45) observes that Cyril has abandoned one of Origen's cherished hermeneutical convictions when arguing that certain passages of the Old Testament offer a literal sense but not a spiritual one. This position allows Cyril to relegate parts of the Old Testament, especially the legislative aspects, to a literal sense completely devoid of mystical signification. Therefore, a scriptural passage that has no relation to the mystery of Christ cannot be spiritual, but only literal.

Cyril also uses the terminology of the literal sense in a wider connotation that embraces various tropes and figurative images. The need for the enigma, parable, and paradigm arises because behind the objects lies an obscure and undetermined sense, and Cyril illustrates this by pointing to the complex imagery of the eagle in Ezek. 17:3-4. By including the metaphorical sense within the category of the literal sense, Cyril also lines up with the Antiochenes. Cyril has clearly been influenced by classical Greek rhetoric, and he seems aware of distinctions between simile and metaphor, but he is not closely bound by classical rules.

The problem of *skopus* that played an important role in the Antiochene exegetical tradition influenced Cyril's hermeneutical approach. For Cyril *skopus* (scope) denotes the purpose and goal of the sacred writers, the angle of vision from which an author views things. Attention to the text's scope applies not only to the literal sense, but to the spiritual sense as well. Kerrigan (pp. 95ff.) points out the hermeneutical importance of Cyril's use of scope when he defends the Mosaic cosmology against the attacks of Julian the Apostate. Against Julian's charge that the Genesis account is inferior to the Greek because it leaves so much out, Cyril argues that Moses wrote only such details as he deemed "useful for orienting one's life" — that is, he had an intentional goal. Kerrigan (pp. 108-9) cites two examples from Isa. 14:29 and 58:1 to illustrate his appeal to the text's scope. It is also significant to observe that for Cyril the spiritual signification is included in the very *skopus* of Scripture. It is an objective component and not merely the subjective interpretation of the commentator.

Finally, Kerrigan (pp. 40ff.) attempts to assess Cyril's esteem for the literal sense. The result of his analysis is somewhat ambivalent. On the one hand, Cyril makes it clear, especially in his prologue to Isaiah (Patrologia Graeco-Latina 70, 9A) and again in interpreting Isa. 7, how important it is to interpret the literal sense of scripture: "Those who reject the literal sense of the inspired Scripture as something frivolous deprive themselves to a certain extent of the possibility of understanding what is written in them." He goes on to argue that only by properly dealing with the literal historical sense can one ascend to the spiritual sense. On the other hand, in terms of his actual interpretation of Isaiah, much less space is given to the literal sense than to the spiritual. Although one can see Cyril's considerable knowledge of geographical matters and trace his frequent use of biblical history, the yield from this is quite small, and not to be compared, say, with that of Jerome. It would almost appear that Cyril felt constrained to deal seriously with the literal, but that his overwhelming interest and real talent lay in expounding the theological content of the text, largely in terms of the spiritual sense. Although profiting from the influence of the Antiochenes and Jerome, Cyril remains basically within the Alexandrian tradition in his hermeneutics.

2. The Spiritual Sense

Cyril's commentaries are filled with exhortations to move beyond the literal sense of Scripture. He frequently repeats his concern to cut down on the "prolixity of the literal sense" in order to expound those elements that prove "the mystery of our Savior." He reckons the spiritual sense to be hidden in the superfluities of the literal sense, "like fragrant flowers of a garden that are closed all around externally within superfluous leaves" (Kerrigan, p. 111). Everywhere one gains the impression that as a commentator Cyril can hardly wait to get to the heart of the task, which is to explore the text's spiritual significance. Indeed, there is a brilliance and richness of thought in his theological reflection that far outstrips anything found in Theodoret or Eusebius.

a. Cyril's Terminology

We turn first to Cyril's terminology when describing the spiritual sense. At the outset it is significant to observe that his vocabulary reflects a very wide diversity of expression in designating the "higher sense." Perhaps surprisingly, the traditional use of the term "allegory," found especially in Philo and Origen, appears rarely. Instead Kerrigan (pp. 109ff.) lists some twenty different expressions characteristic of his usage, including:

1. *theoria* appearing with a variety of qualifying additions, such as *en pneumata*. The frequent term emphasizes that the spiritual sense is attained in the course of a vision, which is an aid given by the Holy Spirit.
2. formulae involving the use of *noēma* (thought or understanding).
3. various combinations with the noun *nous* (mind and its functions).
4. expressions using forms of *mystikos* (mystical, spiritual).

The term *theoria* was, of course, a favorite and widely used expression of the Antiochenes. The issue of how Cyril's usage relates to this school of thought is more important than the effort to trace its original Greek origins. For the Antiochenes, the term *theoria* designated the form of vision considered messianic — namely, those events that pointed toward the future for fulfillment (cf. Theodoret). For Cyril the emphasis does not lie in a series of events standing within a trajectory of eschatological moments, but rather in the discovery of the text's hidden sense with the help of supernatural illumination. Cyril evoked New Testament texts (e.g. John 14:25f.) to support his expectation of the Holy Spirit's future revelation of Christ's mystery. The process of transferring the shadows of the Old Testament into the spiritual knowledge of the New Testament results in an interior transformation reflecting the glory of Christ himself.

b. The Spiritual Sense and its Object

Just as Cyril had argued that the literal sense was determined by its object of referral, so also the spiritual sense was set apart from the *ta aiosthēta* (sense perception). The spiritual sense was signified by such categories as *to alēthes* (truth), *ta anankaia* (necessary, valued), *ta kekrummena* (hidden), and *ta pneumatika* (spiritual). Although many of these terms appeared in Plato and designated a reality removed from change and belonging to a world of ideas, Cyril's usage is too much shaped by Christian theology to be simply identified with classical Greek philosophy. Rather it becomes immediately apparent that for Cyril the objects of the spiritual sense are identical with various realities that belong to Christ's mystery (cf. Kerrigan, p. 131). These realities are those initially made known provisionally and in a veiled form within the Old Testament (creation, law, redemption), awaiting their spiritual transformation onto a higher level. For this reason Cyril's understanding of the spiritual sense is integrally connected to the harmony between the two testaments.

c. The Relation of the Old and New Testaments

Cyril stands in the tradition of both Clement and Origen in stressing the unity of the two testaments. Together they form one single message of salvation. Particularly in his John commentary, Origen argues that the knowledge possessed by the "perfect" in the period preceding Christ's advent was not less than that of the Apostles who were instructed by Christ (John 6, 4, 24, cited in Kerrigan, p. 133). However, Cyril is far more restrained than either Clement or Origen in speaking of the identity of the two testaments. The reason for the difference is that Cyril has enhanced the centrality of the spiritual sense in such a way as to qualify any simple identity between the two testaments. The Old Testament is certainly the source of divine illumination, but it is also accompanied by shadows. Therefore, it is not to be compared with the unadulterated light radiated by Christ. Its light is compared to that of the moon, while the gospel shines with the brightness of the noonday sun (Margerie, p. 246).

It would certainly be anachronistic to describe Cyril's position regarding the two testaments as "dialectical." Yet he can write, "The law is perfect and imperfect as one and the same. It is perfect, if it is understood spiritually (since it speaks to us of Christ's mystery). But it is imperfect, if the mind of those who are being instructed does not go beyond the letter" (commentary on Hosea, cited by Kerrigan, p. 131). Although the Old Testament remains for the Christian the true source of the divine revelation of Christ's mystery, it needs the spiritual sense to render its true meaning. Only the transformed Old Testament translates the prefiguration of Christ into its spiritual reality. The mystical *theoria* bearing spiritual illumination has been buried in the deeds and utterances of history. Of course, Cyril finds his clearest biblical warrant in Paul: "the letter kills, but the Spirit makes alive" (2 Cor. 3:6).

d. Cyril's Doctrinal and Ethical Norms

Standing as he does in the traditions of Clement and Origen, it comes as no great surprise to find Cyril's occasional reference to authoritative norms. These are not directly identified with scripture nor worked out in a rule of faith such as is found in Irenaeus and Tertullian. Yet two terms are used that touch upon a similar subject: *kērygma* and *paideusis*. There is an overlapping of context, with *kērygma* instructing in orthodox doctrine and condemnation of heretics, whereas *paideusis* is concerned largely with ideals of conduct more in line with Clement's educational goals. These terms, particularly the latter, occur usually within the context of the spiritual sense. Thus, the law of Moses serves to point out the sins of wickedness, but it is the spiritual that introduces the Christian to knowledge of virtue and the glory of conduct in Christ. The goal is to be fashioned by spiritual worship. Because there are ethical and doctrinal norms governing the pure life, ugly or unseemly narratives (say, in the Pentateuch) can serve to engender virtue only according to a spiritual reading.

5. The Role Played by the Divine and Human within the Spiritual Sense

Many passages within the Old Testament indicate that Cyril was of the conviction that the spiritual objects were present in the minds of the prophets themselves. At least on some occasions, they were conscious of the spiritual meaning of their oracles. By including the spiritual meaning within the prophet's *skopus,* he implies that it is part of the consciousness of the human author. Yet because the emphasis continues to fall on such illumination being a gift from God, Cyril clearly regards the spiritual sense also as an objective sense of scripture. The spiritual interpretation of the Old Testament derives from God, who in advance attached to the events of the old dispensation the quality of enigma in order to serve future generations in spiritual instruction. The human author was a vehicle through whom the process either proceeded by aid of the Holy Spirit or was blocked by blindness, as in the case of the

Jews. Cyril held that Moses knew Christ's power as Savior and was aware that the law could justify no one apart from Christ's victory over sin and judgment. In the case of Isa. 11:12 ("he will assemble the outcasts of Israel and gather the dispersed of Judah"), its spiritual sense is explicitly attributed to the "conscious intention of Isaiah himself" (Patrologia Graeco-Latina 70, 332B, cited by Kerrigan).

f. The Attitude of the Jews toward the Spiritual Sense

Much of Cyril's running attack on the Jews derived from his understanding of the spiritual sense of scripture. As discussed above, Cyril was unswerving in his evaluation of the Jewish scriptures as containing the enduring revelation of God. Any denial of the revelatory status of the Old Testament, either by Christian or pagan groups, was immediately labeled heretical and a threat to the faith. Rather, the controversy with the Jews turned on the interpretation of the scriptures. The law of Moses was given by God to be understood spiritually. If read only according to the letter, it proves to be unprofitable and its meaning rendered dead and lifeless. Cyril follows the tradition of his Christian predecessors by interpreting the veil on Moses' face (Exod. 34:33) as a symbol of Jewish inability to understand the true nature of the law and their inability to see the rays of divine light pointing to the mystery of Christ (Patrologia Graeco-Latina 69, 536f.). Citing the New Testament, Cyril argues that Jewish contumacy reached its peak during Christ's sojourn among them. John 5:39-40 in particular was used to support Cyril's position. Jesus said, "You search the Scriptures because you think that in them you have eternal life, but it is they that give evidence about me." As a result, the whole of scripture became sealed and its secrets inaccessible to the Jews. (For a detailed study of the challenge of Judaism for Cyril, cf. especially R. Wilken.)

g. Summary of Cyril and the Spiritual Sense

Kerrigan (pp. 165ff.) uses the categories of Daniélou to describe the varieties of the spiritual sense found in Cyril:

1. Cyril shows little interest in the eschatological type of spiritual exegesis. Only rarely does the traditional theme of Christ's return as judge at the end of the age appear.

2. The ethical type of interpretation, sometimes designated as the "interior sense," is well represented, often appearing under the rubric of *paideusis* (teaching, instruction).

3. The ecclesiological type of spiritual exegesis is also prominent, which

focuses on the central role of the church, but in contrast, say, to Eusebius, Cyril retains a very strong Christological focus in stressing the mysteries of Christ throughout.

d) Rarely does Cyril employ the historical type of spiritual exegesis, in which the historical narrative provides access to Christ's mysteries. Cyril followed Origen in not viewing the Old Testament as a figure of historical events connected with Christ's life and mission.

Although this description of Cyril's spiritual Old Testament interpretation is at times useful, with further examination we will see that it does not reach to the heart of Cyril's major contribution to biblical interpretation.

V. Cyril's Interpretation of the Book of Isaiah

One is immediately impressed with the extraordinary length of Cyril's commentary, which far exceeded that of Eusebius or Theodoret among the Greek Fathers. The only collective edition of Cyril's *opera* is that of Aubert, reprinted in the Patrologia Graeco-Latina, vols. 68-77. The Isaiah commentary is printed in Patrologia Graeco-Latina 70, pp. 9-1450. Unfortunately, P. E. Pusey's new edition of certain of Cyril's commentaries did not include Isaiah.

Cyril has structured his commentary into five books, each with five or six subdivisions:

    Book 1, Isa. 1:1–10:32
    Book 2, Isa. 10:33–24:23
    Book 3, Isa. 25:1–42:9
    Book 4, Isa. 42:10–51:23
    Book 5, Isa. 52:1–66:24

The strong differences between this structure and that of Theodoret or Jerome would indicate that there was no fixed common tradition either in the East or West for such an exegetical undertaking of interpreting Isaiah.

Book 1 is preceded by a brief *Prooemium* in which Cyril sets out the scope of the interpretation and his own goals. He begins unequivocally in confessing, "Christ is the end of the law and prophets." Still, he intends to interpret the book according to both its literal and spiritual senses. He is also concerned that his commentary will do justice to the material and prove useful to the reader. He is aware that certain commentators have preceded him — he does not mention names — but he feels that with hard work something new can be found and older truths confirmed.

There are many examples throughout his commentary that demonstrate that Cyril is at times deeply concerned to pursue the literal, historical sense of the biblical text. Moreover, he also clearly shows that he has the literary and rhetorical skills to interpret on this level. When interpreting Isa. 5, he recognizes the first verse as a *stichos* that functions as a kind of superscription: "I will sing to my beloved a song of my beloved concerning my vineyard." At the outset he is aware of a variety of different interpretations that try to sort out the exact referent of the song. He then observes that the expression *di'emou* does not mean "belonging to me," but rather "to the beloved." Although the prophet can then speak of "my vineyard," the claim is not that the vineyard is his, but that he is one of those who is included within the vineyard. Cyril then cites Jer. 9:2 as offering a parallel to this corporate meaning of the vineyard as Israel.

Again, when beginning his interpretation of Isa. 7, Cyril emphasizes the need to deal seriously with the historical sense when this is the chosen manner by which Scripture addresses a given event. He reviews the division of the tribes into Judah and Ephraim, then turns to the reign of Ahaz, the son of Jotham, and relates the attack against Jerusalem by a coalition of the Syrian king and Ephraim. Of course the source of his historical material is confined solely to the various parts of the Old Testament, especially in 2 Kings. When interpreting the phrase "in the year that King Uzziah died" (6:1), Cyril follows the traditional interpretation in building on the account of 2 Chron. 26 of Uzziah's sin and ensuing leprosy, which resulted in God's withdrawing his revelation to his prophets until Uzziah's death.

When interpreting Isa. 7:14-16 Cyril stays within the lines of earlier Christian exegetical tradition (e.g., Eusebius and Jerome) in first briefly addressing the objections of the Jews to his Christological interpretation. However, the influence of Athanasius's attack on the Arian position also emerges with great force: "[S]ince he was God by nature and the Word begotten by God, he was holy as God both from the world and before it, or rather before all ages, seeing that he did not lose his own prerogatives on account of the human nature" (translation by N. Russell, p. 50). In his later period, Cyril would be forced by the Nestorian heresy to even greater clarity in elaborating his Christological definitions regarding the two natures of Christ and their relationship.

In his commentary there are other usages of biblical history to explain particular texts. In Isa. 9:8-10 he summarizes the events of both the northern and southern kingdoms from the reigns of Jeroboam II to Hezekiah and alludes to the destruction of Samaria by Sennacherib on his way to Jerusalem (even though this was actually done by Sargon in the reign of Ahaz). In Isa.

23:1 Cyril refers to a historical incident described in Ezek. 29:18-19 when the ships of Carthage were invited to weep over the fall of Tyre. Or again, in Isa. 30:6ff. Cyril reviews the period of Jehoiakim and the prophecies of Jeremiah. He describes the siege and destruction of Jerusalem and the flight of a remnant into Egypt, incorporating largely the account of the books of Kings and Jeremiah.

Cyril's use of geography reveals a much more critical interest in the subject than that of history. Here Kerrigan's chapter (pp. 322ff.) is largely dependent on F. M. Abel's "La Géographie sacrée chez S. Cyrille d'Alexandri." Both scholars conclude that Cyril takes great pains to explain geographical data and in this compares favorably with Jerome. It seems highly probable that Cyril consulted Jerome, and yet the instances of direct dependency are rare. Not unexpectedly, Cyril's knowledge of Egyptian geography excels and is more extensive than Jerome's. Kerrigan (p. 332) does note the lack of a critical historical perspective when he ascribes to the Alexandria of Isaiah's time a significance it only acquired after Alexander founded the great maritime city on an earlier site of small villages.

Cyril's contribution of textual criticism is minimal. He was unacquainted with the Hebrew language, and his infrequent appeals to Hebrew are completely dependent on sources he only refers to vaguely. Abel makes a strong case for Cyril's dependency on Jerome when he does refer to Hebrew. Cyril occasionally refers to variant Greek readings, but the concern of both Jerome and Theodoret in harmonizing the later Jewish translations is missing in Cyril.

One of the best examples of Cyril's narrative skills is found in his handling of Isa. 36-39. The encounter with the Rabshakeh is analyzed without any appeal to a higher sense; rather, Cyril makes several acute literary observations. He notices that the Rabshakeh omits the title of King when referring to Hezekiah — an obvious sign of disrespect — while then heaping lavish and extravagant praise on the King of Assyria, "the great king." Again, Cyril points out the acuteness of the Assyrian's speech that notes the contradiction between claiming to trust God while calling for aid from Egypt. He recognizes the Assyrian's use of irony: "If your god is so supportive how is it that we have been sent against you by him?" Cyril notes the cleverness of the enemy's deceptive promises.

Of course, Cyril cannot remain purely descriptive for too long. When pointing out the crudity of the Assyrian's speech, he characterizes the words as proceeding from an impure heart. Or when reporting the Rabshakeh's boast that none of the gods of the nations have delivered them, Cyril cannot refrain from mounting his own theological response: these nations were ignorant of the one true living God, the creator of the world. Moreover, God had abandoned Samaria because the people had worshipped the golden calf and were therefore destroyed with the aid of God. Only at the end of the scene does Cyril draw a homiletical application, with Jerusalem described as a type of Christ's church besieged by the enemies of truth.

When treating Isa. 39, the visit of Babylonian envoys to Hezekiah after he had recovered from sickness, Cyril engages in some speculation regarding why the delegates had come. (Of course, because the biblical text is silent on this very matter, the search for the real historical reasons has continued up to the present.) Cyril tries to work from the larger literary context of the preceding chapters. The soothsayers of Babylon had been much impressed with Hezekiah's ability to reverse the direction of the sun's shadow (Isa. 38). They also sought advice on how the attack on Jerusalem by the Assyrians had been repulsed. Finally, Cyril also comments on Hezekiah's response to Isaiah's foretelling of the coming Babylonian captivity. He thinks that it would have been better had Hezekiah asked God's mercy for his posterity rather than being satisfied with peace during his own lifetime. He then extends his comments to a broader moralism on the exceeding weakness of the human heart.

When treating Isa. 13, the destruction of Babylon by the Medes and Persians, Cyril offers a historical review of the period in his preface. God's support for Cyrus against Babylon fulfills biblical prophecy and is the just effect of divine anger in response to Babylon's arrogance and idolatry. He can speak of the imagery as prophetic hyperbole in describing the misery inflicted on women and children. Cyril explains that ultimately it is necessary to penetrate through the crass figure to the true spiritual meaning (*eis pneumatikēn theōrian*, Patrologia Graeco-Latina 70, 345C) but he is prepared first to recount the historical events before penetrating to the substance.

In an earlier chapter, I pointed out that one of the characteristic features of Eusebius's interpretation of Isaiah is the finding of numerous references to the Roman Empire, especially in his commentary. Cyril does so as well, but in a far more restrained manner. Nevertheless, references to Roman rule are included within Cyril's literal sense, even though the New Testament context hovers usually in the background as the implicit fulfillment. Thus Cyril follows church tradition in regarding Isa. 2:1-5 as depicting the conversion of the nations and triumph of the church. Cyril understands the passage as foretelling the universal peace that the Roman rule provided, which also made the proclamation of the gospel easier. Or again, in Isa. 11:15-16 Cyril interprets the oracle as predicting how Caesar Augustus conquered Egypt: "Since it pleased God to hand over Egypt to the scepter of Rome, a violent storm wind blew . . . and the waters of the river were chased into the sea. It was then that God smoothed the way for the Roman army" (Patrologia Graeco-Latina 70, 337B). Then again, in Isa. 19:1-5, the threats against Egypt, Cyril maintains that the oracle alludes to the conquest of Egypt by Rome, even expressly mentioning Vespasian as the conqueror.

In spite of the evidence of Cyril's seriousness in discussing various aspects of the text's literal/historical sense, I believe Cyril's major concern is with the spiritual sense. It is not helpful to lump together his exegesis as "allegorical," if that means a reading into the text of an alien system of doctrine that can basically be dismissed as fully predictable and irrelevant to "honest" biblical interpretation. Rather, I will argue that only when enough empathy is present in the modern interpreter to explore Cyril's method and concerns does his genuine exegetical contribution begin to emerge.

His commentary on Isa. 11:1-3 (Patrologia Graeco-Latina 70, 309ff.) is a good text to use to pursue Cyril's spiritual exegesis: "A rod shall go forth from the root of Jesse. . . ." He begins immediately to reflect on the word "rod" (rhabdos). At first he speaks of the rod or scepter of Aaron as a type of Christ (eis typon Christou), but the appeal to this typology is made almost in passing and serves as a minor and traditional ornament, peripheral to his main concerns in the chapter. Rather, he begins with the theological assumption that the text is a prophetic revelation in which God, who knows all of the future, begins to disclose himself to his prophet. Only by pursuing the interlocking, intertextual references within scripture will the full mystery of God's disclosure be made known.

He commences his study of the word "rod" by tracing its parallel passages. Christ according-to-the-flesh is described as emerging as the rod from the root of Jesse. He sees this as a sign and testimony to Christ's truly earthly nature. Next he begins to play on this theme by expanding the intertextual references. Ps. 132:11 speaks of one from the fruit of David's loins being set on the throne. Then Ps. 45:6 adds a prophetic word: "your divine throne endures forever. Your royal scepter (rod) is a scepter of equity." From this rod springs forth a flower or blossom.

Having recovered a variety of different images associated with the rod, Cyril begins to intertwine them. The rod becomes a means of consolation in Ps. 23:4. It is the staff of the good pastor in Jer. 48:17, and ultimately the staff of Christ, the good shepherd. However, because of human sin, God in Christ as judge also wields the rod in rendering justice and equity. Cyril then pursues the theme of Moses' rod in the deliverance from Egypt of his people. Finally, he concludes with reflection on Canticles 2:1, where the rod becomes a flower, the lily of the valley, and he plays on its fragrance, by which the knowledge of God is instilled. He ends with a homily on 2 Cor. 2:14, 16, which he joins with the work of the Spirit: "Thanks be to God who in Christ . . . through us spreads the fragrance of the knowledge of him everywhere. We are the aroma of Christ . . . to one a fragrance from death to death, to another a fragrance from life to life."

Several things are to be observed in this interpretation:

First, Cyril never intends to explain the "original meaning" of the biblical text. Even this way of formulating the issue would have been incomprehensible to him. Nor is he concerned with the literal sense, since the object to which he is relating the imagery is not confined to sense perception, the hallmark of the literal.

Second, Cyril assumes the theological coherence of scripture in spite of the diversity of the imagery. By seeking to explore the intertextual references to the one word, he gains different avenues into the theological substance, which is spiritual.

Third, to characterize Cyril's approach as allegory, which in one sense it is, does not tell the whole story of what he is doing in this passage. Cyril comes to his exegesis with a knowledge of its substance gained from the whole of the Christian scriptures. He then returns to the Old Testament as if it were a set of musical notes from which he seeks to play a new and different tune in offering a fresh harmonization of Christian truth. This is the process he characterizes as the search for the higher, spiritual sense of scripture. The goal is not to impose upon the passage a theological system, as often claimed, but to move into a form of fresh proclamation to a living audience of hearers (readers) calling for a faithful life in the light of God's great mercy.

Finally, it is crucial to note that Cyril's exegesis is not an uncontrolled activity of creative human imagination. Cyril clearly recognizes a creative component, but he always sees it as a gift of the Holy Spirit. Cyril works materially within the theological norms of interpretation provided by the *kērygma* and the *paideusis* and formally within the church's received scriptures, constantly informed by a *skopus* which shapes both his questions and answers. The point is not to deny the element of spontaneity and fresh imagination in his commentary, but for Cyril this quality is not an independent force serving apart from the context of church tradition and the practice of worship.

Another characteristic example of Cyril's spiritual interpretation is found in Isaiah 19, the vision of Egypt. The first verse of the text provides the context from which Cyril develops his exegesis: "The Lord sits on a cloud and comes to Egypt." On this basis he establishes the intention of the entire chapter: its purpose is to describe how faith in Christ came to transform Egypt. However, first he outlines in detail how Egypt was the most idolatrous and obstinate of all the nations — that is to say, in most need of conversion.

The great change is described in the first verse as Christ comes to Egypt riding on a cloud. Of course, exactly what is meant by this image is controversial, and Cyril briefly outlines some of the interpretive options. Some say that it is the holy flesh of Christ, the temple received from the Holy Virgin. Others understand it to be the Sacred Virgin herself. Cyril expresses appreciation for these interpretations, but takes a different tack when stressing the many-sided quality (*polytropos*, Heb. 1:1) of the prophetic vision of God. The effect is to resist any simplistic identification of the image of Christ being suggested.

Rather, turning to Isaiah 6, Daniel 7, and Ezekiel 1, he reflects on the mystery of God's presence. Next he turns to 1 Cor. 10:1 to pick up the New Testament's resonance: "our fathers were all under the cloud, and all passed through the sea, and all were baptized . . . in the cloud and in the sea." Finally, the theme of eating and drinking leads him to complete his reflection on the mystery of God in Christ with an appeal to baptism and the Spirit. In a real sense, Cyril is offering a theological control of the spiritual sense of scripture in terms of its content or substance. He does not reject outright the allegorical identification of Christ's coming with the Virgin Mary, but seeks to enrich the imagery by appealing to a host of other images from the Old and New Testaments.

Finally, Cyril's interpretation of Isa. 52:13–53:12 provides another excellent example of his spiritual interpretation, which cannot be grasped merely by mechanically pursuing his hermeneutical terminology. He reads the entire chapter, as if by reflex, to be a reflection of the passion of Christ. At the outset in 52:13-15 one is initially taken aback by Cyril's sheer rhetorical elegance. A brilliant contrast is painted between Christ's utterly emptying himself to become human and the resulting richness that is transferred to humanity through his poverty; of Christ's holding back the terror of encroaching death and his translating it into immortality; of liberating those imprisoned in darkest captivity to a vision of true sight for the blind.

Then with the greatest skill and imagination Cyril pursues his goal of constructing a tight morphological fit between the prophetic text and the New Testament by reflecting on a catena of passages from the Gospels and Paul. The approach is, of course, traditional, yet it is remarkable to see with what theological profundity he can render Isaiah in closest resonance with the New Testament. The servant is described in his humility, lacking any appearance to attract favor, but utterly degraded into raw poverty for our sake. Cyril, reflecting the Alexandrian perspective, does not speak of God's suffering, but Christ as the incarnate man enters fully into human suffering as part of his identification with God's fallen creation. Just as the innocent servant of Isa. 53 was falsely accused, so Christ also was unjustly condemned, even though Pilate could find no evil in him. Of course Cyril goes far beyond the Old Testament text when he draws the theological implications of Christ's atoning death and resurrection for those who believe. Moreover, his rhetorical homily makes far more use of the details from Isaiah than the exegesis of either Jerome or Theodoret.

Finally, there is one more aspect of Cyril's exegesis that bears emphasis. One of Cyril's favorite words for the spiritual sense of scripture is *theoria,* which implies a vision. This vision is "pneumatic" because the human mind is aided by the Holy Spirit to transcend the letter when reading. This is a gift given only to the believer, and therefore Cyril never tires of asking God for this prophetic gift for himself and for his audience. Prophecy means for Cyril the divinely given capacity to interpret the Old Testament. Indeed the Christian prophet is one who has received the charism of recognizing the fulfillment of the Old Testament prophecies in the New (Margerie, pp. 245-46). Perhaps it is the charismatic dimension of his interpretation that evokes in Margerie a sense of profound awe: "what [Cyril] finds is often so beautiful, so scriptural in its inspiration, that it would be difficult to follow his argument without falling in love with Scripture itself" (p. 265).

To summarize, Cyril is not simply allegorizing the text, if that is understood as replacing the Old Testament text with a totally alien system arbitrarily forced upon it. Rather, Cyril comes to the text from a holistic understanding of the theological substance of Christian scripture, and then seeks to find further illumination of God's revelation by rethinking the subject matter from within as he intertwines Old and New Testament texts into new configurations. Lying at the heart of this exegetical procedure is the conviction that scripture is a living Word continually activated by the Spirit to speak to each generation of a faithful church.

I am fully aware that this interpretation of the rationale behind the spiritual sense remains an eschatological ideal, and largely unrealized within the Christian church throughout much of its history. Perhaps the most troubling failure of all lies in the persistent attacks on Judaism throughout the centuries, illustrated in a particularly painful form by Cyril. Crucial to the hermeneutical analysis above is the point that the church's spiritual reflection on scripture according to its ontic wholeness falls into the genre of praise, worship, and self-criticism rather than apologetics and polemics. Only in the light of a deeper engagement with the substance of God's will disclosed in scripture will the repentant church be prepared to speak meaningfully of the faith it shares with Judaism.

VI. Summary and Evaluation

At the conclusion of his learned monograph on Cyril's interpretation of the Old Testament, Kerrigan (pp. 435ff.) offers a carefully nuanced evaluation of Cyril's exegetical contribution. He first attempts to place him within the history of Christian biblical interpretation and discusses the sources Cyril used, his advances beyond Origen, and the development within Cyril himself. Of particular interest is Kerrigan's analysis of the influence exerted by Jerome on Cyril, and the continuing impact of Jerome's fusion of elements from both the Alexandrian and Antiochene traditions. When it comes to evaluating the enduring worth of Cyril's interpretation of the literal sense of the Old Testament, Kerrigan feels that it lies not in its intrinsic value, which is actually very limited, but in Cyril's personal witness to the importance of the literal, even if his concern is inadequately realized.

When it comes to assessing the enduring contribution of his spiritual interpretation, the issues become even more complicated. Kerrigan offers a summary of the debate that raged within the Roman Catholic Church in the immediate post–World War II period concerning the interpretation of scripture. The debate was initiated by the encyclicals *Divino Afflante Spiritu* (1943) and *Humani generis* (1950). These ecclesiastical pronouncements, however, served to fuel the discussion rather than to resolve the issues, since even the interpretation of the two encyclicals evoked disagreement as to their precise meaning and intent. Kerrigan sketches quite objectively the diversity of opinion respecting the continuing value of a figurative or spiritual interpretation. On the one side was an important group, largely of French scholars (de Lubac, Daniélou, and others), who sought to revive some form of allegory or typology. On the other side were a growing number of scholars who found support in the encyclicals for applying a modern historical-critical approach to the Bible. In the middle was probably the majority within the church, who opted for a compromise to preserve features of both.

Kerrigan himself seems to be of a genuinely divided mind. He is much impressed with "the enormous progress which has been accomplished in the realm of biblical studies in modern times" (p. 445). Clearly his deepest sentiment lies with those pursuing modern historical criticism. Yet he struggles hard to find some place for Cyril's kind of exegesis other than a purely historical or antiquarian interest. In the end, the basic hermeneutical and theological issue is left unresolved.

It would be grossly unfair to criticize Kerrigan's position of 1950 from the perspective of 2000, since much has happened in the ensuing fifty years to influence judgment. Within the Roman Catholic Church and within most of non-Catholic Christianity as well, the advocates of historical criticism in various forms have clearly won the day. On the periphery it is evident that some theological interest remains in the allegorical/typological interpretation once developed by de Lubac, Daniélou, and others; nevertheless, no new strong voices comparable to these great French interpreters have emerged. However, it would be fair to say that the confidence expressed in the 1950s that modern critical methods would resolve the difficult questions of biblical interpretation has been greatly muted in the years since.

In spite of my deepest appreciation of Kerrigan's accomplishments in studying Cyril's Old Testament exegesis, my major theological criticism of his work turns on the extent to which Kerrigan (usually unconsciously) measured the value of Cyril's exegesis in accordance with the criteria of modern historical criticism, which was just moving to center stage in the Roman church. In spite of his great learning, I seriously doubt whether Kerrigan adequately grasped the theological significance of Cyril's spiritual interpretation within the exegetical tradition of the Christian church. Rather, I would suggest that the moving summary by Bertrand de Margerie of Cyril's exegetical contributions lies much closer to the truth:

> Cyril is the seal of the Fathers . . . the seal that crowns and perfects the teaching of the Fathers . . . opening up new horizons for the Fathers of the future. . . . Cyril is and will remain above all the exegete of the glorious divine nature of Christ which shines forth through his humanity. (*Introduction*, p. 270)

To conclude, the theological dimension of the subject matter being discussed in terms of the spiritual sense of scripture is simply of a radically different order and defies criteria generally employed to gain meaning and measure truth. Therefore, I shall continue to try in this monograph to offer another perspective to the problem of biblical interpretation that lies at the heart of the church's continuing reflection on its scripture.

Bibliography of Cyril of Alexandria

Primary Sources

Opera, Patrologia Graeco-Latina, edited by J.-P. Migne, 68-77.
Commentarius in Isaiam, Patrologia Graeco-Latina 70, pp. 9-1450.
Sancti patris nostri Cyrilli archiepiscopi Alexandrini in XII prophetas post Pon-

tanum et Aubertum edidit, edited by P. E. Pusey. 2 vols. Oxford: Clarendon, 1868.

Deux dialogues christologiques, edited by G. M. de Durand. Sources Chrétiennes, 97. Paris: Éditions du Cerf, 1964.

Cyril of Alexandria: Selected Letters, edited by L. R. Wickham. Oxford: Clarendon, 1983.

"Commentary on Isaiah." In *Cyril of Alexandria,* edited by N. Russell, pp. 70-95. London and New York: Routledge, 2000.

Secondary Sources

Abel, F. M. "La Géographic sacrée chez S. Cyrille d'Alexandri." *Revue Biblique* 31 (1922): 407-27.

———. "Parallélisme exégétique entre S. Jérôme et S. Cyrille d'Alexandrie." *Vivre et Penser,* 1st series (1941): 94-119, 212-30.

Bardenhewer, O. *Geschichte der altkirchlichen Literatur,* 5th ed., vol. 4, pp. 23-77. Freiburg: Herder, 1924.

Bardy, G. "Cyrille d'Alexandrie." In *Dictionnaire d'Histoire et de Géographie Ecclésiastiques,* edited by A. Baudrillart et al., vol. 13 (1956), pp. 1169-77.

———. "Interprétation (histoire de l'), II: Exégèse patristique." *Dictionnaire de la Bible, Supplément,* 1928, pp. 569-91.

Dubarle, A. M. "Les conditions du salut avant la venue du Sauveur chez Saint Cyrille d'Alexandrie." *Revue des sciences philosophiques et théologiques* 32 (1948): 358-62.

Frend, W. H. C. *The Rise of the Monophysite Movement: Chapters in the History of the Church in the Fifth and Sixth Centuries.* Cambridge: Cambridge University Press, 1972.

Guillet, J. "Les exégèses d'Alexandrie et d'Antioche. Conflict ou malentendu?" *Recherches de science religieuse* 34 (1947): 257-302.

Hardy, E. R. "Cyrillus von Alexandrien." In *Theologische Realenzyklopädie* 8, pp. 254-60.

Jouassard, G. "Cyrill von Alexandrien." In *Reallexikon für Antike und Christentum,* vol. 3, pp. 499-516. Stuttgart: T. Klauser, 1957.

Kamesar, A. "The Virgin of Isaiah 7, 14: The Philological Argument from the Second to the Fifth Century." *Journal of Theological Studies* 41 (1990): 51-75.

Kerrigan, A. *St. Cyril of Alexandria, Interpreter of the Old Testament.* Rome: Pontifical Institute, 1952.

———. "The Objects of the Literal and Spiritual Sense of the New Testament according to St. Cyril of Alexandria." *Studia Patristica* 6 (1957): 354-74.

Margerie, B. de. "Saint Cyril of Alexandria Develops a Christological Exegesis." In *An Introduction to the History of Exegesis,* vol. 1, pp. 241-70. Petersham, Mass.: St. Bede's Publications, 1993.

McGuckin, J. A. *St. Cyril of Alexandria: The Christological Controversy.* Leiden: Brill, 1994.

Prestige, G. L. *Fathers and Heretics,* pp. 150-79. London: SPCK, 1940.

Quasten, J. *Patrology,* vol. 3, pp. 116-42. Westminster, Md.: Newman Press, 1960.

Russell, N. *Cyril of Alexandria.* London and New York: Routledge, 2000.

Sellers, R. V. *Two Ancient Christologies: A Study in the Christological Thought of the Schools of Alexandria and Antioch in the Early History of Christian Doctrine.* London: SPCK, 1940.

Torrance, T. F. *Theology in Reconstruction,* pp. 139-214. London: SCM, 1975.

Wilken, R. L. *Judaism and the Early Christian Mind: A Study of Cyril of Alexandria's Exegesis and Theology.* New Haven: Yale University Press, 1971.

Young, F. *From Nicaea to Chalcedon,* pp. 240-65. London: SCM, 1983.

10

Theodoret of Cyrus
(c. 393–c. 460)

I. Introduction to the Antiochene School

In the usual contrast made between the Alexandrians and the Antiochenes, it has been customary to focus on the allegorical speculation of the Alexandrians in contrast to the historical emphasis of the Antiochenes. As we saw in the chapter on Origen, such a portrait has obscured the real distinctions of both schools. Particularly misleading in reference to the Antiochenes has been the contrast between the spiritual concerns of the Alexandrians and the historical concerns of the Antiochenes. Recent scholarship, summarized by Bradley Nassif in 1993 ("The 'Spiritual Exegesis' of Scripture"), has therefore focused on the "spiritual" exegesis of Scripture in the school of the Antiochenes.

The crucial technical term around which the debate has revolved is that of *theōria*, the spiritual hermeneutic at whose center lies the dual concern for both a historical and a Christological reading of the Bible. Heinrich Kihn made the first move toward a correct interpretation of the Antiochene hermeneutic in 1880 ("Über 'Theōria' und 'Allegoria'") when he revised the widespread but erroneous identification of Antiochene *theōria* with Alexandrian *theōria* — that is, with allegory. The next step in correctly describing the essential marks of *theōria* came in 1920 when Alberto Vaccari ("La 'teōria' nella scuola . . . antiochus") outlined four aspects comprising the Antiochene approach:

1. *Theōria* presupposed the historical reality of the events described by the biblical author. These events functioned like a mirror imaging a different reality.
2. In addition to the historical reference, *theōria* simultaneously embraced a second future reality that was ontologically linked to the first.

3. The first historical event stood in relation to the second as the mediocre to the perfect, the small to the large, the sketch to the finished work.
4. Both the present and future events together were described as direct objects of *theōria*, but in different ways. The present functioned as the less significant vehicle through which the prophet knowingly described a greater future event in human history through the use of hyperbolic language.

In the period that followed in patristic research, the full complexity of the Antiochene hermeneutic emerged. First, it became increasingly clear that there was considerable variation in application among the leading commentators within the school (e.g., Theodore, Julian, Chrysostom, and Theodoret). Second, there was debate whether *theōria* should be understood as comprising a single literal sense rather than a double literal sense, or even an additional secondary meaning, as in allegory. Third, a considerable lack of clarity remained in trying to subdivide various forms of *theōria*. Some scholars suggested a difference between "typology," in which the prophet neither saw nor intended to describe the future antitype, and a form of verbal proclamation in which the prophet actually perceived and intentionally announced future messianic realities. Bertrand de Margerie (*An Introduction to the History of Exegesis*, p. 169) cites Chrysostom's distinction between typical prophecy and verbal prophecy as helpful in clarifying this issue: "Prophecy in types is that which takes place in deeds or in historical realities; the other prophecy is one in words. For God has persuaded some by highly insightful words, while he has bolstered the certitude of others . . . through the vision of events."

Finally, beginning in the 1950s, there was much discussion in Roman Catholic circles on how to relate the ancient hermeneutical insights of the Antiochenes to the growing impact of historical-critical methods in the Catholic church. What was the relation of *theōria* to typology, allegory, and the *sensus plenior?* In the light of the present restricted agenda of this study, it is impossible to pursue these further issues in detail. The concern of this chapter is to focus our attention on the Isaiah commentary of Theodoret as an accessible representative of the school of Antioch.

II. The Antiochene Background of Theodoret

This project on the history of interpretation is limited to the book of Isaiah, and Theodoret emerges as the one Antiochene whose complete commentary on Isaiah is extant. (This statement needs to be qualified to some degree by the still contested discovery of Chrysostom's commentary on the entire book of Isaiah in an Armenian translation; cf. chapter 8.) In order to understand the contribution of Theodoret, it is crucial to speak briefly of the influence exerted on him by his Antiochene predecessors, in whose footsteps he confesses to have followed.

The father of the exegetical school of Antioch is usually acknowledged to be Diodore of Tarsus (died c. 390). Although he was the teacher of Chrysostom and Theodore of Mopsuestia, he defended throughout his life the Nicene faith as a pillar of orthodoxy. Yet a hundred years after his death, as a repercussion of the doctrinal struggle with Nestorius, he was accused and condemned of heresy. As a result, in spite of a very large number of works on theological and non-theological subjects, only a few fragments of his works have survived. Sadly, even those reprinted in Migne (Patrologia Graeca 33) are now considered largely of uncertain authorship.

Fortunately, the same fate is not true of Theodore of Mopsuestia (c. 350-428). Although many of his works also perished, enough remains to provide a profile of his exegetical method. Still extant are a complete Greek text of his Minor Prophets, a Latin version of ten minor epistles of Paul, and a Syriac text of his commentary on John. In many ways Theodore represents the farthest extreme from that of Origen, against whose allegorical interpretation he strongly reacted. As we saw in a previous chapter on Origen, the conflict between these two schools of interpretation has often been misconstrued as if the Antiochenes rejected allegory out of hand and adumbrated the modern historical-critical approach of the nineteenth century.

Rather, the two schools shared at the outset many of the assumptions inherited from the earliest Christian tradition: the inspiration of scripture, the theological unity of the two testaments, and the need for careful philological interpretation. However, the two schools differed markedly, especially when contrasting Origen with Theodore, regarding the correct exegetical avenues toward achieving these goals. It is also clear that the larger theological context and doctrinal debates that shaped the third century of Origen and the fourth and fifth centuries of Theodore provided additional influences in shaping the nature of the exegetical debates. Unfortunately, the church tended to read both Origen and Theodore from the perspective of later, polemical controversies (Origenist controversy, Nestorian debate), which greatly muddied the waters.

The main lines of Theodore's exegetical position can be briefly summarized as follows:

1. Central to Theodore is his very different view of history. Because human history has been divided into two successive epochs, history must be

taken with utmost seriousness. This theological evaluation has important hermeneutical and exegetical implications for all of his work.

a) The Old Testament is not viewed as a veiled revelation of the New Testament, which must be allegorically interpreted to reveal its hidden message. Rather, the Old Testament has been inspired by the same Holy Spirit, and its historical context must be carefully respected. In a sense, Theodore challenged the traditional denigration of the Old Testament as, in principle, "carnal" or peripheral to Christian theology.

b) Because the Old Testament addressed primarily the needs of Israel, Theodore eschewed the temptation to find everywhere Christian doctrine hidden in its symbolism. He rejected seeing in the Old Testament trinitarian doctrine, and he greatly restricted the proof-from-prophecy patterns of the Old Testament. He found only four psalms (2, 8, 45, 110) to be predictions of Christ. Indeed, when interpreting the Psalter, he argued for a single referent for each psalm, and therefore he relegated most of the psalms to the events in the life of historical Israel. Texts were interpreted according to contingent historical events. For this reason, Theodore was accused of interpreting the Old Testament like the Jews.

c) As a Christian interpreter, Theodore was, of course, concerned to relate the Old Testament to the New, but he chose a form of restricted typology rather than allegorical techniques as his major device for achieving this goal. He generally employed a move from promise to fulfillment by means of a typological adumbration of real Old Testament events in which the earlier events retained their theological value, but were related as type to antitype.

2. Over against the widespread Platonic contrast between earthly and spiritual realities, Theodore developed a very strong eschatological dimension of history and pointed to successive stages in the purpose of God moving through human history to its ultimate consummation.

At times Theodore's exegesis led him into difficulty. Because of his concern to avoid the danger of excessive symbolic, figurative interpretation, he fell into an overly literal reading that hindered serious attention to the metaphors and similes of John's Gospel. Also, he could not fully attain a consistent interpretation of the Old Testament prediction while affirming a genuine correspondence between the testaments.

III. Theodoret of Cyrus

1. His Life and Works

In comparison with the brilliance of Diodore and Theodore, Theodoret of Cyrus (c. 393- c. 460), often called the last of the great theologians of Antioch, has tended to fall into the background. Emphasis has usually fallen on his ecclesiastical role in the controversy surrounding the heresy of Apollinarius. As a loyal representative of the Antiochene school, he became deeply involved in the controversy between Cyril of Alexandria and Nestorius. However, until rather recently Theodoret's exegetical works were described as unoriginal and as a mediocre imitation of Theodore (cf. Bardy, "Théodoret," pp. 299-325). Fortunately, there has been more recently a sharp reversal of scholarly judgment, spearheaded by the research of J. N. Guinot (L'exégèse de Théodoret, 1995).

The very fact that Theodoret's commentaries have been largely preserved and held in the highest esteem throughout the earlier centuries should have cautioned against dismissing him as unimportant. Moreover, the critical edition of his complete commentary on Isaiah provides a further reason to assess anew his exegetical contribution. A careful study of his commentary will demonstrate his crucial role in mediating between the extremes of the Alexandrian allegorical interpreters and the dangers for Christian theology present in the overly literal, historicist interpretation of Theodore of Mopsuestia. In sum, Theodoret's response to both the left and right of the theological spectrum of his age called forth remarkably sophisticated reflection on proper exegetical methods.

Theodoret was born at Antioch c. 393, and died about 460. He was educated in local monasteries and probably was not a pupil of Theodore. Nevertheless, he was deeply committed to the theology of the Antiochene school. He was elected bishop of Cyrus, a small town near Antioch, and executed his ecclesiastical duties conscientiously for thirty-five years. He entered into controversy with Cyril of Alexandria, suspecting him of the heresy of Apollinarius, and at the Council of Ephesus sided with John of Antioch defending Nestorius. He finally accepted the Union creed, and at the Council of Chalcedon (451), when he reluctantly joined the condemnation of Nestorius, was reinstated in the episcopal office.

Theodoret's extant writings are not only numerous, but reflect a great breadth, including apologetic writings, dogmatic treatises, histories, sermons, and extensive letters. However, it is his exegetical writings that are our present concern. Of particular interest is his interpretation of Canticles, Psalms, Daniel, and above all Isaiah, which offers the best entry into his exegetical approach.

2. *Theodoret's Approach to Exegesis*

Guinot *(L'exégèse de Théodoret)* begins his discussion of Theodoret's exegesis by reflecting on the initial assumptions of Theodoret that undergird his approach. Guinot offers his summary (pp. 252ff.) from a close study of all of Theodoret's commentaries, but it will ultimately be our specific task to illustrate Guinot's points in more detail from Theodoret's Isaiah commentary.

First, and of particular importance for anyone interested in the modern debate over scripture as canon, Theodoret assumes the inspiration of scripture, both Old and New Testaments, by the Holy Spirit. Although the biblical sense can at times be hidden and obscure, nothing in scripture is by accident or haphazard. There is a definite meaning to be discovered, and a careful exegesis demands greatest attention in determining the different witnesses present in scripture. Theodoret's emphasis on the proper canonical context emerges with great clarity in his preface to the Song of Songs. He rejects at the outset interpretations, especially of some Jews, that stand outside the circle of the church's confessions and can only result in a "carnal" misunderstanding.

Second, the text rests on a historical basis that can be verified by the facts *(ta pragmata)*. Then, using many of the favorite patristic terms, he underlines scripture's harmony *(symphōnia)*, its coherence *(akolouthia)*, its intent *(skopus)*, and especially its end *(telos)*.

Third, he stands in the patristic tradition of all Christians, both Alexandrian and Antiochene, in confessing that Jesus Christ is the key to understanding, apart from which the Bible is sealed (cf. Isa. 29:11-12). Of course, how this Christological hermeneutic is to be realized in actual exegesis remains highly debatable.

Finally, Theodoret, both as scholar and pastor, stresses the required spiritual disposition of the reader for properly understanding the sacred text. The need for a desire to receive the truth in sincere openness and humility is not merely a pious convention for Theodoret, but a basic hermeneutical necessity.

3. *Theodoret and the Different Senses of Scripture*

In an earlier chapter on Origen, I traced in the early post–World War II period the new interest in the figurative senses of scripture led by Daniélou,

Hanson, Lampe, and Woollcombe, among many others. A characteristic feature of their proposals was a sharp distinction between allegory and typology. The former was largely rejected as a Hellenistic import with quasi-mythical roots, but the latter was accepted as genuinely biblical in origin. Typology was especially compatible to the modern historical-critical emphasis because of its concern to support the historicity of the original biblical events even when they were later rendered figuratively in relation to subsequent history.

In the period that followed, however, patristic scholars raised many serious objections regarding this construal of the figurative senses. It was alleged that the term "typology" was actually a modern term without ancient roots within Christian tradition. Then again, the sharp distinction between allegory and typology could not be sustained. In addition, the stress on the crucial role of historicity as constitutive of typology in contrast to allegory was judged to be largely anachronistic and not an essential feature in the appeal to figurative readings. Finally, the contrast between the Alexandrian and Antiochene exegesis could not be correctly formulated in terms of timeless ideas or concern for historical events. As a result of these criticisms, there seemed to be little place left for the term "typology," as shown in the work of Andrew Louth *(Discerning the Mystery)*, who strove to rehabilitate the term "allegory" as the appropriate term by which to describe the church's figurative interpretation.

While most of the leading modern patristic scholars would now share these criticisms of the work of, say, Daniélou and R. P. Hanson, there have been some important modifications. A classic example is found in the corrective offered by Frances Young ("Typology" in *Crossing the Boundaries*, p. 42). The issue turns on her fresh analysis of the Antiochene school, initiated first by Sebastian Brock's study of Ephrem, the fourth-century Syrian poet. The effect is that Young now acknowledges that the designation "typology" can be a useful term and, if correctly applied, can indeed aid in distinguishing features of the Antiochene exegesis from that of Alexandrian allegory. The concern of this chapter on Theodoret will be to pursue the positive features of typology in his development of figurative meaning. Much of the credit for a fresh reading of Theodoret redounds to the research of Guinot, whose critical edition of the Isaiah commentary will long remain the standard authority.

Great attention has been paid in recent study of Theodoret's hermeneutics regarding the different senses of scripture. It is here that the sharp differences emerge between Theodoret and his scholarly peers, both on the left and the right. First, in respect to the literal sense of the text, Guinot's excellent discussion (*L'exégèse*, pp. 282ff.) begins with a close analysis of Theodoret's terminology. Theodoret speaks of the literal sense as that which is apparent or obvious *(to phainomenon)* and is set over against the mystical or hidden sense. At times he speaks of a sense "according to what is stated" *(kata to rheton)*. Yet one misses in Theodoret a systematic explanation of the literal sense, even though its role is predominant throughout his commentary. When he uses such terms as *gramma* (writings) or "according to the letter," he often does so to express opposition to Jewish literalism or to articulate a need to transcend the literal for the spiritual. Nevertheless, the literal sense is not denigrated in principle as "carnal," since it remains the human vehicle that God uses in prophecy.

By and large, Theodoret explains the use of the literal sense by means of a paraphrase of the text. On this level, he employs the tools of grammar, lexicography, and stylistic analysis in order to penetrate its meaning. He often focuses on separate words for special attention, and he excels in recognizing irony and other tropes as a property of the literal sense. Also characteristic of Theodoret's exegesis, and often repeated in his initial preface to a section, is his concern to identify the voice or speaker of a passage when it is not evident either in the prophets or in the Song of Songs.

Second, in respect to the figurative sense, the adjective *tropikōs* most often is a designation of the figurative sense, but the frequency of the term is not always a clear indication of its importance. Increasingly, the term *allegoria* has been abandoned, apparently in reaction to Origen. Terms such as *dianoia* or *ennoia* are often employed to indicate a different sense from the literal. *Mystikos* or *pneumatikos* also appear as offering a sense superior to the literal.

What is of special interest in Theodoret is the relation of the figurative to the literal. Theodoret is deeply concerned that the figurative sense is not an arbitrary addition to the literal that springs from the commentator's imagination. Rather, the figurative is above all a metaphorical extension. The style of a text signals to the reader the non-literal quality of its usage. Especially in the introduction to Canticles, Theodoret seeks to establish that the biblical style establishes *idiomata* that determine the rules for figuration. By comparing a whole range of figurative uses of words in the prophets, such as in Ezek. 16-17, he establishes a level of continuity with the same figurative idioms found in Canticles. The result is that the distinction between the literal and the figurative becomes a dynamic and highly flexible one. Although the literal can still be designated at times as "carnal" — this pejorative sense usually attaches to the literalism of the synagogue — in general, the figurative extends rather than denies the significance of the literal. Moreover, the figurative or metaphorical sense embraces a wide variety of genres, such as the moral, mystical, and homiletical.

Third, Theodoret employs a third mode of interpretation that can best be characterized as "typological." Credit for analyzing the nature of this approach largely goes again to Guinot (pp. 306ff.), who has brought a new precision into the discussion and made it possible to recognize the genuine hermeneutical contribution of Theodoret, which belies the characterization of him as an epigone of Theodore.

The appeal to typology is a minor element in his commentaries on Canticles and Daniel. However, it plays an increasingly large role in his later commentaries on the prophets. The appeal to typology derives originally from a Pauline usage as a means to relate the Old Testament and the New. Theodoret extended its usage as a way of checking the allegorical excesses of the Alexandrian school. The figures in the Old Testament were thus construed as types to which the New Testament provided the antitype. The immediate effect of the typological appeal was that the Old Testament type retained its value as an indispensable event or fact, which was not to be denigrated as sub-Christian, but provided a true witness to divine revelation. In addition, the appeal to typology also allowed Theodoret a way to offer a major corrective to Theodore, whose emphasis on the historically conditioned role of the Old Testament largely restricted to Israel's needs threatened to undercut the larger narrative coherence of the Christian gospel, which encompassed both testaments.

Theodoret further developed his use of typology in such a way as to distinguish two different forms of prophetic fulfillment. On the one hand, much like Theodore, he could identify large portions of the Old Testament that offered an "internal" fulfillment within the history of Israel. He thus confirmed the enduring foundation of historical interpretation that could bring a major check to the fanciful tradition of Christian exegesis when it rendered every aspect of the Old Testament into prefigurations of Christ. On the other hand, Theodoret also designated other portions of the Old Testament that could only find their meaning in an "external" fulfillment found in the New Testament. Moreover, he sought to establish hermeneutical rules commensurate with his use of philological and historical tools by which to bring some appearance of exegetical rigor. This distinction allowed him, especially when interpreting the Psalter, to break out of the insistence of Theodore that each psalm reflect only one context, which threatened to sever the psalms from the entire Christological tradition of the church.

IV. Theodoret's Commentary on Isaiah

1. *Formal Features of His Commentary*

In the preface he sets forth clearly his aim. Some passages are clear and obvious, whereas others are obscure, and his focus is to illuminate the latter. The expressed intention emerges in the space he allots to various passages. In several places, Theodoret sets out the reasons for obscurities in scripture, for example in Isa. 28:12 (VIII, 84-90). Obscurities serve to excite the reader's curiosity, point to a deeper meaning, and confirm the hidden treasures of scripture.

Throughout his commentary Theodoret shows much care in establishing the proper historical context and its narrative sequence. He pays close attention to the historical sequence of the Hebrew kings (e.g., 1:1) and also to the Assyrian and Babylonian rulers. In terms of modern critical study, Theodoret's commentary at times gives evidence of some historical confusion and lacunae, especially in the relation of Assyria and Babylon (cf. XIII, 1ff.), but from Theodoret's perspective correct historical dating remains important. He is very careful in trying to show the significance of the placing of the various sections within the book of Isaiah, such as the prophecies of Immanuel (III, 352-56), the positioning of Isa. 36-39 (XI, 1ff.). Theodoret's concern for coherence is further attested by his continuing effort to remove any apparent contradictions (II, 39).

Then again, in his preface he indicates the essential role of focusing his commentary on its subject matter *(hypothesis)*. Especially in the light of his use of a linear commentary *(kata meros)*, he is at pains to keep from undue fragmentation by forming larger themes by which to unite his material. Moreover, his constant attention to intertextual references (cf. Isa. 1:2 = Deut. 31:28; Isa. 14:27 = Deut. 32:39) stems from his conviction that the same Spirit is at work throughout all parts of scripture. Although Theodoret does not spell out in detail any hermeneutical theory, such as the Reformers do concerning *scriptura sui interpres,* the assumptions are very close.

Finally, a special feature of Theodoret's commentary is his ending each section with a paraenesis in which he appeals to his readers to apply in faith the message of the scriptural verses just interpreted. These homiletical concerns account in part for the wide popularity of his commentaries over the years.

2. Substantive Features of Importance in his Commentary

a. Dogmatic Perspective

It is hardly necessary to demonstrate that Theodoret stands in the Christian tradition of the previous Church Fathers in assuming a Christological content to all of scripture. Jesus Christ is the key to all of its understanding (VIII, 320ff.). Isaiah is named the "divine evangelist" (XII, 512). Already in his preface he describes the contents of the book of Isaiah (its *hypothesis*) as the prophetic manifestation of the Savior, his birth from a virgin, his multiple miracles, his passion, death, and resurrection. True interpretation is only possible through "spiritual contemplation" *(pneumatikon theōria)* and is set in contrast to the carnal understanding of the body.

However, it is Theodoret's specific dogmatic perspective on Isaiah that is of special significance. Theodoret's central role in the Christological debates of the fifth century is well known, especially during the Nestorian struggles and his controversy with Cyril. It is obvious that these doctrinal issues are reflected both openly and subtly in his Isaiah commentary. In several places he attacks Arius and Eunomus (VII, 572; XIII, 314) as expressing an erroneous view of the nature of God. However, the debate in relation to Nestorius and Cyril is far subtler and emerges in his defense of the separation of the natures of Christ within the godhead.

Thus, in Isa. 6, in his discussion of Isaiah's having seen God (III, 38-50), Theodoret struggles to demonstrate that there were different forms *(sēmata)* in which God revealed himself, but he had not revealed his nature *(physis)*. Again in his commentary on the passion of Christ in Isa. 53, Theodoret is very precise in his emphasis on the humanity of the Son consisting of two natures in a union without confusion, which was not merely mortal, but indissoluble and essential. In sum, in places that seemed appropriate to him, he used his exegesis of Isaiah to defend the dyophysite Christology of the Antiochene school.

b. Theodoret's Anti-Jewish Polemics

Theodoret's polemics against the Jews share the same features common to almost all the Church Fathers. Much of this attack is conventional and unoriginal, repeating the same accusations of arrogance, blindness, quarrelsomeness, and hardness of heart. Frequently, the Jews are criticized in the Isaiah commentary for refusing to believe (X, 118-23), and in transgressing their own law (II, 100-107).

Of more interest is that Theodoret does make a distinction between believing and unbelieving Jews (e.g., I, 163, 174-75; cf. Guinot's discussion in vol. 1, p. 82). Indeed, Theodoret considered the believing Jews to be in the majority. For Theodoret, this distinction is theologically important in establishing the close continuity between the Old and New Testaments. The Old Testament bears testimony to a faithful Jewish voice.

Theodoret offers frequent references to Jewish (rabbinic) interpretations, but almost always with a negative evaluation. Theodoret derives much of the alleged errors from the Jews' blindness to the revelation of the Incarnate One. However, there is another important reason that emerges in his frequent coupling of Jewish misinterpretations and Theodore of Mopsuestia. The controversy turns on whether or not one sees Old Testament prophecy being fulfilled within Israel's history (an "internal" fulfillment), as both the Jews and Theodore defend, or whether its fulfillment transcends the Old Testament (an "external" fulfillment) and can only be seen as pointing to its Christological fulfillment according to the New Testament (cf. IV, 464ff.; VI, 355ff.; VIII, 128ff.).

We now need to examine more closely examples within Theodoret's Isaiah commentary concerning his hermeneutical approach to the prophetic text in terms of its various senses. One of the important contributions of Guinot's edition of Theodoret's Isaiah commentary is his close attention paid to the parallels in the interpretations of Eusebius, Cyril, and Chrysostom. The similarities and also differences belie any simplistic polarization of the Alexandrian and Antiochene schools of interpretation.

c. The Appeal to the Literal and Historical Senses

At key points in his Isaiah commentary Theodoret offers lengthy historical reviews of the periods at issue, such as the Syrio-Ephriamite war (III, 288ff.) or the Persian period (V, 40ff.). He is concerned to establish that the oracle's prophesying Ephraim's destruction within sixty-five years (Isa. 7:8) be correlated with the Assyrian kings Tiglath-pileser and Shalmaneser. His attempt to establish historical coherence within the book often results in his removing an apparent historical contradiction by suggesting that an exaggeration does not have to involve a historical issue, but is probably due to a stylistic convention (V, 19ff.). To speak of "historicity" in its Enlightenment connotation would be to introduce an anachronism if applied to Theodoret. Nevertheless, one senses Theodoret's concern over the truth of a reported event. In dealing with Isa. 53:5 he emphasizes that the description of the suffering servant does not rest on hearsay, but on the veracity of what was seen.

When Theodoret comes to the oracles against the nations in Isa. 13–23, Guinot expresses some doubts as to whether Theodoret has a clear historical understanding of the relation between Assyria and Babylon. He seems to see the shifting focus from one to the other more in geographical terms of different capitals rather than reflecting differing historical periods. In his handling of the transition from Babylon to Assyria in Isa. 14, Theodoret concludes that this is evidence for the same people being called by different names. Following many of the Church Fathers, Theodoret draws a theological lesson from the dating of Isaiah's vision in Isa. 6 by appealing to the Chronicles' account of Uzziah's transgressions. He concludes that divine revelation ceased in Jerusalem until a new and purer regime took over.

Theodoret's handling of narrative, such as Isa. 36–39, is characterized by a straightforward treatment of the story. He paraphrases the confrontation to bring out the dramatic effects of the speech of the Rabshakeh, and to highlight the full dimension of his blasphemy against the only true God of Israel. It is also evident that Theodoret's historical interest, shared by the Antiochene exegetical tradition, rests on strong theological grounds. Accordingly, the prophetic witness is indissolubly connected with the true humanity of Israel into which the Savior entered. The historical dimension is never seen as a peripheral shell to be removed in order to get to the heart of the message. The point is made explicit in any discussion of the passion of Christ (e.g., Isa. 53), but it is extended far beyond this one topic.

Nevertheless, the persistent concern to do justice to the literal/historical sense of the text derives from a motivation in Theodoret very different from those expressed by the later Enlightenment historians in terms of historical objectivity. Invariably with Theodoret an Old Testament historical passage, as if by reflex, is placed within the larger canonical context of the New Testament, and even within subsequent church history. The issue will become central in the discussion below of his understanding of prophecy and its fulfillment.

Theodoret's exegesis also shows that the line between the literal and the figurative senses of a text is considered to be a fluid one. He seldom first offers a literal reading and then follows with a figurative one, as if these readings were different in kind. Rather, even in a literal interpretation of the prophet's judgment on Israel (Isa. 3:12-15), the voices of the condemned priests are heard crying "crucify him, crucify him." However, Theodoret is aware in his interpretation of the parable in Isa. 5:1-7 and 28:23-28 that a metaphorical reading is the literal sense.

d. The Figurative Sense

The usual term for the figurative sense in Theodoret is expressed by the term *tropikōs*. It is probably best rendered as the metaphorical sense. Theodoret does not regard it as a separate meaning, unlike Origen, but rather as an extension of the word or concept being interpreted. Often it appears as a literary device consisting of the diversity in registering the prophetic vision (VI, 425ff.). Only occasionally does it follow an interpretation of the literal sense or is it set explicitly in contrast to it. However, the oracle of Isa. 57:14 ("to clear the obstacles from the way" is first interpreted "according to the letter" *(kata to rheton)* as referring to the physical barriers, and then figuratively *(kata dianoian)* as the souls of the unbelievers. At times, in order to obtain coherence from a geographical image, a figurative sense is assumed (Isa. 13:2).

The element most typical of Theodoret's figurative or metaphorical use is one that only rarely falls into sheer allegory by assigning different meanings to each separate word (cf. V, 451ff.). Rather, Old Testament words are rendered metaphorically when they are heard to reverberate with the Christian message. In Isa. 1:16 the mention of cleansing with water is immediately identified with baptism, "the bath of regeneration." The mountain of Zion (2:2-4) becomes the image of the church to which the nations are drawn. Although the parable of the vineyard in Isaiah 5 is not rendered allegorically — its initial reference to Judah is recognized — very shortly the context for interpretation becomes a metaphorical one. Even the abandonment of the vineyard to thorns and thistles is related to the thorns made into a crown for the Savior.

Guinot's distinction of this metaphorical interpretation of the figurative sense from a specifically typological one is helpful to an extent, if not pressed too hard. Both the metaphorical and typological usages serve Theodoret well in emphasizing the unity of the two testaments. The major difference between the two figurative techniques is that the metaphorical lacks the explicit appeal to a temporal sequence moving from type to antitype. Rather, in the metaphorical a dimension is called forth that shares in its subject matter, but without an explicit historical referent. In many ways Theodoret's paraenetic endings are simply a further metaphorical extension of the prophetic text to his present Christian audience.

There is an interesting example in Theodoret's interpretation of Isa. 7–8 concerning the two sons, Immanuel and Maher-shalal-hashbaz, that illustrates a remarkable extension of the metaphorical dimension. One could even characterize it as an ontological move in the interpretation of Immanuel. Theodoret is at pains to stress the Antiochene tradition when he focuses on the humanity of the promised Savior who entered into history. Yet how could

Immanuel be a sign of hope for the faithful of Israel in the eighth century and yet be identified with Jesus Christ, the Son of God, born of the blessed Virgin through the work of the Holy Spirit? Theodoret appeals to the example of Levi the priest (Heb. 7:4-9), who paid tithes through Abraham in fulfillment of the law six hundred years before his birth by being in the loins of his ancestor when he met Melchizedek. Accordingly, there was an ontological link between Maher-shalal-hashbaz in the eighth century and Immanuel's birth in the period of Rome. Clearly this move is far more than metaphorical, but it is also quite different from the temporal sequence usually developed by Theodoret between type and antitype.

e. The Typological Sense

As suggested above, Guinot has properly distinguished between Theodoret's metaphorical and typological approach to the figurative sense. Nevertheless, it is important to realize that the term *tropikōs* covers both figurative usages for Theodoret, and the line separating the two techniques is often quite fluid.

The typological approach reflected in Theodoret is, in some form, common to all the Church Fathers because of its New Testament roots, but it is constitutive for the Antiochenes and accounts for the school's deep concern with history. Basically the method is one that tries to guard the theological significance of the events of the Old Testament while allowing these events to be seen as prefigurations of later ones. The Old Testament events in the life of Israel, constituted as prophetic, offer a type that recurs as an antitype within a prophecy-fulfillment pattern.

The refinement offered by Theodoret emerges in his ongoing debate with the Jews and with Theodore. Theodore defended the view that the Old Testament prophecies were largely to be understood within the context of Israel's history, that is to say, by means of an internal Old Testament interpretation. Only rarely were these events prefigurations that received fulfillment only in the New Testament. Obviously the Jews shared the same concern in defending the integrity of the Old Testament apart from Christian interpretation. Theodoret set out to demonstrate with historical, theological, and literary arguments that the limitation of a given Old Testament prophecy only to Israel's history was erroneous.

For example, in Isa. 32, Theodoret seeks to show that the promise of a royal figure could not apply to Hezekiah, Josiah, or Zerubbabel. Such an interpretation "deviates from the truth" (*diamartanei tēs alētheias*, IX, 359-60). Rather, the virtues of the ruler depicted in the biblical text only find fulfillment outside of the Old Testament in Jesus Christ. There is frequently a stress on the hyperbolic nature of the language that indicates to the reader the need to transcend the ordinary historical sense.

Of course, at times Theodoret does appeal to a double fulfillment. The first internal fulfillment was an adumbration of its final fulfillment. Thus the destruction of Jerusalem in Isa. 1:7-9 was adumbrated in the destruction of the city by Nebuchadnezzar, but only received its final fulfillment in the Roman general Titus after the crucifixion of Christ.

In Isa. 40, Theodoret argues that the prophet predicted in advance a judgment in the form of the Babylonian captivity. However, he rejects seeing its fulfillment even in the typological form of Chrysostom's interpretation, which would see in Isa. 40 the return of the exiles from Babylon as an initial adumbration of God's final salvation in Jesus Christ. Rather, Theodoret argues that the scope of a universal salvation offered in Isa. 40 could only be understood in New Testament terms as the message of the gospel. Indeed, for Theodoret the fulfillment of a surprisingly large number of Old Testament prophecies is related directly to the Roman period and confirmed by the New Testament. At least in this respect, Theodoret hardly represents the usual exegetical traditions of the Antiochenes, but shows himself more influenced by the figurative approach of the Alexandrians and is often closer to Eusebius and Cyril than to either Theodore or Chrysostom.

There is an interesting footnote to Theodoret's use of typology. G. W. Ashby, in his dissertation on "Theodoret of Cyrus as Exegete of the Old Testament," closes his analysis by offering a comparison of Theodoret's understanding of typology with that of Gerhard von Rad, who popularized the term in the immediate post–World War II period in the famous essay "Typological Interpretation of the Old Testament." Ashby expresses his puzzlement that von Rad could have developed his view of typology without one mention of a Church Father. From this fact alone it is evident that whatever similarities exist between the two, they reached their positions completely independently of each other, and they arose from very different historical concerns.

Both Theodoret and von Rad used typology in an attempt to overcome an impasse between two competing positions. Theodoret sought a middle way between the allegory of the Alexandrians and the historicism of Theodore, while von Rad sought to overcome a problem arising from the Enlightenment between faith and history. Both Theodoret and von Rad sought to establish the lasting integrity of the Old Testament for Christian theology while at the same time seeking to find an element of continuity in a figurative application akin to the New Testament's usage. Both also tried to overcome the fragmentation of the biblical text by recovering a form of literary coherence. Theodoret opposed the piecemeal application of allegory that disregarded the narrative's sequence. Von Rad resisted an atomization of the biblical text by the excesses of source and traditio-historical criticism.

Nevertheless, while the two shared some significant features of "family resemblance," the differences between the two interpreters remain. First, Theodoret still sought to build his interpretation directly upon the "facts of history" verified from empirical events, while von Rad saw history from a post-Enlightenment perspective, albeit in a highly dialectical fashion that distinguished *Heilsgeschichte* from empirical events filtered through historical-critical analysis. Second, Theodoret assumed that the Spirit-inspired scripture was the vehicle for divine revelation, which was illuminated by intertextual references. Von Rad, in contrast, focused exegetically on the oral tradition undergirding the written text, of which the latter was only a fragile attempt of subsequent editors to actualize the text for the future by an ongoing reinterpretation of these fully human writings. Third, Theodoret spoke of the active and supernatural role of the Holy Spirit in illuminating the sacred Word to faithful recipients. Conversely, von Rad spoke of spirit more in terms of the charismatic dimension of human interpretation seeking to reinterpret the past through fresh and creative applications. In sum, one can only surmise that von Rad might have been aided in his hermeneutical reflections if he had had the occasion to probe deeply into the writing of Theodoret.

Bibliography of Theodoret

Primary Sources

Opera, Patrologia Graeca, edited by J.-P. Migne, 80-84.
Commentaire sur Isaïe. 3 vols. Sources Chrétiennes 276, 295, 315, edited by J.-N. Guinot. Paris: Éditions du Cerf, 1981-84.

Secondary Sources

Ashby, G. W. *Theodoret of Cyrus as Exegete of the Old Testament*. Grahamstown, South Africa: Rhodes University Publications, 1992.
————. "The Hermeneutic (sic) Approach of Cyrrhus to the Old Testament." In *Studia Patristica* 15, pp. 131-35. Berlin: Akademie-Verlag, 1984.
Bardy, G. "Théodoret." In *Dictionnaire de Théologie Catholique* 15 (1946): 299-325.
Crouzel, H. "La distinction de la 'typologie' et de 'l'allégorie.'" *Bulletin de littérature ecclésiastique* 65 (1964): 161-74.

Devresse, R. *Essai sur Théodore de Mopsueste*. Rome: Biblioteca Apostilica Vaticani, 1948.

Greer, R. *Theodore of Mopsuestia*. London: Faith Press, 1961.

Guinot, J.-N. *L'exégèse de Théodoret de Cyr*. Paris: Éditions Beauchesne, 1995.

————. "Theodoret of Cyrus: Bishop and Exegete." In *The Bible in Greek Christian Antiquity*, edited by P. M. Blowers, pp. 163-93. Notre Dame: University of Notre Dame Press, 1997.

Hidal, S. "Exegesis of the Old Testament in the Antiochene School with Its Prevalent Literal and Historical Method." In *The Hebrew Bible/Old Testament*, vol. 1, edited by M. Saebø, pp. 543-68. Göttingen: Vandenhoeck & Ruprecht, 1996.

Kihn, H. "Über 'Theōria' und 'Allegoria' nach den verlorenen hermeneutischen Schriften der Antiochener." *Theologische Quartalschrift* 20 (1889): 531-82.

Lubac, H. de. "'Typologie' et 'Allégorisme.'" *Recherches de science religieuse* 36 (1949): 542-76.

McCollough, C. T. "Theodoret of Cyrus as Biblical Interpreter and the Presence of Jews in the Late Roman Empire." *Studia Patristica* 18 (1985): 327-34.

Margerie, B. de. *An Introduction to the History of Exegesis*, vol. 1, pp. 165-87. Petersham, Mass.: St. Bede's Publications, 1993.

Nassif, B. "The 'Spiritual Exegesis' of Scripture: The School of Antioch Revisited." *Anglican Theological Review* 75 (1993): 437-70.

Quasten, J. "Theodoret of Cyrus." In *Patrology*, vol. 3, pp. 536-54. Westminster, Md.: Newman Press, 1960.

Rad, G. von. "Typological Interpretation of the Old Testament." In *Essays in Old Testament Hermeneutics*, edited by C. Westermann, pp. 17-39. Richmond: John Knox, 1963.

Schäublin, C. *Untersuchungen zu Methode und Herkunft der antiochenischen Exegese*. Köln/Bonn, 1974.

Sellers, R. *Two Ancient Christologies*. London: SPCK, 1940.

Tennant, P. "La theoria d'Antioche dans le cadre des sens de l'Écriture." *Biblica* 34 (1953): 135-58; 354-83; 456-86.

Vaccari, A. "La 'teōria' nella scuola esegetica de antiochus." *Biblica* 1 (1920): 3-36.

Vigouroux, F. "École exégètique d'Antioche." In *Dictionnaire de la Bible*, vol. 1 (1891), pp. 683-87.

Young, F. "Theodoret of Cyrrhus." In *From Nicaea to Chalcedon*, pp. 265-89. London: SCM, 1983.

————. "The Rhetorical Schools and Their Influence on Patristic Exegesis." In *The Evolution of Orthodoxy: Essays in Honour of Henry Chadwick*, edited by R. Williams, pp. 182-99. Cambridge: Cambridge University Press, 1989.

————. "Typology." In *Crossing the Boundaries: Essays in Biblical Interpretation in Honour of Michael D. Goulder*, edited by S. E. Porter et al., pp. 29-48. Leiden: Brill, 1994.

11

Thomas Aquinas
(c. 1225–74)

The purpose of this chapter on Thomas Aquinas is a highly restrictive one. It does not purport to assess the theology of Thomas in any comprehensive way — a daunting enterprise even for the specialist. Nor does it even attempt to analyze in general Thomas's exegetical contribution to biblical studies. Rather, it will continue to pursue the previously announced goal to raise certain basic hermeneutical issues of theological importance by means of a study of selected commentaries on the book of Isaiah. It seeks to discern patterns emerging within the history of the church's engagement with this prophetic corpus as a part of Christian scripture.

Even though the dominant concern of this study is hermeneutical, the nature of the enterprise requires that each work be placed within its larger historical framework in order to appreciate both the diversity and commonality of approach within the church's exegetical tradition. A central concern of this study is to analyze the relationship between the forces exerted on a particular author arising from his historical and cultural context and his creative application of a received canonical text along with its exegetical traditions.

I. The Literal and Figurative Senses according to Thomas

Thomas stood within the traditional fourfold interpretive schema of the church, which had already by the twelfth century gone through a considerable development. As has previously been reviewed, Origen's contribution to biblical exegesis was crucial in developing a powerful theory of the multiple senses of scripture under the influence of both the New Testament and the external impact of Philo and other Hellenistic authors. Origen and his followers within the Alexandrian tradition usually spoke of a sharp distinction between the literal and figurative senses of the text, but there was considerable fluidity in additional figurative senses, such as the allegoricq, anagogic, and tropological senses. As previously described, a somewhat different tradition arose among the Antiochenes, often sharply critical of the alleged excesses of the followers of Origen. Yet as we have previously argued, there was a large measure of agreement on the need to interpret both the literal and the figurative senses, even though the exact relation between the two continued to be debated. Over against the neo-Platonic scheme of Origen that sharply contrasted the earthly (carnal) and the spiritual dimension of a heavenly reality, the Antiochenes focused on a temporal sequence of prophecy and fulfillment within an overarching historical trajectory proceeding from the Old Testament to the New. During the fourth and fifth centuries, Jerome and particularly Augustine sought to combine elements of both approaches in somewhat different ways. In two famous treatises (*On Christian Doctrine* and *The Spirit and the Letter*), Augustine offered a sophisticated hermeneutical synthesis that dominated Christian interpretation well into the scholastic age. The juxtaposition of sign *(signum)* and reality *(res)* became the ruling hermeneutical category by which to move from the biblical text to its theological reality. In the period following Augustine, the threefold scheme of multiple senses was gradually replaced by a fourfold one in a form usually associated with Cassian's historical, allegorical, anagogical, and tropological, but the hermeneutical substance was scarcely affected by this expansion and systematization of the nomenclature.

In his brief review of the history of interpretation, Otto Pesch (pp. 682ff.) offers an important theological argument in an attempt to refute the modern charge that this traditional scheme was arbitrary and an unfortunate adaptation of Hellenistic rhetoric. He maintains that the method relates organically to the Christian faith and correctly reflects not only an explicit New Testament usage (cf. 1 Cor. 10:11), but a profoundly theological insight into the relation of the two testaments and their witness to God, Christ, and the Holy Spirit.

It is at this point in the study of the allegorical approach that a significant debate has arisen. During the period beginning roughly in the 1930s new interest arose in the study of the history of interpretation. It is best represented by the pioneer works of Beryl Smalley, Ceslas Spicq, and Henri de Lubac, among many others. In slightly varying forms the theory has been advanced by some that no significant new hermeneutic emerged until the twelfth century to call into question the traditional form of patristic biblical interpretation, but that beginning in the twelfth century with the Victorenes and culminating in Thomas (1225-1274), a new approach emerged that replaced the interest in the figurative senses with a new focus on the primacy of the literal/historical sense. Smalley highlighted the originality of Hugh of St. Victor (died 1141) in his vigorous recovery of the literal sense. However, it was Thomas who not only systematized his historical approach, but also brought a new and decisive turn to exegesis by replacing the neo-Platonic heritage of Augustine with that of Aristotle. Smalley (pp. 303ff.) offers a very powerful analysis of the change by tracing the interpretation of Exod. 23:19 ("Thou shalt not boil a kid in his mother's milk") from Augustine to Thomas, including the impact of Maimonides.

According to the interpretation of Smalley, followed independently by and large by Spicq, Thomas replaced the Augustinian theory of multiple senses by defending the univocity of biblical words. Thus, in *Summa Theologiae* 1.1.10 he distinguished between the sign that signified things and things that then became signs of other things. A word can mean only one thing, but an additional spiritual sense can derive from a thing *(res)* that signifies in turn a second thing *(res²)*. The Aristotelian impact of Thomas's hermeneutics is thought to be evidence for insisting that the spiritual sense is not hidden behind the text, but only revealed by penetrating through the text to its substance, thus overcoming the separation of body and spirit essential for Augustine. Then again, the influence of Maimonides (1135-1204) was thought to be a powerful force in applying the Aristotelian categories of reason, causality, and essence to the Bible. According to this interpretation, by shifting the hearer of the spiritual senses from the biblical text itself to the substance *(res)*, theology was separated from its direct connection with biblical exegesis.

However, over against this interpretation of Thomas's relation to the church's traditional fourfold exegetical approach, Henri de Lubac has offered a powerful rebuttal in his *Exégèse Médiévale.* With the greatest detail possible, de Lubac has tried to refute this widespread interpretation of Thomas represented by Smalley, Spicq, and many others. De Lubac has argued as follows:

1. First, Thomas often refers specifically to the figurative tradition of the church, usually without any negative assessment. When he praises Gregory's allegorical interpretation of Job, there is no reason to assume his comments were meant ironically or that he intended to distance himself from this tradition.

2. When Thomas explicitly sets forth his interpretation of the multiple senses of scripture (*Quodlibet* 7.6; *Galatians commentary,* Ch. 5 lect. 7; and *Summa Theologiae* 1.1.10), his continuity with the traditional allegorical approach is clear.

3. When Thomas stresses the centrality of the literal/historical sense in interpretation, and insists that no doctrinal implications be drawn that deviate from the literal sense, he is simply affirming a theological position long expressed within the church and vigorously defended by Hugh of St. Victor. Nothing essential to the dogmatic content of the faith can be expected from figurative interpretations.

4. Thomas explicitly dismisses the objection that an appeal to figurative senses of scripture engenders confusion that undermines the objective truth of dogma (*Quodlibet* 7.14. q.6), and points to the exegetical constraints exercised by the text's literal sense.

When offering his own critical assessment of this modern debate concerning Thomas's relation to the fourfold method, Pesch (pp. 701ff.) agrees initially with de Lubac's arguments respecting his continuity with the traditional exegetical approach. Thomas stood basically in agreement with his predecessors in accepting the role of figurative interpretation as a complement to the literal sense. Yet at the same time, Pesch holds that de Lubac has overstated Thomas's continuity with the past, and he has underestimated the genuine hermeneutical innovations introduced by Thomas. Not only did Thomas greatly sharpen the nature of the hermeneutical debate in response to the new challenges of the thirteenth century; he laid a fresh hermeneutical foundation from which to pursue the new philological and historical approaches soon to explode in the Renaissance. It will be part of the purpose of the subsequent analysis of Thomas's Isaiah commentary to pursue this question in more detail.

II. Hermeneutical Issues Related to Thomas's Exegesis

1. Thomas clearly articulates the relation of the divine and human authorships of the Bible at the outset of the *Summa*. Unequivocally for Thomas the author of scripture is God (*ST* 1.1.10). The scriptures are the Word of God chosen by God himself. However, in addition, Thomas does make mention of the human authors of the Bible as the *causa instrumentalis,* that is, as a tool in the hands of the divine author. For this reason the role of the human author of scripture presents no fundamental theological problem for Thomas. There is no tension between the divine revelation and the work of the human author. In a word, Thomas's approach to scripture in this regard remains in a different world from that of the Enlightenment, for which the tension between divine revelation and its scriptural form evokes a crucial and continuing debate.

2. The alleged univocity of words in Thomas raises a number of complex hermeneutical issues. According to Thomas (*ST* 1.1.10), the literal sense is the plain, straightforward sense that the author intends, and is therefore univocal — the words mean only one thing. However — here Thomas makes an important contribution — because the spiritual senses are derived not from the words, in the Augustinian sense, but from the things signified by the words, they can themselves be signs of other things. This multiplicity of senses does not produce equivocation; these senses are not multiplied because one word signifies several different things, but because the words themselves signify other things. For Thomas this is a unique quality of scripture, that it possesses this capacity.

However, there is an additional sentence in Thomas's treatment (*ST* 1.1.10) that has complicated the issue and evoked much recent debate: "Now because the literal sense is that which the author intends, and the author of Holy Scripture is God who comprehends everything all at once in his understanding, it is not amiss *(non est inconveniens)*, as St. Augustine says in *Confessions* XII, if many meanings *(plures sensus)* are present even in the literal sense of one passage of Scripture."

Recently, Eugene Rogers ("Virtues," pp. 65f.), followed by Stephen Fowl (*Engaging Scripture*, p. 39), argues that Thomas's appeal to authorial intention promotes diversity rather than a restriction of readings. He concludes that the literal sense for Thomas is that which commands "communal assent" (George Lindbeck's terminology), and is thus largely indeterminate. My initial reaction to this reading of Thomas is that the complexity of interpreting this particular passage in Thomas has not been adequately faced. At the very least, one needs to engage the lengthy debate among the experts (Synave, Spicq, and Pesch, among others). For my part, I shall defer in offering my own conclusion until after a more detailed study of Thomas's actual interpretation of Isaiah.

3. There is a third controversial hermeneutical problem that has been raised with considerable force by J. S. Preus (*From Shadow to Promise*, pp. 46ff.). The issue turns on whether for Thomas the Old Testament has independent theological meaning apart from its role as offering the promise of the gospel to be fulfilled in the New Testament. This issue is not one that can be easily resolved without first throwing the net very wide to include the *Summa Theologiae* along with his other commentaries. Again I shall defer the discussion in order to see if any light can be thrown on the issue from a closer study of Thomas's Isaiah commentary.

III. An Analysis of Thomas's Isaiah Commentary

1. *Its Structure and Goal*

Thomas wrote his commentary on Isaiah during his second sojourn in Paris (1269-72). The Vatican library possesses an autographed script of his original work on Isaiah, thus putting its authenticity beyond dispute. According to Spicq (p. 300), the commentary was shortly edited and additions inserted at the end of the chapter under the rubric *Notae super illo verbo* or the like.

Thomas's commentary is preceded by his exposition of Jerome's prologue and a *prooemium* in which he sets out his goals and manner of approach. One is immediately struck by the scholastic form of the commentary that Thomas inherited from his predecessors of the twelfth century (e.g., Hugh and Albert). The commentary is carefully divided into a multitude of divisions, subdivisions, and distinctions. The larger intentions of the author are summarized before each smaller unit; even the intentions of individual words are further subdivided according to their logical sequence. Thus in the *prooemium* to Isaiah he focuses immediately on its threefold subject matter: authorship, style, and content. Each rubric is then further divided, and the distinctions are further grounded by the citation of parallel verses.

Thomas sees himself standing in close continuity with Jerome, whose prologue to Isaiah he interprets and uses as a model. He readily accepts Jerome's assessment that Isaiah excels the other prophets by his use of words and beauty of style. Isaiah writes in a plain and open manner. But of more importance, he follows Jerome in characterizing Isaiah more as an evangelist of the gospel than as a prophet whose tongue is the inspired organ of the Holy Spirit. Using the parallel of Isaiah's writing his vision on a large tablet (Isa. 8:1) with that of Hab. 2:2f., he pursues the analogy throughout the *prooemium* of the prophetic vision being far off but pressing toward its goal.

What is striking in Thomas's analysis is his repeated emphasis on the profundity and obscurity of the scriptures. This is because they contain the mysteries of Christ and his church. The difficulty of interpretation does not lie in prophecy regarding the future, but rather with the concealed nature of the past events. Indeed, the content of the book lies in the coming of Christ and the calling of the nations. These mysteries are perceived as distant, but are manifested in visions and revealed to the faithful, "who have greeted it from afar" (Heb. 11:13). Not by chance does Thomas cite Matt. 25:34, calling for the blessed to receive the kingdom "prepared for you from the foundation of the world." Eph. 3:9 is also much cited: "to make all men see what is the plan of the mystery hidden for ages in God."

Although clearly the theological emphasis of the *prooemium* falls on the ontological mystery of the revelation of God concerning his eternal purpose, attention is also clearly paid to the unfolding of a unified narrator encompassing both testaments. The very role assigned to Hab. 2 speaks of the delay of the promise, which was perceived eschatologically from afar by the Fathers (Heb. 11:13), but finally revealed by the Spirit in the incarnation of Christ (John 1:14). Moreover, the mystery of God's hidden plan has been already perceived even under the law and in periods of Israel's idolatry.

The difficulty of understanding the function of Thomas's *prooemium* is that its relation to the actual commentary is not immediately apparent. The goals expressed do not seem to reflect what actually occurs in most of the commentary. Thus, for example, in outlining the mystery of God's judgment against Egypt, he cites Isaiah 19: "The Lord comes to Egypt riding on a swift cloud." This verse is, of course, a favorite among the early Fathers (cf. Cyril) as offering an allegory on the birth of Jesus and his entry into Egypt (Matt. 2:20ff.). However, in Thomas's commentary on Isa. 19 there is no hint of such an allegorical interpretation. In fact, the very lack of figurative exegesis is a hallmark of his approach. One can, of course, argue with de Lubac that this introduction is only a further confirmation of his continuity with the church's allegorical exegetical tradition. However, it seems odd that the introduction seems unrelated to what generally follows in his actual interpretation of Isaiah. In contrast, Jerome's prologue reflects exactly the legacy of his Alexandrian hermeneutics, but joined with his own learned interest in text criticism, history, geography, and philology. Thomas's exposition of Jerome's prologue, while illuminating certain details of his understanding, does not seem to clarify the problem of this puzzling discrepancy.

2. Various Levels of Interpretation

The beginning of Isa. 8 offers a good example of Thomas's exegetical approach. He first provides a careful interpretation of the biblical text *ad litteram*. He starts by reviewing the history of Assyrian aggression against Israel, mentioning by name the different invasions of Tiglath-pileser, Shalmaneser, and Sennacherib, which history he correlates with the accounts in 2 Kings. He next turns to an analysis of the sign in 8:1ff. of the son of Isaiah, Maher-shalal-hashbaz, rendered in the Vulgate as *Accelera spolia, Festina praeclari*. The sign reveals to Judah *ad litteram* through the name the coming destruction of the ten tribes. The sign is triply confirmed by its writing, by its testimony of witnesses, and by the birth of the child. Then each phrase of the sign-act is further explained, usually by citing a parallel verse (e.g., Jer. 36:2; Hab. 2:2; Deut. 19:15).

After offering his own interpretation *ad litteram,* Thomas turns to other unnamed interpreters, who claim that it is impossible to interpret the passage literally. If one recalls at this juncture the long-developed allegorical interpretation of this chapter represented widely in the church's tradition (cf. Cyril), it becomes clear that Thomas is not simply sparring with a few peripheral figures. The first set of objections to a literal reading involves alleged contradictions of a logical or historical nature. Accordingly, one would not need a "large book" to inscribe so few words. Or again, an honorable man would not bring along witnesses for such a private matter involving his wife. Thirdly, Uriah had brought an idol from Damascus into the Jerusalem temple and therefore could not be used as a reliable witness. Finally, Zechariah could not have been still alive at this time according to 2 Chron. 24. In each case, Thomas methodically seeks to refute these arguments.

There then follows another series of positive reasons for preferring a figurative reading to the literal one offered by Thomas. The sign was to be written *per stilum hominis,* which was the manner used by the prophet in order that its meaning not be understood by just anyone, but only by those interpreting its meaning *ex figuris* (citing Hosea 12:10). Then again, the name of the child was a circumlocution for Jesus, the Savior. In response, Thomas rejects these objections to a literal interpretation as not having the authority of scripture, in contrast to the warrant provided by Matt. 1 regarding the child in Isa. 7. However, Thomas does seem more open to an interpretation of the *Glossa* that could see the child as a *figura Christi.*

Viewing Thomas's commentary on Isaiah as a whole, it is a fair assessment to say that the great bulk of his interpretation falls under the rubric of *ad litteram.* Nevertheless this statement must be carefully qualified by the nuances, restrictions, and extension of the term "literal sense."

Thomas's usual method is to offer initially a careful structural analysis of a chapter, followed by subsequent divisions and subdivisions. These serve to clarify the inner coherence of the whole, and usually focus on the logical procession among the various parts of the passage. Not surprisingly, his use of Aristotelian categories such as causality allows him to nuance the text with great precision. He then offers a word-by-word, or phrase-by-phrase interpretation that often amounts to a grammatical explanation or a literary paraphrase to clarify a biblical term. However, rather than expanding a phrase by further exegetical reflection, he usually cites a parallel biblical text. The reader is then forced to study the entire biblical context of the parallels in order to see the connections being suggested, much like a rabbinic midrash. The fact that Thomas was untrained in both Hebrew and Greek limits the lasting value of his philological comments. However, using Jerome's work usually prevents him from grievous mistakes, except when he is led astray by Jerome's own theories of etymology.

The modern reader is often impressed by the exterior details within his literal interpretation that cover geographical, historical, zoological, chronological, and anthropological observations. For example, in Isa. 7 he describes the three water reservations of Jerusalem, assigning to each a particular function within the life of the city. Or again, at the end of chapter 13, he struggles valiantly to identify the various wild beasts and howling creatures that inhabit the desolated land. Finally, in chapter 7 he presents a somewhat novel chronological interpretation of the sixty-five years before the destruction of Ephraim by carefully calculating the years of Jotham's co-regency with Uzziah, his subsequent sole reign over Judah, the years of Ahaz, and the capture of Samaria in the sixth year of Hezekiah in order to acquire the figure of sixty-five years.

Thomas treats the historical chapters (Isaiah 36–39) by and large in a straightforward literal sense. He describes the threat to Hezekiah posed by the coming of the Rabshakeh verse by verse. He offers brief but concise observations, noting the crudity of the Assyrian's mockery. He points out the cleverness of the Rabshakeh in turning Hezekiah's pious acts of purifying Judah's sacrifice into one of sacrilege, thus showing his considerable narrative skill. Then again, when describing the destruction of Babylon by the Medes in chapter 13, he captures the intensity of the historical drama. By an appeal to other parallels of attacking armies and the resulting terror within the city, he is able to give the reader a very realistic feeling for the eschatological dimension of divine judgment as the heavens themselves tremble before God's fierce anger.

One of the ways that Thomas has expanded his understanding of *ad litteram* interpretation is to include the use of metaphor within this category, a practice developed earlier by his predecessors, especially Hugh, among others. He notes, for example, in chapter 4 how the imagery of the tabernacle serves as a metaphor by which to depict the protection from the heat and shelter from rain. The imagery compares the promised divine blessings with those experienced by Israel in the exodus from Egypt. Or again, in chapter 5 Thomas interprets the parable of the vineyard as a metaphor by which to describe Judah's abuses of the continuing care of God for his elected people. Thomas offers an *ad litteram* interpretation of the parable of chapter 5, but he also lists other figurative options, including the "mystical," without any negative evaluation. On occasion Thomas offers a literal interpretation, such as in Isa. 12, which offers a future promise of the return from the captivity of Babylon, but then turns more toward a typological exposition in seeing the text as ultimately addressing the consolation of Christ.

As suggested above, much of the discussion of Thomas's use of figurative senses has focused on the hermeneutical discussion offered in *Summa Theologiae* 1.1.10, yet in his commentary on Isaiah the most important sections of his Christological interpretation come without an explicit appeal to this hermeneutical device. Rather Thomas appears to follow the traditional messianic interpretations of the church in seeing a direct prediction of the coming of Jesus Christ as Messiah in Isa. 7, 9, and 11. Thomas begins his analysis of chapter 7 with a careful review of the historical situation leading up to the threat to Ahaz posed by the Syrio-Ephraimite coalition. Then he interprets the divine offer of a sign of liberation and why Ahaz's refusal was not out of piety, but out of unbelief. Next he distinguishes between the two parts of the sign: a sign of liberation for those believing, but of destruction for those of unbelief. However, the sign offered is the incarnation of Jesus Christ *(Hoc autem signum est de Christi incarnatione)*. Clearly for Thomas this reading is not considered a figurative one, but *ad litteram*.

Thomas stands fully in continuity with the traditional Christian messianic interpretation, so he offers a lengthy refutation of the objections raised by the Jews against this interpretation. Many of his rebuttals arise from traditional Christian apologetics. The sign could not refer to Hezekiah because of the chronological discrepancy. The word *almah* rather than *betulah* was intentionally used in order to emphasize the quality of purity of the *almah*, which is missing in *betulah*. Then again, no son of Isaiah became ruler of Judah, but only Immanuel as the Son of God.

Thomas also seeks to work exegetically in showing that a biblical sign can either precede or follow its fulfillment. Thomas also tries to mount a case theologically that the promise of salvation to Judah in terms of the promise of the incarnate Christ derives logically from God's larger commitment to redeem the entire world (John 3:16), and is therefore not irrelevant to the historical crises of eighth-century Israel. However, Thomas is not just making a logical point, but rather arguing ontologically in relation to the substance of the Incarnation, which transcends the boundaries of temporal limitation.

Perhaps of even more significance hermeneutically is that, although Thomas argues for the messiahship of Jesus Christ according to the literal sense of the text, he buttresses his argument and elaborates its theological significance by using other Old Testament texts figuratively. Thus he cites the familiar texts used by the earlier Fathers, such as Jer. 31:22 and Ezek. 44:2, to demonstrate allegorically the uniqueness of the virgin birth. He also argues that the child's diet of curds and honey (7:15) is an additional witness to the divine and human nature of this promised savior (cf. Canticles 4:11). He also cites St. Bernard in this context as further confirmation of Christ's assuming human flesh apart from any corruption. A similar argument for Christ's human and divine nature is further found in chapter 9.

When Thomas comes to Isa. 11, he pursues the same approach used for chapters 7 and 9. He begins by outlining three different interpretations of the passage. The first option is that of Jerome and all the Fathers, who expound the promise to refer to the restoration through Christ, which he, however, characterizes as a figurative sense *(ut sit figurative dictum)*. The second expounded by some teachers sees the text as referring to Hezekiah or Josiah, clearly a historically time-conditioned referent. Thirdly, the Jewish option accepts the text as referring to their expected Messiah, and they wish to understand the entire passage *ad litteram.* Thomas rejects the second and third options and embraces the first as the only true one, thus aligning himself with the church's traditional interpretation. Thomas also uses this text to refute two Christian heresies that deny Christ's true humanity and genealogical descent from Adam. Once again he uses a catena of traditional Christian prooftexts: Num. 24:17; Cant. 2:1; Jer. 22:5, which he intermingles with New Testament citations.

When one turns to analyze Thomas's handling of Isa. 40–66, certain hermeneutical differences in approach begin to appear. Thomas himself is fully aware that something new occurs within the book. He designates Isa. 40–66 as the "second part" of the book, which he characterizes as Israel's consolation. Moreover, he recognizes that the context of these chapters speaks prophetically of the destruction of Babylon and the restoration of Israel. Of course, Thomas does not speak of a "second Isaiah," but envisions simply the prophet Isaiah's vision of the divine judgment of Babylon that ended Israel's captivity, and the promise of divine forgiveness and restoration of God's chosen people.

In contrast to his interpretation of Isa. 7, 9, and 11 as directly related to the coming messsiahship of Christ, he often joins together a literal and a typological sense in Isa. 40–66. The clearest example is the figure of Cyrus in Isa. 44, 45, and 49. Cyrus was God's servant who was chosen to fulfill God's promise of deliverance. Yet immediately Cyrus is interpreted both as a historical figure and as a type of Christ *(mystice de Christo).* Although one does not gain a very sharp profile of the historical Cyrus, his historical presence is fully recognized. Nevertheless in 41:2, "the victorious one whom God stirred from the east" is interpreted by Thomas as Abraham, following the traditional Christian reading. Yet even here, a note acknowledges that some commentators identify this reference also with Cyrus. Because a main theme of Isa. 41 is the love of God toward the patriarchs, it is easy to see how the typological trajectory of the divine plan overshadows specific historical details. Much of the commentary focuses on the attributes of God's power, mercy, and love. Still, a Christological flavor to his entire interpretation lies always in the background and surfaces explicitly with the intertextual reflections on peace set at the end of the section and subsumed under the rubric of *nota super illo verbo:* "Christ passed by in safety" *(Christus transivit in pace).*

When Thomas comes to the servant passages in Isa. 42 and 49, he initially pays careful attention to the servant's identification with Israel, even though the overarching context is the revelation of God's love through the Son portrayed in John 3:16. When God "sustains his servant," Thomas interprets it "according to his human nature," citing Luke 1:54: "He has helped his servant Israel." However, by and large, his interpretation expounds the text Christologically with citations from the New Testament. Thus, God gave the "judgment" of his Son (John 5:20), and he was "well pleased" with him (Matt. 3:17). That the nations await God's "law" (42:4) is identified with awaiting the "gospel" by means of a citation from Gen. 49:12.

Next, when Thomas comes to chapter 53, he finds here a remedy against all the obstacles impeding redemption. The entire chapter is now understood Christologically. First, it offers God's promise to overcome sin through the passion of Jesus Christ. Second, his exaltation from his humiliation follows. Thomas then pursues the depiction of the rejection, oppression, and shame of the servant, in a sense typologically, with a catena of verses chiefly from the Old Testament. In dealing with the description of the servant's outward appearance — having no beauty but only a form to repel — Thomas is forced to offer a distinction between his external and inward beauty, because Christ's beauty has always been affirmed traditionally from parallels in Ps. 45 and Canticles.

In a real sense, Thomas's interpretation of Isa. 40–66, but especially of chapter 53, is not directed primarily to the text itself — that is, not just to the words, but to their substance. He does not distinguish between literal and figurative senses according to the Alexandrian tradition, but passes through the words of the text to their theological substance, which inevitably transcends the verbal sense of the passage. He thus moves from his earlier mode of explaining the text by means of single verbal synonyms to a theological reflection that wrestles with its ontological dimension. In this sense, one can recognize the positive application of an Aristotelian influence that overcomes some of Augustine's dualism between text and substance.

There is another aspect of Thomas's interpretation that can perhaps best be characterized with the modern terminology of intertextuality. It is a mark of his interpretation *ad litteram* that Thomas usually explains a text by means of a close synonym. Then as a further warrant, he offers a citation of a parallel passage from either the Old or New Testament that contains an identical or similar word. This procedure, later given the term *dicta probantia,* was largely denigrated in the nineteenth century as static and lacking in any sense of genuine literary or historical context.

Yet for Thomas this procedure was anything but mechanical and naïve. The sophistication of his use of intertextual reference emerges especially when Thomas moves from the literal sense to a figurative level of interpretation. For example, in chapter 1, Thomas summarizes at the outset the intention of the main body of the text: the advent of Christ and the calling of the Gentiles. However, what exactly he understands by these two rubrics is revealed by close attention to the verses that follow. Ps. 25:10 begins his interpretation: "All the paths of the Lord are mercy and truth." This is followed by Luke 2:34: "This child is set for the fall and rising of many in Israel." Next the Apostle Paul provides a transition to the Gentiles in Rom. 11:25: "a hardening has come upon part of Israel until the full number of the gentiles come in and so all Israel will be saved." In sum, lest we think that Thomas is only concerned with the advent of Christ and the inclusion of the nations, the intertextual references show that he interpreted the biblical context to address the ultimate joining of the "Old Testament saints" with "those hardened within Israel," who together with the Gentiles comprise the salvation of all of Israel.

Another form of Thomas's application of intertextuality is the addition of *notandum super illo verbo,* which are set editorially usually at the end of a section. Usually this rubric consists of theological reflections focused on a single word or concept that he joins together on the basis of content. This is to say, Thomas makes the association according to his understanding of a resemblance of subject matter that extends to both testaments (cf. chapter 9 on the attributes of the Savior). This procedure, like the *dicta probantia,* consists of a catena of verses without commentary that nevertheless prompts the reader to reflect on the nature of the reality undergirding these different witnesses. To name this an ontological interpretation is probably a terminological anachronism, but it does touch on an essential feature of Thomas's theological approach to the substance of scripture.

3. Biblical Interpretation and Philosophical Categories

At the outset of the introduction to Thomas's exegesis, I briefly attempted to set Thomas within his medieval context. The works of Smalley, Spicq, and de Lubac have done much in revealing Thomas's continuity with the great expositors, especially in the twelfth century, who preceded him. No one contests the formal characteristics common to the scholastic age that Thomas shared but also perfected. Our present concern is to focus on a few topics within the book of Isaiah in which his philosophical concerns, usually developed at considerable length in the *Summa*, play a significant role in his exegesis.

In his interpretation of chapter 1, Thomas addresses the larger issue of the nature of prophecy. It is immediately clear that Thomas has been influenced by Jerome's "Prologue to Isaiah," where he discussed the problem of Hebrew meter and Isaiah's particular style. Thomas quite correctly distinguishes the genre of the historical books of the Old Testament from that of the prophets. Then he begins to talk about various forms of the prophetic vision, and the relation of prophecies concerning the future and those addressing the present. He continues by analyzing the relation of visions to sense perception and to the imagination, and reflects further on prophetic illumination in relation to natural understanding. The discussion is brief, and the reader is forced to return to the *Summa Theologiae* in order to gain a detailed account of Thomas's thoughts on the nature of prophecy, its causes, the manner of prophetic knowledge, and its divisions.

The hermeneutical issue at stake is not in respect to the coherence of Thomas's thought or his adaptation of Aristotelian categories, but to what extent his set of questions serves the immediate exegetical task of interpreting the book of Isaiah. The issue is complex because Thomas, along with the Fathers, made no distinction between biblical and systematic theology. Moreover, Thomas stood partly within the Christian exegetical tradition in assuming the unity of the whole Christian Bible, which allowed him to project New Testament concepts back into the Old Testament.

Yet to the extent that Thomas lays so much emphasis upon the intention of the author as the key to the biblical text's literal meaning, one can raise the question as to whether the distinction between biblical theology (the theology of the biblical writers themselves) and systematic theology can be totally disregarded. That is to say, it remains hermeneutically significant to understand the range of questions that are in accord with the intention of the biblical author and those that are only indirectly related to the writer's concerns. Specifically in terms of Isaiah, many of the questions regarding the quality of prophetic knowledge — an infusion by God of new species or merely new light — seem very far removed from the concerns of the author of Isa. 1.

Another case in point taken from the exegesis of Isaiah is the problem of contingent events. (Thomas discusses the issue in *Summa Theologiae* 171.3.) The issue emerges in several places in the commentary on Isaiah, but especially in chapter 38. Did the prophet speak falsely when he said of King Hezekiah, "You shall die, you shall not recover" (38:2), only later to rescind the judgment?

In order to respond to this problem, Thomas develops his philosophical hypothesis of a twofold form of knowledge — absolute and contingent — which exists simultaneously in the divine mind, but not in prophetic revelation (cf. *Summa Theologiae* 2a.2ae.176.6). The philosophical strength of Thomas's argument in accord with his larger theological understanding of God is apparent. However, it would seem useful from the perspective of biblical theology to recognize that the problem was indeed occasionally recognized within the Old Testament (2 Sam. 24:16; Jer. 26:19; Jon. 3:10). The formula "God repented of what he had done (or said)" would indicate this. However, this "metaphorical" formula by which to address a problem is far removed from Thomas's sophisticated theological resolution.

Within the later history of exegesis, the biblical approach of Thomas and the Fathers came under attack from two different directions. On the one hand, from the side of the Reformers the explicit appeal to *sola scriptura* served to elevate the literal sense of the text above all subsequent theological reflection (though to what extent this goal was actually carried out is another question). On the other hand, the heirs of the Enlightenment argued that serious biblical interpretation required a rigorous separation between the author's historical interpretation and all subsequent theological reflection. Thomas's approach along with the exegetical traditions of the Fathers was rejected as inadequate for the rational critical human consciousness come of age. We shall return to this difficult issue in our final chapter.

IV. Conclusions

1. In spite of Thomas's strong continuity with the church's exegetical traditions so brilliantly analyzed by de Lubac, a study of his Isaiah commentary shows the unique stamp that Thomas has left on biblical interpretation. His emphasis on the literal sense has often been correctly stressed, but equally important is Thomas's largely non-allegorical manner of penetrating to the figurative sense by means of an ontological, intertextual move shaped by the substance of the witness itself. On the negative side, one can also see that his *dicta probantia* method of citation of parallels, when used by commentators less capable than Thomas, could deteriorate into a mechanical device without a true sense of theological context. Unfortunately, this is what so often occurred in later Catholic and Protestant orthodoxy.

2. Thomas's interpretation of Isaiah offers many examples of his successful adaptation of Aristotelian categories that served to illuminate the biblical text and to sharpen the biblical witness with great precision. Neverthe-

less, there are other examples, especially concerning the nature of prophecy and visions, that seem to obscure rather than clarify the biblical text, and to blur the particular concerns of the biblical author. This is of course hardly unique to Thomas, but well serves to illustrate a perennial problem of all interpretation, none of which is immune from subjective mishandling. The central hermeneutical issue turns on the question of whether there is indeed coercion from the biblical text itself in terms of its subject matter to serve as a constraining force. Although expressed in different ways and by means of varying terminology, a strong case can be made that both Thomas and the Fathers would agree with such a theological formulation, especially when the role of the Spirit is emphasized in quickening the Word for every new generation of the faithful.

3. J. S. Preus (pp. 46ff.) has raised the problem whether Thomas's doctrine of justification by grace alone prevents any theological value being accorded to the people of the old covenant. In a word, how does the Old Testament function theologically not simply as a promise pointing to its subsequent fulfillment in the gospel? Is the New Testament the literal sense of the Old Testament that God intended? This issue is obviously too broad to be resolved solely on the basis of a study of Thomas's Isaiah commentary. Otto Pesch (p. 708) rightly questions whether one can adequately assess Thomas's understanding of the relation of the Old Testament to the New without study of *Summa Theologiae* 1–2.98-100 and 102-105. However, even from the limited perspective of his approach to Isaiah, our study has shown Thomas's profound wrestling with the selfsame ontological reality shared by both testaments. Nevertheless, one would also have to say that the issue raised by Preus is not completely without merit. Although Thomas's ontological approach acknowledges the theological substance of the Old Testament, his great emphasis on the New Testament as the goal of the Old Testament promise is such that its theological role can become blurred or even concealed. For example, there is little emphasis on the voice of the faithful Jewish remnant of Isa. 7 and 8 that confesses in its plight that "God is with us." In his reading of Isa. 12 one hears little of the responding answer of a historic Israel professing "God is my salvation. . . . I will trust . . . he has become my salvation." Perhaps of equal significance to this historical question of Thomas's understanding of the theological role of the Old Testament is the widespread acknowledgment in today's Christian church that a true interpretation of the Old Testament as an abiding testimony to God's faithfulness to his people of the covenant is an absolute desideratum for Christian theology.

4. Very recently, as suggested above, E. F. Rogers has argued that Thomas's reflection on the literal sense leaves matters surprisingly undeter-

mined, and that the author's intention functions more to promote diversity than contain it. Rogers's article has been further developed by S. E. Fowl, who not only agrees that Thomas's intention is to promote diversity, but, following Hans Frei, George Lindbeck, and Kathryn Tanner, asserts that the literal sense of Scripture is that which commands "communal assent" (p. 39). The initial warrant for this interpretation of Thomas arises from an interpretation of *Summa Theologiae* 1.1.10 concerning the intention of God as the author of scripture, the effect being that many meanings are present even in the literal sense of one passage.

The issue is far too complex to resolve solely from a study of Thomas's Isaiah commentary. However, I have found little support to affirm that for Thomas the literal sense is that which commands communal assent. Admittedly, Thomas's appeal to the effect of God's authorial intention appears to provide a concession to this otherwise carefully formulated understanding of the literal sense of Scripture in *Summa Theologiae* 1.1.10. However, whatever its exact meaning — its interpretation is far from settled among the experts — I can find no convincing grounds in his Isaiah commentary for seeing therein a warrant for hermeneutical indeterminacy. Even less convincing is the attempt to draw Thomas into the modern theories of meaning as communal assent. What is missing in this discussion is Thomas's careful attention to the ontological force exerted by the subject matter itself (its *res*). This concern allows Thomas to move with great freedom from the literal to the figurative senses without becoming lost and confused in a sea of indeterminacy.

Bibliography of Thomas

Primary Sources

St. Thomas Aquinas. *Summa Theologiae: Latin Text and English Translation.* edited by T. Gilby et al. (Blackfriars Edition). London and New York: McGraw Hill, 1964-81.
———. *In Isaiam Prophetam Expositio, Opera Omnia,* vols. 18-19. Paris: Louis Vivès, 1876.

Secondary Sources

Bouthillier, D., and J. P. Torall. "Quand Saint Thomas méditat sur le prophète Isaïe." *Revue Thomaste* 90 (1990): 5-47.

Chenu, M.-D. *Toward Understanding St. Thomas.* Chicago: Henry Regnery, 1964.

Ebeling, G. "Der hermeneutische Ort der Gotteslehre bei Petrus Lombardus und Thomas von Aquin." In *Wort und Glaube,* vol. 2, pp. 209-56. Tübingen: Mohr Siebeck, 1969.

Elze, M. "Schriftauslegung. Alte Kirche und Mittelalter." *Religion in Geschichte und Gegenwart,* 3rd ed., vol. 5, pp. 1520-28.

Fowl, S. E. *Engaging Scripture,* pp. 38-40. Oxford: Blackwell, 1998.

Frei, H. "The 'Literal Reading' of Biblical Narrative in the Christian Tradition: Does It Stretch or Will It Break?" In *The Bible and the Narrative Tradition,* edited by F. McConnell, pp. 36-77. New York: Macmillan, 1986.

Froehlich, K. "Aquinas, Thomas 1224/5-1274." In *Historical Handbook of Major Biblical Interpreters,* edited by D. K. McKim, pp. 85-91. Downers Grove, Ill.: InterVarsity Press, 1998.

Glorieux, P. "Essai sur les commentaires scripturaires de Saint Thomas et leur chronologie," *Recherches de théologie ancienne et mediévale* 17 (1950): 237-66.

Kennedy, R. G. "Thomas Aquinas and the Literal Sense of Sacred Scripture." Ph.D. dissertation, University of Notre Dame, 1985.

Lindbeck, G. "The Story-Shaped Church: Critical Exegesis and Theological Interpretation." In *The Theological Interpretation of Scripture: Classic and Contemporary Readings,* edited by S. E. Fowl, pp. 39-52. Oxford: Blackwell, 1997.

Lubac, H. de. *Exégèse Médiévale,* vol. 2, pp. 233-302. Paris: Aubier-Montaigne, 1964.

Mailhiot, M.-D. "La pensée de S. Thomas sur le sens spirituel." *Revue Thomaste* 59 (1959): 613-63.

Marshall, B. "Aquinas as Post-Liberal Theologian." *The Thomist* 53 (1989): 353-406.

Martin, R. F. "Sacra Doctrina and the Authority of its Sacra Scriptura According to St. Thomas Aquinas." *Pro Ecclesia* 10 (2001): 84-102.

McGacken, T. "Saint Thomas Aquinas and Theological Exegesis of Sacred Scripture." *Louvain Studies* 16 (1991): 99-120.

Persson, P. E. *Sacra Doctrine: Reason and Revelation in Aquinas.* Philadelphia: Fortress, 1970.

Pesch, O. H. "Exegese des Alten Testament bei Thomas." In *Deutsche Thomas-Ausgabe,* vol. 13, pp. 682-716. Salzburg: Anton Pustet, 1934.

Preus, J. S. *From Shadow to Promise,* pp. 46-60. Cambridge, Mass.: Harvard University Press, 1969.

Reyero, M. Arias. *Thomas von Aquin als Exeget.* Einsiedeln: Johannes Verlag, 1971.

Rogers, Eugene F. "How the Virtues of the Interpreter Presuppose and Perfect Hermeneutics: The Case of Thomas Aquinas." *Journal of Religion* 76 (1996): 64-81.

————. *Thomas and Karl Barth: Sacred Doctrine and the Natural Knowledge of God.* Notre Dame: University of Notre Dame Press, 1998.

Smalley, B. *The Study of the Bible in the Middle Ages.* 3rd ed. Oxford: Blackwell, 1983.

Spicq, C. *Esquisse d'une histoire de l'exégèse latine au moyen age.* Paris: Vrin, 1944.

Synave, P. "Le Doctrine de S. Thomas d'Aquin sur le sens littéral des Écritures." *Revue Biblique* 35 (1926): 40-65.

Synave, P., and P. Benoit. *Prophecy and Inspiration: A Commentary on the Summa Theologica, II-II, Questiones 171-78.* New York: Desclée, 1961.

Tanner, K. "Theology and the Plain Sense." In *Scriptural Authority and Narrative Interpretation,* edited by J. Green, pp. 59-78. Philadelphia: Fortress, 1987.

Torrance, T. F. "Scientific Hermeneutics According to St. Thomas Aquinas." *Journal of Theological Studies* 13 (1962): 259-89.

Vander Ploeg, J. "The Place of Holy Scripture in the Theology of St. Thomas." *Thomist* 10 (1947): 398-422.

Weisheipl, J. A. *Friar Thomas d'Aquino: His Life, Thought, and Work.* Rev. ed. Washington: Catholic University Press, 1983.

Wolterstorff, N. "The Migration of the Theistic Arguments: From Natural Theology to Evidentialist Apologetics." In *Rationality, Religious Belief, and Moral Commitment,* edited by R. Audi and W. J. Wainwright. Ithaca: Cornell University Press, 1986.

Wyschograd, M. "A Jewish Reading of St. Thomas Aquinas on the Old Law." In *Understanding Scripture: Explorations of Jewish and Christian Traditions of Interpretation,* edited by C. Thoma and M. Wyschograd, pp. 125-38. New York: Paulist, 1957.

12

Nicholas of Lyra
(c. 1270–1349)

The importance of Nicholas of Lyra as a biblical interpreter from the late fourteenth century through the seventeenth is attested to by the enormous number of extant manuscripts of his works. Yet until quite recently in the modern era, he has been largely neglected and thought to be, at best, a pale shadow of Thomas Aquinas. No critical edition of his corpus has been attempted. There were a few learned articles concerning his exegesis during the nineteenth century (e.g., Fischer), several studies largely by French Catholics in the early twentieth century (Labrosse and Langlois), and the occasional reference to Nicholas as a source of Luther's rabbinical knowledge.

However, within the last several decades there has been a revival of interest in Nicholas and a considerable bibliography of scholarly research has developed (cf. the bibliography of C. L. Patton). Sections devoted to Nicholas were included in a dissertation by Gerhard Ebeling (1942) and again by J. S. Preus (1969), both in relation to Luther. In 1978 J. G. Kiecker offered a dissertation on Nicholas's hermeneutical principles, and he made Nicholas's three Latin hermeneutical introductions available to a wider audience with an English translation and extensive notes. This publication was followed in 1998 with Kiecker's new translation of Nicholas on the Song of Songs. In 1963 Herman Hailperin presented an extensive treatment of Nicholas that probed deeply into this largely neglected area in relation to rabbinical literature, especially focusing on Rashi. Finally, the breadth of the new interest in Nicholas has been demonstrated recently by a collection of critical essays edited by Philip Krey and Lesley Smith (2000) that covers in detail various aspects of Nicholas's biblical interpretation.

I. Life and Works

Nicholas was born in France on the coast of Normandy around 1270. Little is known of his early education or exactly when and from whom he learned Hebrew. He entered the order of the Franciscans at Verneuile about 1300, studied at Paris, and became master of theology in 1308. He held high administrative positions in his order until he resigned them in 1330 to devote himself to writing. He died about 1349 and was buried at the Franciscan house in Paris.

Although Nicholas produced a goodly number of extant academic and ecclesial tractates, his enduring fame lies in his biblical commentaries. His *Postilla litteralis* covering both Old and New Testaments was written between 1322 and 1332/3. He also produced from 1333-39 a companion volume, *Postilla moralis*, intended for the clergy. Nicholas's reputation rests largely on the *Postilla litteralis*, which includes two prologues. His *Postilla moralis* also has an introduction, which is generally referred to as the third prologue.

II. His Hermeneutical Contribution

For someone who was characterized in the history of exegesis as straightforward and plain *(Doctor planus et utilis)*, there is a remarkable level of disagreement respecting the nature of his work, his hermeneutical principles, and his lasting contribution. Because several lengthy passages from Thomas are included in his various introductions as well as in the body of his *Postilla litteralis*, some commentators have characterized Nicholas as an unimaginative copy of Thomas, but this judgment has recently been called into serious question. Again, the problem arises of establishing the relation of Nicholas's exegetical method stated in his prologues and the actual interpretation offered in the commentaries. Some recent scholars question the extent to which Nicholas was consistent, and various explanations have been suggested to ease the tension. Certainly the place to begin is briefly to review the three prologues, which will immediately raise the issue of the inner coherence of his exegetical approach.

1. The First Prologue

The first prologue concerns the praise of holy Scripture that is evoked by its superiority over all other writing. While human science offers a philosophy concerning well-being in the present life, scripture serves to order the well-being of the future life. Scripture surpasses all other writing because its subject is God and its knowledge is given by divine revelation. Scripture is the source of true wisdom and understanding. Nicholas elaborates on this theme by suggesting four excellencies: singular eminence, general content, visible excellence, and saving efficacy.

In describing scripture's special qualities he offers a basic hermeneutical principle on which he grounds his fourfold mode of interpretation. The defense of the fourfold scheme is, of course, traditional, but its formulation in terms of first and second signification seems closely dependent on Thomas (*Summa Theologiae* 1.1.10). According to this approach, words always signify things, but in scripture the things signified by words signify other things. By this first signification — that is, by the words that signify things — the literal or historical sense is obtained. By the second signification — that is, by the things signified by the things — the spiritual sense is acquired. Nicholas then specifies the three traditional figurative senses: allegorical, tropological, and anagogic. He then proceeds to characterize the "outer" and "inner" meaning of interpretation. In sum, the emphasis of the first prologue falls on scripture's spiritual meaning.

2. The Second Prologue

In contrast, the emphasis of the second prologue falls on scripture's literal sense. Nicholas begins by using again the terminology of the "outer" (literal) and "inner" (spiritual) senses. Then he shifts the focus by stressing that the literal sense provides the foundation for all interpretation. It is absolutely essential for understanding, since the spiritual senses are grounded in the text's literal meaning. He even cites Augustine as a warrant for his insistence on seeing the priority of the literal. In his defense of the literal sense, Nicholas attacks two prevalent exegetical approaches. First, he criticizes those who multiply the mystical sense to the detriment of the literal. Second, he is unhappy with a scholastic method that divides the text into so many parts as to confuse the understanding and to distract the attention away from the literal sense.

Nicholas is aware that his emphasis on the literal sense raises the difficult issue of dealing with a faulty biblical text. He argues that errors arose from poor copyists, but he also recognizes the additional inherent literary problem of determining the length of a biblical verse, which decision greatly influences the meaning. He appeals to Jerome's advice to return to the Hebrew codices to get at the truth of the biblical text. In this context, he commends Rabbi Solomon ben Isaac (Rashi) as usually a good guide in discerning the literal sense. However, since he has reservations about all Jewish readings of the Old Testament's messianic passages, he calls for the use of critical reason and an assessment of the truth of the biblical text in reaching a judgment.

Nicholas next turns to the seven rules of Tyconius, thus following the lead of Augustine, which he attributes to Isidore of Seville. These hermeneutical rules appear under traditional rubrics such as Christ and his church, true and false body, and spirit and letter, and were used to aid in overcoming various interpretive problems. Nicholas's use of the third rule (spirit and letter) is the most significant for him; it addresses how the literal and the spiritual senses are received in the same word. Here he offers his unique formulation of a double-literal sense *(duplex sensus litteralis)*. As an illustration he cites 1 Chron. 17:13, where God names Solomon as his son, whereas in Heb. 1:5 the Old Testament verse is interpreted as referring literally to Christ as son. Accordingly, the verse was first fulfilled in Solomon and more perfectly in Christ.

What seems perplexing in this treatment, which began as a defense of the literal sense, is that all the illustrations offered by Nicholas seem closely akin to the church's traditional spiritual interpretations of these texts. Is the author using the term "literal" in a different sense from that usually intended?

3. The Third Prologue

This prologue introduces the *Postilla moralis,* that is, the Bible's moral or spiritual meaning. Nicholas begins by repeating the analogy of the inner and outer side of scripture, and once again identifies the traditional subdivisions of the figurative before turning his major attention to the parabolic sense of scripture. He argues that the verse in Judg. 9:8, "The trees want to anoint a king over them," cannot be understood literally and still be true. If there is no literal sense in the text, then the parabolic sense becomes the first sense, as it is now contained under the literal sense. This conclusion would seem to indicate that under certain circumstances there is no spiritual sense, but only a literal one. How is this move to be explained? Is he using Thomas's hypothesis that the literal sense is identified with the author's intention, or is he merely calling the spiritual sense the literal? These are the hermeneutical questions that have evoked confusion and call for further analysis.

III. Difficulties in Interpreting Nicholas's Hermeneutics

1. When viewed from the first and third prologues, Nicholas seems to stand in the line of traditional Catholic understanding of the relation between the literal and the spiritual senses, between the inner and outer meanings. Both these prologues distinguish between the literal and the threefold figurative usages. He grounds this distinction in the first prologue in terms of scripture's ability for words to signify things that in turn signify other things. This formulation appears dependent upon Thomas. However, this dependence on Thomas's formulation does not function in Nicholas to blur the distinction between the two levels of meaning.

2. When one turns to the second prologue, which emphasizes the literal sense as the foundation for all true interpretation and even attacks the overemphasis on the spiritual/mystical sense, confusion begins. Nicholas cites the seven rules of Tyconius as an aid in recovering the literal sense, but in each case his exegetical examples of each rule end up providing what seems to be a spiritual interpretation rather than a literal one.

How is this inconsistency to be explained? J. G. Kiecker (*The Hermeneutical Principles,* pp. 64ff.) seeks a solution by arguing from a highly controversial passage in the *Summa* (1.1.10) that Nicholas followed Thomas's interpretation of the first and second signification in order to account for the relation of the literal and figurative senses. The passage from Thomas is as follows:

> Now because the literal sense is that which the author intends, and the author of holy scripture is God who comprehends everything all at once in his understanding, it comes not amiss, as St. Augustine observes, if many meanings are present even in the literal sense of one passage of Scripture. (Kiecker's translation, p. 76)

In other words, according to Kiecker, Nicholas assumes Thomas's hypothesis that because God intends a literal sense, the spiritual sense becomes for God the literal. In the case of Isa. 61:10, the verse is literally about Christ and his church, because this is what God intended.

This interpretation may well explain why Nicholas understands each of his illustrations of the rules of Tyconius to be the literal sense of the text, because God's intention was thus to render the spiritual. The effect is that, according to Kiecker, Nicholas virtually does away with the spiritual sense. There is no literal-spiritual dichotomy, but only a literal-literal sense. Certainly this interpretation of Nicholas is more plausible than simply to suggest that he is basically confused.

Still there remains a problem with this solution. Nowhere within the three prologues does Nicholas directly appeal to the passage in Thomas stating that the literal sense is what the author intends. At best the idea is indirectly implied in the second prologue, but then God's authorship is set in relation to his ability to create in scripture a double signification of words signifying things (the literal sense), but things also signifying other things (the spiritual sense). That God's intention overrides this distinction is not mentioned in the prologues.

In sum, Kiecker's solution remains a reasonable speculation, but one without specific evidence from the prologues. Moreover, the problem remains as to why Nicholas continues to defend the traditional scheme of a threefold figurative sense in the first and second prologues if his intention was ultimately to remove the whole concept of a spiritual sense.

3. The problem of the relation of the literal and the spiritual is closely related to another formulation of Nicholas, judged by many to be his most original contribution. In the second prologue, when discussing the third rule of Tyconius, Nicholas speaks of the same word having a double-literal sense *(duplicam sensum litteralem)*. As we saw earlier, 1 Chron. 17:13 speaks of Solomon as God's son, whereas in Heb. 1:5 Christ is identified as God's son literally. Rather than following the traditional solution of relating the two as the literal and the spiritual fulfillment, Nicholas speaks of both as literal, thus removing the need for an appeal to the spiritual.

This formulation of a double-literal sense would seem to support Kiecker's interpretation that Nicholas arrived at this position by applying Thomas's view of God's intention as determining its true meaning. Still it must again be pointed out that nowhere in Nicholas's text is this connection with Thomas's theory explicitly acknowledged. Moreover, as I shall try to illustrate, the double-literal sense is not the dominant category Nicholas applies to the messianic prophecies of Isaiah.

4. There is one final problem to be discussed respecting Nicholas's hermeneutical theory. The issue arises over his interpretation of the parabolic sense in the third prologue. In his dissertation Kiecker goes to lengths to show that Nicholas's understanding of the Song of Songs reflects a very complex and sophisticated redefinition of the literal sense, one that develops from his understanding of the parabolic form.

Nevertheless, it seems to me that Nicholas's commentary on the Song of Songs does not really resolve the hermeneutical issue of the relation of the literal to the spiritual senses. At the outset of his commentary he argues for the need to establish the proper context for interpreting the Song of Songs. He rejects the Jewish identification of the bride and groom with God and Israel as well as the traditional Christian interpretation of Christ and his church. However, Nicholas's suggested context is only a slight modification of the church's traditional reading: he merely posits as his context for interpretation a historical trajectory that demonstrates the love of God for his church, first during the Old Testament period and then during the New Testament age. In the end, his rather heavy-handed application of this quasi-*heilsgeschichtliche* scheme lacks either great illumination or persuasive force.

Thus, in spite of his sophisticated literary refinements, he returns to a figurative interpretation without providing a significant hermeneutical advance. Moreover, his figurative rendering does not show much promise in interpreting the poetic, literary, and imaginative dimension of this parabolic form.

IV. Nicholas's Commentary on the Book of Isaiah

We turn now to a more detailed examination of Nicholas's interpretation of Isaiah to see if his actual exegesis reflects his hermeneutical understanding of the prologues. We shall also be concerned to see if his commentary aids in illuminating some of the anomalies encountered in the prologues.

The aim of his commentary on Isaiah in the *Postilla litteralis* is declared at the outset: to offer its literal sense and to avoid the multiplication of unnecessary subdivisions. He also makes it clear that he will use Jewish commentators, especially Rashi, when they aid in rendering the plain sense of the biblical text. At the same time, Nicholas says his intention in studying the prophetic narrative is to recover the mystery of Christ, his humiliation, and exaltation. Thus, at the beginning of his commentary one finds the same themes of the prologues, the literal and the spiritual, set forth without apparent tension as the unified goal of his exegesis.

In Isa. 2:1-4, after recapitulating the fall of the kingdom of Judah described in chapter 1, Nicholas turns to portray the reign of Christ in these verses. Both Christians and Jews agree that the subject of the passage is the reign of the Messiah, but he notes that there is a fundamental disagreement between them regarding the identity of the promised, eschatological Savior. Jews reject the Christian claim of Jesus as the Christ. Nicholas then lists the Jewish arguments for rejecting this claim, and why the messianic hope was not fulfilled with the coming of Jesus.

To the objection that the term "latter days" must lie in the future and not in the past, Nicholas mounts a philological case for seeing two different usages of the formula. It could be used in an absolute sense, or in a sequential sense to designate a new beginning in contrast with events preceding it. However, citing Genesis 49, he argues for a non-absolute interpretation that allowed events from the past to be fulfilled by Christ's advent. To the objection that Mount Zion was not physically altered with Jesus' coming, Nicholas appeals to Rashi for a warrant that the passage is to be understood parabolically. The miraculous events were thus fulfilled in the healing ministry of Jesus. To the objection that no universal peace ensued, Nicholas relates the promise of world peace to that afforded by the Roman rule under Augustus and by the conversion of the Gentiles under the reign of Constantine.

Significantly, Nicholas concludes that the Isaianic passage in chapter 2 is to be interpreted literally in reference to the coming of Jesus Christ. Moreover, there is no attempt to interpret an initial fulfillment prior to that offered by the New Testament in reference to Jesus. One is at first surprised to see the large concentration of rationalistic arguments he presents in defense of this position.

Chapter 7 offers another lengthy exposition of a messianic passage. Once again, Nicholas's intention is to demonstrate that the chief purpose of the chapter is to announce the advent of Jesus Christ. His main energy is directed against Jews and against those traditional Christians who do not want to attribute the prophetic text to Christ — *ad litteram*.

He again initially lists the objections to his referring the text directly to Christ. Many arguments have traditionally been used by the Jews and have evoked a long history of Christian apologetics. First, the objection was raised that the sign to Ahaz could not possibly refer to the birth of Jesus some five hundred years later. Second, the Hebrew noun *almah* is not a reference to a virgin. Third, in the New Testament Jesus is always referred to by his personal name, not as Immanuel. Finally, judgment would fall on Israel's enemies before the child was able to call "my mother, my father" (8:4), but Jesus as divine was never lacking in knowledge. This last objection stemmed from a Christian response to Nicholas's literal identification of prophecy and fulfillment.

Nicholas's response is largely traditional, but he does appeal to Rashi's authority in rejecting Hezekiah as the alleged reference of the sign. He also mounts a philological argument that was not unique to him, but that he refined. He argues that the term "sign" can function as a foretaste of a future event, but also as a retrospective recognition of a promise only understood after the event. Finally, the identification of Jesus in the New Testament with Immanuel was made to highlight prophetically the unique qualities of the Savior, and also to point to the dual nature of Christ, human and divine. Nicholas usually retains such theological reflections for his *Postilla moralis* rather than the *Postilla litteralis*. Again what is surprising is that Nicholas does not appeal to a *sensus duplex litteralis,* but comes down strongly with the New Testament's fulfillment as the only true interpretation of the Isaianic text, one that is *ad litteram.*

This same pattern for interpreting the messianic texts of Isaiah continues in his treatment of Isa. 8. Nicholas's interpretation is significant in showing his explicit disagreement with Thomas concerning the role of *ad litteram.* Nicholas begins by repeating and confirming Thomas's objection to a traditional Christian interpretation that advocates a figurative reading of this passage (e.g., Cyril). The arguments defending a figurative interpretation of chapter 8 turned on the inappropriateness of a command to a holy prophet to approach his wife for cohabitation. Again, it was suggested that Uriah was an idolater and not fit for a truthful witness (8:2). Then again, Zechariah the son of Jeberechiah (v. 2) had not yet been born and could not have served as a witness. Thomas succeeded in refuting these arguments and proceeded to opt for a literal reading of the text in which the promised son of chapter 8 was the natural son of the prophet Isaiah. Up to this point Nicholas agrees with Thomas in rejecting a figurative reading, but he strongly disagrees with Thomas's identification of the child in chapter 8 with the prophet Isaiah's son as the proper literal referent of the passage.

Rather, taking his lead from the targum, Nicholas interprets the sentence in 8:4, "I went to the prophetess," not as the voice of the prophet, but rather of God (Cyril followed a similar, but less developed theory). God is addressing the "prophetess" Mary according to Luke 1. The Zechariah of Isaiah 8 is actually the minor prophet, who prophesied at the time of Darius in Ezra 6. Zechariah's prophecy of consolation refers to Zech. 9: "Lo, your king comes to you . . . humble and riding on an ass" (v. 9), which points to the advent of Christ lying still in the future.

As a result of this reading, both imaginative and tortuous, Nicholas is able to claim that Isaiah 8 is a literal reference to the coming of Christ, foretold in Zech. 9. Nicholas thus follows in Thomas's footsteps in rejecting the church's traditional figurative interpretation, but he departs from Thomas in rejecting his identification of the son as Isaiah's. Ironically, Nicholas's literal interpretation accepts many features of the earlier figurative reading, say, of Cyril, but now named by Nicholas as *ad litteram.*

The more significant implication of Nicholas's exegesis is that his interpretation, at least respecting the messianic passages, does not represent a *duplex sensus litteralis,* but identifies the Old Testament prophecy directly with the New Testament's fulfillment. The effect is that in this passage, Isaiah 8 seems to have lost its Old Testament context completely and appears to be a step backwards from that of Thomas. The disturbing question raised by the prologue remains, as to whether or not Nicholas has simply incorporated the church's traditional, figurative readings within the category of the literal.

Finally, Nicholas's interpretation of Isa. 9 once again reveals a similar pattern for handling the prophet's messianic passages. In arguing only for the one *ad litteram* reading of the passage as that which agrees with Matt. 1, Nicholas again launches a lengthy apologetic directed against following those traditional Catholic interpreters who saw in Isa. 9 reference to the two assaults against Israel under Tiglathpileser (2 Kings 15) as an initial fulfillment of divine judgment. Rather, using philological and geographical evidence, he concludes that the passage has its only *ad litteram* fulfillment in Christ, and that the passage addresses Christ's exaltation and act of liberation. Nor does Nicholas shift his perspective in treating Isa. 11, which reads *ad litteram,* as promise to both Jews and Christians of Christ's reign incorporating the conversion of the Jews.

V. The *Postilla Moralis*

Up to this point the focus has been on Nicholas's commentary in the *Postilla litteralis.* Yet Nicholas also wrote a *Postilla moralis,* the approach to which he summarized in the so-called third prologue.

The major contribution of this prologue was Nicholas's development of a theory of parabolic interpretation. This was necessary because many biblical passages appeared to have no literal sense, and the interpreter was forced to move immediately to a non-literal reading. Yet when one turns to Nicholas's treatment of those passages in Isaiah that are most usually associated with a non-literal, parabolic meaning, one is disappointed with the lack of a rich exposition. The parable of chapter 5 seems to be a rather flat and unimaginative exposition that gains little from the parabolic language and style of the genre.

Similarly, chapter 19 ("Behold, the Lord is riding on a swift cloud and comes to Egypt") traditionally affords a rich text for a figurative, Christological reading of Christ's descent into Egypt (cf. Cyril). However, Nicholas attempts to interpret the chapter *ad litteram,* but ends up offering a reading largely in accord with Matt. 2. He speaks of the mystery of the Word of God moving to convert the Gentiles and of the persecution of the apostles according to Acts 13. In sum, just as the figurative senses are absorbed within the category of the literal, once again the genre of the parabolic seems to provide little in the way of a recovery of a fresh dimension.

Of more significance is Nicholas's concern for rendering a moral or homiletical reading of Isaiah. Here one can see Nicholas's deep pastoral concerns and his efforts to address an actual audience of Christian believers. Thus, in his moral commentary on chapter 1 he seeks to apply the Isaianic judgment delivered to the people of Jerusalem to his own historical context. The clergy and those of higher rank are the most vulnerable to the prophet's attack, and Nicholas singles out this class from the simple people who are oppressed by the abuses of the wealthy. In chapter 5, Nicholas uses the parable to attack the evils of the church and those who fail to respond to God's gracious gifts. Almost immediately Christ is identified with the beloved one in the parable, and the text is easily fitted into a Christological pattern.

Chapter 7 of the *Postilla moralis* is significant in showing how different his interpretation is from a carefully developed traditional reading. Rather, in Nicholas's reading, Jerusalem signifies the spirit of faith according to the *sensum moraliter*. Rezin, whose name means iniquity, signifies arrogance, just as Pekah signifies avarice. Is it significant that in his prologues, when contrasting the difference between the literal and the figurative, Nicholas's figurative attempt is far subtler, and he does not hang his non-literal reading on simple linguistic identifications? Occasionally, as in Isa. 11, Nicholas develops the theme of the mystery of Christ by comparing it to a good pastor who carries a staff to protect his flock.

I would suggest that one of the main problems with Nicholas's *Postilla moralis* is that, although he has sought to retain a homiletical and applicative sense of the Old Testament to supplement his earlier emphasis on the literal sense, he in effect has lost any serious hermeneutical linkage between these two levels of scripture. There is no reflection, as one finds in Origen or Augustine, on how one moves from one level of meaning to another. Rather, the practical comments appear to be largely pious aphorisms, not in any sense trivial, but without any organic connection to his main exegetical interpretation of the book of Isaiah.

VI. Summary Reflections and Conclusions

In our previous review of the relation of the literal to the spiritual in Nicholas's understanding, we discussed a series of unresolved anomalies arising from his formulations within the several prologues. Most of these initial difficulties have not received any great clarification from a study of his Isaiah commentary. Instead, the hermeneutical problems seem to have intensified.

Nicholas's exegesis of Isaiah is dominated by his research for the *sensus litteralis*. He inherited from the Christian exegetical traditions a long history of apologetic defenses against Jewish objections to the Christian reading of Isaiah. Nicholas expands his apologetic defenses in an effort to undercut interpretations of the messianic passages that would find a first fulfillment in the Old Testament period. The result is that the literal meaning of Isaiah's oracles has been increasingly identified solely with the New Testament's interpretation. In the second prologue there is talk of a double-literal sense, but in the Isaiah commentary little use is made of this hermeneutical device. Rather, the literal fulfillment is consistently identified with the advent of Christ.

The effect of Nicholas's approach is that often interpretations that were once understood as the spiritual or figurative meaning of the text have been largely retained, but now have been incorporated within the rubric of the literal. Kiecker ("The Hermeneutical Principles," pp. 76-77) argues that the blurring of the distinction between the literal and the spiritual in Nicholas derived from Thomas's theory of meaning as divine intention. Kiecker's hypothesis remains plausible, but the Isaiah commentary provides no further evidence to support it. There are no explicit references to authorial intent as the force effecting the shift from a literal/spiritual polarity to the literal/literal scheme. At best one can see Thomas's influence in Nicholas's preoccupation with the literal sense.

Again, like Thomas, Nicholas stands within a Christian exegetical tradition that inherited a concern for scripture's figurative senses. Earlier we traced the subtlety with which Thomas used intertextual references largely taken from the New Testament to signal his theological concern to forge continuity between the two testaments in a unity of substance derived from the extension of the literal sense into the spiritual. Unfortunately, much of this hermeneutical skill seems lacking in Nicholas.

Of course, Nicholas reveals his active interest in the spiritual dimension of scripture in his *Postilla moralis.* Yet as emerges from his Isaiah commentary, these homiletical remarks seem strangely isolated from his exegesis of the literal sense, and lack the organic link between the different dimensions of scripture's meaning. Moreover, when occasionally there is attention paid to the spiritual or mystical level in his *Postilla litteralis,* the comments seem often flat, conventional, and lacking in the sustained brilliant exposition found in Origen or Cyril. The only obvious exception to this assessment is found in his commentary on the Song of Songs, which offers a serious, often profound interpretation of its spiritual sense, even when it is, in fact, rendered as its literal, parabolic sense.

Bibliography of Nicholas of Lyra

Primary Sources

Biblia Sacra cum Glossa Ordinaria. 6 vols. Antwerp, 1617.

Biblia Latina cum Glossa Ordinaria, edited by K. Froehlich and M. J. Gibson. 4 vols. Turnhout: Brepols, 1992.

For manuscripts and printed editions of Nicholas's works, cf. P. Glorieux, *Répertoire des maîtres en théologie de Paris au XIIIe Siècle,* vol. 2, pp. 215-31, Études de philosophie médievale 18. Paris: Vrin, 1933.

Secondary Sources

Bunte, W. *Rabbinische Traditionene bei Nicolaus von Lyra: Ein Beitrag zur Schriftauslegung des Spätmittelalters.* Judentum und Umwelt, 58. Frankfurt, 1994.

Ebeling, G. *Evangelische Evangelienauslegung.* Munich: Albert Lempp, 1942.

Fischer, M. "Des Nicholaus von Lyra postillae perpetuae in Vetus et Novum Testamentum in ihrem eigenthümlichen Unterschied von der gleichzeitigen Schriftauslegung." *Jahrbücher für Protestantische Theologie* 15 (1889): 403-71, 578-619.

Froehlich, K. "Nicholas of Lyra (c. 1270-1349)." In *Dictionary of Biblical Interpretation,* vol. 2, edited by J. H. Hayes, pp. 206-8. Nashville: Abingdon, 1999.

Hailperin, H. *Rashi and the Christian Scholars,* pp. 137-246. Pittsburgh: University of Pittsburgh Press, 1963.

————. "Nicholas de Lyra and Rashi: The Minor Prophets." In *Rashi Anniversary Volume,* pp. 115-47. Texts and Studies, vol. 1. Philadelphia: Jewish Publication Society, 1941.

Kiecker, J. G. "The Hermeneutical Principles and Exegetical Methods of Nicholas of Lyra, O.F.M. (c. 1270-1349)." Ph.D. dissertation, Marquette University, 1978.

————, ed. *The Postilla of Nicholas of Lyra on the Song of Songs.* Milwaukee: Marquette University, 1998.

Krey, P. D. W. "Nicholas of Lyra: Apocalypse Commentator, Historian and Critic." *Franciscan Studies* 52 (1992): 53-84.

Krey, P. D. W., and L. Smith, eds. *Nicholas of Lyra: The Senses of Scripture.* Leiden: Brill, 2000.

Labrosse, H. "Nicolas de Lyre." *Études Franciscaines* 16 (1906): 383-404; 17 (1907): 489-505, 593-608; 19 (1908): 41-52, 153-75, 368-79; 35 (1923): 171-87, 400-432.

Langlois, C. V. "Nicholas de Lyre, Frère Mineur." *Histoire littéraire de la France* 36 (1927): 355-400.

Lubac, H. de. *Exégèse Médiévale. Les Quatre Sens de L'Écriture,* vol. 2-2, pp. 345-37. Paris: Aubier, 1964.

Merrill, E. H. "Rashi, Nicholas de Lyra, and Christian Exegesis." *Westminster Theological Journal* 38 (1975): 66-79.

Patton, C. L. "Nicholas of Lyra (c. 1270-1349)." In *Historical Handbook of Major Biblical Interpreters,* edited by D. K. McKim, pp. 116-22. Downers Grove, Ill.: InterVarsity Press, 1998.

Preus, J. S. *From Shadow to Promise: Old Testament Interpretation from Augustine to the Young Luther,* pp. 61-71. Cambridge, Mass.: Harvard University Press, 1969.

Smalley, B. *The Study of the Bible in the Middle Ages.* 2nd edition. Oxford: Clarendon, 1952.

Spicq, C. *Esquisse d'une histoire de l'exégèse Latine au Moyen Age.* Paris: Vrin, 1944.

13

Martin Luther
(1483–1546)

I. Introduction

To enter into the arena and to wrestle with Luther's exegetical approach to the Old Testament is an awesome task, and much beyond the capacity of any one scholar. Not only is the sheer range of his biblical writings quite overwhelming, but the amount of secondary literature that engages in continual controversy over Luther's contribution evokes a sense of the enormity of the enterprise. Even to recall again Heinrich Bornkamm's provocative characterization, "If one could divide Luther's professorship . . . into two fields . . . , one would have to call Luther a professor of Old Testament rather than of New Testament exegesis" (*Luther and the Old Testament*, p. 7), highlights the impossibility of avoiding the challenge in relation to this project.

The only way for us to enter this field in these pages is to focus on a very limited number of issues. Therefore, the goal of this chapter, as in previous sections, is restricted to an analysis of the hermeneutical issues involved in Luther's exegesis of the book of Isaiah. The primary text remains Luther's lectures on Isaiah in 1527-30 (*Martin Luthers Werke. Kritische Gesamtausgabe* [*WA*] 31, II; *American Edition of Luther's Works* [*LW*], vols. 16 and 17) as well as his two later studies in 1543-44 of Isa. 9 and 53 (*WA* 40, III).

II. Luther's Exegetical Tradition

One of the features of the modern study of Luther has been the rediscovery of his medieval roots. Previously the sharp break with the past — religious, cultural, political — that the Reformation evoked tended to render peripheral the inherited medieval aspects of Luther's background. Moreover, it was often assumed that the new Reformation theology was a return to the pristine New Testament church, and that the medieval period with all the accretions of Catholicism had little of significance for interpreting the revival of the true Christianity in the sixteenth century. Of course, this perspective has greatly changed thanks to the work of several generations of Luther scholars, and the shift in perspective has been ably summarized by numerous volumes such as Heiko Oberman's *The Harvest of Medieval Theology* (1963) or J. S. Preus's *From Shadow to Promise: Old Testament Interpretation from Augustine to the Young Luther* (1969).

Considerable attention has focused on Luther's use of earlier sources in his biblical exegesis. There is a general agreement that the most important source was the *Glossa Ordinaria,* including both the marginal and interlinear notes. It is also evident that Luther made use directly of certain of his favorite Church Fathers, especially Augustine and Ambrose. He had a passing acquaintance with Origen, to whom he consistently voiced his strong disagreement. His relation to Jerome was quite different in spite of the elements of shared Alexandrian theology, and Luther, like most previous Christian interpreters, was often dependent on him as the source for much of his technical, philological, historical, and geographical information. However, Luther was generally critical of Jerome's actual interpretation as being too much under the allegorical influence of Origen. To what extent Luther was influenced by German mystics continues to be debated, but certainly there was some, and the sermons of Bernard and Tauler were held in much esteem, which also served as a source of this piety. From the medieval period the *Postillae perpetuae* of Nicholas of Lyra was a major influence in transmitting in great detail not only the Christian exegetical tradition, but especially the Jewish rabbinical traditions of Rashi and others.

One of the most significant debates in regard to Luther's relation to medieval tradition turns on his use of allegory. The issue is complex for a number of reasons. On the one hand, early in his career, Luther had harsh things to say in rejecting the allegorical method. On the other hand, Luther continued to employ various forms of allegory in his biblical interpretation throughout most of his career, as Gerhard Ebeling has pointed out (*Evangelische Evangelienauslegung,* pp. 44ff.).

Ebeling introduces his study of the subject by first summarizing the general consensus among Luther scholars that developed in the late nineteenth century and extended into the early decades of the twentieth century. It has been argued that, although in principle Luther rejected the fourfold medieval exegetical approach by 1517, he was never fully consistent in his actual practice. Under the pressure of habit and from practical needs arising from his preaching, he continued to fall back on the old tradition. Others suggest that in treating certain rhetorical forms he used allegory as a complement to enrich his grammatical sense of the text. Still others argue that he retained elements of allegorical exegesis as a sort of escape mechanism when his literal interpretation of a passage seemed unsatisfactory. Finally, there is widespread agreement that in his mature period, he used allegory less and less, and that it was pushed to the periphery as a result of his focus on the theological content. It is also clear that the use of allegory assumed a somewhat different function in respect to the Old Testament from that of the New.

In his 1942 Zurich dissertation, Ebeling pursued the subject of Luther's approach to allegory within the broad perspective of an analysis of Luther's hermeneutics. By narrowing his scope to his handling of the Gospels, Ebeling was able exhaustively to analyze Luther's use of allegory in his preaching from 1522 to 1529, and then beyond to 1540. What emerged from his study was that indeed the appeal to an allegorical approach greatly diminished. Yet at the same time there was never a systematic pronouncement that in principle set forth his rejection of the medieval tradition. Rather, the shift occurred gradually as a corollary to Luther's own theological and hermeneutical development.

Some of the complexity of the problem emerges from the diversity of terminology Luther used. He spoke of "allegory," "figurative," "mystical," "secret," and "spiritual" without making any clear distinctions. Luther was certainly aware of the metaphorical use of language, and from the beginning he showed great literary skill. He objected to the rigidity of the fourfold medieval approach to exegesis as blunting the full force of scripture as plain speech, unencumbered with subtle levels of figuration. Yet while rejecting the traditional model, Luther did retain along with the literal, plain sense of scripture a tropological sense that called for the proper moral response to the commands of God. This concern did not arise from an intentional hermeneutical adjustment, but flowed from the content of the scriptures that always possessed an existential dimension for its readers.

Ebeling struggled hard to arrive at a precise definition of the term "allegory." In spite of Luther's widely varied vocabulary, he clearly recognized the difference between the parable/simile and the allegory/metaphor. In the former, meaning is concealed in words but is revealed by following the leads of the words themselves. Thus, the real meaning of the parable of the vineyard in Isa. 5 is at first hidden, but then exposed by a reading of the text itself. In contrast, an allegory is an extended metaphor whose meaning is only unlocked by a key provided outside of the text. The allegory says one thing but means another.

The complexity of the use of allegory occurs when a non-figurative passage without any apparent figurative speech forms is rendered as an allegory on the assumption that the divine author, namely the Holy Spirit, intended something different from the verbal sense of the words. After considerable reflection, Ebeling accepted Adolf Jülicher's definition of allegory:

> Allegorical interpretation is the rendering of a text under the assumption that what it says clearly hides something else which obtains its meaning from somewhere else. The effect is that the actual words and larger units of the text have been replaced more or less completely by a comparative rendering by means of concepts which belong to a foreign sense of the text and derive from an intention independent of its literary composition. (*Evangelische Evangelienauslegung*, p. 48)

There are several problems with Jülicher's definition of allegory. First, even though Jülicher's formulation serves to define allegory with considerable clarity when allegory is largely conceived of in the narrow sense of the traditional threefold/fourfold scheme, it reflects elements of modernization and rationalism that prejudge its results from the outset. It is one thing to make a literary judgment that allegory says one thing but means something else. (This definition is indeed shared by Luther: "Allegoria est, das man ein dingk furgibt und verstehts anders, den die wortt lauten." *WA, Tischreden* 2; 2772a, cited by Ebeling, p. 47). It is quite another to suggest that the allegorical rendering is by definition "foreign" to the text. Clearly a value judgment is at work that measures the worth of a figurative sense in terms of its correspondence to the text's literal meaning. In contrast, the Church Fathers measured the truth of the figurative sense not as foreign, but as stemming from the *res* (substance) of the text itself. The source of the figurative was not separated from the text and assigned to an alien "from somewhere," but rather regarded as a different and true dimension of the selfsame reality. Implied in Jülicher's definition is that the literal/historical is the one true interpretation, and the figurative is a substitute and alteration falsely imposed from some other source than the text.

Secondly, for Jülicher allegory is defined almost exclusively in terms of the medieval fourfold scheme, which greatly narrows the scope of the analysis, particularly in respect to Luther. Although in his earlier period Luther focused his criticism of allegory according to the narrow definition (cf. the summary of Gen. 1-3, *LW*, vol. 1, pp. 231-33), increasingly he employed a different sense of allegory used in the broadest sense of figuration to designate the hidden, spirit-filled understanding of the text's true meaning. Luther's move is clearly not from the literal/historical meaning to a fourfold allegory, but the text is understood by means of a theological dialectic of flesh and spirit. The same text has a different referent depending on its context and on the activity of the Spirit. A major criticism of Origen targets his separating the literal/historical from its figurative sense, and thus losing the one true Christological content — whether in the Old Testament or the New — that is found in the concrete form of the scriptures when illuminated by the Spirit and seen through the eyes of faith. Later, as we shall see, this same dialectic was increasingly formulated in terms of law and gospel. In this chapter, I shall argue that Luther, along with the Church Fathers, shares this allegorical tradition in which the true meaning of the scripture is different from interpretation only through the eyes of unbelief apart from its Christological content revealed by the ever-present Christ.

III. Luther's Exegetical Approach

In spite of the recent recovery of Luther's medieval roots, one must still speak of the Reformation as a turning point in the history of exegesis. Accordingly, much effort has been expended in trying to determine the major forces at work, especially in the shaping of Luther's biblical interpretation.

In his essay "Luthers Bedeutung für den Fortschritt der Auslegungskunst," Karl Holl reviews Luther's break with the traditional allegorical method in which he had been trained. Holl describes Luther's massive intellectual achievement in sensing the organic connection between the objective grammatical, literary structure of the biblical canon and the inner experiential world of the author. With great care he pursues the development of Luther's hermeneutical circle between Word and Spirit in his battle with the Protestant enthusiasts. He also traces Luther's enormous literary achievements in penetrating to the heart of scripture by both recovering and transforming scripture's inner and outer world, which he then filtered through his own subjective emotions. In the end, Holl concludes that it was Luther's contribution to the literary art of interpreting a text, pursued by Matthias Flacius, that stands out and made possible the development of the science of hermeneutics. In a word, he anticipated the intellectual breakthrough that culminates in the Enlightenment, reaching its pinnacle in Schleiermacher.

While I do not for a moment denigrate Holl's brilliant analysis, and I embrace with appreciation the breadth and depth of his portrait of Luther, in the end I do not think that he has penetrated to the heart of Luther's exegetical contribution, which was in every respect driven by a burning theological passion, namely, to see the presence of Christ in all of scripture. Indeed Luther and Erasmus shared much in common in the sixteenth century, but their differences now emerge far greater than their similarities. The same judgment must also be passed on Luther and Schleiermacher. There are certainly lines connecting Luther with the Enlightenment, but the discontinuities in this broken history are more significant than the continuities.

In Luther's early period, a fundamental concern of his fell on delineating the antithesis between letter and spirit. His sustained objective was to understand scripture in such a way that it did not remain merely letter (cf. Ebeling, *Luther,* p. 98). Of course, Paul had first formulated this contrast in 2 Cor. 3:6: "The letter kills, but the spirit gives life." In this passage the Apostle was drawing a sharp distinction between the law of the old covenant and the spiritual nature of the new. However, in the subsequent Christian exegetical tradition, especially as interpreted by Origen, the antithesis was understood in the Platonic sense of the letter being the sphere of sense perception, whereas the spirit was that which reached beyond the letter by means of allegorical interpretation. The letter was therefore construed as outwardly oriented, whereas spirit was inwardly or heavenly directed.

Luther rejected in strongest terms this Platonic interpretation of Paul. He then extended the biblical terminology far beyond Paul's original context to express a fundamental distinction by which to understand scripture as a whole. The letter that kills is an interpretation apart from the life-giving Spirit that makes the text come alive. The commands of God in the Decalogue can be rendered according to the letter that kills, but the same text can become life-giving if its true Christological content is understood. Therefore for Luther the literal sense is not the historical *per se,* but the Christological incorporated within the historical. Thus, Luther can state that the basic meaning of all of scripture is that which concerns Christ.

The biblical text does not consist of four separate layers, each possessing its own independent meaning, but is rather the one unified voice of God addressed to its hearers. Its meaning is not to be abstracted through an allegorical filter; it remains in all its concrete, historical particularity. In this form it both reveals and conceals its true subject matter. Because of its historical particularity, scripture shares in the language, customs, and literary style of its time, which therefore demands the most careful philological, historical, and literary analysis. Luther's continual emphasis on the importance for biblical exegesis of language, style, and structural analysis thus stems from a basic theological concern and was never an end in itself. The same motivation was the basis of his desire to translate the Bible into vernacular speech, to make the text "speak German."

As mentioned above, Luther attacked the traditional fourfold method of exegesis for blunting and confusing the living, preached Word. The objective Word of scripture was an active and dynamic voice of proclamation, not first written, but spoken and heard. Moreover, it was a word that evoked a response and was consistently existential in its intention. Luther joined to his emphasis on the objective force of the preached Word a tropological dimension, not as a separate, moral level of the text, but as part of the essential role of scripture in calling for an answer to the divine imperatives.

With his understanding of the category of letter and spirit, Luther was able to wage an exegetical war with both the Roman Catholic Church on the right, and the new spirit-filled Protestant enthusiasts on the left. Against the Roman Catholic tradition he rejected the claim that the institutional church possessed the key to the correct interpretation of the Bible. Once scriptural meaning was understood as a relationship between Word and faith, the traditional role of the church as the only legitimate vehicle by which divine authority was transmitted was destroyed. In his *Preface to St. James and St. Jude* Luther gave his bold and radical formulation of his case:

> All the genuine books agree on this, that all of them preach and inculcate Christ. . . . Whatever does not teach Christ is not yet apostolic, even though St. Peter or St. Paul does the teaching. Again, whatever preaches Christ would be apostolic, even if Judas, Annas, Pilate and Herod were doing it. (*LW,* vol. 35, p. 396)

Against the left-wing enthusiasts who denied in principle all the elements in the outward forms of Christian faith, and subordinated the objective word to personal claims of the Spirit, Luther argued that there was no Spirit apart from outward form. The unity of the letter and the spirit remains in a dialectical tension, and the Spirit cannot be individualized and abstracted from tradition and doctrine. Clearly it was extremely painful for Luther to have his earlier message of the liberating power of the Spirit now turned against him.

In Luther's middle and late periods, the categories of law and gospel largely replaced those of letter and spirit. He did not see this move as a fundamental shift of perspective, but rather as a more useful rubric performing the same hermeneutical task, broader in its theological implications. This category also served him forcefully in his continuing disputations, and lent itself to an immense theological expansion within this dialectic. Where Christ is preached, the distinction radically defines the different natures of the gospel as the Word of faith and the law as the religion that kills.

Luther conceived of this distinction as a flexible one, in the sense that the recovery of the gospel within scripture was never a static given, lest it itself turn once again into law. For this reason scripture remains the active, dynamic preached Word that continues to free. Within the homiletical task allegory can serve as a useful tool for embroidering a text to creative application, but it is never a substitute for the literal, plain sense on which it is based.

In a real sense, Luther's understanding of history is "pre-critical" in nature. That is, when the Bible depicts an event, he assumes that it is historical. Luther had no developed sense of *Heilsgeschichte* in the modern manner of distinguishing between *Historie* and *Geschichte*. Nevertheless, even here, certain important observations are to be made. For Luther, biblical history was not literal in the modern sense of historical-factual interpretation, but in the "literal, prophetic sense" (cf. Bornkamm, p. 88) of pointing to the coming of Christ. For Luther, biblical history was the history of the people of God recounted in order to reveal the purpose of God in redeeming Israel and the nations. Therefore, when interpreting Gen. 1–3, Luther was at pains not to follow the allegorical leads of Origen and Augustine, but to retain the biblical depiction of events in its plain, straightforward sense. He constantly ruled out as idle speculation questions that had been raised regarding elements of the creation, and he reminded his hearers that scripture speaks in a language directed to the uneducated, simple people of God.

The changing relationship between Luther and Erasmus provides an important commentary on their strikingly different hermeneutical positions. In his early period Luther expressed admiration for Erasmus's great learning, and he used his critical Greek text of the New Testament with gratitude. Yet before long, he became highly critical of Erasmus's biblical interpretation. He recognized a new and threatening front opening up in a form of humanistic learning personified in Erasmus. At first Erasmus appeared to share in Luther's criticism of the Catholic church's use of scripture. However, shortly he found that Erasmus's learned and witty interpretations never reached to the true theological content of scripture, but rather fragmented its meaning into confusion by proposing multiple options of interpretation that seemed to Luther either trivial or irrelevant. Thus the issues at stake in this controversy went far beyond differing individual temperaments, but were substantial in nature. It is interesting to note that Erasmus continued to champion allegorical interpretation as edifying and useful, and thus in this respect was hardly a precursor of the eighteenth-century Enlightenment.

Any discussion of Luther's hermeneutical approach to scripture must focus at some point specifically on his Old Testament interpretation in contrast to his New Testament interpretation. Earlier I suggested that Luther's view of history did not contain a developed theory of *Heilsgeschichte* akin to the modern view, in which sacred history is distinguished in some manner from ordinary secular events. Nevertheless, Luther stood firmly within the ancient Christian tradition in seeing the Old Testament as containing the divine promises of the gospel that were only fulfilled in the New. At times Luther expressed clearly a supersessionist view of the relation between the testaments:

> The promises of Moses . . . do not last longer than the statutes and judgments served. For that reason the Old Testament finally had to become obsolete and had to be put aside; it had to serve as a prefiguration of the New and eternal Testament which began before the ages and will endure beyond the ages. The Old Testament, however, began in time and after a time came to an end. (*The Deuteronomy of Moses*, 1525; *Luther's Works*, 9, p. 63)

Two questions will have to be addressed in order properly to evaluate this characterization of the Old Testament. First, to what extent did Luther's development of theological categories such as letter and spirit and law and gospel seriously alter his early supersessionist view? Secondly, is there any evidence that he was led to modify and to alter this position in his later period?

Luther reflected traditional Christian interpretation of the Old Testament in his direct application of its text to Jesus Christ. In his treatise *How Christians Should Regard Moses* (1525), Luther listed the messianic prophecies found in the Pentateuch. His list includes all the familiar passages: the Protoevangelium of Gen. 3:15, the blessing of Abraham's seed (Gen. 22:18), the promise of a prophet like Moses to be sent (Deut. 18:15, 18), and the prophecy concerning Judah (Gen. 49:10). However, Luther went far beyond this conventional list and found dozens of Christological promises that were not strictly messianic, such as David's last words (2 Sam. 23:1ff.), and a large number of psalms that he interpreted as predictions concerning Christ, his suffering, death, resurrection, and kingdom. Particular emphasis fell on Pss. 2 and 110. Then again, the prophets were a main source for expressing the promise of the coming divine ruler (Isa. 9:6; 51:4-5; 53:1ff.; 60:19ff.).

However, Luther's interpretation of the Old Testament was far from traditional, and received a major shaping by means of his new theological categories that transformed his reading. This hermeneutical shift is most clearly discerned in his understanding of law and gospel. In his early exegesis Luther followed the Christian tradition of identifying the law with the Old Testament and the gospel with the New. This divide certainly explains why, in his

Deuteronomy commentary cited above, once the gospel was fulfilled in the New Testament, the Old Testament as bearer of the law was rendered obsolete. He compared it to the Old German *Sachsenspiegel,* and accordingly viewed the Old Testament as a set of laws restricted in its place and authority only to the Jews.

However, once the law/gospel contrast was no longer identified with the formal division between the two testaments, but was defined in terms of its Christological content, the relationship of the two was fundamentally altered. The Old Testament contained gospel, whereas the New Testament could also be the bearer of the law. Of course, this dialectical understanding received its powerful warrant from the Apostle Paul. The patriarch Abraham, far from being a figure buried in Jewish history, was designated the father of Christian faith. He was justified not by the law, but by faith in Jesus Christ. As a result, the entire Old Testament could be read as a witness to the one unified plan of God for the salvation of Israel and the nations. Of course, the Old Testament as well as the New Testament could be misinterpreted according to the letter, or it could be heard as gospel according to the life-giving freedom of the Spirit.

Still the hard question remains whether the Old Testament as bearer of the gospel was only an eschatological promise to be fulfilled and thus experienced in the New Testament with the coming of Christ. In 1969 J. S. Preus (*From Shadow to Promise,* pp. 212ff.) offered an interesting proposal. He argued that in Luther's early period, as exemplified by his first Psalm lectures, the medieval Luther still understood the Psalms as speaking about a promise addressed to the future church. However, by the time of the second Psalm lectures Luther began to speak of the "faithful synagogue" as a remnant of Israel that actually received and experienced the promised divine grace. Therefore, we see a parallel between faithful Israel, who has embraced God's salvation while continuing to long for Christ's spiritual advent, and the true church of the New Testament, which continues to live in the same tension between being already redeemed, but not yet. In sum, according to Preus, Luther's supersessionist theology respecting the Old Testament was radically altered by a new grasp of a faithful witness to Christ preceding the period of the new covenant. It will be a concern of this chapter to test Preus's theory, which he based largely on the Psalms, with Luther's early and late exegesis of Isaiah.

Finally, one of the most frequent charges brought against Luther's biblical exegesis, which was first sharply formulated in the period of the Enlightenment, is that his exegesis was dominated by prior dogmatic decisions. These were imposed upon the Bible apart from its true historical context and were foreign to any evidence obtained from a plain reading of the text itself.

Moreover, it is certainly true that Luther found a warrant in the Old Testament for most of the central doctrines of the Christian church, including the divinity and humanity of Jesus Christ, his ascension to the right hand of the Father, the establishment of the church through the righteousness of faith, and even the Trinity.

Indeed, it was the doctrine of the Trinity that appeared to evoke the greatest scorn from Luther's critics. It was alleged that this Christian doctrine was not found in the New Testament, nor could one even speak of its presence in the Old. The traditional Christian appeals to the appearance of the plural form of address in Gen. 1:26, or the three figures visiting Abraham at Mamre in Gen. 18:2, or the plural form of God's name, Elohim, were increasingly dismissed as trivial.

In the light of this widespread critical attitude, it comes as a surprise to see the new scholarly research respecting Luther's understanding of the Old Testament in terms of Luther's trinitarian hermeneutic. In "Luther's Trinitarian Hermeneutic and the Old Testament," Christine Helmer has mounted the case that the textual basis for the Trinity can only be treated once the argument for the trinitarian substance *(res)* in the Old Testament is advanced. In other words, the basis for the doctrine in Luther's thought does not hinge on arbitrary appeals to certain Old Testament verses, but arises from the rendering of the divine subject matter itself. Luther focused particularly on the intra-trinitarian mystery revealed in the speech patterns within the Old Testament. He even privileged Hebrew as the language used to refer to the theological subject matter in which the mystery of the coequality between the Father and Son is grounded. Great weight was attributed to parsing with much philological precision the intra-trinitarian speech structures of Pss. 2 and 110, and of 2 Sam. 23:2ff., in which the literary exchanges signify the trinitarian reciprocity between Father and Son. These speech structures render transparent the intra-trinitarian relations and the interplay between the outer and inner speech in the divine discourse, thus providing access into the mystery of the eternal Word. With respect to the Trinity, the only material used in his analysis is the literal sense of scripture that points beyond itself to a subject matter in eternity. In sum, Luther's exegesis emerges as an exegetical model in which careful philological and theological attention to the Old Testament text recovers the true biblical grounds on which trinitarian doctrine rests.

At the conclusion of this chapter, I shall return to the issue of recovering the enormous gap that presently exists between modern biblical studies and Christian dogmatic theology, and seek to draw some implications from Luther's hermeneutics.

IV. Luther's Exegesis of the Book of Isaiah

We now turn to a more detailed focus on Luther's handling of Isaiah. Initially the focus will fall on his lectures of 1527-30 before including his final studies of 1543-44 on Isa. 9 and 53.

1. Formal Characteristics of Luther's Isaiah Exegesis

Luther's exegesis of Isaiah shows throughout that these were originally lectures. He strives to address his audience, and his concern is much in evidence. One can see often when a lecture ended, at times right in the middle of a chapter or topic.

The intensity of his lectures varies according to the nature of the subject matter. In his commentary he occasionally refers to the Church Fathers, but rarely cites them by name. At most he announces his disagreement with, say, Origen or Jerome. Later he uses a recurrent polemic against Erasmus, Zwingli, and Oecolampad in a stereotyped way to indicate various fronts on which he has done battle.

In his commentary he makes mention of Nicholas of Lyra, but usually in a negative sense, that Nicholas fails to recognize a spiritual dimension beyond the historical. Yet in his later period, particularly in his lengthy exposition of Isaiah 53, it is clear that he has engaged Nicholas in a far more detailed manner and often cites the interpretation of Jewish exegesis of Isaiah 53. It is evident that Luther's knowledge of Rashi is completely dependent on Nicholas. He cites, for example, Lyra's observation that the early rabbis understood Isaiah 53 as messianic, a position still reflected in the targum, but later rabbis substituted a corporate interpretation. In both the earlier and later periods Luther's running controversy with the Jews remains fully negative and is more akin to the vocabulary of John's Gospel than that of the Synoptics.

The intensity of Luther's focus on philological references varies greatly. In the preface to his Isaiah commentary, he states at the outset with much force that two kinds of knowledge are necessary for biblical interpretation: knowledge of grammar and knowledge of the historical background of the text. The latter is necessary not only to interpret the events reported, but also to provide a source of Isaiah's rhetoric and dialectic. Of course, what Luther means by historical background is largely confined to the Bible's own words. Still, he was not averse to employing occasional material from Josephus and selected classical writers. Luther makes passing linguistic comments throughout the Isaiah commentary, contrasting at times the Hebrew with the Latin sense of a word. His philological analysis of the difference between *mishpat* and *sedek* (Isa. 1:17) is precise and illuminating. At several places he observes that the Hebrew verbs rendered in the past tense are best translated in German in the present tense, but this is hardly a new discovery for him. However, when treating Isa. 53 in his later exegesis of 1540, there is much more serious exegetical use of the Hebrew text. In his treatment of the term "servant" he cites the Septuagint and Vulgate texts along with parallel passages elsewhere from Isaiah in order to confirm his interpretation.

Throughout his Isaiah commentary Luther makes constant references to literary forms he gained from classical writers. He speaks of metaphor, simile, paronomasia, and irony. Certainly this interest in literary conventions assumed an even greater significance following his debates with Zwingli and the enthusiasts over the alleged metaphorical rendering of "This is my body." However, in his Isaiah commentary the literary feature that appears most frequently and with great effectiveness is the paraphrase. Frequently, after a close interpretation of a passage, Luther will introduce a phrase such as "It is as if he were saying" to render the passage in a fresh and powerful recapitulation (cf. 1:2, 5, 24). His paraphrases are neither abstractions of the biblical verses nor applications of homiletical adaptations, but rather down-to-earth reformulations that seek to bring out the exact meaning with great precision. His rich vocabulary is filled with abundant images and stems from everyday activities of agriculture, commerce, and family life (1:19).

Another feature of Luther's style shared in his Isaiah commentary is the tendency to summarize a biblical passage by formulating patterns that correspond to the wise ways of God with the world. So, for example, "the best laws are worthless if there are no good judges, but it is God who provides good magistrates" (1:26). "This is the method of our God, that he permits the enemies to climb up to the highest level . . . and then he throws them down" (33:1). "God first gives himself to the godly, and only then does he provide all good things" (1:2). "This is Scripture's way" (1:2).

In his Isaiah commentary there is not much attention paid to larger literary structures. Certainly there is little critical analysis according to the norms of later historical criticism. He observes that the prophecies of Isaiah fall into two parts (1–39 and 40–66), not on the basis of style and authorship, but according to the changing subject matter. Occasionally he corrects the traditional chapter divisions, observing that 4:1 really belongs to chapter 3 and 52:13-15 belongs to chapter 53. However, it is in his theological dialectics that Luther's critical ability emerges, not in any literary critical innovation. At the beginning of chapter 40, when he attempts to give an overview of the book of Isaiah as a whole, he views the material completely from a theological perspective. The first part of Isaiah functions as historical prophecy concerning Christ and the defeat of Assyria. In the second part, there is only prophecy. At first it is external in nature concerning Cyrus; then it is of a spiritual nature concerning Christ. The last four chapters are the most joyful, and speak only of Christ and the present church. In sum, when viewed in terms of strictly structural analysis, Luther's interests are less developed than those of Thomas or Nicholas.

2. The Nature of Prophecy

According to Luther's preface to the book of Isaiah, the leading theme of all the prophets is to keep the people in eager anticipation of the coming Christ. The prophet is one who hears the Word of God and thus says, "Thus saith the Lord." The book begins with an announcement of Isaiah's vision, but this vision is expressed not in a mystical experience, but in the oral proclamation of the living, preached Word.

The goal of all the prophets is directed to the people capable of receiving the gospel. The good news of God's salvation in Jesus Christ is the center of all prophecy. Isaiah's ministry was therefore correctly interpreted by 1 Peter 1:10: "The prophets . . . searched and inquired about this salvation." The prophet is therefore charged by the Holy Spirit to move on the people with a powerful proclamation of God's great deeds of salvation. The prophet's message also provides the grounds for establishing continuity with the task of every succeeding preacher in urging hearers to await eagerly the coming of the Savior. There is no way to deal directly with the naked godhead; Christ is our only way to God (Isa. 4:6). Therefore, the message of both the biblical prophet and his evangelical successor must be highly existential and filled with burning passion from the Holy Spirit.

Luther summarizes the historical scope of Isaiah's message in three sections: 1) the preaching of the coming of the Babylonian captivity; 2) the return from captivity; 3) its consequence for Christ's coming kingship (ch. 1). Yet behind these various stages of history is the one unified theological focus of all prophecy on Jesus Christ. Isaiah's approach, according to Luther, was not to deal in generalizations or in outlining broad schemata within history, but rather to plunge immediately into the specifics of Israel's life with words of judgment and promise. Thus chapter 1 begins with a divine judgment on a sinful nation that has forsaken the Lord and is unable to repent.

It is particularly characteristic of Isaiah according to Luther's reading to move back and forth between the spiritual kingdom of Christ and the physical kingdom of earthly rulers and powers. It is crucial, for example, when treating Isa. 9, to see that the first part of the chapter is about Christ's kingdom before the prophet turns his attention back to the rebellious kings of Israel. The spiritual and the physical intertwine whether he is addressing worship, politics, or matters of business.

3. Luther's Dialectical Method

Luther was not a systematic theologian if judged by the medieval scholastic traditions in which he was trained. He increasingly appealed to the sole authority of scripture in his early disputations with Cajetan (1518) and Eck (1519). It is therefore hardly surprising that his theological development would have affected his approach to scripture and his method of writing a commentary.

In a very real sense, Luther's approach to theology and to biblical interpretation was dialectical. (I am using the term not in the classical medieval sense, but according to its modern hermeneutical usage.) Two related but opposing terms are juxtaposed and held in tension. The theological truth being sought lay not in one philosophical abstraction, but in the subtle and ongoing interaction of the two realities confronted in an irreducibly concrete form. Most familiar in Luther's theology are the rubrics of spirit and letter, gospel and law, spiritual and physical kingdoms, external and internal, old and new creation, sin and righteousness, faith and works, hidden and revealed, old and new Israel, and finally Old and New Testaments. It is also obvious that these categories greatly overlap and in a profound sense continue to form the one central confession of the Christian faith.

Nevertheless, Luther, both in his theological treatises and in his biblical exegesis, often found a given rubric most appropriate in bringing out the central teaching of a particular subject. One must also reckon with the fact that Luther's dialectical method also meant that contradictions emerge when the arguments are abstracted from the concrete debate and interpreted as a static, harmonistic whole. So, for example, when Luther contrasted the radical newness of the gospel over against the law as old and obsolete, one could suppose at times that the same polarity obtained between the New and Old Testaments, but such an interpretation would be deeply erroneous, as can be shown by its flat denial in other contexts.

a. The Spiritual and Physical Kingdom

In the first two chapters of Isaiah, Luther uses the contrast between the spiritual and earthly kingdoms. He begins with the sinful state of Judah and Jerusalem in the days of four of its kings. The people of God have become sick, alienated from the Holy One. Their worship is corrupt; they lie desolate under God's wrath; they are comparable to Sodom and Gomorrah, except for a few survivors. But then sharply juxtaposed is the picture of Zion, the faithful city. This city redeemed by justice is deemed righteous because of God's righteous Word. Zion is the city of God because from it goes forth the Word of the Lord that establishes justice and peace between the nations.

In this portrayal the prophet moves from the physical kingdom to the spiritual. In chapter 1 the physical kingdom suffers because of sin and godlessness. But there follows the prophecy concerning the kingdom of Christ, which Luther at first ascribes to the period following the captivity. However, then Luther notes that Isaiah speaks of the spiritual kingdom whenever he describes the church of Christ. Wherever the gospel is proclaimed, there is the kingdom of Christ. The two kingdoms are not two entities, separated in time and space, for it is only out of the physical mountain that the spiritual kingdom emerges. Thus the prophet Isaiah, after speaking about Christ's spiritual domain, turns back to the kingdom of Israel, back to the temporal world (Isa. 9:8). The message that influences the nations to stream to Zion is the proclaimed Word, namely of Christ the king, of his mercy and peace. Whereas when Moses preaches the law, he is the minister of sin and death.

In other chapters the earthly and spiritual kingdoms are contrasted in terms of the spirit and the flesh (Isa. 35), or between the hidden and revealed church of Christ. Often in this context the transference from the physical to the spiritual is in terms of the church's emerging out of the remnant of the synagogue (Isa. 34). In Isaiah 60 the spiritual kingdom of Christ is described in terms of light over against darkness. "Arise and shine," light has come and the glory has appeared. The light attracts the nations to the gospel.

Often the term "allegorical" occurs in this context to illustrate the imagery of the opening of the eyes of the blind, or the ears of the deaf who now accept the gospel (35:5). Life in the spiritual kingdom is one of Christian liberty and freedom of conscience. Sin, Satan, and the law cannot subjugate it. A favorite text of Luther is Isa. 28:16, which speaks of the precious cornerstone, the foundation of Zion. Luther follows the New Testament's interpretation of Christ, the hidden stone, rejected by humanity, but the grounds for Christian faith.

Since for Luther any description of the spiritual kingdom is identified almost by reflex with the reign of Christ, the result is that all the promises of the coming redemption of Israel in so-called "Second Isaiah" (Isa. 40–66) are interpreted as prophecies concerning Christ the king. The words of comfort and the cessation of warfare are interpreted in terms of Christ's pardon. The "voice of one crying in the wilderness" is not only understood as the voice of John the Baptist, but the entire imagery of revelation of God's glory, of the transformation of the desert into a garden, is expanded upon with a running commentary from the Gospels. The contrast between the old and the new teaching is especially proclaimed from these chapters, and 2 Cor. 5:17 becomes a favorite verse to emphasize the radical newness of God's creation.

b. Law and Gospel

Luther uses the rubric contrasting law and gospel most frequently to interpret the many chapters of the prophet's attack on the sins of Israel, resulting in divine judgment. At times in Luther the contrast is stated in absolute terms:

> The Apostles are clearly entrusted with a new kind of teaching by the Holy Spirit, namely, with the Gospel. . . . For until now before the Gospel nothing was taught but the Law, terrifying and killing. (40:1)

However, most often the divine judgment is specifically directed toward the Jews, who typify life under the law. The law was given to prepare them to receive Christ, but when Christ was rejected, the law became the means of Israel's destruction (Isa. 3), and the promises of the gospel were transferred to the church. In Isa. 1 the prophet attacks Israel for its misunderstanding of the laws of sacrifice. The prophet agrees with David in Ps. 40:6, who rejected the sacrifices as a means of appeasing God. Although sacrifices were commanded by God through Moses, these are not works of merit, but when used by the godly they testify to faith. Thus the Jews are condemned by the prophet in misusing sacrifices and obscuring thereby the good institution of God by engaging in festivals of their own creation.

Life under the law is a tyranny (9:4), to use Paul's phrase. The law served first to terrify and reveal sin. When it succeeded in driving to despair, then the consolation of the gospel was offered. Christ fulfilled the demands of the law, and thus there is Christian liberty, since the law can no longer accuse and render guilty (9:8).

The dialectical relation between law and gospel comes out clearly in Luther's interpretation of Isa. 6, the prophet's vision of God. The prophet was terrified at the appearance of God as smoke filled the house. The severe judgment of an awesome God evoked the prophet's despair over his sinful condition before the Holy One of Israel. Then the seraph, the bearer of the gospel, promised the forgiveness of sins for Christ's sake and imparted to him Christ's righteousness. Through the law came the knowledge of sin, but through the gospel came the gift of grace and promise of resurrection.

According to Luther's reading, the message of Isa. 40–66 is the announcement of the gospel: "Comfort, comfort my people." Her warfare is ended because the law of sin and death has been finished through Christ's advent. God's people have been forgiven and cleansed, and apart from works of the law, forgiveness and divine freedom have been granted. What then follows in "Second Isaiah" is the portrayal of the life in the Spirit, the gospel of restoration to the new people of God.

In the preceding introduction to Luther's theology, the point was made that the rubric of spirit and flesh initially played a crucial role in formulating his dialectic, but in his middle and later periods law and gospel tended to replace his earlier emphasis. By the time of Luther's commentary on Isaiah this change became apparent. Only rarely does the use of the Spirit function as a hermeneutical device closely akin to law and gospel (but cf. 61:1). Rather, the spirit is the Holy Spirit now joined with the Word. In 59:21 Luther cites his Larger Catechism to explain the relation of the Spirit to the Word as the third member of the creed. The church confesses its faith because of the work of the Spirit and Word in effecting the forgiveness of sins. In Isa. 11, the Spirit plays a leading role in equipping the promised Messiah with its gifts: wisdom, understanding, counsel, might, and knowledge. Then Christ's fulfillment of the messianic promise in chapter 11 is illustrated with a catena of New Testament verses.

4. The Messianic Hope of Isaiah

It is hardly surprising that a commentary on Isaiah would be concerned with the topic of messianism. On the one hand, Luther's interpretation of the messianic passages of Isaiah is quite traditional. He follows, by and large, the lines established by the Church Fathers regarding chapters 7, 9, and 11. Yet on the other hand, the way in which Luther's exegesis of the Messiah flows together with his other rubrics of physical and spiritual kingdom, law and gospel, and the hidden and revealed Savior gives his treatment a somewhat unique shape.

When treating Isa. 7, Luther interprets the sign as containing one hidden and another open. To the unbelief of Ahaz the sign points to his destruction, but to the faithful it is a sign of the Messiah, the son born of a virgin and yet God and man, Immanuel. This sign was given for the sake of the remnant that the kingdom/Judah should not be destroyed until Christ would come. However, for the unbeliever, it remained concealed.

In Isaiah 9 the prophet predicts the coming of a child who will become the head of the kingdom of peace. Then the attributes of the promised Messiah are given: Wonderful Counselor, God almighty, Everlasting Father, Prince of Peace. He will reign upon the throne of David, but whereas David's reign over the Jews was physical and earth-bound, Christ has inaugurated the spiritual reign that will last forever. Christ prepares and strengthens this kingdom in the world through the Word and faith, but he does this in a hidden, concealed manner.

Isaiah 11 speaks of the spiritual king, or a shoot growing out of the stump of Jesse. Then the Spirit of God will rest on him to indicate that his kingdom will be spiritual, not physical. He will be given the spirit of wisdom and understanding. This spirit will fill him and insure a kingdom for the poor, for the lowly and faint-hearted. According to Luther his messianic reign is portrayed in "allegories": "the wolf will dwell with the lamb . . . the leopard will lie down with the kid." The church will convert the nations not by force, but by the goodness of the Word. Luther then supports the prophetic portrait throughout with citations from the Gospels showing the fulfillment in Christ's ministry.

Following the tradition of the ancient church, Luther extends the portrait of the coming Messiah throughout the entire book of Isaiah. Particularly chapters 60 and 61 are of great significance, and Luther's exegesis follows the leads of the New Testament's interpretation. Isaiah 60 is interpreted completely as a prophecy concerning Christ and his kingdom. Jerusalem is commanded to "arise, shine," to greet the light of the gospel that breaks into the darkness. The parallel to Eph. 5:14 is cited: "Await and Christ will give you light." The stark antithesis between the darkness of the law and the brightness of the gospel is developed throughout Isa. 60. The dialectic of the law and gospel is continually highlighted. To the believer the message is life, salvation, and Christ; to the unbeliever, death and darkness. Moreover, the light of the gospel attracts the nations, removing all the restrictions of the synagogue and extending to the Gentiles. Then the description of the church follows, according to both its outward and inward appearance. The foolishness of God is hidden under the cross, and the world and its rulers cannot perceive its eternal glory.

If Isa. 60 focuses on the kingdom of Christ, chapter 61 describes the head of the kingdom. Luke 4:18 teaches that Christ himself used this text as a most clear witness to his own person: "The Spirit of the Lord God is upon me, because the Lord has anointed me to bring good tidings to the afflicted." What clearer description of Christ and his ministry! He is anointed by the Spirit as the Messiah. The anointing is not a physical one, but a divine unction. He was sent to bring good tidings to the afflicted, poor, and oppressed, and to heal and bind up the brokenhearted, and to bring liberty to the captives. For Luther the morphological fit between the two testaments was indisputable.

The Messiah comes to proclaim "the year of the Lord's favor." He frees those bound by the law with the promise of forgiveness. But the year of the Lord's favor is also the day of vengeance upon the ungodly. The prophet proclaims a hard message to the hardened, and a soft, gentle one to the afflicted. The same theme of the angry Christ who executed the divine threat of the gospel (Mark 16:16) is developed at great length in Isa. 63. The prophet uses metaphorically a dreadful personification of a fearsome giant taking revenge on his enemies. Then almost immediately the prophet returns to the praise of God whose steadfast love to the house of Israel is repeated. This is his promise: God has always been the Savior.

5. The Remnant

A difficult problem within Luther's interpretation of the Old Testament turns on his understanding of the role of the remnant. The issue has broad implications for the relationships between the two testaments. We touched earlier on the subject in the preceding section on Luther's exegetical approach, and reviewed the provocative thesis of J. S. Preus respecting Luther's use of the terminology of a "faithful remnant." Our concern is now to return to the problem and discuss it in terms of Luther's Isaiah commentary.

First, it is important to see how he distinguished sharply between two types of people according to his rubric of law and gospel. In 43:21 Luther writes: "Now [God] begins to make a distinction between people and people, between the people of the Church and the people of the Law." The people of the old law formed and fashioned themselves. They praise their own works and are their own people. But the people of the New Testament are "my people, formed by me." They understand true worship. In this passage there is the sharpest distinction made between the people of the Old and those of the New Testament, which threatens all lines of continuity.

However, in other passages, Luther's approach to the problem of the old and new peoples is far more nuanced. The issue focuses on his understanding of the role of the remnant. In 43:14 God reminds the Chaldean fugitives that "He had bestowed this blessing (on them) for the sake of the kingdom of Israel, which he had to preserve until Christ. . . . There had to be an Israel until Christ. All deeds and acts were a prelude before Christ." Or again, in Isa. 2:1: "After the Babylonian Captivity, a part of the Kingdom of Judah was preserved in order that it might be the seed of the coming reign of Christ, to whom it was bound. Therefore, this people could not be completely rejected until the lawful reign of Christ had come." Then again in 7:3: "Shear-jashub bore the image of the people, of whom a remnant has always been preserved . . . for whose sake the king with the rest of the ungodly experience the mercy of God." Finally, in 9:7, one reads: "David's reign over the Jews was physical . . . but finally Christ has begun his spiritual reign." Christ's reign is different from David's, yet it is a reign over the same people.

The point being made in these passages is that there is a historical continuity between the old physical people and the new spiritual people. The term "remnant" is not only those who are the godly seed for the new, but the physical remnant of the old Israel is necessary for the coming of the spiritual kingdom.

The question then arises: in what sense was the spiritual kingdom of Christ only a promise for the future and not an Old Testament reality itself? Once again the evidence seems conflicting for Luther's interpretation. On 12:1 Luther writes, "The prophet foresaw this future preaching and confession of the gospel, which did not take place in the Old Testament." The kingdom of Christ appears to be only a promise. In Ps. 118, Luther hears the same note sounded: "The cry to open the gates of righteousness for them to enter is said in the spirit of the dear fathers in the Old Testament, who longed for the kingdom of Christ (cf. Luke 10:23), but it is still closed and the Gospel and Christendom are not yet revealed."

However, in Isa. 1:14, Luther, building on Rom. 9:29, finds that "God has promised that He would be the God of Abraham and of his seed forever. Because of this promise there always remain among the Jews those who belong to Christ." In other words, a faithful remnant already experienced the reality of Christ's salvation in the Old Testament period, since Abraham was indeed the father of Christian faith.

In the light of this mixed evidence from Luther's Isaiah commentary, we return to the thesis of Preus that in his later period Luther shifted from seeing the gospel as only a promise, but rather spoke of a faithful remnant already experiencing Christ's presence in its reality. There remains from the Isaiah corpus of Luther another set of Luther's late exegesis of Isaiah, namely of Isa. 9 and 53. How does this evidence affect the question? Can one discern, say, in his commentary on Isa. 53 (1544) any change respecting his understanding of the remnant from that found in his early commentary of 1529?

A careful study of Luther's later exegesis of Isaiah, especially when compared with his earlier commentary, does reveal some development. However, the evidence either to confirm or to deny Preus's theory of a change regarding a faithful remnant within the Old Testament is not forthcoming from the exegesis of Isaiah 9 and 53, for several reasons:

1. Neither chapter 9 nor chapter 53 focuses on the subject of a remnant within Israel. Rather, the theme that dominates Isa. 9 is the inbreaking of the eschatological kingdom of God and the contrast between the darkness of the old world and light of the new. Similarly, Luther's focus in chapter 53 turns on the suffering, death, and resurrection of the Messiah, rather than how faithfully Israel responded.

2. The major themes of the early Isaiah commentary are largely continued in the later exegesis. The major difference in treatment is that Luther's later exegesis develops the arguments in far greater depth and erudition. There is much more use of Hebrew and of the various Greek translations, and he shows a far greater knowledge of the early Christian interpreters, and especially of Jewish interpretation. However, the rubrics of the kingdom of the world opposed to that of the Spirit, salvation by works or faith, and law versus grace are expanded, but not substantially altered.

3. Luther's handling of the Jews has grown in ferocity. In both chapters much continues to be made of Jewish blindness to the gospel, and the inability to see that Isaiah is promising a spiritual kingdom, not a physical one. The Jews are accused of awaiting a glorious, triumphant king and therefore failing to see the true identity of the suffering servant. In his exegesis of Isaiah 53 Luther debates at length with the so-called "collective" interpretation of the servant defended by Jews in referring the servant to the entire people of Israel. Here Luther is largely dependent on Nicholas's reading of the rabbis.

4. Luther continues to commend the lives of certain crucial Old Testament figures: Adam, Abraham, and David. He speaks of the flesh and blood character of the descendents of Abraham who constitute the people of Israel (WA 6, p. 328). These share in the promised blessing of the kingship of David. Yet he appears to distinguish, perhaps even unconsciously, between the children of Israel as heirs of the blessing and the Jewish people who have rejected the blessing. At one point Luther contrasts the wisdom of the Jews living in Christ's day who held to God's messianic promise, and those of his own day who were totally intransigent and scornful (WA 2, p. 165). This outburst would reflect Luther's growing disappointment and frustration with the Jewish rejection of Christ, which caused his increased anger.

In sum, the issue raised by Preus will have to be pursued within a broader survey that encompasses the entire corpus of Luther's writings.

V. Biblical Theological Reflections on Luther's Exegesis

There are several larger implications to be drawn from our analysis of Luther's interpretation of Isaiah. First, it is highly significant to observe how he altered the traditional function of allegory within Christian interpretation by means of a theological dialectic involving letter and spirit and law and gospel. The effect was that he was able to maintain, at least in theory, a unity of the physical and spiritual side of the Bible. Moreover, the spiritual (kerygmatic) witness of the text remained in a dynamic relation to the physical (historical) and was not assigned to a static level of an allegorical sense.

Second, Luther attempted by means of a Christological interpretation of the Old Testament to recover its witness to the living presence of Christ within Christian scripture. His exegesis sought both to do justice to the ontological dimension of the Old Testament's Christian witness and to stress the existential force of the text, which continued to exert a vertical role of divine address in the Christian community of faith. Although Luther's exegetical hermeneutic was often visceral rather than reflective, he sought to give the Old Testament text in practice a new life when he read it, not to recover events just of the past, but to give a fresh and living voice to the entire corpus of sacred scripture.

Third, Luther left some extraordinary examples of Old Testament exegesis, which demonstrated a theological richness as he read the ancient text within the context of Christian tradition. In modern parlance, what he offered in his interpretation, say, of Isa. 42, 53, 60, and 61 was an exercise in biblical theology's reflection on both testaments. Of course, Luther as a sixteenth-century interpreter did not make the clear distinction between an exegesis that worked from an original historical context, and one that had consciously shifted to a theological context provided by the full corpus of canonical scripture. Ever since the Enlightenment, Luther's Christological approach has often been rejected as a naïve distortion of the text's true meaning because he imposed an alien dogmatic system on the biblical text. Such a criticism has failed to grasp the heart of Luther's approach. Rather, in chapters such as Isa. 42, 53, and 61, he was able to evoke from the ancient text a rich Christian texture in a fresh, close reading of its words. Or, to change the metaphor, Luther took the old notes of the Old Testament's score and played a new song from the older libretto.

Of course, the relation between a genuinely historical reading of the Old Testament incorporating the original authorial intent of its human writer and a confessional Christian approach within its new and enlarged canonical context remains a pressing and yet unresolved problem of the post-Enlightenment age. An important component to the problem is to determine not only the proper function and role of such a reading, but also the community of faith in which such a reading is practiced and celebrated. At present the closest analogy lies in the church's liturgy and hymnology, in which the scriptures function in various creative applications for Christian instruction and edification.

Bibliography of Martin Luther

Primary Sources

Martin Luthers Werke. Kritische Gesamtausgabe (WA). Weimar: Bohlau, 1883–.
American Edition of Luther's Works (LW), edited by J. Pelikan and H. T. Lehmann. Philadelphia and St. Louis: Muhlenberg, Concordia, 1955–.

Secondary Sources

Bauer, K. *Die Wittenberger Universitätstheologie und die Anfänge der deutschen Reformation*. Tübingen: Mohr Siebeck, 1928.
Bayer, O. *Promissio: Geschichte der reformatorischen Wende in Luther's Theologie*. 2nd ed. Darmstadt: Wissenschaftliche Buchgesellschaft, 1989.
———. "Oratio, Meditatio, Tentatio: Eine Besinnung zu Luthers Theologieverständnis." *Luther Jahrbuch* 55 (1988): 7-59.
Beutel, A. *In dem Anfang war das Wort: Studien zu Luthers Sprachverständnis*. Tübingen: Mohr Siebeck, 1991.
Bizer, E. *Fides ex Auditu*. 3rd ed. Neukirchen-Vluyn: Neukirchener Verlag, 1966.
Bluhm, H. *Martin Luther: Creative Translator*. St. Louis: Concordia, 1965.
Bornkamm, H. *Luther's Doctrine of the Two Kingdoms in the Context of His Theology*. Philadelphia: Fortress, 1966.
———. *Luther and the Old Testament*. Philadelphia: Fortress, 1969.
Ebeling, G. *Evangelische Evangelienauslegung: Eine Untersuchung zu Luthers Hermeneutik*. Munich: Albert Lempp, 1942.
———. *Luther: An Introduction to His Thought*. London: Collins, 1970.
———. *Lutherstudien*, vol. 1. Tübingen: Mohr Siebeck, 1971.

————. "Die Anfänge von Luthers Hermeneutik." *Lutherstudien*, vol. 1, pp. 1-68. Tübingen: Mohr Siebeck, 1971.

————. "Luthers Auslegung des 44. (45) Psalms." *Lutherstudien*, vol. 1, pp. 196-220. Tübingen: Mohr Siebeck, 1971.

————. "Karl Barths Ringen mit Luther." *Lutherstudien*, vol. 3, pp. 428-573. Tübingen: Mohr Siebeck, 1985.

Elert, W. *The Structure of Lutheranism*. St. Louis: Concordia, 1962.

Gerrish, B. A. *Grace and Reason: A Study in the Theology of Luther*. Oxford: Clarendon, 1962.

Hailperin, H. *Rashi and the Christian Scholars*. Pittsburgh: University of Pittsburgh Press, 1963.

Helmer, C. "Luther's Trinitarian Hermeneutic and the Old Testament." *Modern Theology* 18 (2001): 49-73.

Hermann, R. *Von der Klarheit der Heiligen Schrift: Untersuchung und Erörterungen über Luthers Lehre von der Schrift in De servo arbitrio*. Berlin: Evangelische Verlagsanstalt, 1958.

Holl, K. "Luthers Bedeutung für den Fortschritt der Auslegungskunst." *Gesammelte Aufsätze*, vol. 1, pp. 544-82. Tübingen: Mohr Siebeck, 1927.

Joest, W. *Gesetz und Freiheit*. 4th ed. Göttingen: Vandenhoeck & Ruprecht, 1968.

Jülicher, A. *Die Gleichnisreden Jesu*. 2 vols. Tübingen: Mohr Siebeck, 1888-89.

Kähler, E. "Beobachtungen zum Problem von Schrift und Tradition in der Leipziger Disputation von 1512." In *Hören und Handeln: Festschrift Ernst Wolf*, edited by H. Gollwitzer and H. Traub, pp. 214-29. Munich: Kaiser, 1962.

Kohls, E. W. *Die Theologie des Erasmus*. 2 vols. Basel: F. Reinhardt, 1966.

Koopmans, J. *Das altkirchliche Dogma in der Reformation*. Munich: Kaiser, 1955.

Lohse, B. *Mönchtum und Reformation*. Göttingen: Vandenhoeck & Ruprecht, 1963.

————. "Die Bedeutung Augustins für den jungen Luther." *Kirche und Dogma* 2 (1965): 116-35.

————. "Luther und Erasmus." In *Lutherdeutung Heute*, edited by B. Lohse, pp. 47-60. Göttingen: Vandenhoeck & Ruprecht, 1968.

————. *Martin Luther's Theology*. Edinburgh: T. & T. Clark, 1999.

Marshall, B. "Faith and Reason Reconsidered: Aquinas and Luther on Deciding What Is True." *The Thomist* 63 (1999): 1-48.

Oberman, H. A. *The Harvest of Medieval Theology*. Cambridge, Mass.: Harvard University Press, 1963.

————. *The Roots of Anti-Semitism in the Age of Renaissance and Reformation*. Philadelphia: Fortress, 1984.

Østergaard-Nielsen, H. *Scriptura Sacra et Viva Vox: Eine Lutherstudie*. Munich: Kaiser, 1957.

Pelikan, J. *Luther the Expositor*. St. Louis: Concordia, 1959.

Preus, J. S. *From Shadow to Promise: Old Testament Interpretation from Augustine to the Young Luther*. Cambridge, Mass.: Harvard University Press, 1969.

Rothen, B. *Die Klarheit der Schrift*. 2 vols. Göttingen: Vandenhoeck & Ruprecht, 1990-92.

Scheel, O. *Documente zu Luthers Entwicklung*. Tübingen: Mohr Siebeck, 1929.

Steinmetz, D. C. *Luther and Staupitz: An Essay in the Intellectual Origins of the Protestant Reformation*. Durham: Duke University Press, 1980.

———. *Luther in Context*. Grand Rapids: Baker, 1995.

Vogelsang, E. *Die Anfänge von Luthers Christologie*. Berlin: de Gruyter, 1933.

Wolf, E. *Peregrinatio*, vol. 1. *Studien zur reformatorischen Theologie und zum Kirchenproblem*. Munich: Kaiser, 1954.

Zahrnt, H. *Luther deutet Geschichte*. Munich: P. Müller, 1952.

14

John Calvin
(1509–1564)

I. Introduction

In the nineteenth century it was common to refer to John Calvin, the French Reformer, as the man of one book, namely, his magisterial *Christianae Religionis Institutio (Institutes)*. No one would contest the importance of his work, which appeared in several editions until his death in 1564. It shaped the theology of the non-Lutheran Protestant churches within the sixteenth-century Reformation, not only in Europe, but also in England, Scotland, and especially the New World. Yet during his lifetime Calvin's contributions were hardly confined to his *Institutes*. In addition to his heavy administrative duties as chief pastor in Geneva and the countless letters, tractates, and polemical pamphlets that flowed from his pen, the extent of Calvin's preaching and lecturing is mind-boggling. In the midst of this activity, Calvin managed to produce commentaries on almost the entire New Testament and a large portion of the Old Testament. In the sixteenth century these volumes were considered as important as his *Institutes*.

The study of Calvin's commentaries has been greatly aided by the masterful studies of T. H. L. Parker (*Calvin's New Testament Commentaries*, 1971; *Calvin's Old Testament Commentaries*, 1986; and *Calvin's Preaching*, 1992). In these volumes, which have no close parallel in either French or German, Parker has provided an exhaustive study of the exact dates, editions of publication, translations, and historical background of all of Calvin's commentaries.

Following the initial publication in the sixteenth century of individual volumes, Calvin's commentaries were collected in two great editions, the Geneva edition of 1617 and the Amsterdam edition of 1667. In the early nineteenth century F. A. G. Tholuck reprinted his New Testament commentaries from the Amsterdam edition along with a few Old Testament commentaries, which served to revive interest in his exegetical work. Then, in 1863 the critical edition of the *Corpus Reformatorum* began to appear. During the sixteenth and seventeenth centuries there were some English translations of individual commentaries, but the standard English edition appeared in the mid-nineteenth century published by the Calvin Translation Society. In spite of some criticisms, especially of the notes added, these volumes continue to be the most readily available English translations. The rediscovery and ongoing publication of Calvin's sermons are peripheral to our present concerns, but are thoroughly discussed in Parker, *Supplementa Calviniana* (1962).

Surprisingly enough, it has only been rather recently that renewed interest in Calvin's commentaries has emerged and they have become a source of much debate. The nature of the debate has been helpful in bringing the central hermeneutical issues sharply into focus.

II. Calvin's Exegetical Method

During the nineteenth century interest in Calvin's commentaries was somewhat sporadic. His contributions were usually set in the context of the achievements of the modern historical-critical approach to the Bible, which had established the widely accepted norms within the discipline. Thus F. A. G. Tholuck, who was one of the leading pietistic theologians of the early nineteenth century and editor of Calvin's commentaries, praised Calvin for his sober, historical, and philologically oriented exegesis. F. W. Farrar, who usually preferred Calvin over Luther, had some positive things to say about his rejection of allegory and his attention to the text's historical context (*History of Interpretation*, 1886, pp. 342ff.). However, in the end, he judged Calvin's contributions to be of minor significance when compared to the major advancements of non-dogmatic, historical-critical interpretation, which he assumed to be the wave of the future.

In the period immediately preceding and following World War II, there was again a strong resurgence of interest in Calvin's exegesis, stimulated in large part by the rebirth of confessional theology in Germany under the leadership of Karl Barth and others. In an influential article of 1977 ("Calvin's Exegetical Principles"), Hans-Joachim Kraus sought to summarize eight exegetical principles that could be derived from Calvin's work. Among these were his well-known principles of brevity and clarity, the determining of the intention of the author, the establishing of the historical, geographical, and institutional background, and the analyzing of the literal and grammatical meaning within its larger literary context. Kraus was also interested in Calvin's typological interpretation, which he claimed was an eschatological extension of the literal sense. More controversial was Calvin's expressed concern that the Old Testament be read with the purpose of finding Christ there. For Kraus there remained some vagueness and lack of clarity on just how this was to be accomplished without falling into the pitfalls of allegory. In this same post–World War II period, when there developed a heated debate over the role of typology, Calvin was usually related to the school of the Antiochenes, but interest in him among French Catholics who were pursuing a fuller sense of the biblical text was minimal.

III. Calvin's Exegetical Consistency

One of the most interesting and important debates related to Calvin's exegesis has recently surfaced in such a way as greatly to sharpen the hermeneutical issues. The controversy relates to the consistency of Calvin's exegetical method. It had long been recognized that Calvin was a French humanist in his literary training. The excellence of his education in the classical languages is everywhere evident. In addition, he acquired a competent knowledge of Hebrew from some of the great Renaissance scholars of the day. The publication of a critical edition of his early work on Seneca's *De Clementia* (1969) made abundantly clear that there was a strong continuity between his early critical analysis of Seneca and his later biblical commentaries. Both demonstrated the same concern for philological precision, historical background, and close attention to the literal sense of the text as reflecting the intention of the author. In the light of this powerful, early influence on Calvin's literary method, the obvious question arises regarding the relation of this side of Calvin's work to his later overwhelmingly theological purpose undergirding the writing of commentaries, which he time and again explicitly emphasized. In his Introduction to Isaiah, he speaks of this book "as containing no human reasoning, but the oracles of God . . . revealed by the Spirit of God." Scripture is the Word of God and the authoritative source of the divine will for his church.

In 1965, Edward Dowey spoke of seeing "two Calvins," the theologian and the humanist scholar, the one affirming the verbal inerrancy of the Bible, the other able to acknowledge mistakes (Dowey, *Knowledge,* p. 104). He concluded that Calvin was inconsistent. He was unable to assimilate traditional doctrine and the newer, critical approach to scripture.

David Puckett (1995) further highlighted this problem of consistency within Calvin's exegesis by reviewing the striking disagreement between two modern scholars in their assessment of this tension. On the one hand, in 1919 Kemper Fullerton called Calvin's "the first scientific interpretation in the history of the Christian church" (cited by Puckett, p. 10), since he embraced the exegetical principle of the grammatical-historical approach. He then argued that frequently Calvin disregarded this principle in spite of his basically correct historical sense. On the other hand, H. J. Forstman argued that Calvin could not be viewed as a practitioner of historical interpretation because his exegesis was never independent of his doctrine of divine inspiration, unity, and perfection of scripture (cited p. 11). Puckett made the interesting observation that, in spite of reaching radically different conclusions, Fullerton and Forstman had one thing in common: both saw a serious tension between Calvin's doctrine of scripture and his historical exegetical method.

Puckett's own theory about this tension in Calvin encompasses Calvin's concern to do justice both to the divine intention within scripture and the human intention of its author. First, he explores Calvin's humanistic approach, emphasizing the philological, historical, and literary focus to recover the intention of the author. Next, he pursues Calvin's theological concern to interpret the Old Testament in such a way as to find Christ within the progressive nature of God's revelation. He explores various hermeneutical devices such as his theories of accommodation, typology, and shadow versus substance by which to extend the divine intention beyond the literal sense of the text. However, in the end, Puckett concludes that Calvin was unable to resolve the tension, and he sees a middle way that sought to avoid the opposing extremes of Jewish historical liberation and Christian allegory.

Although one can certainly acknowledge the force of Puckett's case, nevertheless, it seems to me that there are some important factors in Calvin's biblical interpretation that have not been adequately handled, and which could offer a major corrective to his concluding estimate of Calvin's exegesis as a middle way.

IV. Hermeneutical Reflections on Calvin's Exegesis

1. The Plain Sense

Recent research (such as that of Kathryn Greene-McCreight) has revealed the complexity of Calvin's understanding of the literal or plain sense of the biblical text. He uses a variety of terms to express the literal sense (*sensus literalis*), including "the genuine," "the simple," "the true," and "the natural." As stated above, most treatments of Calvin's exegesis have rightly stressed his humanistic education, and many have inferred that his attention to the literal sense offers the clearest evidence of this background. When Calvin's early edition of Seneca's commentary appeared in 1969 in a critical edition, the similarity between his editing of Seneca and his subsequent biblical commentaries appeared to confirm the highest level of continuity.

Yet it is precisely at this juncture that a basic confusion entered. Indeed there was a methodological continuity in his use of philology, style, and literary context, but Calvin was explicit in his early Romans commentary (1540), and always thereafter, to express the uniqueness of sacred scripture as containing the very Word of God. As Parker writes (*O.T. Commentaries,* p. 66), "[F]or Calvin the Bible, the whole Bible, and every nook and cranny of the Bible, is the Word of God as completely as if God himself had spoken the actual words." In summary, because the content of the Bible is unique, the approach to its interpretation is also unique. Indeed, because the Bible is a written text of a human author, its words can be studied grammatically as any other writing. However, this is only part of the task; the relation between the human and divine nature of scripture requires a much more subtle approach.

It would be a mistake, however, to suppose that Calvin simply joins the humanistic study of the literal sense of a biblical text with an additional theological step. Rather, it is crucial to understand that what Calvin means by a text's literal sense is not simply identified with its verbal or historically reconstructed meaning.

A central concern of Greene-McCreight's study of Calvin's exegesis is to explore exactly what is involved in his "plain sense" of scripture. She designates it as a "ruled reading." By this she means that there are two restraints at work in interpreting the literal sense of scripture. On the one hand, there is a verbal sense shaped by the concerns of a humanistic training that includes the grammatical meaning, the narrative structure, and the author's intention. On the other hand, the doctrinal content of the divine will is expressed in a coherent narrative. The storyline of the Christian faith stretches from the creation in the beginning to the eschatological consummation of the kingdom of God. This larger theological framework, which embraces the history of divine redemption through Jesus Christ, constitutes a rule of faith *(regula fidei)*. These two restraints do not constitute two different levels of meaning, but embrace the one literal sense. Calvin's notion of the literal sense is deep enough not to need another textual level to carry a spiritual meaning by means of allegory. Rather, the literal sense is the true and genuine meaning of scripture. In contrast to Luther, Calvin does not relate the two aspects of the literal sense in a dialectical fashion between the spiritual and the carnal, nor does he hold to an unresolved tension, a *via media*. Of course, as we shall see below, the literal sense is not only authored by the Holy Spirit, but stands in constant need of quickening by the rendering of the letter into the spirit. The theological restraint of the rule of faith is not an independent dogmatic component, different in kind from the verbal, but derived from the substance *(res)* of the scriptures and providing a framework encompassing the whole within a divine harmony.

2. Human and Divine Intentionality

It is an essential component of Calvin's humanistic training that he is deeply concerned with understanding the literal meaning as an expression of the intention of the human author *(mens authoris)*. Throughout his biblical commentaries he continually affirms that a major task of the interpreter of scripture is to discern the intentions of the author, whether of Moses or one of the prophets. Indeed in his letter to Grynaeus *(Preface to Romans)*, he writes as if the highest priority of the exegete is to unfold the mind of the writer *(mentem scriptoris)*. Much of the harshest criticism of other commentators arises when their interpretations "would never have entered the mind of the author." Moreover, Calvin is fully clear that the personalities of the human writers were not denied or obscured. Their mental faculties were intact, and even their innermost thoughts and emotions were an essential part of their message.

Yet at the same time, indeed often in the same passage, Calvin wants to identify true meaning with that which reflects the intention of God *(Dei consilium)*. God is the acknowledged author of scripture. The reader is constantly admonished to strive to understand the intention of the Holy Spirit. In his commentary on Dan. 12:4, Calvin rejects an interpretation offered with the comment: "I think the Holy Spirit has a different intention here" (cited in Puckett, p. 32).

Of course, the difficult and perplexing question is to understand the relation of the divine and the human intention. In an excellent chapter (pp. 35ff.) Puckett pursues the issue with skill, giving great care not to make the task easy with premature harmonizations. Puckett points out that for Calvin there is little difference between attributing words to the prophet or to the Holy Spirit. A word of Moses can be looked at as his own assertion or that of the Holy Spirit. Calvin's choice of words seems to suggest that the intention of the prophet and that of the Holy Spirit are so closely related as to be virtually interchangeable. Puckett concludes that Calvin is unwilling to divorce the intention of the human writer from the meaning of the Holy Spirit and that there is no practical means by which to distinguish them.

Although this assessment is certainly true for Calvin, there is also within the ruled reading a strong force exerted to extend the meaning by adapting the biblical text to the present usage of the church. This bridge or act of application is by means of a transference, that is, an *anagōge* (literary analogy). This is a form of figuration that Calvin denied was an allegory in the traditional sense. It is not to twist the simple sense of Scripture when the interpreter seeks to extend its meaning both in time and in reception. While it is not the case that Calvin restricts his use of analogy to those texts identified with the Holy Spirit's authorship, the extension through analogy often derives from a holistic reading of the larger corpus of scripture, that is, one that transcends an individual writer. One inference to be drawn from this use of figuration is that the extension derives from the overarching purpose of God with Israel and the world into which the messages of human writers are absorbed.

3. Calvin's Understanding of History

Calvin's understanding of Old Testament history is shaped completely by his theological stance that it is the divine will that gives meaning and direction to all earthly events. Moreover, this divine purpose is the story of Israel, which was adopted also to be that of the church. Whereas the choice of Israel is the revelation of God's special love and mercy toward his elected people in the mystery of predestination, equally important is the providential activity of God in the world for the welfare of God's creation and the safety of the church. Parker (*Calvin's Old Testament Commentaries,* p. 84) insists that covenant in Calvin is not the all-embracing doctrine that it later became in some Reformed circles, but was restricted, by and large, to the covenant with Abraham and was therefore ultimately focused on the calling into being of the church. The period before Christ's incarnation was the childhood of the church, which reached its maturity after the advent. The election of Abraham set Israel off from the rest of the nations of the world, but the ensuing history of Israel called forth both divine promise and divine judgment. The covenant was not made with the physical descendants of Abraham, but with faithful, invisible Israel within the empirical, historical nation.

In his treatment of the Old Testament stories, Calvin shows literary skill in handling the material as a narrative that uses rhetorical devices. He is not averse to rearranging the biblical sequence (cf. the details in Parker, *Calvin's*

Old Testament Commentaries, pp. 93ff.), yet when it comes to factual matters, Calvin, with few exceptions, accepts a direct historical referentiality. At times, when the difficulties of an Old Testament story seem to appear insurmountable, such as the preserving of all living creatures in the ark, Calvin resorts to an appeal to the miraculous.

A far more sophisticated hermeneutical understanding in respect to interpreting history can be found in Calvin's concept of accommodation (cf. Ford Lewis Battles, "God Was Accommodating Himself to Human Capacity"). It is one that Calvin employs in more than one context. Basically he argues that God condescends in his dealing with fallible human beings by accommodating his teachings to mankind's limited capacity. Particularly in his treatment of the creation account of Genesis, Calvin acknowledges that Moses wrote in such a way to accommodate his knowledge to the simple, uneducated people for which he wrote. Calvin also used this concept to restrict the attempt to speculate on details of the biblical account that only serve to distract the reader from the truth of the biblical account concerning God's activity.

However, it would be a mistake, as one finds, for example, in H. Jackson Forstman (*Word and Spirit,* pp. 13ff.), to suppose that the appeal to accommodation was simply an escape hatch employed whenever a historical event seemed in irreconcilable conflict with scientific knowledge or common sense. Rather, it demonstrates one way in which Calvin was able to modify his usual assumption of a direct historical referentiality to all events of biblical history. By assigning an apparent contradiction to an intentional restructuring of the event for a theological reason, Calvin was struggling toward formulating a theory of truth that was not dependent on an exact correlation between biblical and non-biblical sources.

Closely akin to accommodation was Calvin's understanding of the role of typology. This form of figuration plays a major role in establishing the relation between the two testaments, but it also serves in shaping Calvin's understanding of history. Because history is the unified expression of the will of God for his creation, Calvin envisions a meaningful pattern of events within God's unfolding purpose. Calvin did make a sharp distinction between typology and allegory, but not in terms of a theoretical principle or by means of terminology. Rather, he attacked the fanciful, arbitrary speculation associated with allegory while supporting a typological figuration that extended and reinforced the factual truth of the original event. In many ways, Calvin's use of typology recalls several of the hermeneutical problems that were at issue in the early church between the Alexandrian and Antiochene Church Fathers as well as the concern that resurfaced in the post–World War II period, when a new literary critical defense of typology was developed as a protest against the widespread rejection of figuration in the name of scientific biblical exegesis.

There is one final aspect of Calvin's understanding of history that needs mentioning. When discussing the rubric of law and gospel in Luther, we noted the centrality of this dialectical relation to his overall interpretation of the Old Testament. But Calvin's emphasis on the role of the law is quite different. According to Calvin, the redemption of Christ had already been revealed through promise to the people of the old covenant. The Old Testament sinners were saved by the same atoning work of Christ no less than New Testament saints. The role of the law was to serve as an addition, which according to Gal. 3:17 was given four hundred years after God had offered Abraham his promise in a covenant of grace. The purpose of the law was not to provide a new way to salvation through works — Calvin agrees fully here with Luther — but to encourage his people to look eagerly for Christ's coming. The law was a schoolmaster pointing to Christ. It served to instruct Israel of the old covenant pedagogically until the church had grown up from its period of childhood to full maturity. Rather than pursuing the sharp contrasts of law and gospel according to Paul's theology in Galatians, Calvin found the book of Hebrews more compatible, and he adopted freely the imagery of light and shade, of shadow and reality. The law adumbrated in its imagery the reality concealed until Christ's advent.

4. The Relation of the Two Testaments

In two well-known chapters in his *Institutes* (book 2, chapters 10 and 11), Calvin sets forth his understanding of the relation between the testaments, first treating the similarities and next the differences between the two. It is unnecessary for our purposes to review in detail his position other than to recognize that his exegesis of the Old Testament is dependent in every sense upon this understanding. Crucial to his argument is that there is no difference in substance and reality *(substantia et re ipsa)* between the two covenants, but the administration of God's unified will varies. The Old Testament promises are couched as earthly blessings in contrast to the heavenly blessings of the New Testament. The old covenant is one of shadow and is temporal; the new covenant is clear and eternal. The old covenant is of the letter rather than the spirit. Finally, whereas the old covenant is made with only one nation, in the new covenant the distinction between Jew and Gentile has been removed.

In my judgment, it is Calvin's connection of the similarity in substance between the testaments that has fundamentally shaped his Old Testament exegesis. Indeed, Calvin continues to use the traditional category of promise and fulfillment, especially in the familiar messianic passages of Isaiah, but his marked reservations in exploiting a direct Christological application from the Old Testament set him apart not only from most of the Church Fathers, but also from the other Protestant Reformers, especially from Luther and his followers. Constantly Calvin objects to traditional Christian exegesis as using weak arguments to support Christian doctrine that subject the church to the ridicule of the Jews. Instead Calvin lays his emphasis on the similarity of substance between the testaments, namely, on the ontological identity of the one purpose of God (cf. below for examples from Isaiah). By frequently appealing to the trope of synecdoche, Calvin is able to extend a single instance of a teaching to a broad, underlying Christian doctrine that sees in God's vengeance on Israel (Isa. 15) an illustration of the enduring wrath of God against all human pride and arrogance.

Although the God of the Old Testament is always understood as the God and Father of Jesus Christ, very rarely does Calvin evoke the visible presence of Jesus Christ within the Old Testament. Even in his exegesis of John 12:41, "Isaiah said this because he saw his (Christ's) glory and spoke of him," Calvin objects to a narrow Christological identification with the person of Christ, but he identifies the glory of Christ seen by the prophet in a trinitarian sense with the image of the invisible God.

One of the more controversial aspects of Calvin's exegesis is his use of the New Testament's citation of Old Testament passages as offering the true intention of the Old Testament. At times Calvin does recognize the difficulty of reconciling an Old Testament passage in its plain sense to its New Testament context. He allows, for example, Paul considerable freedom in applying an Old Testament text to his new historical situation. At other times, he appeals to the sense of the text rather than to its exact verbal wording. However, there are times when Calvin seems forced to harmonize the texts or even to twist their meaning in order to achieve a coherent reading. From a modern critical perspective, Calvin's approach to the two testaments is often attacked in failing to do justice to the multiple and diverse witnesses within the various parts of scripture.

There is one final issue to be discussed regarding the relation between the two testaments in the exegesis of Calvin. He takes his lead from several passages in the New Testament that speak of the people of the old covenant living in constant expectation of the advent of Christ. 1 Peter 1:10-11 speaks of the prophets who "searched and inquired about this salvation; they inquired what person or time was indicated by the spirit of Christ." Or again, Hebrews

11:10 describes Abraham as one who "looked forward to the city which has foundations, whose builder and maker is Christ." As a result, Calvin often attributes a Christian motivation to the saints of the Old Testament. Thus, David knew that he was only a type of the promised Messiah. Others are said to live by their hope in immortality. Finally, the faithful priests of the old covenant fully understood that their practice of sacrifice only gained its meaning from the expectation of the advent of Christ.

In my opinion, Calvin is fully right in formulating a biblical theology of both testaments in which there is an overarching unity between the two. In a real sense, the formation of a Christian canon provides the theological warrant for exploring the underlying themes that unite the scriptures of the church. My exegetical caveat is that Calvin's approach runs the danger of projecting backward into the biblical narrative a meaning that is not derived from the Old Testament. The effect is that he christianizes the Old Testament by a form of psychologizing the unexpressed motivation of its characters. In a concluding chapter, a case will be made that a more developed understanding of the hermeneutical implications of the Christian canon can overcome many of the exegetical problems raised when seeking to maintain the unity of the scriptures.

5. The Homiletical Use of the Old Testament

One of the most impressive aspects of Calvin's interpretation of scripture, particularly in respect to the Old Testament, is his constant attempt at adapting its message to his own time and to his Christian audience. At the very moment when Calvin is using his humanistic skills to recover the historical context of a passage, he invariably strives to apply the passage beyond its original context to that of the present needs of the church. Of course, it is not by chance that Calvin is so skillful in this endeavor. Because his search for the plain sense of scripture is shaped by the restraints of the verbal sense and by the rule of faith, there is no insurmountable obstacle separating the literal sense of the texts from its theological application. Indeed, one is frequently astonished by the ease with which the transference is made. Because of his understanding of the substance of the entire biblical witness, he can extend a particular biblical event or teaching to the selfsame Christological realities from which the church lives. Moreover, Calvin is everywhere conscious that the need for existential application does not depend on a clever rhetorical process. Rather, his preaching remains fully dependent upon the activity of the Holy Spirit, the spirit of the living Christ, to bring the substance of the text alive and to evoke from its reader and hearer a response of Christian faith.

V. An Analysis of Calvin's Commentary on Isaiah

1. The Formal Side of his Interpretation

Even a quick perusal of Calvin's handling of the book of Isaiah immediately reveals his humanistic training. In his comment on Isa. 6:13 he freely admits some obscurity in the words. Then he proceeds, "but let us first ascertain the meaning, and we shall easily find out the signification of the words."

His initial recourse was to turn to the Hebrew text to establish the meaning of the biblical words. There is a general modern consensus that Calvin's knowledge of Hebrew was adequate, especially for a Christian scholar of the early sixteenth century, but was not on the level of later Hebraists like Drusius or Vatablus. Still T. H. L. Parker speaks of Calvin's custom of preaching from the Old Testament using only a Hebrew Bible as his text (*Calvin's Old Testament Commentaries*, p. 20). Calvin's reference to the Hebrew of Isaiah was always explicitly oriented to a specific text, and its goal was a practical one of offering direct aid in determining a word's meaning. There is no hint of simply offering a display of learning. His practical orientation is also reflected in his continual use of paraphrases that seek to remove any erudite obscurities. In his Isaiah commentary he seldom makes use of the Septuagint or the other Greek translations, the exceptions being when he refers to a New Testament's citation that construed the Old Testament text differently from the Hebrew. So regarding Isa. 10:22, he notes that Paul's citation of the text in Rom. 9:27 according to the Septuagint is different from the Hebrew, and he struggles to reconcile the two readings.

When Calvin comes to the difficult text of Isa. 46:8 with an unusual verbal form often translated as a denominative of *ish* = man as "show yourself men," he reviews several options derived from Hebrew roots, but ends up siding with Jerome's rendering "to be ashamed." In contrast, when interpreting the prophet's response to the theophany of Isa. 6:5, he disagrees with Jerome's rendering of *damah* as "I was silent," and stresses the passive sense of the verb: "I have been reduced to silence," to signify Isaiah's terror resembling that of a dead man. At times, when considering the issue unimportant, Calvin is content to list various options without offering his own preference. When a decision is offered, the crucial factor does not rest solely on a Hebrew etymology, but whether the sense is the "true and natural one" (8:2) or the one that best agrees with the larger context (2:9).

In his commentary there are many signs of Calvin's literary concerns. He continually mentions the need to attend to the "mode of expression" (2:9). He is aware of "an elegant allusion or play on words" often lost through translation from the Hebrew. He is especially attentive to literary figures of speech: metaphor (5:7), synecdoche (2:3), paronomasia (5:7), and hypallage (1:19). He notes the "highest skill expressed" in the composition of poems by Isaiah (e.g., 5:1-7).

Calvin pays much attention to the structuring of the larger units. He notes that in the collecting of the prophetic oracles, chronological arrangement is often disregarded (1:7). In his treatment of the vision of Isaiah in chapter 6, he enters into the debate regarding its alleged displacement and seeks to justify a purposeful role for its present position in the book. Already in his preface he attempts to address the issue of how these prophetic writings were compiled and established into a book, but in the end he does not pursue this issue beyond the briefest sketch of a literary reconstruction.

Finally, in respect to Jewish interpretation, Calvin's acquaintance, particularly in his Isaiah commentary, seems even more distant than Luther's. When it comes to substantive questions of interpretation, Calvin's comments are overwhelmingly negative regarding rabbinical exegesis, but the mention of specific Jewish authors rarely appears. Nicholas's commentary does not seem to play a role. Only in relation to the formal matter of establishing the Hebrew text does Calvin show respect and interest in rabbinic tradition. In Isa. 9:6 he notices that, contrary to the usual manner of writing Hebrew, there appears the final form of the *mem* in the middle of the word *le marbeh*. He is puzzled about whether the prophet intentionally wrote it in this manner, and reflects, "since the Rabbins were so close observers of the minutest position of a letter, we cannot avoid thinking that this was not rashly done." This attitude of respect is a far cry from frequent Christian accusations — both early and late — that the Jews deliberately falsified the Hebrew text in order to oppose Christian claims.

2. Calvin's Exegetical Method in Isaiah

a. Methodological Consistency

Our initial analysis stressed the apparent contradiction between Calvin's humanistic training in the use of the critical tools of philology, history, and classical literature and his larger theological approach. I tried to make the case that this alleged tension was not something ever sounded by Calvin himself. Certainly he did not ever intimate that he was using two different approaches. Rather, it was argued that Calvin's understanding of the plain sense involved a critical search from the literal sense that was encompassed within a rule of faith. What does the study of Calvin's Isaiah commentary add to this debate?

In his preface Calvin clearly states that the office of the prophet lies in the role of explaining the law. Of course, by law he includes a doctrine of life, threats and promises, and a covenant of grace. Indeed, what Moses expresses in general terms, the prophet describes in detail. In Isa. 1 he continues this theme that there is nothing in Isaiah's book not revealed by God himself. The prophet does not speak of his own accord or imagination.

Isaiah's calling as a prophet is given at the outset. His message concerns Judah and Jerusalem; everything else is peripheral. Yet it is clear that the subject matter extends beyond one historical situation. The plain or literal meaning of the biblical text addresses a subject matter that encompasses God's complete salvific purpose for the church and the world. In other words, the context from which Isaiah speaks involves a content that embraces the anticipated kingdom of God and the covenant of grace. The prophet, inspired by the Spirit, envisions past, present, and future. However, the distinction between the kingdom of the world and the kingdom of Christ, that is, between the visible world of human affairs and the heavenly dimension of divine sovereignty, is revealed only through the eyes of faith (60:5). What is particularly characteristic of the commentary on Isaiah is the ease with which Calvin moves between the earthly and heavenly kingdoms. He is adamant that the spiritual world is not entered by an appeal to allegory, but is revealed in the plain sense of the text.

From the context of faith Calvin can move freely from addressing the Jews of Jerusalem in the eighth century to an appeal to a future people of God. His ability to extend the meaning of the historical text is not accomplished by the traditional techniques of allegorical figuration, but within the restraints afforded by the subject matter itself. This extension can be expressed ontologically, that is to say, in terms of the eternal presence of God found in both the Old and New Testaments, or in terms of a historical extension that moves eschatologically to fulfill God's will.

It is in this context of Calvin's understanding of the plain sense of Scripture as embracing both the verbal and the confessional that one finds some of his strongest rejections of the allegorical method (5:2; 19:1; 63:1). Calvin objects to allegory for a variety of reasons, but especially for separating into two levels the earthly/historical and the spiritual/heavenly dimensions of God's kingdom.

As we mentioned earlier, there is an interesting discussion in both Parker (*Calvin's Old Testament Commentaries*, pp. 72ff.) and Puckett (pp. 108-9) regarding Calvin's use of the term *anagoge*. The discussion arises from Galatians 4, in which Paul uses the term "allegory." Calvin argues that Paul is not using allegory in the traditional sense, but simply drawing a comparison between the church and the family of Abraham. This figurative usage thus involves no departure from the plain sense of the text. Calvin is also concerned that many Christians have tortured passages of scripture by appealing to allegory to contest the Jewish claims, but as a result have only evoked ridicule by their weak arguments (4:3; 6:3; 7:14).

b. Divine and Human Intentionality

Much has been written in recent years about the relation of divine and human intentionality in Calvin. The issue is important because of Calvin's insistence on both aspects. Yet when reading his Isaiah commentary, the reader does not sense that Calvin saw a contradiction or even a tension between the two. On the one hand, the prophet spoke the Word of God; he did not speak of his own accord or draw from his own imagination (1:1). Yet Calvin recognized that the prophet exercised freedom, imagination, and human skill in faithfully conducting his office as a messenger of God. His task often evoked his anger and frustration because of the persistent resistance of Judah's kings and people (7:13; 22:4). Therefore, the role of the interpreter is to recover the true sense of the prophet's words with every means possible. On the other hand, for Calvin God alone is the author of scripture, and he constantly refers in his exegesis of Isaiah to what "the Holy Spirit intended by this word" (2:8). In sum, the human and the divine intention are virtually identical, and in no instance is one played against the other in his interpretation. Nor is the integrity of the prophet's words ever denigrated or relativized.

The hermeneutic that undergirds Calvin's position arises from his understanding of the role of the Holy Spirit. "Faith alone opens for us the gate of the kingdom of God . . . it is the Spirit of God alone who can make us partakers of that fellowship" (6:7). Or again, it is the Spirit that enlightens by his word and illuminates by the light of understanding (29:24). Finally, Calvin stresses the indissoluble unity between the divine and human intention when he writes, "[B]oth ought to be united, and the efficacy of the Spirit ought not to be separated from the preaching of the gospel" (49:22).

The hermeneutical implications of this understanding of the Spirit are that for Calvin, the Spirit-inspired Word of God in scripture has its own voice. Scripture is not an inert artifact awaiting human creative imagination to give it life, but its voice goes forth from God's mouth with power (53:11), exerting a coercion upon its hearers for salvation or for judgment. It should be obvious that this hermeneutical understanding of the Word of God, supported by most of the Church Fathers, is entirely anathema both to the heirs of the Enlightenment as well as to postmodern detractors.

In the earlier discussion of Calvin's exegetical method found in his introduction, I mentioned his use of an interpretive device by which God was seen accommodating his teachings to the limited capacity of human beings. There are several illuminating examples in his commentary on Isaiah that illustrate this exegetical move (1:24; 40:18). One of the most extensive occurs in his interpretation of Isaiah's vision in chapter 6. Calvin first raises the obvious question: How could Isaiah actually see God, who is spirit without a visible shape? He responds with an exposition of God's manner of revealing himself not as he actually is, but according to Isaiah's capacity to perceive his inconceivable majesty. Thus, the prophet attributed to God a throne, a robe, and a bodily appearance. Then Calvin is quick to add that this representation was not deceitful, but only a limited one. He did not see the essence of the Spirit, but was offered a clear proof to see that God's Spirit rested in Christ, as the Evangelist had correctly stated (John 1:32).

c. Prophetic History in Isaiah

At first sight, Calvin's understanding of history would be described as "precritical." That is to say, Calvin views biblical accounts of historical events uncritically as truthful and directly referential to commonly experienced occurrences accessible to all. In his exegesis of the prophecies directed to the nations in Isa. 13–23, Calvin uses every available secular source along with the Bible to interpret the prophecies concerning the destruction of Tyre, Moab, and Babylon. Moreover, he also finds confirmation of the truth of Isaiah's prophecy in his prediction of the coming of Cyrus some two hundred years before his arrival (chapter 45). Similarly, the prophet foretold the fall of Babylon many centuries before it happened (13:4).

Yet upon a closer reading of his Isaiah commentary, a much more complex, reflective understanding of history emerges. In the first place he distinguishes between historical events and the shape they received in the biblical narrative. Thus, in 36:3 he notes that the narrative often alters the chronological sequence in order to make its own point. Again, the prophet intertwines earlier and later events and views historical events as prelude to future redemption whose significance is determined by their relation to a larger eschatological end (45:6). Finally, when interpreting Isa. 10:5, Calvin argues that the same event can be perceived as both present and future, depending on the perspective of the viewer. God's promises are concealed for a time from unbelievers and only visible to those with the eyes of faith. Although Calvin did not develop a dialectical form of *Heilsgeschichte*, he adumbrated certain features that emerged in the nineteenth century.

To enter into the heart of Calvin's theology of history, it is necessary to pursue his sustained effort to extend the significance of historical events beyond their initial occurrence. In spite of his rejection of an allegorical reading of prophetic passages and his emphasis on a literal, historical reading of the biblical text, within his concept of a text's plain sense was its ability to extend its theological significance from the past to the future.

There are two central theological moves that undergird Calvin's understanding of this extension. First, Calvin developed a sophisticated approach to the traditional pattern of prophecy and fulfillment. Rather than stressing the supernatural effect of a later fulfillment corresponding exactly to its earlier prediction (e.g., Justin), Calvin employed a dynamic understanding of historical events that unfolded in a process that anticipated in stages the full realization of the initial promise. Although the term "typology" is a more modern formulation, Hans Frei (*Eclipse*, p. 2) sees Calvin's approach as an extension of the literal interpretation of the text at the level of the whole biblical story. Prophecy is not limited to single events in history, but encompasses the entire historical intervention of God into the future. Calvin's concern (much like the Antiochenes whom he does not mention) is to maintain the theological significance of the prior individual events in the history of Israel while also extending their function into the future as the final consummation of the divine promise. His view of prophecy and fulfillment is also highly Christological, because such events as the freeing of Israel from its Babylonian captivity are viewed as a foretaste of the divine deliverance in the reign of Christ.

Secondly, and closely intertwined by Calvin with the first move mentioned above, is the extension of historical events by an appeal to the theological substance undergirding the divine intention for all of history. Thus, Isaiah warns the people of Judah not to fix their eyes on the present conditions of their history, which was only a shadow, but "on the Redeemer, by whom the reality would be declared" (2:2). Again, in Isa. 42:1 he speaks of Christ as the "perpetual Redeemer." The covenant made with Abraham and his posterity had its foundation only in Christ (42:6). When the sign of Immanuel was offered to Ahaz (7:14), it served to confirm the promise that "whenever God assisted his ancient people, he reconciled them to himself through Christ at the same time." This ontological argument is often interwoven with the promise-fulfillment pattern in his commentary. As we shall see shortly, Calvin's understanding of the progressive, eschatological extension of prophetic events had wide implications for other aspects of his exegesis.

d. The Relation of the Two Testaments in Isaiah

As one would expect from our earlier discussion of Calvin's exegetical method, the relation of the two testaments of the Christian Bible would play an important role in his Old Testament commentaries, especially that of Isaiah. In speaking of God's revelation to Abraham, Moses, and the rest of the Fathers, Calvin writes, "It is one and the same faith that has been held by us and by our fathers, for they and we have acknowledged the same God, the Father of our Lord Jesus Christ" (40:21). He writes that God addresses "the believers who were concealed in the kingdom of Israel and joins them with the Church" (17:14).

Calvin's use of the New Testament in his Isaiah commentary is constant and takes many forms. Great significance is placed in his exegesis of Isa. 61:1 on the fact that Christ explains this passage with reference to himself (Luke 4:18). Christ is introduced as speaking as if the entire Old Testament passage related to him alone. As the head of the prophets, he holds chief place and alone makes all these revelations.

Frequently the relation between the testaments is made with a typological link. The deliverance from captivity in Babylon, indeed the whole period of divine rescue, is understood as the entrance of the reign of Christ. Isa. 40:3 is applied to John the Baptist in Matt. 3:3, Mark 1:3, and Luke 3:4. According to Calvin, "What is here described metaphorically by the Prophet was at that time actually fulfilled" (40:4). Moreover, the prophet does not address merely the people of his own time, but all of posterity. Sometimes the connection between two passages arises from only a loose analogy. In John 15:1 the Evangelist speaks of Christ as the true vine, and the imagery of Isaiah's song in chapter 5 is everywhere present, but developed Christologically.

Most frequently the direct citations of Isaianic passages by a New Testament writer to which Calvin draws attention are those of Paul. This is hardly surprising because already in Isa. 1, Calvin notes, "Paul is the best interpreter of this passage" (1:9). He is also aware that Paul uses considerable freedom in his citations from Isaiah; nevertheless, he is unswerving in his assurance that the original meaning of the Hebrew text has not been destroyed. When interpreting Paul's use of Isa. 28:16 in Rom. 9:33 ("He that believeth shall not be ashamed"), Calvin acknowledges the change that occurred in Paul's using the Greek translation, but argues that Paul used such liberty in not quoting the exact words from the Hebrew without changing the essential meaning of the original. A similar assurance is given in his comment on Isa. 40:18 in relation to Paul's use of the verse as a proof against idolaters in Acts 17:29. Again, in his interpretation of Isa. 9:3 Calvin implies that Paul's use of Hosea in Rom. 9:25 actually serves to bring forth the real design of the Old Testament prophet.

Quite frequently Calvin notes that a New Testament author (e.g., 1 Peter 3:14) draws a general doctrine from a passage such as Isa. 8:12. Peter warns his hearers also not to fear. Calvin concludes his remarks homiletically: "If that warning of Peter was ever necessary, it is especially so in the present day."

In sum, Calvin, as a linguistically trained scholar, is fully aware of the semantic alterations often effected by the translation of Hebrew into Greek or Latin. He uses several techniques to accommodate the changes: the substance rather than the letter is central, or the original Hebrew meaning has been intentionally extended. However, as far as I am aware, in no case does Calvin question the truth or authority of the New Testament's interpretation of Isaiah.

e. Exegesis and Doctrine

One of the most striking features of Calvin's Isaiah commentary, and one that sets him apart from virtually every commentary since the Enlightenment, is his understanding of the relation of Old Testament exegesis and Christian doctrine. Although Calvin consciously structured his theological corpus in such a way as to divide his dogmatic *opus (Institutes)* from the theological task of writing biblical commentaries, he used his exegesis to provide an explicit link with Christian doctrine. Constantly, and throughout the entire Isaiah commentary, Calvin pauses, as it were, before and after interpretation, to draw a direct line from his exegesis to what he names doctrine *(doctrina)*.

Calvin seeks to draw out the broader theological implications by reflecting on the larger contours of the material into which his detailed exegesis has entered. His goal is not simply to systematize or summarize his exegesis, but rather to point out to his readers the practical dogmatic yield that has been provided to them through scripture. His reflections are thus far more oriented to pastoral care than to systematic theology.

Moreover, Calvin is exploring the range of Christian theology, which he directs to the everyday life of Christians, and in his Isaiah commentary he uses almost entirely the content gained from the Old Testament. It is particularly significant when, addressing the question of the law containing the doctrine of salvation (Isa. 8:20), he appeals to Christ's words in Luke 16:29: "They have Moses and the prophets, let them hear them . . . for although Abraham is brought forth as the speaker, still it is a permanent oracle which is uttered by the mouth of God." To speak somewhat anachronistically, Calvin is constructing a biblical theology formed almost entirely from the Old Testament. So, for example, he speaks of the hope of eternal life, which hope appears to be concealed during the attack of Sennacherib (36:16). Again in Isa. 59:16, he calls to remembrance the "universal doctrine" that our salvation is by grace, "a wonderful blessing bestowed by God alone, and not the industry of men." Further, in his commentary on Isa. 26:8, he names "a very beautiful doctrine" that turns out to concern the perseverance of the saints: "God will be our guide during the whole of life."

Several times in the commentary he addresses the doctrine of salvation (e.g., 8:20) that is contained within the law. It provides the rule for a good and happy life. The law consists of three parts: a doctrine of life, threats and promises, and a covenant of grace. The role of the prophet is to explain these parts of the law that have been misunderstood, for the law is a "perpetual rule" for the church (preface). Then again, he speaks of a "highly useful doctrine" (8:16) that concerns the office of teacher and minister, encouraging them to persevere in discharging their duties. Frequently there is added an admonition that these doctrines are to be inculcated "at the present day" (5:7).

I think it fair to say that there are few elements in Calvin's biblical exegesis more alien to the heirs of the Enlightenment and the postmodern era than his view of biblical doctrine. It has become a truism in many contemporary theological circles that doctrine is rigid, oppressive, and authoritarian. It only serves to stifle human imagination and to destroy creative spirituality. In contrast, Calvin speaks of these Christian doctrines as useful, joyous, comforting, and liberating. These doctrines are a sign of God's gracious guidance that, when embraced, lead to a good and happy life (8:20). Could it be that this quality of exegesis explains in part why Calvin's commentaries continue to be widely used in the church and have remained in print into the twenty-first century?

f. The Application of Exegesis

Closely allied to the subject above, but deserving a separate paragraph, is the manner in which Calvin sought to apply his study of Isaiah to the lives of his readers.

Calvin's pastoral concerns are everywhere evident in his commentary. He offers advice, gives consolation, exhorts his people to follow a good conscience. He does not scold, or resort simply to moralisms, but roots his homiletical applications to the substance of their faith, appealing at times again to central doctrines. Usually at the end of a passage, he turns to its application with a variety of formulae: "we ought to learn . . ." (1:7); "let us understand that the same things are addressed to us . . ." (5:8); "such is the manner therefore in which we ought always to deal with men who are estranged from God" (1:16).

Because Calvin is much concerned with well-regulated governance (3:4), much of his advice is addressed to Christian behavior within a civil society. He writes that nothing in life takes place by chance. God has a concealed bridle by which he restrains sinful men and prescribes limits beyond which they cannot go (7:20): "Let us then be assured that violent attacks are under his control." Although Calvin is fully aware that the prophetic comfort offered in Isa. 40 applies first of all to the Jewish captives in Babylon, he does not hesitate to extend the comfort "to ourselves whenever our strength fails" (40:30).

One of the effects of Calvin's biblical exegesis is that there never developed for him "an ugly ditch" (Lessing) that separated scientific, historical interpretation from the existential needs of his hearers. The ease with which he moved from the past to the present and to the future would confirm that he not only assumed the unity of the Christian Bible, but applied the ancient prophet's message as a living and truthful Word of God that had not lost its relevance in instructing and guiding his own people.

Bibliography of John Calvin

Primary Sources

Ioannis Calvini Opera Supersunt Omnia, edited by W. Baum, E. Cunitz, and E. Reuss. 59 vols. Braunschweig: Brunsvigae, 1863-1900.
The Commentaries of John Calvin. 46 vols. Edinburgh: Calvin Translation Society, 1843-55. Reprint, Grand Rapids: Eerdmans, 1979.
Institutes of the Christian Religion, edited by John T. McNeill. 2 vols. Philadelphia: Westminster Press, 1960.
Calvin's Commentary on Seneca's "De Clementia," edited by F. L. Battles and A. M. Hugo. Leiden: Brill, 1969.
Sermons sur le livre d'Esaïe, chs. 13–29. Supplementa Calviniana, vol. 2, edited by G. A. Barrois. Neukirchen: Neukirchener Verlag, 1961.

Secondary Sources

Barth, K. *Calvin.* Theologische Existenz Heute, 37. Munich: Kaiser, 1936.
Battles, F. L. "God Was Accommodating Himself to Human Capacity." *Interpretation* 31 (1977): 19-38.

Berger, S. *La Bible au XVIe Siècle: Étude sur les Origines de la Critique Biblique* (1879). Reprint, Geneva: Slatkine Reprints, 1969.

Bohatec, J. *Budé und Calvin: Studien zur Gedankenwelt des französischen Frühhumanismus.* Graz, 1950.

Bouwsma, W. J. *John Calvin: A Sixteenth Century Portrait.* New York: Oxford, 1988.

Breen, Q. *John Calvin: A Study in French Humanism* (1931). Hamden, Conn.: Archon, 1968.

Cramer, J. A. *De Heilige Schrift bij Calvijn.* Utrecht: Oosthoek, 1926.

Dowey, E. A., Jr. *The Knowledge of God in Calvin's Theology.* New York: Columbia University Press, 1965.

Duffield, G. E., ed. *John Calvin: A Collection of Distinguished Essays.* Grand Rapids: Eerdmans, 1966.

Farrar, F. W. *History of Interpretation.* London: E. P. Dutton, 1886; reprint, Grand Rapids: Baker, 1961.

Forstman, H. J. *Word and Spirit: Calvin's Doctrine of Biblical Authority.* Stanford: Stanford University Press, 1962.

Frei, H. *The Eclipse of Biblical Narrative.* New Haven: Yale University Press, 1974.

Fullerton, K. *Prophecy and Authority.* New York: Macmillan, 1919.

Gamble, R. C. "'Brevitas et Facilitas': Toward an Understanding of Calvin's Hermeneutic." *Westminster Theological Journal* 47 (1985): 1-17.

Ganoczy, A. *The Young Calvin.* Philadelphia: Westminster, 1987.

Ganoczy, A., and S. Scheld. *Die Hermeneutik Calvins: Geistesgeschichtliche Voraussetzungen und Grundzüge.* Wiesbaden: Franz Steiner, 1981.

Ganoczy, A., and K. Müller. *Calvins handschriftliche Annotationen zu Chrysostom: Ein Beitrag zur Hermeneutik Calvins.* Wiesbaden: Franz Steiner, 1981.

Gerrish, B. A. "The Word of God and the Words of Scripture: Luther and Calvin on Biblical Authority." In *The Old Protestantism and the New,* pp. 57-68. Chicago: University of Chicago Press, 1982.

Greef, W. de. *Calvijn en het Oude Testament.* Groningen: Ton Bolland, 1984.

Greene-McCreight, K. E. *Ad Litteram: How Augustine, Calvin, and Barth Read the "Plain Sense" of Genesis 1–3.* Bern and New York: Peter Lang, 1999.

Haroutunian, J. "Calvin as Biblical Commentator." In *Calvin's Commentaries,* pp. 15-50. Philadelphia: Westminster, 1958.

Kraus, H.-J. "Calvin's Exegetical Principles." *Interpretation* 31 (1977): 8-18.

Lane, A. N. S. "Calvin's Use of the Fathers and the Medievals." *Calvin Theological Journal* 16 (1981): 149-205.

Lehmann, P. "The Reformers' Use of the Bible." *Theology Today* 3 (1946): 328-44.

Muller, R. A. "The Hermeneutic of Promise and Fulfillment in Calvin's Exegesis of the Old Testament." In *The Bible in the Sixteenth Century,* edited by D. G. Steinmetz. Durham: Duke University Press, 1990.

Neuser, W. H., ed. *Calvinus Reformator: His Contribution to Theology, Church and Society.* Potchefstroom: Potchefstroom University Press, 1982.

Parker, T. H. L. *Supplementa Calviniana.* London: Tyndale Press, 1962.

———. *Calvin's New Testament Commentaries.* London: SCM, 1971.

———. *Calvin's Old Testament Commentaries.* Edinburgh: T. & T. Clark, 1986.

———. *Calvin's Preaching.* Edinburgh: T. & T. Clark, 1992.

Puckett, D. L. *John Calvin's Exegesis of the Old Testament.* Louisville: Westminster John Knox, 1995.

Schellong, D. *Calvins Auslegung der synoptischen Evangelien.* Munich: Kaiser, 1969.

———. *Das evangelische Gesetz in der Auslegung Calvins.* Munich: Kaiser, 1968.

Steinmetz, D. G. "John Calvin on Isaiah 6: A Problem in the History of Exegesis," *Interpretation* 36 (1982): 156-70.

Tholuck, F. A. G. "The Merits of Calvin as an Interpreter of the Holy Scriptures." *The Biblical Repository* 2 (1832): 541-68.

Torrance, T. F. *The Hermeneutics of John Calvin.* Edinburgh: Scottish Academic Press, 1988.

Vischer, W. "Calvin, exégète de l'Ancien Testament." *Études Théologiques et Religieuses* 40 (1965): 213-31.

Weber, H. E. *Reformation, Orthodoxie und Rationalismus,* vol. 1, pp. 217-57. Gütersloh: Bertelsmann, 1937.

Woudstra, M. H. "Calvin Interprets What 'Moses Reports': Observations on Calvin's Commentary on Exodus 1–19." *Calvin Theological Journal* 21 (1986): 151-74.

Wright, D. F. "Accommodation and Barbarity in John Calvin's Old Testament Commentaries." In *Understanding Poets and Prophets: Essays in Honour of George Wishart Anderson,* edited by G. Auld, pp. 413-27. Sheffield: Sheffield Academic Press, 1993.

15

Seventeenth- and Eighteenth-Century Interpreters

The widely used term "post-Reformation period" attempts to bridge the historical development of theology during the seventeenth and eighteenth centuries. It is useful in recognizing the entrance of a multitude of new forces at work in Europe. However, the terminology offers a one-sided focus on theology and fails to reckon with a host of other new directions. One thinks, for example, of the influence of French and German philosophies of the Enlightenment, the impact of English deism on the European continent, the tumultuous effects of religious conflicts, and the new political, social, and economic configurations within Europe.

Nevertheless, for our particular study, the term is helpful in highlighting the enormous diversities that emerged in relation to the interpretation of the Bible. Our concern is not to be exhaustive, but rather to offer a selection of typical interpretations that would continue to have an impact in understanding the role of the past as well as in the shaping of the future. As before, the choice of scholars will be restricted to those who have written either commentaries or treatises on the book of Isaiah.

I. Grotius and Calov

We begin with an example of two diametrically opposed biblical scholars of the seventeenth century, Hugo Grotius and Abraham Calov.

Hugo Grotius (1583-1645) at first might seem to be an unlikely choice. His great reputation arose from his broad humanistic learning in philology and the classics, perhaps only paralleled by Erasmus. Grotius was primarily trained in law and served in several important political and diplomatic offices during his lifetime.

His international reputation was established with his epoch-making volume of 1625, *De iure belli ac pacis,* which sought to define the boundaries of international law governing states in war and peace. His second important book, *De veritate religionis Christianae* (1627) was an apologetic defense of Christianity in terms of an appeal to the trustworthiness of scripture. It was also an attempt to overcome the bitter doctrinal strife within Holland by establishing a rational basis for Christian unity. In addition, Grotius was also a biblical scholar trained especially in the classics, but also with a knowledge of Hebrew and Syriac. His goal was to write annotations on all of the books of the Old Testament and the New, which project he largely achieved before his untimely death in 1645. Our focus will fall on his Annotations on Isaiah (reprinted, *Critici Sacri,* vol. 4).

The most notable contribution of Grotius was his attempt to establish philologically the precise meaning of biblical words and phrases. Toward this end, he appealed directly to the Hebrew text, which he compared with the various Greek translations along with the Jewish targums. Frequently, he was highly critical of the Vulgate's rendering of the Hebrew text. In addition, Grotius was also committed to recovering the historical background of each biblical text, and he employed his extensive knowledge of Greek and Latin sources in the task. Finally, Grotius sought to combine a rational and imaginative reading of controversial texts, which often appeared to his critics as unwarranted speculation. Although he was not overtly antagonistic to Christian tradition after the manner, say, of Gesenius in the nineteenth century, he gave the tradition no privileged status, and continually substituted his own exegetical construal in its place, much to the anger of his opponents.

In sum, perhaps one of the most penetrating evaluations of Grotius's exegetical work remains that offered by Ludwig Diestel (*Geschichte des Alten Testamentes,* 1869, pp. 430ff.). Diestel acknowledged the usefulness of his succinct annotations, which excelled with incisive and learned philological precision. However, the weakness of Grotius's approach was that the reader never received insights into the larger context of an entire passage, which was unfortunate because his avowed aim was to write for the laity. Nevertheless, Diestel evaluated Grotius's contribution to biblical studies as "epochmaking" for several reasons. First, with extraordinary freedom he sought to break with Christian exegetical tradition and to treat the biblical text purely as a scientific object to be critically analyzed. Second, he disregarded all appeals to the New Testament's use of the Old Testament as possessing any exegetical authority. Third, he spoke occasionally of a "mystical sense" only as a concession to his audience, but made it clear that it did not represent his own opinion. In our subsequent analysis of Grotius's commentary on Isaiah, we shall return to several points of Diestel's evaluation.

Abraham Calov (1612-86) represented the exactly opposite position from that of Grotius. He received a classical training within the tradition of strict Lutheran orthodoxy. He held various university positions both in philosophy and theology, ending up with a call to the University of Wittenberg in 1656. During much of his career Calov was deeply involved with various religious controversies, in which he opposed vigorously any overtures of a union proposed by Calixt. He regarded Socinius as an archenemy of Christianity. He wrote a variety of books and tractates in systematic theology, but he is best known for his biblical commentaries published between 1672 and 1676 entitled *Biblia Testamenti Veteris illustrata* and *Biblia Novi Testamenti illustrata*. In an astonishing display of polemics, Calov printed the complete text of Grotius's *Annotationes* along side of his own commentary. As a result, his *Biblia illustrata* is an extremely convenient tool by which to compare the differing interpretations of these two scholars on the book of Isaiah.

During the nineteenth century Calov was the subject of harsh judgments. Diestel *(Geschichte des Alten Testaments)* dismissed him utterly as an anachronism without any redeeming qualities (p. 403). However, the recent treatment by Reventlow (*Epochen der Bibelauslegung,* vol. 3, pp. 203-33) offers a more balanced assessment that is fairer in respect to his strengths.

We turn now to treat some specific examples of the debate from the book of Isaiah.

1. The problem of understanding the reference in Isa. 7:8 to sixty-five years until Ephraim would be destroyed, has long been an exegetical crux. One of the most frequent explanations is to start the chronology with Amos's prophecy against Israel rather than within the context of Isaiah's prophecy. Grotius will have none of this ploy. He makes a brilliant but speculative textual emendation reading "six" instead of "sixty-five," which would correlate well with the destruction by Shalmaneser of Ephraim as reported in 2 Kings 17:3-6.

Calov's response is to reject the emendation as "audacious," and he returns to the traditional harmonization. However, there then follows an argument that indicates a dogmatic hardening never present either with Luther or Calvin. Calov appeals to the truth of the *Hebraica veritas* and to divine providence, which has preserved the text uncorrupted.

2. A second feature characteristic of Calov's interpretation of the Old Testament is to assume that any New Testament citation from the book of Isaiah is the correct and normative understanding of the Old Testament text.

For example, the vision of the prophet of God in the temple (chapter 6) is interpreted in John 12:41: "Isaiah saw his glory (Christ's) and spoke of him." Grotius understands the object of the vision to be a *fulgorum eximum* ("an extraordinary flash of lightning"). Calov responds: *perversa depravatio!* Then he proceeds to demonstrate by citations from the Church Fathers that the church has always held that Isaiah saw the glory of Christ the Son of God. This then leads him into a theological discussion of the church's understanding of the Trinity and its adumbration in the liturgy of the seraphim: *"sanctus, sanctus, sanctus."* Calov not only attacks the Socinians, but also Calvin for his tendency to downplay a Christological reference in the Isaiah passage.

3. Calov frequently attacked opponents he characterized as "Judaizers." Grotius is the chief example of this error, but Calov extends his list much wider to encompass the Socinians, humanists, and many Reformed scholars — including, at times, Calvin. The term applies to Christians who consciously or unconsciously interpret an Old Testament passage after the fashion of the Jews. Usually this entails seeking an immediate historical reference to a prophecy deemed messianic by Christian tradition.

An early example of the controversy appears over the interpretation of Isa. 2:2-4. Grotius describes Isaiah's prophecy as one depicting a time "afterwards" *(posthac)* in which the city of Jerusalem would be delivered from the siege of Rezin of Syria and Pekah of Ephraim, initiated during the reign of Ahaz. In contrast, Calov understands the passage as offering an eschatological prophecy concerning the last days with the divine exaltation of Jerusalem, the gathering of the nations to Zion, and the entrance of universal peace under the reign of Christ.

Another classic example is the reference in Isa. 9:6 to a child on whose shoulders will rest the government and whose name will be called "Wonderful, Counselor, Mighty God, Everlasting Father, Prince of Peace." Grotius follows the Jewish tradition in identifying the figure with Hezekiah. Calov is horrified and cannot imagine how this fully obvious reference to the Messiah could be rejected. However, he does calm down and offer several pages of exegetical evidence to prove why the exalted names could only refer to a divine figure and certainly not Hezekiah. A similar debate occurs in Isa. 11:1 with the "shoot from the stump of Jesse," whom both the Jews and Grotius again identify with Hezekiah.

The interpretation of Isa. 7:14 was somewhat more complex even among Jewish interpreters. Rashi had abandoned the earlier identification of the child with Hezekiah because of a chronological inconsistency, and the child was seen rather as a later son of the prophet. Grotius developed a rather elaborate theory, building on an earlier Jewish midrash of a second marriage of the prophet Isaiah, since the *almah* of chapter 7 could not have been the same woman who gave birth to Shear-jashub. By identifying the same child in chapters 7 and 8, he finds further evidence that the son was indeed the son of Isaiah's wife, the prophetess.

Calov first responds by offering literary evidence that the style in which the sign was given in chapter 7 was far too elevated and mysterious to refer to an ordinary child. He cited other Old Testament passages as evidence that a prophetic sign also transcended the ordinary. However, behind all these arguments was Calov's basic concern to discount any intermediate stages of fulfillment, which he regarded as undermining the ultimate Christological fulfillment. As a result, any appeal to an ongoing *Heilsgeschichte,* or a continuing process of fulfillment, was unacceptable to Calov. It is significant that such orthodox Reformed scholars as Cocceius and Vitringa took a very different direction even in the seventeenth century.

Of course, the problem of providing a genuinely historical referent for Isaiah's prophecies was still far from being solved by Grotius. One begins to note the inadequacies of his approach when turning to his interpretation of chapters 40–66. For example, when he begins to comment on the servant passages in chapters 52:13–53:12, Grotius follows his earlier exegetical practice and speculates on some well-known historical figure in this case, identifying the servant with Jeremiah. His choice is not irrational, since there are several literary parallels between Jeremiah's sufferings and those of the servant. However, the problem arises for Grotius that in chapters 40–66 he is really unable to reconstruct any genuinely historical context. He recognizes events which seem to be late post-exilic, but he remains confused about why the prophet has skipped over all the kings who followed Hezekiah.

Of course, this historical and exegetical problem was later resolved when "Deutero-Isaiah" was identified as a later exilic author. However, this critical option was not available to Grotius. He still assumed the eighth-century prophet Isaiah was the author of the entire book and spoke of the clairvoyant quality of the prophet even to provide the name of Cyrus.

4. There is one final issue of dispute between Grotius and Calov that turns out to be of considerable hermeneutical significance. After offering his identification of the promised child in chapter 7 as the son of Isaiah the prophet, according to the literal sense of the text, Grotius suddenly introduces another term. He appeals to a "mystical sense" in arguing that in some manner Christ could nevertheless be clearly perceived (*Christum agnoscentibus liquido apparere, Biblia illustrata,* vol. 3, p. 52). Then again, after he identifies the servant of chapter 53 as Jeremiah according to the literal sense, he adds

that the mystical sense speaks of another. Accordingly, the Isaiah text does not relate to Christ *sensu literali,* but only mystically *(tautum mystico).*

Calov responds in a furious attack. How can one have a mystical sense that contradicts a literal? Calov further points out that Grotius is not appealing to the church's tradition of multiple senses. Nor does he suggest that the relationship is between a type and its antitype. Rather, the mystical hangs over the text in a vague, unexplained manner, in which the two contradictory senses are left disconnected. At one point in chapter 7, Calov offers the hypothetical suggestion that, from one perspective, every liberation of the Jewish people could be considered a prefiguration of the spiritual liberation effected by God through Christ, but then he is quick to add that this is not what Grotius intends by a mystical sense. Calov might have pushed Grotius toward some form of ontological interpretation of prophecy, but he cut off this option as well as the typological. As a result, a profoundly Christian exegetical tradition present in both the Church Fathers and Reformers is missing in both protagonists.

II. Johannes Cocceius (1603-1669)

Few scholars have remained so controversial in the history of biblical interpretation as has Johannes Cocceius. On the one hand, he has been named the most significant Reformed theologian of the seventeenth century (Faulenbach, *Weg und Ziel,* p. 1). On the other hand, he has been consistently dismissed as an advocate of the wildest form of allegorical typology for his extension of Old Testament prophecy to include references to historical events even up to the seventeenth century (cf. the examples in Schrenk, *Gottesreich,* p. 29). It is this paradox that I shall attempt to address when assessing his contribution to biblical studies.

1. Life and Works

Cocceius was born in Bremen in 1603 to a distinguished academic family. He began his training in Bremen, and in the gymnasium he learned Latin, Greek, Hebrew, Syriac, and Arabic. In addition he pursued the study of rabbinics and Talmud. When he moved to Franeker, he received training in theology by leading scholars including Maccovius and Ames. In 1643 he became professor of theology in Franeker, and later in Leiden until his death in 1669. Although Cocceius's contribution to theology has usually focused on his influence in developing the Reformed school of federal theology (cf. Schrenk, pp. 82ff.), our present concern will center on his biblical and exegetical writings and will only peripherally touch on his role in federal theology.

The scope of his writings is truly enormous. His *opera omnia* were published in eight folio volumes from 1673-1675 in Amsterdam, and then expanded to twelve volumes in the third edition of 1701-1706. Beside several huge tomes in systematic theology, numerous polemical and apologetic works, and a Hebrew lexicon (1669), he succeeded in writing commentaries on virtually every book of the Old and New Testaments. Even such a critical scholar as Ludwig Diestel, who dismissed Calov as insignificant and reactionary, had much positive to say of Cocceius, and was impressed with his enormous philological and rabbinic knowledge.

Another sign of Cocceius's significance is reflected in the number of students who subsequently directed his exegetical approach in many new and fresh directions. Among the next generation of biblical scholars, the names of Campegius Vitringa, Hieronymus Witsius, and Friedrich Adolf Lampe come to mind. Again, of particular interest has been the impact of Cocceius on the Lutheran church and the support he offered to the various forms of German pietism. More controversial is the proposed relation between Cocceius and the *heilsgeschichtliche* school of Carl Kraft and J. C. K. von Hofmann represented in Erlangen in the nineteenth century.

2. Cocceius's Understanding of Scripture and Theology

When viewed from a purely formal perspective, Cocceius seems to be a representative of classic seventeenth-century orthodox Reformed theology. In his *Summa Theologiae* (1662) and again in the preface to his commentary on Isaiah, the familiar components of Protestant scholasticism appear: The Bible as the infallible Word of God, the divine revelation of Jesus Christ in scripture, the perspicuity of God's eternal will, and the continuous guidance of the Holy Spirit in conveying its message to the believer.

Yet this initial impression of Cocceius can lead to a serious misunderstanding of his theology. Actually Cocceius, more than any other contemporary theologian, broke the back of the older form of scholastic Protestantism. However, he did not do so after the manner of Grotius, who foreshadowed the Enlightenment in his attack on the church's tradition. Rather, Cocceius rejected the dogmatic system of his Reformed predecessors, which was grounded on various philosophical assumptions (e.g., Polanus), and he sought a new approach by means of a direct appeal to biblical exegesis. Of course, an appeal to the Bible was hardly new, but Cocceius rejected its traditional usage as simply prooftexting through the means of *dicta probantia*.

In contrast, he set forth the exegetical steps of a philological study of scripture, on which his hermeneutics was grounded. He began with a study of the individual words of the biblical text and sought to find their significance within the integrity of the oracle. However, it was in the larger composition *(tota compages orationis)* that he placed his major emphasis. Moreover, this plain, grammatical sense was not seen in opposition to its broader and deeper meaning, but was the source from which he could discern the complete spirit of the Bible. Indeed, he did not refrain from drawing the logical consequences that he thought reflected the intent of its divine author. Significantly, Cocceius was highly critical of Origen's method of contrasting the spiritual sense with the literal (cf. the discussion in Schrenk, p. 30).

However, even more crucial to Cocceius's approach was its unswervingly Christological focus in every sphere of his interpretation. Although Schrenk *(Gottesreich)* certainly was aware of Cocceius's Christological emphasis, it was actually Faulenbach *(Weg und Ziel)* who recovered the centrality of the knowledge of Jesus Christ for his theology. Faulenbach cites a typical formulation of Cocceius: "The principal matter of the gospel is this: Jesus is the Christ promised to the Fathers, in whom the Fathers hoped and in whom they received life." Then Faulenbach concludes, "In these words lies the entire understanding of Scripture, indeed they contain the entire theology of Cocceius from its onset" (p. 45).

Accordingly, the purpose of the Bible is to serve as the means of divine revelation, but it can only be this vehicle when the Word of God is opened under the guidance of the Holy Spirit. The content of this Word is Jesus Christ alone; he is the Light. The goal of life is the pursuit of the knowledge of God in Christ. This knowledge is not merely an intellectual activity, but an experience of being transformed within a divine salvation produced solely by the power of God, not human reason. In the person of Christ, the believer grasps the trinitarian nature of God as revealed by the Son.

In the preface to the *Gesamtausgabe* of his works, Cocceius sets forth the theological foundation of his exegesis. What Moses and the prophets have written is interpreted to us through the gospel. The gospel is the center and starting point for the scriptural interpretation. One does not move in chronological sequence from Old Testament to New, but in reverse, because the key to understanding the Old lies in the New. Only through its fulfillment in the New Testament is an Old Testament prophecy made clear. This Christological Word is never subservient to dogmatic systems, but remains free and unrestrained to exercise its direct authority. Faulenbach continues to insist that Cocceius's theology cannot be understood until one recognizes the Christological interpretation of scripture as the foundation for all of his work (p. 54). Of course, this Christological position evoked great opposition from both sides of the theological spectrum, namely, the older Reformed orthodoxy on the right, and the followers of Grotius on the left. He was given the nickname *"Scripturarius"* by his opponents, who further satirized his position with the aphorism

> *"Grotius nusquam in literis sacris invenit Christum,*
> *Cocceius ubique."*

(cited from Diestel, p. 429)

3. Cocceius and Heilsgeschichte

During the nineteenth century Cocceius was often described as one of the originators of the school of *Heilsgeschichte* and closely aligned with Bengel. Some of the evidence for this description was derived from Cocceius's attack on the scholastic categories of Reformed orthodoxy and his appeal to the historical sequence of scripture. In 1923 Gottlob Schrenk *(Gottesreich und Bund)* further made the case for interpreting Cocceius in terms of *Heilsgeschichte*. He argued that the two foci of his theology were the concepts of covenant and the kingdom of God. Scripture was a harmonic system in which all the stages of its *heilsgeschichtliche* development were dominated by these major themes. Particularly within the Old Testament there were clearly stages distinguishing different aspects of the divine economy and ordered in a fixed *ordo temporum*. The initial stage marked the freedom of the patriarchs, followed then by the Mosaic law through which servitude entered. Next followed the period of the judges, the concession to the rule of kings, and the destruction of the earthly rule of David's house through the Babylonian exile. The goal of all this development was reached by the coming of Jesus Christ in fulfillment of the Old Testament's promises, with the installation of God's covenant of grace.

In 1973 Faulenbach *(Weg und Ziel)* incisively attacked this widely accepted interpretation of Cocceius. Of course, certain elements of Schrenk's characterization of Cocceius's theology were sustained: the unity of scripture within the one purpose of God, the importance of covenant and kingdom, and the sharp contrast between the Old and New Testaments. However, Faulenbach argued that Schrenk had failed to see clearly enough the centrality of Cocceius's Christology and as a result had misunderstood his interpretation of history. First, the idea of a process of development, even an evolution, was completely alien to Cocceius, and stemmed from later German idealistic philosophy. Second, Cocceius never spoke of a *Heilsgeschichte,* nor did he ever focus on the phenomenon of history in itself. Instead he spoke of God's action on human beings. The one historical event of the incarnation of God in Christ alone constituted the covenant of grace; it was not a final stage of an historical development. In sum, the divine will is revealed in its Christological reality, not in a horizontal growth within history. The Old Testament has the character only of promise. In Christ alone was the eternally ordered covenant of grace made visible.

4. Cocceius's Apocalyptic Understanding of History

In 1869, Diestel summarized his analysis of Cocceius with a penetrating observation: "The basic error of Cocceius's exegesis can be decisively characterized: he acknowledges no actual prophecy, rather only apocalyptic" (*Geschichte,* p. 429). For Diestel this perception was so obviously a fatal mistake that he wasted no time in understanding its rationale or in exploring its ramifications. In contrast, the work of Schrenk and Faulenbach in the twentieth century has sought to pursue the exegetical, theological, and historical implications of Cocceius's apocalyptic reading of the Bible, rather than simply dismissing it as too bizarre to warrant further reflection.

In his exegesis of Isa. 2:1-4 (*Curae Majores, Opera,* vol. 3, pp. 64ff.), Cocceius sets forth clearly his apocalyptic scheme. History is divided into two kinds: the present age and the age to come (or age of the Messiah). The former is the age of sin and darkness; the latter is the rule of God and light. For his biblical warrant he cites passages from Dan. 8:19; 9:24; 10:14; Isa. 54:1; 61:2; 63:4, and Hab. 2:3-4. However, his categories and terminology are largely taken from the New Testament: 1 Cor. 2:6; Gal. 4:24-31; Eph. 1:21; and Heb. 2:5. The Old Testament belongs to the period before the advent of salvation in Christ, but faithful Israel lives in anticipation of the coming covenant of grace. His apocalyptic view of history thus sees two patterns of events: oppression versus redemption, the rule of Satan versus the rule of Christ, the covenant of works versus the covenant of grace.

As we observed above, the true knowledge of God is revealed in Christ by the entrance of his redemptive acts of grace. There is an eschatological sequence of these events that forms a pattern of God's unfolding will. For this reason attention to numbers is important. This divine intervention moves from promise to fulfillment, but the events are not linked by any development or growth within the sphere of ordinary history. God's action in the world of time and space is different in kind from that of imminent historical sequence. It is apocalyptic, because it has no causal connection with profane history, but stems solely from the divine will in the mysterious unfolding of redemptive action. The historical pattern is that from Daniel, Matthew 24, and Revelation. It is of the saints hard pressed by earthly rulers who are encouraged to endure, for the end of the old age is near.

There is, however, another aspect of Cocceius's apocalyptic emphasis. Cocceius was not interested merely in speculating about God's eschatological timetable. Rather, his whole approach was deeply theological and was intent on shaping the obedient life of the believer in the light of the knowledge of Christ. Christians lived in constant expectation of the entrance of God in their own history, and were continually confronted by the study of scripture to respond in their lives in the profane world with utmost moral seriousness. In a word, Cocceius's exegesis of scripture was highly existential. It served unswervingly to confront believers with the imperatives of life under grace. Knowledge of the patterns or stages allowed the simple, uneducated Christian to interpret his own life's journey within the stages of God's unfolding purpose. It was undoubtedly for this reason that Cocceius exerted a wide influence among various groups of German pietists, starting in the late seventeenth century and increasing during the eighteenth (cf. Schrenk, pp. 300ff.): not only his call for pious living, but also his appeal to life lived in constant expectation of God's surprising interventions.

One of the most consistent criticisms of Cocceius's exegesis, rehearsed by Diestel (p. 429) among others, is that he exploited biblical prophecy in the wildest kind of historical speculation by finding its fulfillment in the details of European history even in the sixteenth and seventeenth centuries. For example, he related Isa. 19:2 to the controversies after the death of Constantine, chapter 23 to events concerning Charlemagne, and 32:7 to the death of Gustavus Adolphus. These criticisms are serious, especially in the light of speculative, apocalyptic interpretations of the Bible that are still widespread in the twenty-first century (cf. Hal Lindsey, *The Late, Great Planet Earth*).

In response, I would suggest that a very different explanation of Cocceius's exegesis in regard to contemporary events is possible when seen in the context of his larger understanding of scripture. We have already noticed the Christological center informing his apocalyptic reading. He saw "God's history" as a sequence of moments of direct divine intervention that were linked not by historical development, but solely by the divine action within the rule of Christ. The individual Christian lived in two different spheres, in this present age and in the messianic. Following the New Testament's lead, the kingdom of God had arrived, but was not yet consummated within God's eschatological purpose.

Cocceius sought to discern in his exegesis a Christological key by which to see the hand of God at work both retrospectively and in the future. There was a pattern or sequence within these redemptive events. In this sense, Cocceius had a concept of *Heilsgeschichte*. The reference for example in Isa. 33:7 to the death of Gustavus Adolphus, the Swedish hero of the Thirty Years' War, was used to illustrate a component of a divine eschatological pattern, namely, that God was faithful in raising up a human deliverer, but then also allowed his bitter and untimely death. In sum, Cocceius's goal was not to engage in senseless speculation, but homiletically to illustrate for his hearers the recurring pattern of mystery within God's plan for his people.

5. Cocceius's Interpretation of Isaiah

Cocceius's exegesis of the book of Isaiah appears in three different forms in his *Opera*. The major commentary is found in his *Curae majores in prophetiam Esaiae*. In addition, there are two shorter expositions in his *Synopsis Prophetiae Jesaiae* and *Meditationes primae in prophetam Jesaiae*.

a. Isa. 2:1-4

Cocceius begins his interpretation in a debate with Jewish exegesis, but focusing mainly on a response to Abarbanel, because he also understands the prophetic text eschatologically. Abarbanel identifies the last days with the day of the Messiah, which will come after the time of Israel's punishment and the gathering of the exiles. Cocceius offers a different sequence of the last days and finds in chapter 2 a warrant for holding that salvation, divine blessing, and the announcement of justice precede rather than follow the final consummation. Both commentators share a common apocalyptic vocabulary.

The singularity of Cocceius's apocalyptic interpretation of Isa. 2:1-4 emerges quite sharply when it is compared with that of Vitringa, Cocceius's best-known student. For Vitringa the passage is to be taken metaphorically, and he follows the church's traditional reading in seeing here a messianic promise of the reign of Christ. However, Vitringa identifies an initial fulfillment of the prophecy in the rise of the Christian church, the spread of Christianity in the Roman Empire, and the converts from a multitude of nations within the peaceful rule of Rome.

For Cocceius the Isaianic language is not metaphorical, but he sets the passage within an apocalyptic context of the entrance of the new age. He uses as prooftexts Hab. 2:3 and Dan. 10:4. The prophetic passage has no fulfillment in imminent historical events, but relates directly to the entrance of Christ's reign. It speaks of the new Jerusalem of Zech. 8:3, the manifestation of the Spirit in Acts 2:33, 36, and the preaching of the apostles in Rom. 10:14-15.

b. Isa. 7–8

Cocceius's interpretation of chapter 7 generally follows the lines of traditional Christian exegesis. He gives much attention to the philological evidence of the *almah* (v. 14), and he rehearses the earlier debates with Jewish interpreters respecting chronology, the identification of the son, and the function of the sign. (Cocceius's most detailed philological arguments are given in his lexicon, p. 617.)

Only when Cocceius turns to his interpretation of chapter 8 does a characteristically apocalyptic reading emerge. At the outset, he deals with the mystery of writing on a tablet (Hab. 2:2) and the role of numbers. Then he argues that 8:1-4 is closely related to chapter 7, and is another sign supporting the earlier prophecy of Isaiah concerning Jesus Christ. He establishes his case by his interpretation of the two witnesses mentioned in 8:2, Uriah the priest, and Zechariah the son of Jeberechiah. Who were these two witnesses? According to his interpretation neither were born at the time of King Ahaz. Uriah the priest could not be the one used by Isaiah as witness because according to 2 Kings 16:10 he was an idolater who brought the Assyrian altar to Jerusalem. Rather, the passage in chapter 8 refers to Uriah the prophet who served during the reign of Jehoiakim and was killed for prophesying evil against the city (Jer. 26:20). Zechariah, cited by Matt. 23:35, is identified with the prophet living during the period of Darius the Persian (Zech. 1:1), who predicted the coming of Christ to Jerusalem (9:9) and the rebuilding of the temple. As a result, the two witnesses coming at a subsequent period after King Ahaz confirmed the Isaianic prophecy of chapter 7 as referring to Jesus Christ and his coming reign.

c. Isa. 19:1-15

This chapter is an oracle concerning Egypt. Cocceius takes his lead from Rev. 11:8, which pictures the last series of woes ushering in God's final apocalyptic judgment of the world. The beast that ascends from the bottomless pit will make war upon the people of the great city, "which is allegorically (spiritually) called Sodom and Egypt." Using this text for his warrant, Cocceius argues that not just Egypt of the Nile is meant, but the entire land area that encompasses the realm of the Roman Empire. Then he proceeds verse by verse to identify the references. God comes in a cloud to judge the idols of Rome and to judge those who set themselves against the Christian religion. This judgment was executed by Constantine the Great. Verse 2 signifies the many wars waged in the empire among the successors of Constantine because of the numerous heretics. The drying up of the Nile predicted in verses 5ff. is confirmed by the Turks being able to cross the rivers and lakes of Asia and Africa. Verses 13ff. relate to civil wars waged at the time of Henry III and Henry IV and the peace that finally emerged between Spain and Gaul. Cocceius concludes with an assurance that historical reports concerning all these events are readily available.

It is significant to note that Vitringa, certainly the most important biblical scholar in the school of Cocceius, offers a detailed refutation of Cocceius's "mystical" interpretation. He does, however, concede that Cocceius had some earlier allies in Eusebius, Cyril, and Theodoret, and to some extent even in Jerome. Vitringa's interpretation of Isaiah 19 (cf. below) is highly significant hermeneutically because he tries to offer a detailed historical interpretation in opposition to Cocceius while at the same time developing his own version of a spiritual fulfillment of chapter 19.

6. Summary and Evaluation

We began the study of Cocceius by noting the controversial quality of his work. He was a scholar of tremendous learning, wideness of scope, and great influence throughout the seventeenth century. Yet even during his lifetime his approach to biblical interpretation evoked heated disagreement.

By placing his apocalyptic approach to prophecy within the larger framework of his Christological focus, we have sought to interpret rather than to justify the theological rationale behind his biblical exegesis. But even a sympathetic scholar like Schrenk is openly reluctant to pursue in detail his apocalyptic position, judging it to be too far removed from the critical world to afford any real value to the modern reader.

Nevertheless, it seems to me there are aspects of Cocceius's biblical interpretation that call for serious reflection when judging his contributions to biblical exegesis:

1. First, it is important to be aware that Cocceius's prophetic interpretation was not a completely isolated, peculiar aberration, but that he stands

within the broad parameters of the Christian exegetical tradition even though he moved to its outer limits.

2. Second, Cocceius strove to maintain the tension between secular history and the story of God's rule — to speak anachronistically, between *Historie* and *Geschichte*. Because he chose to focus almost entirely on the latter and failed to see that these two dimensions of history could not be ultimately separated, his resolution was ultimately unsatisfactory. Yet he raised a central hermeneutical issue that would continue to erupt in the subsequent centuries as an abiding problem for Christian exegesis.

3. Third, he correctly envisioned the task of biblical interpretation to engage the reader directly with the unfettered Word of God and to maintain an existential dimension that would call forth a serious, moral response commensurate with the imperatives of the reign of Christ. His apocalyptic reading serves to enforce the urgency of the gospel message: we must be awake and alert, lest we miss the coming of the bridegroom.

However, there are glaring deficiencies in Cocceius's exegesis that emerge with great clarity when we compare it with the Isaiah commentary of Vitringa. As a loyal pupil of Cocceius, he gently offers a rejection of many of his teacher's interpretations. In his own exegesis of chapter 19 he demonstrates with no uncertainty that this chapter cannot be understood, especially in its theological richness, unless it is set in the context of ancient Near Eastern history, in spite of all the difficulties involved in an exact reconstruction of the events described.

For this reason, it seems appropriate that the next section focus on Vitringa and his attempt to join secular and sacred history as together giving evidence of God's promised sovereignty over the nations.

III. Campegius Vitringa (1659-1722)

1. Life and Works

Campegius Vitringa was born in 1659 in Leeuwarden, Frisia, a province in the northern Netherlands. He was educated at the universities of Franeker and Leiden. In 1681 he became professor of oriental languages at Franeker and remained there until his death in 1722. He was an avowed Reformed theologian of orthodox persuasion and engaged in many of the doctrinal controversies of that period. He wrote various tractates on subjects from both the Old and New Testaments, including a commentary on the book of Revelation. However, by far the most important work for which he is remembered is his massive, two-volume Latin commentary on the book of Isaiah (1714-20). A major characteristic of Vitringa was his attempt to chart a middle course between the extremes of Grotius on the left and Cocceius on the right.

2. *Vitringa's Approach to Exegesis*

In the preface to his Isaiah commentary, Vitringa summarizes his exegetical approach in a few succinct pages. First, he emphasizes the need to explain the exact meaning of the prophet's words by the use of philological means in order to grasp the *sensus genuinus* of the biblical text. He focuses on determining the literal sense and makes virtually no use of traditional allegorical methods. Although he is generally critical of Cocceius's typological/apocalyptic approach, he does on occasion appeal to the "mystical" or "spiritual" sense *(mystice)*. He expresses his preference for the Masoretic text over the Septuagint, but acknowledges the value of the early Greek translations and the role of rabbinic interpretation.

Second, he seeks to determine the subject matter of the oracle *(sensus realis)* and to engage the object of which the words speak *(objectum vaticinii)*. He tries to clarify his position by contrasting his understanding of prophecy with those of both Grotius and Cocceius. He expresses a major concern of his interpretation in setting forth his basic preference for seeing the nearest historical period as providing the prophecy's fulfillment rather than the distant future.

Third, he stresses that the fulfillment of each prophecy must be carefully determined and compared with its historical reference, chiefly by means of a critical analysis of the classical Greek, Latin, and rabbinical sources. Thus, there are frequent references to *themata collecta comparanda cum historia*. It is very clear that the fulfillment of prophecy, and especially its historical verification, forms a central component of his exegesis.

3. *Commentary on Isaiah*

In the interpretation of the first section of the book (chapters 1–12), one is initially surprised that his emphasis on the historical verification of Isaiah's prophecies is somewhat muted. Vitringa largely follows the lines of traditional Christian interpretation, with the result that his particular stress on historical verification appears restrained. For example, Isa. 2:1-4 is interpreted as a picture of the coming of God's reign and the victory of true faith over the heathen gods. The portrayal of transformed Mount Zion is set over against Mount Sinai, the symbol of the old covenant of law. He argues that this eschatological prophecy received its first fulfillment *(implementum prophetiae primum)* in the early history of the Christian church, for which he uses Acts 21:16-19 as his prooftext. However, the ultimate fulfillment is identified with the reign of Christ.

In chapter 4 of Isaiah, he interprets the prophecy to be describing the persecution of the church by hostile rulers, and he identifies a first fulfillment in the destruction of the evil rule of Herod Agrippa according to Acts 12:23. Isaiah 6 is again interpreted as pointing to the kingship of Christ, and as announcing harsh judgment against the Jews. Although he takes his main cue from John 12:41, he does try to retain some reference to Isaiah's mission as a prolepsis of future judgment. He sees the prophecies of chapters 9 and 11:1-9 as references to the messianic rule of Christ, but in the last verses of chapter 11 he finds a direct fulfillment of the promised destruction of Egypt, Arabia, and Mesopotamia. In sum, the traditional Christian reading of Isaiah's prophecies as fulfilled in Christ remains so strong that Vitringa's interpretation of the chapters fits largely within this inherited pattern. Only occasionally does he insist on seeing a multiple fulfillment of prophecies in earlier events of history.

A similar observation can be made regarding his interpretation of chapters 40–48 and 49–66. The first group of chapters is a revelation of the rule of God and the exercise of his power, wisdom, and might against all false deities. These chapters speak of the restoration of true faith. Vitringa rejects the view that these chapters describe the conditions of the Jews exiled in Babylon awaiting deliverance. Rather, he thinks the prophet Isaiah wrote these prophecies soon after the deliverance from Sennacherib's attack on Jerusalem. The reference to the coming of Cyrus is understood as an accurate prediction spoken 170 years before his appearance. Chapters 49–66 are regarded as the most important section of the book of Isaiah. The ecstatic prophet *(propheta hic extra se raptus)* reports both what God and the Son speak, and their words comfort the church with the promise of the coming Messiah. The earlier format used in the commentary that succinctly summarizes the verification of each prophetic fulfillment at the end of each section has usually been omitted because all the prophecies are seen as directed to the rule of Christ in the future.

In striking contrast, only when one comes to the oracles against the nations in chapters 13–23 does one not find an effort made to demonstrate in the greatest detail possible the historical fulfillment of these prophecies. Vitringa begins his analysis of chapter 13 by seeking to prove from history the literal fulfillment of Isaiah's prediction of Babylon's destruction. Accordingly, Babylon would be destroyed completely, forever, and by the Medes. In attempting first to establish an exact date for the destruction, he refutes Grotius's contention that the fall of Babylon occurred in the period between Sennacherib and Nebuchadnezzar. He argues that parallels from Jeremiah 51 prove conclusively the Persian dating and can only be understood in relation to Cyrus's campaign. Then pursuing many minutiae, he engages in harmonizing the accounts of Xenophon and Herodotus regarding Cyrus's relation to both the Medes and the Persians.

Vitringa encounters a problem when it appears that the city was indeed captured but not fully destroyed by Cyrus. He counters by arguing that Cyrus's victory was only the first fulfillment of the prophecy, and that its complete fulfillment took place through various stages. The destruction that Cyrus began was continued by Darius Hystaspes, and again by Xerxes, who tore down the pagan temple. But certainly by the fifth century A.D. the complete destruction of Babylon was attested to by Jerome. Vitringa concludes that Isaiah predicted exactly the fall of Babylon some 200 years before the fulfillment started to unfold.

Then again, Vitringa's attempt to establish the historical verification of the prophecy of the fall of Tyre in Isaiah 23 is one of his most elaborate and complex discussions. He begins by showing from his classical historical sources that both Grotius and Abarbanel were wrong in arguing that Tyre was destroyed before Nebuchadnezzar's attack. Rather, in his opinion, the evidence is clear that the fulfillment of the prophecy refers either to the Babylonian destruction of Tyre or to the destruction of the city by Alexander. The initial difficulty is that there is no conclusive extra-biblical evidence to prove the case for Nebuchadnezzar, even though Isa. 23:13 links the destruction to the Chaldeans, as does Ezek. 26.

Moreover, Isa. 23:15 speaks of the destruction of the city lasting only seventy years, whereas Ezek. 26:14, 19-21 announces unequivocally that the destruction will endure forever. How is this contradiction to be explained? For a time Vitringa toys with a clever distinction that had previously entered into the debate, namely, between the ancient land-based city of Tyre and the more recently constructed island city of Tyre. Could it be that Ezekiel was prophesying concerning the ancient city that was indeed destroyed forever, whereas Isaiah 23 was speaking of the island city? This later fortification had been captured by Alexander, who built a dam in order to take the city, but afterwards this city had revived. However, Vitringa was too careful a historian to accept uncritically this way out of the dilemma. He remained convinced that the imagery of Isaiah 23 refers to Nebuchadnezzar's attack on the ancient, land-based city.

Next Vitringa gets further involved in elaborate calculations regarding the date when Nebuchadnezzar first assaulted Tyre. He sets the time at five years after the destruction of Jerusalem, but then this dating calls for further adjustments within the complex rise of Persian hegemony. Vitringa's theory certainly reflects a series of careful calculations, but in the end his reconstruction depends on a host of historical projections that may or may not be true. In a word, Vitringa has translated the biblical category of prophecy and fulfillment into a very different genre of complex historical speculations.

Before we turn to assess the hermeneutical contributions of Vitringa's exegesis, there is one further aspect of his method to consider. In the above examples, we have seen his great concern to pursue the literal sense of the prophetic text, usually along a historical trajectory. His major criticism of both Grotius and Cocceius was their failure to interpret Isaiah's prophecies according to the historical evidence available. It therefore comes as an initial surprise to discover that in a number of cases, after he has completed his historical interpretation according to the literal sense, he concludes his study with an appeal to the "mystical" sense. What does he mean by this, and what is its exegetical function?

First, it is important to observe that Vitringa does not include as part of his mystical interpretation the recognition of figurative tropes used by the author. For example, in opposition to Cocceius's apocalyptic rendering of the vision of a transformed Zion elevated above all existing mountains (Isa. 2:1-4), Vitringa interprets the passage according to its literal sense as an extended metaphor. He means something very different by his mystical interpretation, and its function is distinct. Invariably it comes at the close of his historical interpretation, and occasionally it is explicitly characterized as not undermining the literal sense. Moreover, it is not a return to the earlier traditional, allegorical method. Nor does he suggest a higher level of meaning beyond the literal, although very rarely he does use the terminology of the tropological reading (30:29-33).

A typical example of Vitringa's appeal to the mystical sense is found in Isa. 22:15-25, the oracle concerning Shebna and Eliakim. The fate of both of these men is set in the Assyrian period, but the details remain somewhat murky. Vitringa notes that language similar to the Isaianic oracle is used in the New Testament, especially in reference to the one who has "the key of David, who opens and no one shuts" (Rev. 3:7). He then joins this passage with Luke 16:1-9, the parable of the dishonest steward, to construct an analogue with Shebna. Finally, he draws some moral reflections on unfaithful servants among God's people.

Then again, at the conclusion of his interpretation of Isaiah 23, the oracle concerning Tyre, he connects the reference in Ps. 45:12-17 (the wealth of Tyre and the golden-woven garments) with Rev. 18:23 (the great merchants) to find a picture depicting heathen Rome and the similarity between Tyre and the pope. Finally, following his interpretation of Isa. 30:29-33, Vitringa reminds his readers that the passage refers to the divine punishment of Assyria according to its literal sense. Then he suggests an analogy between the Eastern church, symbolized by Assyria, which appeals for help from the Western church, and Egypt being a type of the corrupt Western church, otherwise called Babylon, unable to help.

To conclude, several observations come to mind in assessing Vitringa's appeal to a mystical sense. First, it has been undertaken without any of the careful rigor characteristic of his historical and philological exegesis. There is a casual atmosphere of a loosely attached homily. Second, one can only speculate whether it has arisen as a concession to his audience, or remains as a vestige inherited from his mentor, Cocceius. For whatever reason, these attempts at a "mystical" interpretation seem singularly unsuccessful and only detract from his otherwise impressive exegetical accomplishments.

4. An Evaluation of Vitringa's Hermeneutical Contributions

a. Vitringa's major contribution hermeneutically was his construal of the pattern of prophecy and fulfillment as a historical process in which the correspondence between the two could be rationally proven. He did not seek to redefine biblical history in any way, but employed a commonsense understanding of the occurrence of events in time and space that could be ascertained by anyone applying rational analysis to historical sources. Vitringa's massive apologetic defense of the literal coherence between biblical text and historical reference became widespread by the early eighteenth century, especially in England, Scotland, and North America. A multitude of books in this genre flooded the British market in the works of Thomas Sherlock, Thomas Newton, and Alexander Keith, to name but a few. However, in 1875 Abraham Kuenen wrote his exhaustive study of prophecy (*The Prophets and Prophecy in Israel*) that included three lengthy chapters exploring "the unfulfilled prophecies." Ironically, Kuenen offered almost a mirror image of Vitringa's hermeneutics before reaching exactly opposite conclusions.

b. I earlier criticized Cocceius's apocalyptic approach for having lost all theological interest in secular history, which he rendered peripheral to the redemptive actions of God. The reverse criticism can be made of Vitringa. He lost all sense of a dimension of *Heilsgeschichte*, that is, the eschatological entrance into time and space of the kingship of God in Christ that formed the prophetic witness to the mysterious will of God. Vitringa sensed no dialectical tension within the biblical story, but placed all events within a single historical trajectory. Even his attempt to resort to a "mystical" sense lacks any eschatological component, but reflects timeless moralisms and arbitrary analogies.

c. Finally, an existential dimension of biblical interpretation is largely missing in Vitringa. This loss is not after the manner of Grotius, whose historical skepticism blunted his hearing of the biblical message. Rather, Vitringa's horizontal reconstructions failed to serve as a vehicle of faith, but dissipated into speculations and endless hypotheses. There was no sense of a vertical imperative in receiving a Word of God. The homiletical skills of Cocceius that attracted generations of Reformed and Lutheran pietists were not apparent in Vitringa in spite of his largely conservative, orthodox theology.

IV. Robert Lowth (1710-87)

Up to this point, our study of the hermeneutics involved in the interpretation of the book of Isaiah has focused largely on European authors. However, this selection is not to suggest that nothing of importance in biblical interpretation occurred in England and Scotland during the Reformation and post-Reformation periods.

The publication of the great collection of commentaries in the *Critici Sacri* (London 1660, 9 vols.) indicated the intense English interest in the works of the leading international scholars of that period. This publication was followed shortly by Matthew Poole's *Synopsis Criticorum* (London, 1669, 5 vols.) which not only offered more commentators, but also changed the format to make the material more accessible, especially to Puritan preachers. The English Puritan influence on the European continent was felt by the migration of scholars, such as William Ames, to Franeker to become one of Cocceius's teachers. Major textual critical work was done in England not only by the publication of the London Polyglot, which followed the lead of the Spanish *Complutensian Polyglot* (1522), but especially in the work of Benjamin Kennicott and Robert Holmes. Finally, the impact of English deist writers offered a profound challenge to German orthodox scholars in a radically new form of biblical interpretation (e.g., Anthony Collins and John Spencer). The powerful impact of Scottish philosopher David Hume on Europe should also not be underestimated.

However, when it comes to the exposition of the book of Isaiah, one English scholar stands preeminent above all others: Robert Lowth, bishop of

London. His highly original study of the Old Testament signaled a major new exegetical paradigm whose effect was shortly to be felt throughout Europe.

1. Life and Works

Robert Lowth was educated at Winchester College and New College, Oxford. He was appointed professor of poetry at Oxford in 1741, the year in which he gave his first lecture in his famous series on Hebrew poetry. In the early 1750s he served various ecclesiastical offices, and afterward as bishop of Oxford (1766-77) and bishop of London (1777-87). His widespread reputation as one of the most influential Old Testament scholars in the English-speaking world of his day was based, above all, on his two most famous works: *de sacra poësi Hebraeorum praelectiones academicae* (1753), and *Isaiah: A New Translation with a Preliminary Dissertation and Notes* (1778).

2. Lowth's Exegetical Approach to Isaiah

In 1753, in his epoch-making book, Lowth set forth his analyses of Hebrew poetry. Then in 1778, in the introduction to his commentary on Isaiah, he briefly reviewed the results of his earlier work. Whereas it had previously been largely assumed that the Old Testament prophets were written in a form of prose, Lowth sought to demonstrate that Isaiah — indeed, the prophets in general — had written in a style that had to be called poetry. Building on his study first of the Psalms, he sought to show the peculiar features of Hebrew prophecy, pursuing the problems of meter and rhythm, and the structure of verses and stanza. Above all, he repeated his arguments for holding that the essence of Hebrew poetry lay in parallelism, which he distinguished into three different types.

Next, in his "Preliminary Dissertation" with which he introduced his commentary, he set forth the goals of his exposition: "to give an exact and faithful representation of the words and of the sense of the Prophet, by adhering closely to the letter of the text." But then he included an important addition: "to imitate the air and the manner of the author, to express the form and fashion of the composition, and to give the English Reader some notion of the peculiar turn and cast of the original" (p. 1). In practice this meant for Lowth that a translation must reflect the various elements that make up the uniqueness of the author's literary style. In a word, Lowth proposed to give an aesthetic reading of the book of Isaiah.

One can sense immediately the revolutionary effect of this new paradigm. Lowth speaks of the prophet's use of striking imagery taken from nature, "of the remarkable beauty, strength, variety of images" (p. 254). In his notes on Isaiah 13, he affirms, "[T]here is no poem of its kind extant in any language, in which the subject is so well laid out in such a richness of invention, with such images, persons, and distinction. For beauty of disposition, strength of colouring, greatness of sentiment, it stands among all the monuments of antiquity unrivalled." Or again, when discussing the portrait of peace envisioned by the prophet in chapter 11, he first compares the biblical style with Vergil and Horace, concluding that Isaiah's style is indeed superior. He calls chapter 17 "One of the boldest Prosopopoeias that was ever attempted in poetry." In this respect, the contrast with Calvin, Cocceius, and Vitringa could hardly be greater. Needless to say, his translation of Isaiah stands in a class by itself in its use of the English language, rivaled only by the authorized version.

There is, however, another aspect to his commentary on Isaiah that sets it apart from traditional translations. Lowth took great pains critically to restore the best Hebrew text possible. In his introduction he expresses his dismay at the received Hebrew texts of the Masoretes. He argues that when knowledge of Hebrew had died, only the unpointed consonants of the original author remained. With only consonants extant, any number of possible interpretations were now possible. When in the eighth century A.D. the Masoretes pointed the Hebrew text, they offered only one interpretation, which Lowth regarded often as helpful, but never authoritative. Rather, it was the task of the commentator critically to reconstruct the best text possible using all the tools at his disposal, especially the various Greek translations, the Latin, the Syriac, and the Targums. He also made wide use of the rabbinic commentators, particularly of Kimchi, Rashi, Ibn Ezra, and Abarbanel. The result is that Lowth felt free to propose a constant stream of emendations. He once observed that he had discovered fifty examples in the book of Isaiah where a word had been inadvertently dropped out. When commenting on chapter 20 and Isaiah's walking naked for three years, Lowth finds the text unlikely and conjectures that the period of three days be read.

Lowth's exegetical contribution has tended to be limited by later readers to his literary skill and aesthetic reading. Nevertheless, his other exegetical strengths were many. He showed an impressive philological knowledge, intensive interest in the details of ancient history, and constant attention to the *realia* of the biblical texts. For example, he describes the architecture of the city of Babylon, which he has gleaned largely from Greek sources. Often, however, he draws from his own experience information regarding the sequence of various crops, the house furniture within a typical dwelling, and the techniques of capturing a wild beast by snares or nets. He seems equally intrigued in describing different kinds of bows and arrows used in the ancient world. His attention fluctuates between the biblical world and classical culture, and his comparisons remain of much interest.

3. Lowth's Hermeneutical Contributions

In spite of Bishop Lowth's ecclesiastical office, the focus of his commentary rarely fell on specifically theological issues. His attention was predominantly on philological, historical, and literary matters. Still it is obvious that he had read widely in the Greek and Latin Church Fathers, but again when he cites them it is often on a philological or geographical problem. He also had studied Cocceius and Vitringa, but his references were largely to their philological contributions, and especially in the case of Cocceius, to his Hebrew lexicon, not to his Isaiah commentary.

This characterization is not to suggest that Lowth's exegesis was completely lacking in matters of theological content. Often he made judicious observations that greatly clarified an ongoing theological debate. For example, when treating chapters 40–49, he notes three themes that some commentators have thought highly contradictory: the deliverance of the Gentiles from their state of ignorance and idolatry; the deliverance of humanity from the captivity of sin and death (notes on 42:13); and the deliverance of the Jews from the Babylonian captivity. Lowth sought to demonstrate that these themes were coherently intertwined as distinct parts of a larger literary composition.

In general, his handling of the so-called messianic passages of Isaiah (chapters 7–11, 42, 53, etc.) was conservative and supported a traditional Christian interpretation. However, when treating chapter 53, he opposed those Christian expositors who saw no contemporary reference whatever to an actual context within Israel's history, but only understood the passage in relation to Christ's passion. Lowth spoke of a primary and secondary meaning, but avoided entering further into the controversy.

In several places Lowth insists on the primacy of the literal sense of the text, which he believed provided the foundation for all other figurative readings. He even suggests that the "mystical or spiritual sense is very often the most literal sense of all" (Isa. 52:13). However, once this rule is noted, he allows a legitimate role for the traditional categories of the tropological, allegorical, and mystical sense. Clearly it is the abuse, not the use, of the figuration to which he objects.

In regard to the question of understanding the book of Isaiah as Christian scripture, Lowth offered little direct reflection on the subject. He remained a pious Anglican clergyman, always referring in his commentary to Jesus as "our blessed Saviour" or the like. He simply assumed that Isaiah was part of the church's sacred writings and felt no tension to be resolved. On this issue one finds in his work no sense of struggle.

However, when we view Lowth's contribution from a modern perspective, particularly in terms of its effect on the discipline, we see that he did raise some basic exegetical problems that have continued to evoke serious hermeneutical reflection. For at least two centuries of critical study of the biblical text, non-Jewish scholars have generally accepted Lowth's position on the Hebrew text, namely, that there is nothing sacred about it, especially in regard to its Masoretic pointing. It has become a critical axiom that the Hebrew text has suffered serious textual corruption in its transmission, and is therefore in much need of reconstruction. Lowth attributed the sad state of the biblical text of the Old Testament to ignorant copyists and to the loss of Hebrew as a living language.

However, much has changed since the eighteenth century regarding the state of the Hebrew text, not least because of modern archaeological discoveries. In addition, a new hermeneutical issue has surfaced within the last half-century as to the significance of the Hebrew Bible's function as canon, an issue of course never raised by Lowth. Some scholars would now argue that the Masoretic text has a privileged status, not primarily because of its intrinsic quality of purity (although its condition is far better than ever envisioned by Lowth), but because of its role as authoritative, canonical scripture for its Jewish adherents.

Then again, of equal importance, if not more so, is the hermeneutical effect of the scholarly reconstructing of the allegedly original poetic forms of the Hebrew text, which has been largely if not completely disregarded by its rabbinical transmitters (cf. Kugel, *The Idea of Biblical Poetry*). The hermeneutical issue is somewhat akin to the philological one of using a modern approach to comparative Semitics to penetrate the Masoretic text in the hopes of discovering, say, homonyms lost or unrecognized by the rabbis. In both cases, the implications of such literary and philological reconstructions — endeavors brilliantly defended by Lowth — remain ongoing topics of critical debate, but in the meantime they continue to affect the interpretation of most contemporary commentaries and translations, conservative and liberal alike.

V. Augustin Calmet (1672-1757)

For many it might be considered odd to include Augustin Calmet as an important representative of biblical exegesis in the seventeenth and eighteenth centuries. For at least 150 years he has fallen into virtual oblivion. He was never considered a major player by German scholars, and by the nineteenth century he was dismissed as a pious Catholic traditionalist. Diestel (*Geschichte,* pp. 441-42) recognizes his great learning, but complains that his work was crippled by his orthodoxy and strict adherence to the Church Fathers. Within modern British and American scholarship he has been largely forgotten. J. H. Hayes evaluated his contribution in 1999: "The commentary broke no new ground and generally confronted issues from a fideistic position" (*Dictionary of Biblical Interpretation,* vol. 1, p. 156).

These negative evaluations stand in striking contrast to his reputation, especially in France and England, during the eighteenth and early nineteenth centuries. T. H. Horne (*Introduction to the Critical Study of the Holy Scriptures,* Vol. 5, 1846) cites approvingly Adam Clarke's judgment respecting Calmet: "This is without exception the best commentary on the Sacred Writing ever published, either by Catholics or Protestants" (p. 290). James Darling (*Cyclopaedia Bibliographica,* 1854, p. 548) lists in great detail Calmet's entire corpus with the comment, "immense learning, good sense, sound judgment and deep piety."

These conflicting evaluations are reason enough to assess once again his contribution, particularly in the light of his lengthy commentary on the book of Isaiah. Could it be that the present dismissal of Calmet is more a commentary on the present state of the biblical discipline than on Calmet himself?

1. Life and Works

Dom Augustin Calmet was born in Ménil-la-Horque, France, in 1672, studied in the local Benedictine college, and entered the Benedictine order in 1689. He continued his course of philosophy at the abbey of St. Evre, afterwards devoting himself to Hebrew, which he studied under Fabre, a Reformed clergyman. In 1704 he moved to the abbey of Münster to teach. His lectures formed the initial basis for his commentary on the Old and New Testaments, which he wrote with the help of eight to ten colleagues. The commentary was published in twenty-three volumes between 1707 and 1716, entitled *Commentaire littéral.* His other most important work was his biblical dictionary, later published as *Dictionnaire historique* (1730).

2. The Purpose, Structure, and Style of the Commentary

In his general preface to the books of the Old Testament (vol. 1, pp. i-viii), Calmet sets out the purpose of his commentary. He acknowledges that there are many learned expositions of the Bible, but for most clergy and for the ordinary laity of a congregation these are too technical, diffuse, and largely inaccessible. He therefore seeks to aid the reader in providing the Latin text of the Vulgate and de Sacy's French version in parallel columns. His philological comments are generally assigned to brief footnotes. In addition, he confines his more technical discussions to separate prefaces and dissertations in order to maintain the bulk of his expositions in a lucid narrative style. Throughout the commentary he provides chronological tables, maps, and a précis of ancient Near Eastern history to instruct the reader.

He is aware of the difficulty of interpreting the Old Testament to those without a knowledge of Hebrew, but he thinks that this obstacle can be overcome with an exposition of "brevity and clarity." Moreover, the pastoral side of Calmet emerges in his initial preface; he is deeply concerned to revive a love of the study of scripture both in the clergy and the simple reader (p. iv).

The heart of his hermeneutical approach is expressed in the title of the commentary, *"Commentaire littéral."* Although he acknowledges freely his commitment to the teachings of the Church Fathers and to the traditions of the Catholic faith, he wants to focus his interpretation on the literal, historical sense of the text, which he holds as the grounds for all other goals of exegesis. However, he then offers an important qualification: by the literal sense he does not mean simply a grammatical, philological exercise, or a focus on isolated Hebrew words, which only shifts the interpretation to dry and tedious minutiae. True exegesis must seek to penetrate to the mystery and profundity of the biblical message of the text. A truly historical interpretation can be a genuinely spiritual one at the same time.

Calmet next seeks to develop his understanding of the relation between the literal and the spiritual. Scripture has a double sense (vol. 1, p. 565). The first is the literal-historical; the second is spiritual, elevated, and messianic. These two senses are not two separate levels of meaning, but remain in a fluid state of dependency. At times the literal meaning flows into the spiritual in a simple extension. At other times one must understand the spiritual in order truly to grasp the historical meaning. The connection is never arbitrary, but sustained by the nature of biblical language and its symbolic potential. There is an obvious, historical context to the figures of Solomon or Cyrus; yet their significance cannot be restricted to the historical dimension, but transcends the literal-historical to resonate with a Christological intent.

In a certain sense, Calmet's understanding of the relation between the literal and the spiritual can be compared to the Jewish commentator Rashi. He is known for his search for the literal or plain sense of the text that is recovered by careful attention to the literary and historical context in its broadest sense. Yet Rashi also continued to cite midrashic traditions, usually without comment on their relation to the plain sense. The result was that his exegesis reflected both a sober exegetical precision and also a homiletical richness rare among the classic rabbinical expositors such as Ibn Ezra. Calmet also continued to refer to the non-literal interpretations of the Church Fathers, but usually without expressing his agreement or disagreement. In his preface he states that this style is intentional. Not only does it avoid unnecessary controversy; it serves to stimulate readers to reach their own decision as to its truth.

3. Calmet's Interpretation of Isaiah

If one were to read only Calmet's preface to Isaiah (vol. 5, pp. 569ff.) in his article on Isaiah in his *Dictionary*, it would be easy to see why he has been characterized as a traditional Catholic eighteenth-century commentator. He repeats the Jewish traditions regarding Isaiah's life with slight reservations, correlates the various chapters chronologically, and finds a consistent theological pattern of messianic expectation. The chapters following chapter 40 are understood as the consolation of Jerusalem with the coming of the Messiah, his suffering and passion in chapter 53, and the inclusion of the Gentiles in the coming victorious reign of Jesus Christ. Yet such an estimation of Calmet would seriously underestimate the quality of his exegesis and would fail to grasp some of his most creative contributions. Rather, careful study of three of his dissertations relating to Isaiah that precede his actual commentary provides more space to expand on the hermeneutical issues undergirding his commentary.

a. Dissertation on Isaiah 7:14

At the outset Calmet argues that one cannot understand the figure of the Messiah from a single passage, especially not just from Isa. 7:14, but the interpreter must take into consideration the whole range of passages within the larger narrative context that together encompass a true profile. He then cites a long string of passages, many of which are the traditional Christian prooftexts. However, he makes a strong case for the range of diverse events and remarkable imagery with which Israel's expected redeemer was described: from the lineage of Abraham, the tribe of Judah, and the royal line of David. He includes the attributes of a righteous life, his exercise of justice, and kingly qualities, often tapping the hyperbolic language of the Psalms. He draws the implication that one cannot match these elevated features with those of an ordinary human being.

Next he argues that the Jewish interpretation of chapter 7 is correct in stressing the fully human component of the prophetic passage. The biblical text speaks of a genuinely historical event occurring in recognizable time and space. There is a real child promised, an earthly father and a wife, probably of the prophet rather than of Ahaz. However, these earthly, historically concrete elements of the passage do not mean that the birth of Jesus would not be accompanied by extraordinary, mysterious, and divine elements.

This argument then leads Calmet to the heart of his hermeneutical stance. The Isaianic passage, like so many other prophetic oracles, has a double sense: there is the historical and the spiritual. One does not exclude the other; the two flow together. There are two children intertwined in the passage: a historical son of Isaiah, and a promised Son of God. These are not two separate levels, but are portrayed as a unity. The two portraits are linked by figurative language and are not merely artificially joined. The birth of the Messiah is represented by the birth of the young child, the miraculous birth of Immanuel by the fecundity of the maiden in 7:14, and the divine redemption of the human race by the impending deliverance of Judah from the Syrians. Although these two children are literarily fused in this passage, there are clear linguistic keys to distinguish them. The child described in 8:1-4, whose birth establishes a temporal sequence, is distinguished from 7:14-16 by the interpretation of Immanuel offered in Isa. 8:8, 10.

Finally, perhaps his most interesting exegetical ploy is his handling of the term *almah* (maiden). He begins by conceding to Jewish interpretation that the element of virginity is not primary in the word. In fact, the passage provides the potential for ambiguity. It is possible to read the passage as if it spoke of an ordinary birth of a maiden shortly to conceive a child from the prophet. Yet it is also possible to read it according to the traditions of the church. He then defends this approach as supported by the larger literary context and by the elevated tone of mystery and surprise. However, he concedes that neither of the two interpretations can make an ironclad case, but the perspective of the reader influences both. Christians need the eyes of faith to see the coherence of the promise. He denies that such a confession rests on an irrational fideism.

b. Dissertation on the Defeat of the Army of Sennacherib, Isa. 37:36

The exact cause and nature of the destruction of the Assyrian army before the walls of Jerusalem has long evoked controversial theories. Calmet begins his analysis by carefully reviewing the various interpretations (vol. V, pp. 590ff.).

1. The confusion of the battle, particularly during the darkness of night, caused the Assyrians to turn on themselves, thus effecting a military catastrophe.
2. The angel of death encountered in Exod. 12:29 was the agent of God's slaughter of the enemy. Other passages such as Ps. 78:49 and Sirach 48:21 are given as prooftexts.
3. According to the report of Herodotus, during the night a troop of field mice swarmed over the Assyrian camp. They ate their quivers, bowstrings, and the leather handles of their shields, so that on the following day, having no arms with which to fight, the Assyrians fled, suffering great losses during their retreat (*Histories* 2, 141).

Calmet does not rule out any of these theories, but he takes another tack. He turns to various passages within scripture that describe violent actions of God in doing battle with enemies, such as Isa. 29:6-7; Isa. 30:30-32; and Ps. 76:6-10. He then argues that these are part of a peculiar biblical idiom expressing the power of God over death set within a literary genre. These are not descriptions of any one particular historical event, but are used for overarching theological concerns. In sum, he does not resort to a rationalistic interpretation of the destruction of the Assyrian army, but he shifts the focus to discerning the particular force of biblical imagery to depict the identity of God in wrath.

c. Dissertation on the Beauty of Jesus Christ, Isa. 53:2

Calmet returns to an old interpretive problem that troubled Christian commentators since the Church Fathers. He assumes with the tradition that Isaiah 53 depicts the humiliation, suffering, and passion of Jesus Christ. But then he is faced with the difficulty of explaining the prophet's description of him: "He had no form or comeliness . . . and no beauty that we should desire him." How is this description of Jesus to be understood and reconciled with the very different, winsome portrait of the New Testament?

Calmet reviews at great length the solutions to the problem offered by the Church Fathers and schoolmen. He acknowledges the force of the argument that Christ's incarnation involved his assuming all the common defects of human nature, according to which he also suffered hunger, thirst, fatigue, and the need to rest. Yet he also responds positively to the interpretation that the beauty of Christ was not an earthly beauty, but unique, spiritual, and radiating goodness. In the end, Calmet does not attempt to harmonize the seemingly contradictory reports respecting Christ's beauty, but addresses the issue with some profound, theological reflections on the dual witness to the mystery of the incarnation.

To summarize, the remarkable characteristic of Calmet's exegesis is his ability to combine the literal and the spiritual dimensions of the Bible into a rich unity without the arbitrariness of his predecessors. Calmet brought to the task enormous learning in the fields of the empirical sciences. He was unrivalled in his knowledge of ancient geography, chronology, and archaeology. At the same time, he was deeply committed to using this knowledge to illuminate the spiritual aspects of scripture on which the Christian church was grounded. To use again an anachronistic analogy, it is as if he combined the historical expertise of Père Roland de Vaux (1903-71) and the hermeneutical skills of Henri Cardinal de Lubac (1896-1991).

Bibliography of Seventeenth- and Eighteenth-Century Interpreters

I. Grotius and Calov

1. Grotius

PRIMARY SOURCES

Opera Omnia theologica. 3 vols. Amsterdam, 1697.

Annotations in Vetus Testamentum, edited by G. J. L. Vogel. Halle, 1775-76.

De Veritate Religionis Christianae (1622), *Opera Omnia,* vol. 3, pp. 1-98.

The Truth of the Christian Religion. London, 1719.

SECONDARY SOURCES

Guggisberg, H. R. "Grotius, Hugo (1583-1645)." In *Theologische Realenzyklopädie,* vol. 14, pp. 277-80. Berlin: de Gruyter, 1985.

Kuenen, A. "Hugo Grotius als Ausleger des Alten Testaments." In *Gesammelte Abhandlungen zur biblischen Wissenschaft von Abraham Kuenen,* pp. 161-85. Freiburg: Mohr Siebeck, 1894.

Reventlow, H. "Humanistic Exegesis: The Famous Hugo Grotius." In *Creative Biblical Exegesis: Christian and Jewish Hermeneutics through the Centuries,* edited by B. Uffenheimer and H. Reventlow, pp. 175-91. Sheffield: Sheffield Academic Press, 1988.

————. *Epochen der Bibelauslegung,* vol. 3, pp. 211-25. Munich: Beck, 1997.

Unnik, W. C. van, "Hugo Grotius als uitlegger van het Nieuve Testament." *Nederlands Archief voor Kerkgeschiedenis* 25 (1932): 1-48.

2. Calov

PRIMARY SOURCES

Biblia Veteris Testamenti illustrata. 2nd edition. 3 vols. Dresden/Leipzig: J. C. Zimmermann, 1719.

SECONDARY SOURCES

Appold, K. G. *Abraham Calov's Doctrine of Vocation in Its Systematic Context.* Tübingen: Mohr Siebeck, 1998.

Diestel, L. *Geschichte des Alten Testamentes in der christlichen Kirche,* pp. 430-34. Jena: Mauke, 1869.

Hoffmann, G. "Lutherische Schriftauslegung im 17. Jahrhundert dargestellt am Beispiel Abraham Calov." In *Das Wort und die Wörter: Festschrift Gerhard Friedrich.* Stuttgart: Kohlhammer, 1973.

Kunze, J. "Calovius." In *Realenzyklopädie für protestantische Theologie und Kirche,* 3rd ed. (1897), vol. 3, pp. 648-54.

Reventlow, H. *Epochen der Bibelauslegung,* vol. 3, pp. 225-33. Munich: Beck, 1997.

Tholuck, F. A. G. *Der Geist den Lutherischen Theologen.* Wittenberg, 1852.

————. "Calovius." In *Theologische Realenzyklopädie,* 2nd ed. (1878), vol. 3, pp. 73-77.

Wallmann, J. "Calov, Abraham (1612-1688)." In *Theologische Realenzyklopädie,* vol. 7, pp. 564-68. Berlin: de Gruyter, 1981.

II. Cocceius

PRIMARY TEXTS

Opera Omnia. 3rd edition. 12 vols. Amsterdam: J. C. Zimmermann, 1701-6.

Lexicon et Commentarius sermonis Hebraici et Chaldaici. 9th edition. Frankfurt/Leipzig, 1714.

SECONDARY SOURCES

Bengel, J. A. *Bengelius's Introduction to His Exposition of the Apocalypse*. London: Ryall & R. Withy, 1757.

Bizer, E. "Die reformierte Orthodoxie und der Cartesianismus," *Zeitschrift für Theologie und Kirche* 55 (1958): 306-72.

Diestel, L. *Geschichte des Alten Testamentes in der christlichen Kirche*. Jena: Mauke, 1869.

Faulenbach, H. *Weg und Ziel der Erkenntnis Christi: Eine Untersuchung zur Theologie des Johannes Coccejus*. Neukirchen-Vluyn: Neukirchener Verlag, 1973.

Hirsch, E. *Geschichte der neueren evangelischen Theologie*, vol. 1, pp. 237-44. Gütersloh: Gerd Mohn, 1949; 5th ed. 1975.

Kraus, H.-J. *Geschichte der historisch-kritischen Erforschung des Alten Testaments von der Reformation bis zur Gegenwart*. Neukirchen-Vluyn: Neukirchener Verlag, 1956; 2nd ed. 1982.

Moltmann, J. "Geschichtstheologie und pietistisches Menschenbild bei Johannes Coccejus und Theodor Undereyck." *Evangelische Theologie* 19 (1959): 343-61.

————. "Jacob Brocard als Vorläufer der Reich-Gottes-Theologie und der prophetischen Schriftauslegung des Johann Coccejus." *Zeitschrift für Kirchengeschichte* 71 (1960): 110-29.

Müller, E. F. K. "Coccejus." *Realenzyklopädie*, 3rd ed. (1898), vol. 4, pp. 186-95.

Peterson, E. "Das Problem der Bibelauslegung im Pietismus des 18. Jahrhunderts." *Zeitschrift für Systematische Theologie* 1 (1923): 468-81.

Ritschl, O. *Dogmengeschichte des Protestantismus*. Bd. 3: *Die reformierte Theologie des 16. und des 17. Jahrhunderts in ihrer Entstehung und Entwichelung*. Göttingen: Vandenhoeck & Ruprecht, 1926.

Schrenk, G. *Gottesreich und Bund im älteren Protestantismus vornehmlich bei Johannes Coccejus*. Gütersloh: Bertelsmann, 1923.

Stoeffler, F. E. *The Rise of Evangelical Pietism*. Leiden: Brill, 1965.

Vitringa, C. *Commentarius in librum prophetiarum Jesajae*. 2 vols. Leeuwarden: F. Holma, 1714-1720.

Weber, H. E. *Die philosophische Scholastik des deutschen Protestantismus im Zeitalter der Orthodoxie*. Leipzig, 1907.

III. Vitringa

PRIMARY SOURCE

Commentarius in librum prophetiarum Jesajae. 2 folio vols. Leeuwarden: F. Holma, 1714-1720.

SECONDARY SOURCES

Childs, B. "Hermeneutical Reflections on Campegius Vitringa, Eighteenth-Century Interpreter of Isaiah." In *In Search of True Wisdom: Essays in Old Testament Interpretation in Honour of Ronald E. Clements,* edited by Edward Ball, pp. 89-98. Sheffield: Sheffield Academic Press, 1999.

Collins, Anthony. *The Scheme of Literal Prophecy Considered.* London, 1727.

Diestel, L. *Geschichte des Alten Testamentes in der christlichen Kirche.* Jena: Mauke, 1869.

Keith, A. *Evidences of the Truth of the Christian Religion derived from the Literal Fulfillment of Prophecy.* Edinburgh, 31st ed., 1844; reprint, New York: Harper Brothers, 1858.

Kuenen, A. *The Prophets and Prophecy in Israel: An Historical and Critical Inquiry.* London: Longman, 1877.

Newton, T. *Dissertations on the Prophecies which have been remarkably fulfilled and are fulfilling.* London: W. Tegg, 1759; 10th ed., 1804.

Sherlock, T. *Discourses on the Use and Interpretation of Prophecy.* 4th ed. London: J. Pemberton, 1744.

IV. Lowth

PRIMARY SOURCES

De sacra poësie Hebraeorum praelectionis. 2 vols. London, 1753.

Isaiah: A New Translation with a Preliminary Dissertation and Notes. London: J. Nichols, 1778.

SECONDARY SOURCES

Cripps, R. S. "Two British Interpreters of the Old Testament: Robert Lowth (1710-1787) and S. Lee (1783-1852)." *Bulletin of the John Rylands University Library* 35 (1952/3): 385-404.

Hunt, W. "Robert Lowth." *Dictionary of National Biography* 34 (1983): 214-16.

Kugel, J. *The Idea of Biblical Poetry: Parallelism and Its History.* New Haven: Yale University Press, 1981.

Marrs, R. R. "Lowth, Robert." In *Dictionary of Biblical Interpretation,* edited J. H. Hayes, vol. 2, pp. 89-90. Nashville: Abingdon, 1999.

Smend, R. "Lowth in Deutschland." In *Epochen des Bibelkritik. Gesammelte Studien,* vol. 3, pp. 43-62. Munich: Kaiser, 1991.

V. Calmet

PRIMARY SOURCES

Commentaire littéral sur tous les livres de l'Ancien et du Nouveau Testament. Various editions. 26 vols. Paris: Emery et al., 1707-16. 8 volumes in 9, Paris, 1724.

Dictionnaire historique, critique, chronologique, géographie et littéral de la Bible. 2 vols. Paris, 1720-21. English translation, 5 vols., London: Holdsworth and Ball, 1829.

SECONDARY SOURCES

Darling, J. *Cyclopaedia Bibliographica,* pp. 548-52. London: Darling, 1854.

Diestel, L. *Geschichte des Alten Testamentes in der christlichen Kirche,* pp. 441-42. Jena: Mauke, 1869.

Hayes, J. H., ed. *Dictionary of Biblical Interpretation,* vol. 1, pp. 158-59. Nashville: Abingdon, 1990.

Horne, T. H. *An Introduction to the Critical Study and Knowledge of the Holy Scriptures,* vol. 5, p. 290. London: Longman, Brown, Green, 1846.

Schmitz P. "Calmet, Augustin." In *Dictionnaire d'Histoire et de Géographie Ecclésiastique,* vol. 11, pp. 450-54. Paris : Letouzey et Ané, 1949.

16

The Nineteenth and
Twentieth Centuries

I. Historical Critical Commentaries
of the Early Nineteenth Century

The contributions of three critical biblical scholars, very different in style and method, shaped the analysis of Isaiah during the first half of the nineteenth century. However, none of these scholars were concerned directly with the issue that has occupied this study, namely, the struggle to understand the book of Isaiah as Christian scripture. Indeed all three, more or less consciously, set their work in opposition to the church's tradition of a corpus of privileged sacred writings.

1. Wilhelm Gesenius (1821) applied new philological tools to the book of Isaiah gained from comparative ancient Near Eastern philology in order to establish the true grammatical meaning of the text. No longer was he dependent on inherited exegetical tradition, especially the rabbinical readings, as much previous Christian interpretation had been. He avowedly directed his new critical approach, largely conducted independently of Jewish tradition by means of comparative philology, against many traditional Christian interpretations. Gesenius introduced into his exegesis a heavy dose of Enlightenment rationalism. Ironically, all subsequent commentaries on Isaiah — conservative as well as liberal — were consciously or unconsciously indebted to Gesenius, who established the modern study of Hebrew for many generations to come.

2. Ferdinand Hitzig (1833) offered a brilliant and radical application of a historical-critical literary analysis of Isaiah. He called into question many easy assumptions of Isaiah's literary unity as he exacerbated the presence of contradiction and tension within the prophetic text. In his highly subjective

but remarkably imaginative commentary, he unearthed a host of problems previously unseen. Throughout his distinguished career he remained extremely hostile to traditional Christian interpretation, which he regarded as an enemy to genuine exegesis.

3. Heinrich Ewald's exegesis of Isaiah (1869) was not of the same breadth and intensity as the two scholars above, but was rather only a part of a larger multi-volume work on all of the Old Testament prophets. His literary analysis was as radical as Hitzig's in reconstructing the alleged historical order and development of the book's composition. Still, Ewald left a powerful and positive impact on the field by continuing in the creative spirit of Herder. Ewald's brilliant romantic and intuitive grasp of the biblical literature came as a great relief to those expositors who had grown weary of the arid rationalism of Gesenius and his followers, but Ewald contributed little to the understanding of Isaiah. For him, the religious dimension of the prophets was not transmitted primarily in its written canonical form but on different levels of spontaneous experience, which he often described in philosophical terminology.

II. The Conservative Reaction of the Nineteenth Century

The nineteenth-century conservative response to the critical biblical scholarship of the end of the eighteenth century and especially the beginning of the nineteenth was set forth most thoroughly by E. W. Hengstenberg. He wrote no commentary on Isaiah (though he devoted an extensive chapter in his *Christology of the Old Testament* to the so-called messianic, Christological sections of Isaiah). For this reason, the Isaiah commentary of J. A. Alexander is a better representative of the conservative position. Alexander had studied under Hengstenberg in Berlin and aligned himself thoroughly with his perspective. His commentary represents the most complete and scholarly commentary on Isaiah in the English-speaking world during the mid-nineteenth century. Although Alexander was far less imaginative than Hengstenberg and in general would have been considered his epigone, he does offer an impressively thorough response to the historical critics' interpretation of Isaiah.

1. J. A. Alexander

The biblical interpretation in Alexander's commentary does not entirely reflect the traditional approach of the Protestant Reformers, but it is largely an apologetic attempt to refute the critical approaches of the preceding two centuries. Although Alexander does quite often briefly restate traditional Christian theology, most of his commentary is devoted to outlining the full range of competing options and then attempting to refute them with rational arguments. Very rarely does he respond with emotional polemics, or by personal attacks on his opponents. Rather, using their same tools — philological, historical, and literary — he mounts a logical case for a traditional reading of the Old Testament prophets, especially Isaiah. The detailed and exhaustive conservative exegesis of, say, Vitringa has been replaced with various forms of apologetics supported by largely historical and philological arguments. As a result, there is very little new in Alexander's exegesis, but instead an entrenchment and defense of traditional readings.

It is significant to note that Alexander rarely refers to the exegesis of the Church Fathers or the Schoolmen. Occasionally he records Jerome's comments on a place name or regarding a specific geographical tradition, but little attention is paid to his later expositions. Alexander has no place for allegory, and very little for even typology in his exegesis. He is highly critical of Grotius in his appeal to a double sense in Isa. 9:6. Thus seldom do the Church Fathers appear as dialogue partners, and the range of issues that concern him does not overlap with many of the major questions raised by the church's earliest traditions. In a real sense, his commentary is a reaction to the Enlightenment.

The servant passages are all identified with the Messiah, which he assumes from the usage of the New Testament. Chapter 53 is interpreted much in the fashion of Hengstenberg when it stresses "the wonderful agreement of the terms of the prediction with the character and history of Jesus Christ." The servant in Isaiah 42:1-6 and 49:1-9 is identified with the Messiah, but presented "in his own personality rather than in conjunction with his people." Alexander maintains that his position was held by the church from the beginning until the end of the eighteenth century, when it was abandoned by the German critics along with the doctrines of atonement and prophetic inspiration.

The final chapters of Isaiah starting with chapter 40 are understood as presenting the glorious change awaiting the church. In chapter 65 he uses the apocalyptic language of the New Testament to depict the radical shift in dispensations, symbolized by the new heavens and earth.

In sum, it would be difficult to characterize Alexander's interpretation of Isaiah as a struggle to understand it as Christian scripture. For him, no real struggle is evident; he simply assumes without debate that the Old and New Testament form a unity that points to the salvation of the church according to the promise and fulfillment in Jesus Christ. Most of his energy, however, is used in a vigorous apologetic defense of this tradition against the theologians, largely German, in the period from the late eighteenth century to the mid-nineteenth. One cannot rightly say that his interpretation is a repristination of the Reformers, since his scope is much narrower and little memory of issues such as the church's catholicity remains.

2. Joseph Knabenbauer

Joseph Knabenbauer was a German Roman Catholic scholar of the next generation after Hengstenberg and Alexander. His Latin commentary on Isaiah first appeared in 1881 (revised edition 1923). His contribution is important not only in representing a conservative Roman Catholic response toward the end of the nineteenth century, but also in showing a very different stance to a host of serious theological and hermeneutical issues usually associated with Protestant conservatives.

At the outset, it is significant to note that Knabenbauer's opposition to the historical criticism of the nineteenth century is neither initially nor primarily focused on the issue of biblical historicity. Rather, his overriding concern is the perceived attack on the traditions of the Christian church. Therefore, he begins with a review of the Church Fathers and medieval Schoolmen, who unanimously supported the authorship of the book of Isaiah by the one designated prophet. Knabenbauer's appeal to the Church Fathers does not just serve to sustain the church's exegetical tradition, but is used throughout the commentary as an integral part of his own interpretation. This is in sharp contrast to both Hengstenberg and Alexander, whose review of past scholarship seems to begin with the Reformers with only rare exceptions.

When Knabenbauer does turn to the historical components of the prophetic text, he tries to defend his conservative position not by appealing to church dogma, but rather by establishing the serious concerns with dates and authorship evidenced throughout the Old Testament. Then he mounts rational arguments against the critics' appeal to anonymous authors and careless historical referencing. Knabenbauer is fully aware of the whole range of both Protestant and Catholic interpretation, and in general he handles his opponents with fairness.

In one of his more interesting sections Knabenbauer attempts to refute the critical argument that the addressee of chapters 40–66 could only be an exilic or post-exilic audience in Babylon. Knabenbauer seeks to show that eighth-century Judah had already experienced such destruction and oppression during the lifetime of the prophet Isaiah as to account for the themes of judgment and salvation found first in chapters 1–39 and continuing in chapters 40–66.

Then, again, he demonstrates a good literary sense in starting with the larger structure of the book before focusing on the peculiar problems raised by individual passages. In spite of his resistance to seeing different literary levels, he is quite successful in retaining literary coherence even in the final form of chapters 1–39.

Finally, he attempts throughout his commentary to hold the exegetical and theological dimensions of the text together. As a result, there is a wholeness to his interpretation that is generally lacking in Protestant commentaries of the same period, whether liberal or conservative. His commentary is well organized, and the reader is not distracted by endless digressions.

However, there are serious problems with the conservative Catholic position represented by Knabenbauer's Isaiah commentary. First, the New Testament perspective often overshadows the witness of the Old Testament itself. For example, the assumed identification of the suffering servant of "Second Isaiah" (chapters 40–50) with the Messiah of "First Isaiah" (chapters 1–39) does not rest on a close reading of the biblical text, because messianism is not an obvious theme in chapters 40–55. (Many critics would deny its presence completely.) Or again, his sophisticated reading of the threefold *sanctus* in chapter 6 in accordance with trinitarian terminology goes beyond the literal sense of the Hebrew text. Although I would fully agree that there is a legitimate role for a biblical theology of the whole Christian Bible, it must not be an uncritical or unconscious introduction of Christian theology without first hearing the Old Testament's own voice.

Secondly, Knabenbauer's use of linguistic parallels from Jeremiah to prove the pre-exilic age of Isaiah chapters 40–66 fails to reckon with the highly likely possibility that the book of Jeremiah has been redacted in the post-exilic age. The recognition of parallels has exegetical significance in terms of the intertextual relation between the two canonical books, but it does not convincingly serve as a historical apology for an early dating of "Second Isaiah." Then again, his uncritical use of certain psalms traditionally regarded as messianic in order to support his messianic interpretation of Isaiah needs a more critical application, rather than mere prooftexting.

Thirdly, while Knabenbauer's philological evidence is very thorough and often impressive, and his insistence on giving priority of meaning to a word's usage in context rather than to its etymology is sound, the question remains whether he has taken seriously enough Gesenius's arguments on the interpretation of Isa. 7:14 (*Commentar über den Jesaia*, vol. 1, pp. 297ff.), which undercut the etymology of Jerome respecting *almah*. Knabenbauer's very learned review of the history of exegesis of this passage is of interest but does not address arguments based on modern comparative Semitic languages.

Finally, I have spoken with appreciation of Knabenbauer's use of the Church Fathers as an important part of the Christian exegetical tradition. It is interesting to note that although Knabenbauer restricts himself entirely to interpreting the literal sense of the biblical text, his citing of the Church Fathers serves indirectly to appropriate a figurative sense to the text. My question is whether he has reflected adequately on the hermeneutical issues at stake in the tension between the literal and the figurative sense.

In sum, Knabenbauer's contribution serves as an important reminder of the Christian church's powerful exegetical tradition, which was in great danger of being forgotten by the end of the nineteenth century. Yet Knabenbauer is also forced into an apologetic defense of a conservative position at times akin to Hengstenberg's that has not successfully come to grips with the theological and hermeneutical challenges of the Enlightenment. Moreover, he has lost much of the freshness of a holistic sense of the biblical narrative so skillfully represented by Augustin Calmet a century earlier.

III. Mediating Confessional Positions:
J. C. K. von Hofmann and Franz Delitzsch

It is difficult to evaluate the contribution of Franz Delitzsch without some attention to the colleagues and opponents in relation to whom he shaped his own interpretation. On the right was the orthodox Lutheran party of Hengstenberg. On the left were the brilliant and learned commentaries of Gesenius and Hitzig. Yet in the middle of these two extremes was another option, more difficult to define precisely. It stemmed from the German *Erweckungsbewegung* (spiritual awakening) and from the rise of romanticism, but it also remained eclectic, developing in different directions.

One of the pivotal figures of this middle ground was J. C. K. von Hofmann of Erlangen, who waged a battle against positions to his right and left. Unfortunately, he did not write a commentary on Isaiah and thus falls outside the parameters of this study. Still, serious attention must be paid to him. The broad lines of his thought on the Old Testament prophets can be seen in his two important works, *Weissagung und Erfüllung* and *Der Schriftbeweis*, both of which contain sections on Isaiah.

My concern here is simply to draw a few lines by which better to understand Delitzsch, but also to focus on the issue of *Heilsgeschichte* (sacred history), which has some connection with the earlier works of Cocceius and Vitringa (cf. chapter 15), but which also continued to exert a powerful influence well into the twentieth century in the theologies of Gerhard von Rad and Oscar Cullmann.

1. J. C. K. von Hofmann

J. C. K. von Hofmann (1810-1877) is widely recognized as one of the most creative and influential of the confessional scholars of Germany in the middle of the nineteenth century. He was a colleague of Delitzsch in Erlangen from 1859-1867. More than anyone, he was the heart of the so-called Erlangen school, in spite of the presence there of other impressive scholars.

In recent years there have been many attempts to trace the various influences at work on Hofmann (cf. Wendlebourg, "Die heilsgeschichte Theologie," and the analysis of J. W. Rogerson, *Old Testament Criticism,* pp. 104ff.). Among these influences are the work of Ranke, Hegel, Schelling, and Schleiermacher, but Hofmann's work also has a relation to theosophic currents found in such leaders as Boehme, Bengel, and Oetinger (cf. Diestel, *Geschichte des Alten Testamentes,* pp. 704ff., and R. A. Harrisville, *The Bible in Modern Culture,* pp. 123ff.). Von Hofmann's thought is a complex combination of pietistic elements and strains of idealistic philosophy, and it reflects the impact of Ranke's historical method as well. Yet to imply that von Hofmann was merely an eclectic mixture is seriously to misunderstand his contribution. There is a focus, consistency, and brilliance to his writings that only derive from his own profound theological reflection.

Our concern in this chapter is limited to his influence on biblical interpretation, especially in relation to Delitzsch. Hofmann's immediate context was shaped by theological battles waged on two fronts. On the far right was the scholastic Lutheranism of Hengstenberg, who understood biblical prophecy as contingent predictions about the future and their fulfillment. On the left were the higher critics, such as De Wette, Hitzig, and Ewald, who dismantled the unity and authority of the scriptures.

Hofmann's great contribution lies in his redefining biblical history in terms of a *Heilsgeschichte* joined to divine revelation in an organic relation. For Hofmann, history is a sacred process, embedded in secular history, which gives all of creation its ultimate meaning. This sacred history is the gradual unfolding of the divine purpose in salvific events that stretched from the creation of the world to its full consummation in Christ. Coupled with this historical process of teleological events was the revelation of the divine goal of salvation of the whole creation, which formed the other side of the same coin.

The presentation of Christ in the world is the substantive content of all history. This unveiling of Christ involves both history and revelation *(Weissagung)*: history that shapes the communion of God and man; revelation that reveals in specific moments the final shape of this fellowship. These two movements of history and revelation are joined in an indissoluble relation with Christ, who is the source of both. The advance of prophetic history is continually adumbrated by Old Testament types pointing forward to New Testament antitypes. Revelation is not doctrine, but history. Old Testament prophecy does not consist of isolated predictions awaiting a fulfillment in the future; instead the entire *Heilsgeschichte* is prophetic. This sacred history gradually unfolds through different stages in an organic whole, moving toward a goal. The Bible is the record of this *Heilsgeschichte,* but it is not to be read "externally." Rather, the meaning of its history only comes through the experience of the new birth, which confirms that Christ is the goal of all biblical history.

2. Franz Delitzsch (1813-90)

Franz Delitzsch was a pivotal biblical scholar in the last half of the nineteenth century until his death in 1890. He combined special training, an outgoing personality, and an intense interest in Judaism that set him apart in many ways from other Old Testament scholars of his generation. He was also a romantic who wrote essays and monographs on music, flora and fauna, Jewish artisan life, and studies on colors in the Bible. His photographs show him always carrying a flower when lecturing. He wrote numerous commentaries both on the Old Testament and the New Testament, including Genesis, Psalms, Isaiah, Proverbs, and Hebrews. However, what especially distinguished him was his lifelong study of Judaism, both ancient and contemporary. His commentaries are filled with citations from the rabbis. He remained one of the few Old Testament commentators in the nineteenth century who still paid careful attention to the accentuation system of the Masoretes.

Not surprisingly, he was involved in a project for the translation of the New Testament into Hebrew that continued to occupy his attention throughout his entire life. Above all, he was an orthodox Lutheran scholar who was a biblical theologian at heart and wrote several monographs on messianism. Few scholars of his period wrestled harder than Delitzsch in seeking to relate deep Christian faith to the new insights and challenges from the expansion of historical-critical research into every area of biblical study. Fortunately, in 1978 Siegfried Wagner produced a magnificent volume entitled *Franz Delitzsch: Leben und Werk,* on which all future study of Delitzsch will be dependent. Wagner not only provides exhaustive data of Delitzsch's life and work — his use of Delitzsch's many letters is especially illuminating — he offers a probing evaluation of his theological contributions as well.

As a confessional Christian theologian, Delitzsch strongly opposed the wooden, even rationalistic, understanding of prophecy as mere prediction and as the supernatural fulfillment of contingent events. Likewise, he was highly critical of the radical skepticism of many of the newer critics. Delitzsch was often identified with the *heilsgeschichtliche* school of Hofmann in Erlangen, and even accused of being Hofmann's epigone. It is true that Delitzsch was one of the first to recognize the significance of Hofmann's provocative book *Weissagung und Erfüllung* in 1841, and he wrote a long review both praising and criticizing it. Moreover, Delitzsch continued to struggle with Hofmann's position, and in several books, letters, and essays he made very clear his agreements and disagreements.

Delitzsch was very appreciative of Hofmann's emphasis on a *Heilsgeschichte* that encompassed both the Old and New Testaments within a dynamic movement culminating in Christ. He also agreed in seeing a typological component that preserved the unity of the unfolding events by adumbrating the anticipated restoration of God's creation through a process of fulfillments. Finally, he shared with Hofmann the emphasis of earlier German pietism that true understanding of scripture was unlocked by means of the personal, subjective, religious experience of the interpreter.

Nevertheless, there were other important issues in which Delitzsch heatedly disagreed with Hofmann. These were expressed often in Delitzsch's correspondence, but particularly in lengthy sections of his book *Die biblisch-prophetische Theologie* (pp. 170ff., 195ff., 208ff., 257ff.). In his detailed exposition one can see that, although he accepted such terms of Hofmann's as *Heilsgeschichte, Typologie,* and *Erfüllung,* Delitzsch frequently defined this terminology in a different way from Hofmann. For example, he objected to Hofmann's view of sacred history as an organic process that unfolds independently of human response. Indeed, for Delitzsch God offers salvific prophecy through history, but history in itself is not revelation ("die Geschichte nicht an sich eine weissagende ist," p. 180). Delitzsch also disagreed with Hofmann's downplaying the role of sin and underestimating the freedom of the individual to decide in faith. In the end, Delitzsch appealed to the Lutheran formulation of the relation of nature and grace, and felt that Hofmann's misunderstanding of the latter stemmed from the unfortunate influence of philosophical idealism. In sum, Delitzsch's criticism of important features within Hofmann's theological system belies the characterization of Delitzsch as Hofmann's epigone.

The actual exegesis in Delitzsch's commentaries also shows his striking differences from Hofmann. It is characterized by rigorous philology, historical analysis, and literary attention to exegetical detail. Of course, such features are not lacking in Hofmann's *Schriftbeweis,* but the elements of philosophical speculation are lacking in Delitzsch, whose interests remain text-oriented. Therefore, he is critical of a view of sacred history that appears detached from the written text. He strove to keep close to the biblical text — usually focusing on the Masoretic text — and his continual revisions show his constant concern for exegetical improvement.

There is a final important aspect of the relation of Hofmann and Delitzsch that can only be seen clearly in hindsight. Hofmann's worldview was shaped in the early nineteenth century by various idealistic philosophies of history (Fichte, Schelling, Hegel) that stressed the organic unfolding of the ideal Spirit. However, beginning with De Wette and culminating in F. C. Baur and J. Wellhausen, a very different understanding of biblical history began to emerge. What would happen if the true historical development of Old Testament history would appear to be very different from the trajectory of *Heilsgeschichte* assumed by Hofmann? What would it mean if *Heilsgeschichte* and *Weltgeschichte* (secular history) were pulled apart by radical literary (source) critical reconstructions that reordered the sequence of biblical history? What would be the effect of supporting multiple authors of the biblical books that differed from those traditionally assigned by the canon? In a word, Delitzsch faced a very different nest of problems from those of Hofmann, and shortly he would be challenged by a far greater threat than that merely contained in the sterile rationalism of Hengstenberg and the far right.

In his introductory preface to the English translation of the fourth edition of Delitzsch's Isaiah commentary (1889; English translation 1894), S. R. Driver makes much of the change in Delitzsch's critical estimate of the authorship of the book of Isaiah. In his earlier editions he had defended the unity of the Isaianic authorship, whereas finally in 1889 he offered an accommodation respecting the origin and authorship of the book when he acknowledged the authorship of a Deutero-Isaiah. In sum, Delitzsch appeared to align himself with the modern historical-critical approach long advocated by Driver.

Although it is clear that Delitzsch had undergone a change in his perspective from the first edition of 1866, it is far from certain that Driver drew the correct implications from this shift. Delitzsch's change allowed Driver to make two observations. First, it confirmed the cogency of the grounds upon which the historical-critical view of the Old Testament rested. Second, it furnished evidence that critical research is perfectly consistent with a firm belief in the reality of revelation contained in the Old Testament.

It may be that Delitzsch would have accepted Driver's interpretation, at least in part, for he was always irenic in his responses. However in his new introduction to chapters 40–66, Delitzsch offers a different emphasis. He downplays his shift regarding the authorship of Second Isaiah, claiming that for him it involved little of hermeneutical significance. He suggests that he had never found anything objectionable in the view that the book of Isaiah contained prophecies later than Isaiah's. Indeed, he had always treated chapters 40–60 as addressed to the exiles. (This response seems a bit disingenuous considering the intensity of his earlier opposition to dual authorship.)

More significant are the paragraphs that follow, in which he sets out how he differs hermeneutically from the usual critical approach. The crucial issue for him turns on how one understands the unity of the book regardless of dual authorship. He argues that First and Second Isaiah were not joined together by accident. The later chapters were really a continuation of Isaiah's prophecy, equal in quality and value. All parts of the book bear the stamp of Isaiah, whether directly or indirectly. The prophet Isaiah lives among the exiles, not in such a tangible manner as Ezekiel, but like a spirit without visible form, *"Jesaia's Doppelgänger."*

According to the form and content of chapters 40–66, "Isaiah's spirit reigns, Isaiah's heart pulsates, Isaiah's fiery tongue speaks" (cited in Wagner, p. 251). The Christian message of the book remains a unity. Regardless of whether another is the immediate author, the book is the outcome of impulses springing from Isaiah. Moreover, the book contains a consistent eschatological message extending from the promised Messiah, to the suffering servant, to its Christological fulfillment in the New Testament. In sum, it is entirely clear that Delitzsch's approach is very different indeed from that of Driver, Cheyne, and their critical colleagues. (This judgment is implicit in his final introduction to chapters 40–66, but Delitzsch, who died before the English edition appeared with Driver's preface, never stated it confrontationally.)

There are several places in his commentary of Isaiah that best characterize Delitzsch's overarching theological concerns. First, he is at pains to see the larger unity of the book even when recognizing that certain sections were later than Isaiah. He agrees that chapters 24–27 could not have been written by the prophet himself, but by a disciple "who in this case surpasses his master" (vol. 2, p. 419). Then he argues at length that they form a finale to chapters 13–23. One of the most effective ways of achieving the book's unity was in

Isaiah's use of intertextuality. Delitzsch often traced the parallels between the legal portions of the Pentateuch and Isaiah's application of the laws in a conscious effort to call into question the Wellhausen axiom that prophecy always preceded law (vol. 1, p. 2). Then again, with great effectiveness he traced the linguistic parallels between chapters 1-39 and 40–66, not in order to establish claims for single authorship according to Hengstenberg's approach, but to show the continuity of the prophetic message in spite of multiple authorship.

Second, Delitzsch labored hard in describing a literary and historical sequence in chapters 7–11. He sought to escape the restrictions of the traditional Christian interpretation of Isa. 7:14, and yet not to be satisfied with the rationalistic historization of Gesenius and his Jewish predecessors. In the end, Delitzsch was able to mount a case for seeing a *heilsgeschichtliche* connection between the messianic hope of chapters 7, 9, and 11, which culminated in a song of praise (Isa. 12) parallel to the redeemed people on the other side of the Red Sea: "The address is directed to the people of the future as contained in the people of the present" (vol. 1, p. 290).

Third, Delitzsch wrestled hard in his interpretation of the servant figure in Second Isaiah. He resisted the effort of traditional Christians to identify the servant immediately with Jesus Christ, but paid closest attention to the corporate references to Israel as the servant in chapters 41 and 42. Then in the middle section (chapter 49), he observed that the servant was also sent to redeem Israel, and therefore could not be simply identified with the nation as a whole. Finally, in chapter 53 he felt that exegetically it was impossible to avoid the overwhelmingly individual references ascribed to the servant. Thus, Delitzsch spoke of the figure of a pyramid, the lower base being the nation of Israel, the middle section Israel "after the spirit," and the summit as "the Person of salvation" arising out of Israel (vol. 2, p. 165). He continued, "Isaiah 52:13–53:12 proclaims the suffering and resurrection of Jesus Christ as clearly as if the prophet stood under the cross and had seen the resurrected One."

Finally, Delitzsch's commentary on Isaiah in its fourth and final edition never swerved from an all-pervasive Christological focus that had characterized his earlier work. This passionate conviction is noteworthy, especially in the late nineteenth century, because it unleashed a ferocious barrage of criticism from his contemporaries. It struck many as incomprehensible how Delitzsch could emphasize the absolute need for a sober, grammatical-philological exegesis, and then add, "Christ, the crucified and resurrected One, is the active goal of the entire Word of God, and thus also its final meaning" (cited in Wagner, p. 325). Or again, in an essay translated into English (*The Old Testament Student,* pp. 77-78) he writes, "Without the New Testament, the Old Testament would be a labyrinth without a clue, a syllogism without a conclusion, a torso without a heart, a moon without the sun, since Christ is the proper interpreter of the Old Testament." From such statements it is obvious that Delitzsch did not share the widespread opinion of the late nineteenth century that biblical exegesis should be without theological presuppositions.

IV. Late Nineteenth-Century British Commentaries on Isaiah

The late nineteenth century produced a spate of Isaiah commentaries by British scholars that shaped the understanding of the book for the English-speaking world for many decades. It is generally recognized that Britain, and certainly North America, lagged far behind German scholarship during most of the nineteenth century. When British commentaries began to appear, they tended to be at first conservative in comparison with those of the Germans. They cautiously adopted aspects of higher criticism, and even so continued to meet resistance in Britain until the late nineteenth century.

Nevertheless, certain characteristics of British scholarship emerged that set it apart from Germany and provide an important contribution to our overarching hermeneutical concerns in this study. First, these writers were highly successful in introducing a new critical paradigm in respect to the Old Testament, both in Britain and North America, within a few decades, roughly from 1880 to 1910. Second, these British scholars — both English and Scottish — were all members of the Protestant clergy. They were all trained in theology, usually had an ecclesiastical appointment, and continued consciously to address members of the Christian church as their primary audience. It is therefore with much interest that we turn to these commentators to see how they wrestled with the book of Isaiah as Christian scripture.

1. Thomas Kelly Cheyne (1841-1915)

It is fitting to begin with Thomas Kelly Cheyne, Oriel Professor at Oxford. Cheyne began his critical study of Isaiah as early as 1868, when he published a textual-critical study of the book. This effort was followed shortly in 1870 with an attempt to arrange the book of Isaiah chronologically. At this point, Heinrich Ewald's influence was still strong on him. His modification of Ewald was such that he caused no great offense among the conservatives in England.

Then in 1880 the first edition of his Isaiah commentary was published in two volumes.

In the later years Cheyne was widely regarded as the most radical of English scholars, but in 1880 he was still remarkably conservative in approach. Most of his energy went into offering a careful and somewhat unexciting commentary centered on historical, philological, and literary comments. There is strikingly little theological discussion in spite of his earlier dependence on Delitzsch. What is surprising is the caution with which he handles the critical problems. For example, he states that the issue regarding the Isaianic authorship of chapters 40–66 was still an open question, but adds that a decision is not crucial as long as "we maintain the divine inspiring and overruling influence for which I have pleaded" (vol. 2, p. 231). He also defends the position that a suffering Messiah is at least germinally in the Old Testament.

In the fifth edition of his commentary (1889) one notices a growing uncertainty regarding his conservative stance. He follows closely the more advanced critical theories of Julius Wellhausen and W. R. Smith, but still hesitates to embrace them. Then in 1891 S. R. Driver's famous *Old Testament Introduction* appeared, which affirmed unequivocally the anonymous author of chapters 40–66 and the very late dating of chapters 24–27. Shortly thereafter Cheyne began to embrace a much more radical stance in his new critical analysis of Isaiah in 1895. Then in a series of articles republished in *Founders of Old Testament Criticism,* Cheyne actually attacks Driver for his conservative and timid positions respecting Isaiah.

Even more interesting for our hermeneutical concerns is the essay Cheyne published as an appendix to his 1889 edition entitled "The Christian Element in the Book of Isaiah." The essay reveals clearly Cheyne's continuing interest in the theological content of Isaiah in spite of his slowly evolving critical judgments on the book's compositional growth. Cheyne also seems aware that he has not adequately treated the theological dimension of the prophet in his technical commentary.

At the outset, he acknowledges "the full supremacy of the grammar and the lexicon" as an axiom universally accepted (vol. 2, p. 193). Nevertheless, he finds definite Christian elements in the Old Testament of two kinds. First, there is a foreshadowing of special circumstances in the life of Christ, occurring casually in the midst of apparently rhetorical descriptions. These were not conscious prophecies and may seem purely accidental were it not for Christian belief in a special providential guidance. The object of these circumstantial features in an Old Testament description was to symbolize the character and work of Jesus Christ. Second, there are distinct pictures of Jesus Christ, the suffering Messiah. The Divine Spirit ruled in such a way in the mental process of the prophet that he chose expressions that, while completely conveying his own meaning, also correspond to a future fact in the life of Christ. Especially in Second Isaiah's portraits of the teaching, suffering, and triumphant Messiah is the life of Jesus Christ prefigured.

It is important to notice what Cheyne is *not* saying: 1) It is not an issue of Old Testament prediction and New Testament fulfillment, 2) nor is there any *Heilsgeschichte* moving from the Old Testament to the New, 3) nor is the New Testament the culmination of our Old Testament ideal. Rather, there is a certain kind of correspondence between the Old Testament and the New especially visible in the Psalms and Isaiah, which correspondence can be maintained only on the basis of a strictly grammatical, philological reading. It emerges quite clearly at this point that Cheyne is attempting to harmonize the older, traditional view of the Old Testament as a witness to Jesus Christ with the newer historical-critical interpretation of the biblical text.

An initial problem with this effort is that Cheyne seeks to maintain a relation between the testaments not in terms of a special theological movement within the church's scriptures, but according to a general philosophical theory of a foreshadowing of great events for the purpose of later generations being able better to perceive history's significance. Then again, the problem arises whether one can combine the two different readings of a biblical text, the historical/grammatical and the spiritually foreshadowing, without deeper reflection on the context from which biblical interpretation is conducted. In the end, Cheyne's theological compromise does not satisfy either the secular historian or the confessing Christian believer.

2. Andrew Bruce Davidson

Andrew Bruce Davidson, Professor of Old Testament at Edinburgh University, wrote no commentary on Isaiah, yet his influence on the interpretation of Isaiah during the latter part of the nineteenth century in the English-speaking world was of singular importance. He was widely considered the doyen of the study of the Old Testament, and was the teacher for a whole new generation of critically oriented younger scholars, including William Robertson Smith and George Adam Smith. He was regarded as a learned, wise, and trustworthy leader of the Scottish church — he himself belonged to the Free Church of Scotland — and his slow and cautious move from a traditional, conservative stance toward an openness to the newer, critical German scholarship carried great authority toward the acceptance of a new paradigm among the Reformed, Anglican, and Free churches.

In an important article in 1884 ("The Book of Isaiah Chs. XLff."), he set forth his reasons for departing from the traditional authorship of the eighth-century prophet. Of particular interest were his hermeneutical reflections on chapter 53. Although his approach differed from Cheyne's, he shared a concern to legitimate a traditional Christian reading with newer critical analyses.

He begins by conceding unequivocally that the servant of the Lord in chapter 53 was fulfilled in Jesus Christ. Clearly this identification was asserted by the New Testament and affirmed in Isaiah 61 by Christ himself. Davidson then proceeds to argue that everyone except the Jews agree that the figure of the servant was expressed in Christ, and that "the spirit of Christ which was in the prophet led his mind to the great thoughts which he expressed with a view to Christ" (p. 450).

However, Davidson then sets forth a second question that he claims must be sharply distinguished from the first, namely, what subject had the prophet in his own mind when speaking of the servant? He then suggests that the answer to this question may be quite different. Indeed, "it can hardly be doubted that the prophet's thought is national . . . the servant is a creation of the prophet's mind, the ideal Israel itself" (pp. 358-59). The modern reader is left with the impression that Davidson is struggling with great difficulty to hold together two very different positions respecting the servant, and that he has not yet been successful in this compromise. Moreover, the history of the interpretation of chapter 53 after Davidson showed that this tension in the manner formulated by Cheyne and Davidson could not long be sustained in Britain.

Although it is beyond the scope of this monograph to pursue the struggle of the synagogue to understand the book of Isaiah as Jewish scripture, there is an interesting parallel to the tension that developed in the late nineteenth century among Christian interpreters. When the famous *Jewish Encyclopedia,* published by Funk and Wagner, appeared in 1904, the entries on each of the Old Testament books contained two very different analyses. Usually the traditional, orthodox Jewish view respecting a given book was presented, but it was then followed by a second entry, often written by a well-known German scholar, that presented the modern critical assessment of the same book. What is striking is that there was no attempt made to reconcile the two contradictory perspectives. They remained simply juxtaposed and unresolved.

3. Samuel Rolles Driver (1846-1914) and John Skinner (1851-1925)

In 1891 Samuel Rolles Driver published his epoch-making *Introduction to the Literature of the Old Testament*. Its significance is not that his analysis was itself groundbreaking; from the perspective of German scholarship, his book contained very little that was new or previously unknown. Still, before long Driver's *Introduction* was translated into German and praised for its precise and solid presentation of the historical-critical position, which was given with thoroughness and fairness.

However, for the English-speaking world the impact of his volume was of crucial importance. It marked the end of the major resistance to critical Old Testament scholarship by the mainline Protestant Christian churches, and this lack of resistance was increasingly taken for granted by a flood of popularizations throughout the English-speaking world. Driver also succeeded in silencing the earlier impression that historical criticism was a radical, agnostic importation from Germany. (Prime Minister Gladstone was not convinced, and regretted his appointment of Driver as Regius Professor. Cf. J. A. Emerton's essay on Driver in *A Century of British Orientalists*, pp. 122-25.)

There is no better way to describe the sharp break in the English exegesis of Isaiah represented by Driver and Skinner at the end of the nineteenth century than to compare it with the conservative Anglican commentary of William Kay of 1875 in the "Speaker's Commentary." Kay stands firmly within a venerable Anglican exegetical tradition grounded in the Church Fathers, and is more distant from Hengstenberg than J. A. Alexander. Yet even in Kay, the apologetic temper of his commentary is evident as he seeks to assure his Anglican constituency of the enduring truth of the traditional position against the threats to the ecclesiastical establishment arising from *Essays and Reviews* of 1860.

The positions of Driver and Cheyne were clearly not identical, but by the end of the nineteenth century there had emerged a wide consensus on most of the major historical-critical issues among the leading British scholars, and both Driver and Skinner had played an important role in achieving this level of agreement. But because Skinner wrote a two-volume commentary on Isaiah, and Driver's only written comments on Isaiah were a lengthy chapter in his *Introduction* and a semi-popular book entitled *Isaiah: His Life and Times*, this chapter will give primary attention to Skinner and only in passing register Driver's position where there is some disagreement.

At the conclusion of his introduction (p. lxxiii), Skinner summarizes what he considers the critical consensus regarding the authorship, structure, and literary development of the book of Isaiah: "The book bearing Isaiah's name is in reality a collection of prophetic oracles, showing a composite authorship, and completed literary history. Approximately two-thirds of it consists of anonymous prophecies, all of which are of an age subsequent to Isaiah. To this class belongs the whole of the latter part of the book after chapters 40ff., but even within chapters 1–39 great diversity of authorship exists." Driver's *Introduction* reveals his full agreement with this description.

Both Skinner and Driver give much attention at the beginning of their analysis to outlining the historical background of the book of Isaiah in which crucial sources are provided by ancient Near Eastern data. It is assumed that a true chronology of the Hebrew kingdoms must be based on the synchronism established by the Assyrian monuments. The apparent rationale for the priority given ancient Near Eastern history is that the framework in which a prophetic book functions is historical. The Hebrew prophet is understood as offering a religious commentary on the affairs of the world, and without a proper knowledge of this history, the prophetic message is incomprehensible and fragmentary. Driver, when treating chapter 15, characterizes it as a "misfortune" that the prophecies of Isaiah have not been arranged in chronological order, and a chronology must be reconstructed with varying levels of difficulty. His interpretation follows his historical reconstruction.

For both Skinner and Driver, biblical history has no dialectical dimension, and thus the hermeneutical tensions between the biblical portrayal and a secular reconstruction have vanished. It should be recalled that both Cheyne and Davidson still retained at least a vestige of a hermeneutical importance in the tension. In this context, it is significant to bear in mind that in the understanding of the early church, history was what was recorded in the Bible; it was understood theocentrically as the testimony of God at work in the world. Of course, the theologians of the church were acutely aware of the secular world and how it impacted on the kingdom of God, but the latter was always secondary to the former, namely, the unfolding of the divine will throughout his creation. One of the great effects of the Enlightenment was in reversing this priority. Whereas once history was understood in the light of biblical prophecy, by the seventeenth century prophecy was being interpreted as a corollary of secular history. For a time, both in the eighteenth and nineteenth centuries, theologians such as Cocceius and Hofmann sought to keep the priority of biblical history by appealing to a concept of *Heilsgeschichte*. However, by the end of the nineteenth century the secular historical perspective had long since achieved hegemony.

Another component of interpretation that is shared by both Skinner and Driver is a pervasive influence of philosophical idealism, which substitutes for the church's earlier appeal to some form of *Heilsgeschichte*. One hears in Skinner the frequent appeal to a growth of spiritual truths (p. xxvi), of religious values, of God's moral personality (p. liv), and of "simple but comprehensive principles" (p. xlvii) undergirding the prophet's consciousness. In discussing Isaiah's use of the concept of holiness, Skinner traces a development starting with a much lower level of religious thinking, but slowly filled with ethical content and moral perfection (p. li).

When discussing his interpretation of Isa. 7:14, Skinner concludes that the sign given Ahaz was, in short, the actual birth of the Messiah. Then he writes, "It is no objection to this view to note that the sign did not come to pass. Unfulfilled predictions are a standing phenomenon of the Old Testament. If the sign had been merely a particular event in history, it would have been rendered invalid by its failure to realise itself . . . [but] it retains its religious value as long as the ideal to which it points remains an object of faith and aspiration" (vol. 1, p. 67). Driver's view regarding Isa. 7:14 is somewhat more traditional. He conceives of the focus of Immanuel as "an ideal one, projected by him upon the shifting future" (p. 42).

Finally, it comes as no surprise within the framework of philosophical idealism that biblical prophecy is interpreted completely in anthropocentric categories. Skinner speaks continually of the "genius of Isaiah," as does Driver. The prophet was a visionary possessed with unusual sensitivity to persons and nature. "His perceptions of spiritual truth were such as we call intuitive and were frequently accompanied by experiences of an ecstatic kind" (p. lxxi). Following the lead of Matthew Arnold, Skinner applies to Isaiah the distinctive qualities of Homer's genius: "Plainness of thought, Plainness of style, Nobleness, and Rapidity" (p. lxxi). Little wonder that Isaiah emerges as a "hero of faith" (p. xlii). Driver's characterization of the prophet varies little from Skinner's (pp. 107ff.), though he does stress a bit more that Isaiah clothed his ideas "in noble imagery and most often interpreted symbolically rather than literally" (p. 111). Isaiah's prophetic conceptions were "independent of time" and thus capable of being detached from their original context. However, Isaiah's ideal remained.

It is time to return to our major question: How did Skinner and Driver contribute to the struggle to understand the book of Isaiah as Christian scripture? It would be unkind and wrong to suggest that they had neither a struggle nor a concept of Christian scripture. The battle they fought at the end of the nineteenth century was quite different from the beginning of the twentieth century. To most academics it appeared fully obvious that critical biblical scholarship had completely won the day. The older defensive lines of Hengstenberg and even of Delitzsch had been breached. It was within this context that these sincere Christian scholars sought to hammer out a solution from which the church could address a new generation. However, the haunting question remains: Was the price paid too high?

4. George Adam Smith (1856-1942)

There are several different ways of evaluating the contributions of George Adam Smith to the field of Bible. He was an esteemed academic (Prof. of Old Testament, Free Church College, Glasgow), principal of the University of Aberdeen, a lecturer of international repute, and, above all, a preacher. As a young scholar he was assigned the task of writing a two-volume commentary in the *Expositor's Bible* on the Book of the Twelve, which proved enormously successful and evoked much approbation. Later in 1888-90 he wrote a two-volume commentary on Isaiah in the same series.

At the time of the publication of the first commentary a heated controversy still raged in Britain regarding the place of historical criticism, especially surrounding a commentary series such as the *Expositor's Bible,* which was directed primarily to the clergy and general public. Some of the commentaries, especially in the New Testament, proved to be very conservative in orientation. In contrast, Smith's work was avowedly critical in approach and demonstrated his mastery of the field, particularly in respect to current German scholarship. Two features of Smith's commentary emerged immediately that overshadowed any initial suspicion. First, his commentary was written in an elegant and compelling English prose, even with occasional flashes of brilliant Victorian hyperbole. Second, his detailed critical learning was carefully balanced with profound and moving theological reflection on the biblical text, including the New Testament.

a. Smith as a Critical Old Testament Scholar

Smith was well-trained in Latin, Greek, and Hebrew, which he used throughout his commentary; however, he made no pretense of rivaling the philological expertise of Skinner, Driver, or G. B. Gray. His originality rather surfaced in his literary skills. His concern with prophetic structures, poetic style, and metrical cadence were consistently fresh and probing. His translation of much of the book of Isaiah is also often brilliant in bringing the text alive in a fresh fashion. In terms of the higher critical questions of authorship, he offered an extended account of why he felt compelled to embrace the hypothesis of an anonymous author of chapters 40–66. Again, in the first volume of his commentary, he reviewed carefully the debate on messianism before reaching his own somewhat moderate view, which was akin to that of Delitzsch.

Throughout his commentary Smith, like both Skinner and Driver, paid close attention to Isaiah's historical background. Clearly Smith regarded the task of historical investigation as having great theological significance, since one of his major themes was the activity of God in history. In his analysis of chapters 1-5, he argued that the historical experiences gained by the young prophet in the early circumstances of Judah's history were directly reflected in his vision of chapter 6 at the death of Uzziah. It is significant to note that in the revised edition of his Isaiah commentary, made thirty-nine years after its initial publication, some interesting aspects of Smith's approach came to light. In his revised edition he retained most of his earlier moderately critical judgments on dating Isaiah's oracles, but in his newer footnotes he showed concern that his earlier historical position on Isaiah had become quite vulnerable on the basis of the more radical theories of Bernhard Duhm and Karl Marti. He worried that the historical foundation of his interpretation could become a slippery slope if there were no limits to historical skepticism.

b. Smith as an Expositor

In terms of Smith's approach to biblical exegesis, he greatly developed a feature that appeared only sporadically in Cheyne, Skinner, and Driver: the psychologizing of a text. That is, he interpreted a biblical text in such a way as to bring it into conformity with ordinary human behavior. A classic example is his interpretation of Isaiah's commission to harden his people (chapter 6). To explain this dreadful command, Smith argues as follows: "No prophet, we may be sure, would be asked by God to go and tell his audiences that in so many words, at the beginning of his career. It is only by experience that a man understands that kind of commission" (*Isaiah,* vol. 1). The effect of this ploy is certainly to blunt the force of the divine imperative to the prophet. Furthermore, Smith shows great interest in exploring the personality of the prophet, even when he is forced to speculate from texts that are largely silent. And Smith's frequent reference to conscience (cf. chapter 1) is disconcerting, since the term is strikingly absent in the Old Testament.

Closely akin to these features is Smith's use of terms arising from nineteenth-century philosophical idealism. Of course, this sort of appropriation was hardly unique to Smith; it was widespread during the nineteenth century in Britain, Germany, and America. Still, it is particularly noticeable in Smith. He speaks of Israel's developing religion as one with deep roots in primitive culture slowly moving toward a "spiritual doctrine." Particularly in the prophets, the moral content begins to replace the crude elements of Israel's early religion. He traces a trajectory of growing spirituality that, of course, makes it a foreshadowing of the New Testament. Messianism is the prophet's attempt at a personification of ideal Israel, which increasingly focuses on the noble figure in whom Israel's hopes are fulfilled. The cultic, ritualistic, and legal language is de-emphasized in favor of the spiritual and existential experience of confronting the sovereign God of the universe.

c. Smith as Theologian and Preacher

It would be easy to continue to describe aspects of Smith's approach to the Old Testament, which anchor him firmly in the late nineteenth century. His Beecher Lectures at Yale University (*Modern Criticism*, 1901) broke little new ground, and reflected a mild theological liberalism of the period. Yet to continue with this line is to miss by far Smith's most important and unique contributions. Moreover, up to now we have not seriously addressed our central question, namely, the nature of Smith's struggle to understand the book of Isaiah as Christian scripture.

An overwhelming feature of Smith's exegesis is the seriousness with which he wrestles with the theological content of Isaiah's message to the people of Judah. Although he has impressive chapters on important topics such as messianism, servant of the Lord, and politics and faith, even more significant is the way that he deals with the theological dimension of the subject matter throughout his entire commentary. Even when handling details of historical issues, he does not end his discussion as if it were merely talk about history, but carefully interweaves history, geography, and philology with the implications for theology, ethics, and doctrine.

Smith does not have any explicit references to his larger understanding of Christian scripture. He does not discuss in any detail how he understands the relation between the two testaments. Yet it is in his actual practice of interpretation that one discerns an understanding that undergirds his entire commentary. The prophet experiences in his call a vision of the holiness and majesty of God, not a God only of Israel, but the maker of heaven and earth. He did not receive a call like Moses, but he heard from the divine lips the need for messengers, and he immediately responded in a decision of self-surrender. Isaiah did not become an empty vehicle for the divine oracle, but as an obedient and suffering human being he carried to Israel God's terrifying judgment joined with an unswerving confidence in God's ultimate victory. Smith does not cite the New Testament in a catena of prooftexts, but his struggle with the theological content invariably drives him to include in his interpretation the

New Testament's witness to the selfsame divine purpose. His references are never casual, nor merely rhetorical, but are seen as the culmination of God's one will for the salvation of the entire world.

A classic example of Smith at his best is found in the six chapters in the second volume of his Isaiah commentary entitled "The Servant of the Lord." He begins his study with a careful review of the critical issues related to the figure of the servant in Second Isaiah. He describes the changing identity and mission of the servant, which moves from a personification of the nation, to an ideal remnant, and finally to a single individual. Although his overarching view is somewhat akin to Delitzsch's, he presents it in a far more fluid and dynamic fashion. There then follows a chapter on the New Testament's use of the imagery of servant. His study climaxes with three chapters on a careful theological exposition of chapter 53 accompanied by a brilliant, fresh translation.

Finally, both in these chapters and throughout the commentary, one sees another of Smith's greatest contributions in his application of the Old Testament text to his audience. Invariably, and with great subtlety and much passion, Smith draws the reader in. The imperative mode is interspersed with the discursive: "Let us understand that we are sent forth like the great Servant of God" (p. 324). "We are not warriors but artists . . . after the fashion of Jesus Christ who came not to condemn . . . but to build life up to the image of God" (p. 325). In this respect, Smith is in a class by himself compared to his British contemporaries. The only other possible rival would be A. B. Davidson, who, however, separated his commentaries from his sermons.

Perhaps the major implication for our persistent question regarding the struggle to understand Isaiah as Christian scripture is that Smith's work reflects many of the same theological concerns of previous generations: careful attention to the literal sense of the text, intense wrestling with the theological content of the Old Testament, a profound commitment to the New Testament's understanding of the one divine purpose brought to fulfillment in Jesus Christ. Smith's approach to biblical interpretation bore the stamp of the nineteenth and early twentieth centuries in which he worked. Yet even in its completely time-conditioned form, it bears a clear family resemblance to the best of the Christian exegetical tradition.

Bibliography of the Nineteenth- and Twentieth-Century Interpreters

I. Historical Critical Commentaries of the Early Nineteenth Century

PRIMARY SOURCES

Ewald, H. *Die Propheten des Alten Bundes erklärt,* neue Bearbeitung. 3 vols. Göttingen: Vandenhoeck & Ruprecht, 1867-68.

————. *The Prophet Isaiah, Chapters 1–33.* London: Deighton Bell, 1869.

Gesenius, W. *Geschichte der hebräischen Sprache und Schrift. Eine philologisch-historische Einleitung in die sprachlehren und Wörterbuch der hebräischen Sprache.* Leipzig: F. C. W. Vogel, 1815.

————. *Commentar über den Jesaia.* 2 vols. Leipzig: F. C. W. Vogel, 1821.

Hitzig, F. *Der Prophet Jesaja.* Heidelberg: C. F. Winter, 1833.

SECONDARY SOURCES

Smend, R. "Über die Epochen der Bibelkritik." In *Epochen der Bibelkritik. Gesammelte Aufsätze,* vol. 3, pp. 11-32. Munich: Kaiser, 1991.

II. Conservative Reaction of the Nineteenth Century

PRIMARY SOURCES

Alexander, J. A. *Commentary on Isaiah.* 2 vols. New York: Wiley & Putnam, 1845-47. Rev. edition. Edinburgh: T. & T. Clark, 1875. Reprint, Grand Rapids: Kregel, 1992.

Hengstenberg, E. W. *Christology of the Old Testament.* 4 vols. Edinburgh: T. & T. Clark, 1854.

Knabenbauer, J. *Commentarius in Isaiam Prophetum.* Paris: Lethielleux, 1881. Revised edition by F. Zorell, 1923.

SECONDARY SOURCES

Bachmann, J., and T. Schmalenbach. *Ernst Wilhelm Hengstenberg. Sein Leben und Wirken nach gedruckten und ungedruckten Quellen.* 3 vols. Gütersloh: Bertelsmann, 1876-92.

Mehlhausen, J. "Hengstenberg, Ernst Wilhelm (1802-69)." In *Theologische Realenzyklopädie,* vol. 15, pp. 39-42. Berlin: de Gruyter, 1986.

Reventlow, H. *Epochen der Bibelauslegung,* vol. 4, pp. 278-90; 290-95. Munich: Beck, 2001.

Taylor, M. A. "Joseph Addison Alexander." In *The Old Testament in the Old Princeton School (1812-1929),* pp. 89-166. San Francisco: Mellen Research University Press, 1992.

III. Mediating Confessional Positions

1. J. C. K. von Hofmann

PRIMARY SOURCES

Hofmann, J. C. K. von. *Weissagung und Erfüllung im Alten and im Neuen Testamente.* 2 vols. Nördlingen: Beck, 1841-44.

———. *Der Schriftbeweis.* 2 vols. Nördlingen: Beck, 1852-56.

———. *Biblische Hermeneutik.* Nördlingen: Beck, 1880. English Translation, Minneapolis: Augsburg, 1959.

SECONDARY SOURCES

Diestel, L. *Geschichte des Alten Testamentes in der christlichen Kirche,* pp. 704-5. Jena: Mauke, 1869.

Harrisville, R. A. and W. Sundberg. "Johann Christian Konrad von Hofmann." In *The Bible in Modern Culture,* 2nd ed., pp. 123-45. Grand Rapids: Eerdmans, 2002.

Hübner, E. *Schrift und Theologie. Eine Untersuchung zur Theologie J. C. K. von Hofmann.* Munich: Kaiser, 1956.

Kraus, H.-J. *Geschichte der historisch-kritischen Erforschung des Alten Testaments,* pp. 207-10. Neukirchen-Vluyn: Neukirchener Verlag, 1956; 3rd ed., 1982.

Rogerson, J. W. "Hofmann and Delitzsch: Confessional Scholars with a Difference." In *Old Testament Criticism in the Nineteenth Century, England and Germany,* pp. 104-20. London: SPCK, 1984.

Steck, K. G. *Die Idee der Heilsgeschichte.* Zürich-Zollikon: Evangelischer Verlag, 1959.

Wendlebourg, E.-W. "Die heilsgeschichtliche Theologie J. Chr. K. von Hofmanns in ihrem Verhältnis zur romantischen Weltanschauung." *Zeitschrift für Theologie und Kirche* 52 (1955): 64-104.

Weth, G. *Die Heilsgeschichte.* Munich: Kaiser, 1931.

2. Franz Delitzsch

PRIMARY SOURCES

Delitzsch, F. *Die biblisch-prophetische Theologie, ihre Fortbildung durch Chr. A. Crusius und ihre neueste Entwicklung seit der Christologie Hengstenbergs.* Leipzig: Gebauerische Buchhandlung, 1845.

———. *The Prophecies of Isaiah* (1867). 2 vols. 4th ed., 1889. Edinburgh: T. & T. Clark, 1894.

———. "Must we follow the New Testament Interpretation of Old Testament Texts?" *The Old Testament Student* 6 (1886-7): 77-78.

————. *Old Testament History of Redemption.* Edinburgh: T. & T. Clark, 1880.
————. *The Messianic Prophecies.* Edinburgh: T. & T. Clark, 1880.

SECONDARY SOURCES

Kraus, H.-J. *Geschichte der historisch-kritischen Erforschung des Alten Testaments von der Reformation bis zur Gegenwart,* pp. 210-21. Neukirchen-Vluyn: Neukirchener Verlag, 1956; 3rd ed., 1982.
Rogerson, J. W. *Old Testament Criticism in the Nineteenth Century,* pp. 104-20. Philadelphia: Fortress, 1985.
Wagner, S. *Franz Delitzsch. Leben und Werk.* Munich: Kaiser, 1978.

IV. Late Nineteenth- and Early Twentieth-Century British Commentaries

Cheyne, T. K. *Notes and Criticisms on the Hebrew Text of Isaiah.* London: Macmillan, 1868.
————. *The Book of Isaiah Chronologically Arranged.* London: Macmillan, 1870.
————. *The Prophecies of Isaiah.* 2 vols. London: Kegan Paul, 1880-81; 5th ed., 1889.
————. *Founders of Old Testament Criticism.* London: Methuen, 1893.
————. *Introduction to the Book of Isaiah.* London: A. C. Black, 1895.
Davidson, A. B. "The Book of Isaiah Ch. XLff." In *The Expositor,* series 2, vol. 8, pp. 250-69; 351-61; 430-51. London: Hodder and Stoughton, 1884.
Driver, S. R. *Isaiah: His Life and Times.* London: Nisbet, 1888.
————. *Introduction to the Literature of the Old Testament.* Edinburgh: T. & T. Clark, 1891.
————. "The Permanent Religious Value of the Old Testament." In *The Higher Criticism,* pp. 71-88. London: Hodder and Stoughton, 1912.
Emerton, J. A. "Samuel Rolles Driver, 1846-1914." In *A Century of British Orientalists* 1902-2001, edited by C. E. Bosworth, pp. 122-38. Oxford: British Academy, 2001.
Kay, W. *Isaiah* ("Speaker's Commentary"). London: John Murray, 1875.
Skinner, J. *The Book of the Prophet Isaiah.* 2 vols. Cambridge: Cambridge University Press, 1896; rev. ed., 1915.
Smith, G. A. *The Book of Isaiah.* 2 vols. New York: Armstrong & Son, 1888-90; rev. ed., New York: Harper and Brothers, 1927.
————. *Modern Criticism and the Preaching of the Old Testament.* London: Hodder and Stoughton, 1901.
Smith, W. Robertson. *The Prophets of Israel.* Edinburgh: T. & T. Clark, 1882; 2nd ed., 1895.

17

Postmodern Interpretation

I. The Nature of Postmodern Interpretation

Postmodernism is a somewhat loosely defined term that describes a method of interpreting texts that emerged during the last few decades. A. K. M. Adam, trying to chart the beginning of the cycle of postmodernism in biblical studies, suggests, "[W]e may estimate that the discipline of biblical studies intersected 'postmodernism' roughly twenty years ago" (*Handbook of Postmodern Biblical Interpretation*, 2000, p. vii). There is no consensus about what constitutes postmodernism, but as Barry Harvey notes (*Handbook*, p. 1), it is possible to identify traits that are common to most candidates for the title. Many are negative: there is no single substantive concept of rationality, no method leading to a scientific concept of the whole of reality, no single determinate meaning accessible to later generations of interpreters, no sort of semantic property with which texts are imbued.

George Aichele (*The Control of Biblical Meaning*, p. 100) adds two other features: "Language no longer denotes extratextual truth, but instead language is an exercise of power. . . . History is understood to be a fragmentary, subjective, and profoundly ideological fiction that is created in response to present interests." Clearly postmodernism is in no way a return to traditional methods of interpretation, but it is an extension of the historical-critical approach of the late nineteenth and early twentieth centuries, which has however been consciously radicalized by attacking the assumptions of the alleged objectivity of the scientific, historical-critical methodology. Whereas the critical approach of the past centuries appeared completely successful in destroying all traditional approaches, it was itself inconsistent in failing to grasp its own time-conditionality.

Working on the assumption that all literary interpretation is an activity involving an imaginative construction of the author in shaping a text, postmodernism denies that there is only one determinate sense of a text, but rather postulates meaning as an ongoing creation of the reader in dialogue with a given composition. Because the context of the reader is always changing, the interpretive activity involves a continuous process of shifting construals. Moreover, postmodernism has radicalized the earlier recognition of other factors influencing a reading by greatly expanding the scope to include sociological, economic, and political forces, gender, class, and ethnic biases, and the unconscious psychological elements affecting any textual reading. In adopting features from deconstruction, postmodern interpreters deny any overarching categories of historical or literary coherence, finding discontinuity and tension a part of every literature, which forces a continuous exploration of conflicting tropes within the tradition.

Of course, there remain many serious methodological differences within those groups that identify with postmodern interpretation. In large measure, postmodernists pride themselves on their uncompromising secularity. Theirs is a "coming of age" that radically disassociates itself from any privileging of religious or ethical value systems. Yet there is another group of postmodern interpreters who consciously stand within religious communities, usually either Judaism or Christianity.

For our immediate concerns, Walter Brueggemann (b. 1932) is the most important example of an interpreter of the book of Isaiah who is an avowed Christian theologian and consciously identifies himself as a postmodern interpreter. But even here, many further modifications are needed in order not to distort his profile. Brueggemann, as with many postmodernists, shares features of his interpretation with other approaches not dependent on postmodernism in origin, goals, and techniques. His two-volume commentary on Isaiah (1998) reflects at times his early training in the post–World War II "Biblical theology movement" when he speaks of a divine purpose in history, and of the prophet's "unfailing attention to Yahweh." Again, Brueggemann shares features from the classic historical-critical approach in his form-critical comments. Then again, one often finds evidence of elements of modern literary and redactional criticism, whether it is in the mode of his esteemed teacher, James Muilenburg, or the recent work of M. A. Sweeney. Finally, one can see a further development of his use of postmodern categories in his *Theology of the Old Testament* (1997) that reflects a more radical postmodern formulation than found in his Isaiah commentary (pp. 707ff.). Readers should also acknowledge Brueggemann's brilliant homiletical interpretations, which are often fresh, probing, and skillfully applied.

Our concern in this chapter will not be to offer an evaluation of his Isaiah commentary as a whole, but will rather focus on those elements that are distinctly postmodern in emphasis. The intent will be to relate his interpretive approach to our central question, namely, the church's struggle to interpret the book of Isaiah as Christian scripture. For many postmodernists of a secular commitment, this question is rejected at the outset as meaningless and of no interest. However, for Brueggemann, a confessing Christian with deep commitments to the church, the issue is an important one, even if his work represents a repudiation of much that has in the past constituted Christian exegetical tradition.

II. Characteristic Traits of a Postmodern Interpretation of Isaiah

There are certain characteristic features of Brueggemann's interpretation of the book of Isaiah that can be described as postmodern.

1. There is no one correct interpretation of an Old Testament text. This position stems from a hermeneutical principle. A critical evaluation does not rest on the interpreter's inability to reconstruct a text's original meaning because of the lack of historical sources, nor is it caused by the untrustworthy quality of its textual transmission. At this juncture, postmodernism differs sharply from the historical-critical approach arising from the Enlightenment and greatly perfected in the nineteenth and twentieth centuries. These scholars believed that a proper use of modern critical tools could often come very close to a text's original meaning, which was usually identified with authorial intent. In contrast, Brueggemann's postmodernism works on the assumption that no one interpretation can be "monopolistic" (*Isaiah*, vol. 2, p. 149), or be regarded as a final, closed reading. All interpretations are considered "tentative" (vol. 1, p. 75) and rhetorically open. Every interpretation is subjective, provisionary, and in constant flux because of the endless contexts available at any given moment, both personal and communal.

2. Brueggemann is at pains to describe the biblical text as "generative," that is, there are limitless possibilities and potential that can be evoked by creative imagination. Since every construal is subjective and there is no determinate meaning, no textual interpretation is unaffected by the biases of its individual or communal reading. Postmodernism in the form advocated by Brueggemann condemns both the church's traditional understanding and the practitioners of historical-critical, scientific analysis as "hermeneutically innocent" in their failure to see the radical fluidity of changing contexts operating both consciously and unconsciously.

3. Brueggemann is particularly harsh in his rejection of traditional Christian interpretations. Constantly there is an attack on a "preemptive reading" of the Hebrew Bible. He flatly repudiates any claim that the book of Isaiah predicts or anticipates Jesus Christ (vol. 2, p. 6). He argues that such a claim not only "fails to respect Jewish readers" (vol. 2, p. 6), but is a distortion of the book itself. Indeed, there is nothing whatever that is intrinsically Christian in the Old Testament. Brueggemann appears to be nervous when even speaking of a Messiah or messianic figure in the book of Isaiah. In fact, actual references to a Messiah in the commentary are virtually non-existent; he fears that it would be considered anti-Jewish. Accordingly, one does not read an "Old Testament," but the Hebrew scriptures, which do not privilege any one religious reading.

4. Brueggemann has much to say about the relation of the Hebrew Bible to the New Testament's usage. He frequently cites from the New Testament as offering an imaginative construal of an Old Testament parable or apocalyptic saying. However, the New Testament's use of the Old Testament does not rest on any textual basis derived from the Old Testament itself. Rather, the New Testament writers have consistently read back into the Old Testament a Christian interpretation. There is nothing in the Old Testament literature itself that can objectively claim to be Christian in any meaningful sense of the term. That is to say, the pattern of prophecy and fulfillment does not move from the Old Testament to the New, but only from the "fulfillment" in Christ backward to the Hebrew scriptures. Old Testament texts are only creatively construed to be related to the New Testament. Even the use of the category itself is a preemptive move. Similarly there is no *Heilsgeschichte* present in the sense that there are genuine elements of historical continuity or adumbrations of theological concepts later claimed by the church as central to Christian theology. For example, to find any notion of "vicarious suffering" would be inadmissible. There is no ontological connection linking the two testaments; Brueggemann repeatedly asserts that there is nothing besides Israel's speech that undergirds the Hebrew scriptures (*Theology of the Old Testament*, p. 723). Any overarching meta-history such as Paul's, or a trajectory of unfolding clarity in revelation (Heb. 1:1), is rejected as unwarranted and offensive.

III. Theological Implications
of a Postmodern Interpretation

1. With much sadness, I am forced to conclude that Walter Brueggemann's postmodern interpretation of the Old Testament offers a serious break with

the entire Christian exegetical tradition that I have sought to pursue from the earliest period to the present. The struggle to understand the book of Isaiah as *Christian* scripture is seen by him as largely misplaced, because the attempts to find substantive continuity between the Old and New Testaments, or to discover the Christian gospel prefigured in the Old, are rejected in principle at the outset.

2. Accordingly, the relation between the two testaments derives not from anything arising from the literal sense of the Old Testament, but stems from the imaginative construal of the New Testament communities. The biblical text serves to provide a potential for the endless generation of new meanings. There is no history of divine revelation within the Christian Bible, but the connection is one derived solely from the side of human creativity. The very questions that evoked a search for theological understanding of the relationship — namely, the figurative sense of the Church Fathers, the ontological substance of the Schoolmen, and that *Heilsgeschichte* of the modern period — are all deemed in principle an illusion. Rather, the Hebrew scriptures are largely a disjunctive corpus, often incomprehensible in themselves, requiring human ingenuity to project meaning. The literary corpus is, at best, a rhetorical deposit of imagery awaiting its rebirth, facilitated by the human spirit of Jewish and Christian interpreters.

3. The theological relationship between Jews and Christians is also deeply affected by the assumptions of postmodernism. A central issue that caused the break between Jews and Christians was the latter's claim that the Old Testament spoke of Jesus Christ. The great debate arose when Christians sought to appropriate the Jewish scriptures in support of their own confession. Obviously for Christians and Jews the identification of Jesus as the Christ remains today an enduring point of greatest disagreement. The conflict cannot be trivialized or sidetracked. It is simply theologically unacceptable for Christians to argue that the church's appeal to the Old Testament as a witness to Jesus Christ must be repudiated because of an offense caused to Jews (Brueggemann, *Isaiah,* vol. 2, p. 6; *Theology of the Old Testament,* pp. 733ff.). There is a genuine confessional disagreement here that must be respected.

However, this does not mean that there can be no further meaningful dialogue between Christians and Jews because of this theological disagreement regarding a crucial issue. The two faiths share much in common. The writers of the New Testament did not formulate a new doctrine of God, but accepted completely that Christians worship the one God of Abraham, Isaac, and Jacob. The New Testament identified fully with Judaism in its rejection of all forms of polytheism and paganism. Finally, in deep contrition, the Christian church has been forced to acknowledge that too often Christians who confess the name of Christ do not follow his call for love and reconciliation, whereas there are Jews who do not identify with Jesus Christ but strive to live lives that in fact reflect his demands for justice and righteousness toward the oppressed of the world.

4. Brueggemann's use of postmodern categories calls into question the Christian confession of a unified Word of God in an Old and New Testament that together constitute the Christian Bible. Central to this confession is the belief that the two testaments together reveal the true will of God for his people. The one redemptive purpose of God from the creation shaped the world's history toward its eschatological fulfillment according to God's sovereign power. To suggest that the Hebrew scriptures are a "neutral" source of imagery waiting to be construed at will by various pluralistic readings strikes at the heart of the Christian faith. In a word, the characterization of the Hebrew Bible as "generative" is an inadequate theological formulation of the Christian understanding of its scriptures.

5. According to traditional Christian theology, the Bible is God's means of "telling God's story." The main character is God, and thus its interpretation must be theocentric if it is to be faithful to the biblical text. Brueggemann's concept of imaginative construal serves to exacerbate the error of nineteenth-century theological liberalism in replacing this theocentric focus with an anthropocentric one. Recall his title *In Man We Trust: The Neglected Side of Biblical Faith* (Atlanta: John Knox, 1972). Human imagination, not the divine Spirit, is assigned the role of quickening the biblical text. In contrast, when the early church spoke of the coercion or pressure exerted by the biblical text on the reader, it was a formulation grounded on the conviction that the written Word possessed a voice constantly empowered by God's Spirit. *(Credo in Spiritum Sanctum.)* To confuse the divine Spirit with human imaginative creativity is to introduce a serious distortion into the entire theological discipline.

Selected Bibliography of Postmodern Interpretation

Adam, A. K. M. *What Is Postmodern Biblical Criticism?* Minneapolis: Fortress, 1995.
———. "Post-modern Biblical Interpretation." In *Dictionary of Biblical Interpretation*, vol. 2, edited by J. H. Hayes, pp. 305-9. Nashville: Abingdon, 1999.
———, ed. *Handbook of Postmodern Biblical Interpretation*. Saint Louis: Chalice Press, 2000.

Aichele, G. *The Postmodern Bible.* New Haven: Yale University Press, 1995.

————. *The Control of Biblical Meaning.* Harrisburg: Trinity Press, 2001.

Aichele, G., and G. A. Phillips, eds. *Intertextuality and the Bible.* Semeia 69. Atlanta: Scholars Press, 1995.

Barthes, R. *The Semiotic Challenge.* New York: Hill and Wang, 1988.

Brueggemann, W. *Theology of the Old Testament.* Minneapolis: Fortress, 1997.

————. *Isaiah* (Westminster Bible Companion). 2 vols. Louisville: Westminster John Knox, 1998.

Cahoone, L., ed. *From Modernism to Postmodernism.* 2nd ed. Oxford: Blackwell, 2003.

Caroll, R. B. "Poststructuralist Approaches: New Historicism and Postmodernism." In *The Cambridge Companion to Biblical Interpretation,* ed. J. Barton, pp. 50-67. Cambridge: Cambridge University Press, 1998.

Docherty, T., ed. *Postmodernism: A Reader.* New York and London: Harvester/ Wheatsheaf, 1993.

Exum, J. C., and D. J. A. Clines, eds. *The New Literary Criticism and the Hebrew Bible.* Valley Forge: Trinity Press, 1993.

Fish, S. *Is There a Text in This Class? The Authority of Interpretive Communities.* Cambridge: Harvard University Press, 1980.

Fowler, R. "Postmodern Biblical Criticism." *Forum* 5 (1989): 3-30.

————. *Let the Reader Understand.* Minneapolis: Fortress, 1991.

Ingraffia, B. D. *Postmodern Theory and Biblical Theology.* Cambridge: Cambridge University Press, 1995.

Jencks, C. *What Is Postmodernism?* 4th edition. London: Academic Editions, 1996.

Jobling, D., and S. Moore, eds. *Poststructuralism as Exegesis.* Semeia, 54. Missoula: Scholars Press, 1992.

Kristeva, J. *Revolution in Poetic Language.* New York: Columbia University Press, 1984.

————. *Language — The Unknown: An Initiation into Linguistics.* New York: Columbia University Press, 1989.

Levenson, J. D. "Is Brueggemann Really a Pluralist?" *Harvard Theological Review* 93 (2000): 265-94.

Lyotard, J.-F. *The Postmodern Condition: A Report on Knowledge.* Minneapolis: University of Minnesota Press, 1984.

McKenzie, S. L., and S. R. Haynes, eds. *To Each Its Own Meaning: An Introduction to Biblical Criticisms and Their Applications.* Rev. ed. Louisville: Westminster John Knox Press, 1999.

McKnight, E. V. *Postmodern Use of the Bible: The Emergence of Reader-Oriented Criticism.* Nashville: Abingdon, 1988.

Melugin, R. F. "On Reading Isaiah 53 as Christian Scripture." In *Jesus and the Suf-*

fering Servant, edited by W. H. Bellinger and W. M. Farmer, pp. 55-69. Harrisburg: Trinity Press, 1998.

Norris, C. *Deconstruction: Theory and Practice: New Accents.* New York: Methuen, 1982.

Steins, G. *Die "Bindung Isaaks" im Kanon (Gen 22). Grundlagen und Programm einer kanonisch-intertextuellen Lectüre.* Freiburg: Herder, 1999.

Stout, J. *The Flight from Authority: Religion, Morality, and the Quest for Autonomy.* Notre Dame: University of Notre Dame Press, 1981.

Tracy, D. *The Analogical Imagination: Christian Theology and the Culture of Pluralism.* New York: Crossroad, 1981.

Vanhoozer, K. *Is there a Meaning in This Text? The Bible, the Readers, and the Morality of Literary Knowledge.* Grand Rapids: Zondervan, 1998.

18

Hermeneutical Conclusions

I. The Goals of the Analysis Reviewed

The purpose of this study of the church's struggle to understand the book of Isaiah as Christian scripture is to address a number of crucial hermeneutical problems arising from my historical analysis. Can one speak meaningfully of a "family resemblance" in the church's exegetical traditions? What is the nature of this resemblance, and how can such a claim be sustained? It is my hope that from serious theological reflection on the history of interpretation we can draw some conclusions that will both illuminate the exegetical endeavors of the past and afford some aid regarding the hermeneutical challenges facing the interpreters of the Bible today.

At the outset, in the light of the enormous cultural and historical diversities that have emerged in every period of the church's life, it would seem easier to say where the agreement does *not* lie. There is no single creedal formulation on which a consensus can be found. No one philosophical or theological system extends throughout the ages. Although the formation of the Christian Bible shortly became a central focal point for all Christians, its completion emerged some centuries after the church's inception, and even its exact scope remains in flux.

Gerhard Ebeling once spoke of church history as the exposition of scripture (*Die Geschichtlichkeit,* p. 81). Indeed, a study of the history of interpretation does afford much promise in a search for larger patterns of theological coherence. The advantage of focusing one's analysis on a single, albeit crucial, biblical book lies in the hope that by restricting the scope of the investigation, the material being studied does not overwhelm the interpreter by its sheer mass. However, there are obvious dangers of misconstruing the larger subject matter because of this somewhat arbitrary limitation. I am also fully aware that the decision to focus on the hermeneutical issues of interpretation entails the omission of much relevant historical background material, which leaves one vulnerable to the criticism of the specialists.

Nevertheless, I have tried to show in my study that there are discernible characteristic features that constitute and identify a family resemblance within the Christian exegesis of the Old Testament. My initial task will be not only to describe these features, but to pursue the full range of both similarity and diversity within the ongoing struggle, often occurring in the context of bitter strife among fractured and contentious leaders, when theology and politics were frequently inseparable.

II. Characteristic Features of the Christian Exegetical Tradition

1. The Authority of Scripture

A basic characteristic of Christian exegesis has been its acknowledgement of the authority of scripture, but how this conviction is expressed and interpreted varies greatly. Widespread is the confession that God is the author of the Bible's Word. It contains the Word of truth calling for the "obedience of faith." Yet for long periods in the history of the church the authority of its scripture was simply assumed without the need for a defense. The authority of the sacred scriptures was inherited by the early church from the synagogue and in the later second century was extended also to the New Testament as the oral transmission of the gospel gradually received a written form.

In spite of the widespread, conventional formulae praising the scriptures as the source of divine revelation — Irenaeus and Origen were typical — one usually discerns the authoritative role of scripture when debating with adversaries. Justin and Trypho disagreed on how to interpret the oracles of Isaiah, but their dialogue was made possible and also serious because of a shared reverence for the inspired prophet. In contrast, Irenaeus became incensed with the Gnostics, who denigrated the sacred writings with mythological speculations. In the confrontation of early Christianity with Greek Hellenistic thought, there was occasionally an effort made by apologists like Clement to offer rational proofs of scripture's truth and antiquity, but ultimately this tack was undercut by the growing conviction that true comprehension of scripture depended on a "God-given grace to understand" (Justin).

In the early church biblical authority was manifested, above all, in its usage in shaping the life of the congregation through preaching, liturgy, and catechesis. One of the greatest contributions of Irenaeus was in his joining all parts of scripture into a single vision of both testaments as a unified and authoritative telling of the one story of salvation through Jesus Christ. He provided a framework within which the one divine plan of God unfolded in a progressive revelation from creation, to incarnation, and then to final redemption. The authority of Christ was thus demonstrated by God's summing up all things in himself.

The development of the Christian canon from the second to the fifth century was an attempt to safeguard the privileged status of sacred scripture by restricting its use in worship to a designated range of Old Testament and New Testament books. This process was evoked both by internal and external forces relating to the preservation of the truth of the apostolic gospel. The Gnostics emerged as a major threat to the faith already by the second century by rejecting the God of the Old Testament as the Father of Jesus Christ. Significantly, the fluid state of the Christian canon, especially respecting the tension between the narrow (Jewish) and larger (Greek) forms of the Old Testament corpus, did not play a decisive role in challenging the family resemblance of the Christian faith. Rather this tension, later formulated in terms of the Catholic versus Protestant Bible, surfaced in the post-Reformation period within the context of dogmatic controversies. Although it was obvious that increasingly during the Middle Ages the New Testament gained a major dominance over the Old within the Christian church, the debates over biblical interpretation did not in principle destroy the Old Testament's canonical status. The book of Hebrews provided a New Testament warrant for speaking of the "shadows" and provisionary status of the old covenant, but without denying its authoritative role as part of the one sacred story culminating in the divine revelation in Jesus Christ (Heb. 1:1). In sum, the two testaments were universally accepted as Christian scripture. In spite of the bitterness of the Reformation debates between Catholics and Protestants, the authority of scripture was not at issue, but rather the relation of biblical authority to subsequent church tradition.

Only in the period preceding and following the Enlightenment did the explosion of new scientific knowledge and the new critical analysis of the Bible, along with philosophical rationalism, begin to call into serious question the assumptions of its divine authority. Yet even at this stage of the church's history, the acceptance of its authority within the church was in general retained, even though its interpretation gradually was being altered and broadened. The Bible's prophetic role was reformulated within the academy; it shared with non-biblical sources common ethical ideals, moral direction, and values that both reason and human experience could also affirm.

The difficult question remains when defining biblical authority as a basic characteristic of the Christian exegetical tradition: Does this authority have any meaning outside the context of a worshipping community of faith, who await a fresh Word of God in shaping an obedient Christian life? In sum, the theological understanding of biblical authority as constitutive of a Christian family resemblance is not a static dogmatic "given" within the history of the church, but receives its true meaning within a specific context in which its message is proclaimed and received in the obedience of faith. When seen in the light of this confessional stance, the Bible's authority provides an essential and foundational feature of Christian exegesis. Thus, interpreters of Isaiah such as Theodoret could affirm that the prophet's meaning was at times hidden and obscure, yet its authority was never compromised or rendered inoperative by the working of the Spirit.

2. The Literal and Spiritual Senses of Scripture

Although the Jewish scriptures — later named the Old Testament — were from the inception of the church understood as divine and authoritative, these writings were always read and interpreted from the context of the Christian gospel. Rowan Greer speaks correctly of a "transformed Old Testament." One only has to reflect on the extent of the numerous quotations and paraphrases of the Old Testament in the New Testament to see the importance of the relationship. It had become such a reflex of Christian interpretation that when Grotius first proposed the need to interpret the Old Testament apart from the New, his exegesis was largely received with deepest suspicion. Even Calvin was attacked by some extreme Lutherans as being a "Judaizer" because of the emphasis he placed on reading the literal sense of the Old Testament. Actually this misconstrued attack failed to recognize the fundamental difference between Calvin and Grotius, since Calvin everywhere sought to hear the gospel in the Old Testament even when making no explicit reference to the New Testament.

I would further argue that a basic characteristic of Christian exegesis has been its recognition of both a literal and a spiritual dimension of scripture. Of course, the warrant for this hermeneutical decision was found in the New Testament itself (John 3:14; Matt. 16:4; 1 Cor. 9:9; Romans 3:31ff.; etc.), and could not be explained as a late Hellenistic intrusion. Andrew Louth (*Discerning*, pp. 96-131) is certainly correct in asserting that allegory, used in its broadest sense, is constitutive of Christian interpretation as a means of discerning the mystery of Christ. It is, therefore, a basic error to dismiss it as an escape hatch used to avoid difficulties within the text.

Yet at the same time during much of the church's history, enormous energy, reflection, and debate has gone into the effort to understand exactly the relation between the literal and the spiritual dimensions of the biblical text. Usually the extravagant development of the allegorical method within Christianity has been assigned to Origen, whose influence of course has been enormous. Nevertheless, as we have seen, the interpretation of Origen has undergone serious revision during the last decades, and the earlier attempts to describe allegory as a Gnostic innovation, basically alien to Christianity, have not been sustained. A more balanced way of understanding the hermeneutical issues involved emerged from an analysis of the historic tensions between the Alexandrian and Antiochene schools. The earlier misconstrual of the relationship, as if the Alexandrians were fanciful allegorists while the Antiochenes adumbrated modern historical criticism in stressing the historical context, has been replaced by careful study of both the similarities and differences regarding the issue of multiple textual meanings. Both schools fully agreed in recognizing both a literal and spiritual dimension, and both sought to develop subtle strategies by which to guide and control the interrelationship of the two. The great variation in the hermeneutical terminology — *theoria, allegoria, skopus, nous* — reflects the continuing struggle for exegetical precision. The Alexandrians were passionate in believing that the literal sense apart from the spiritual killed its meaning. However, the Antiochenes feared the biblical historical sequence could be lost in timeless symbolism. It is important to note that by the fifth century elements of the best from each exegetical tradition had been appropriated by Christian expositors (Jerome, Theodoret, Cyril).

The great strength of Irenaeus, in spite of certain ambiguities in his approach, was in providing a rule of faith *(regula fidei)* as a framework for Christian interpretation that emphasized the theological content of scripture. He did not impose a rigid dogmatic system on the biblical material; rather, he offered a holistic summary of the apostolic faith of the church from its beginning for preserving the truth of the faith according to a biblical order. It also served to test the rival claims of various new teachings being offered as Spirit-filled construals of the gospel.

The search to understand both the literal and spiritual levels of scripture received a fresh impetus from Thomas, who stressed the need for a literal interpretation *(ad litteram)* of the author's intention. Yet Thomas's actual exegesis of Isaiah continued to make homiletical use of traditional allegory in his commentary, a point rightly emphasized by Henri de Lubac. Among the Reformers, both Luther and Calvin directed much criticism against the traditional fourfold form of multiple meanings within scripture. Their attacks focused on the theological dangers that they perceived in the allegorical method. Luther argued with much force against the threat of blunting the power and clarity of God's Word by offering endless spiritual options. Calvin objected to seeing the literal and the spiritual senses pulled apart rather than in a single, straightforward meaning. Yet in actual practice, both Luther and Calvin were able to extend their interpretation of the literal/historical sense to apply existentially to the needs of contemporary congregations.

The great strength of the Reformers' interpretation was in recovering the living voice of God in the written Word that called forth a response from a people fully anchored in time and space. Particularly Calvin's understanding of the "plain sense" of the text allowed him to balance the restraints of the Bible's literal/historical sense with the theological contours of the Christian faith. Luther's appeal to a dialectical reading of the book of Isaiah moved between the letter and the spirit in a dynamic fashion and allowed him to hold in a fruitful theological tension the literal and spiritual dimension of the text. Both Reformers continued in different ways the earlier patristic concern that the interpreter strive to maintain the prophetic vision according to its proper *skopus*. In the debates between Luther and Erasmus regarding the interpretation of scripture, one can see an early adumbration of many of the hermeneutical issues that would explode in the Enlightenment's claim for the interpreter's rational autonomy in developing an allegedly objective reading independent of Christian tradition.

Perhaps the greatest challenge to the church was not the discovery that a myriad of other secular interpretive options were available for reading the Bible. Rather, it was the growing loss of confidence within the church itself as to whether it actually possessed in the Bible a sacred scripture given as a gracious gift of divine revelation to guide and instruct in the way of salvation.

3. Scripture's Two Testaments

An essential component shaping the family resemblance within the Christian exegetical tradition is the conviction that the Christian Bible consists of both an Old Testament and a New Testament. There are several important reasons for this scriptural terminology. The Christian scriptures bear a unified witness to one divine story that has a narrative sequence of a beginning and an end. Moreover, both testaments share an eschatological perspective pointing towards history's final *telos,* the reign of God. The sequence with the terminology is not just a historical one, but is grounded on a trinitarian theology that confesses the one triune God at work in the different divine economies:

preparation, old covenant, incarnation, new covenant, and consummation. The recently suggested substitution of the terminology of first and second testaments is therefore theologically inadequate (cf. Seitz, *Word Without End,* pp. 61-74).

The problem arises that, in spite of the universal assent within the Christian church to two testaments, the exact nature of the relationship between the two has never received one definitive interpretation. Indeed in the New Testament a variety of different theological strategies have been employed in joining the Old and the New.

One of the most persistent attempts to resolve the problem has been to subordinate the Old Testament to a peripheral role. Although the attempt of Marcion and his followers to remove the Old Testament from the Christian canon was rejected as heretical, the church's rendering of the Old Testament by means of allegory tended at times virtually to silence its voice. Even the characterization of the book of Isaiah as the fifth Gospel ran this same danger.

Another more fruitful attempt took its lead from the Apostle Paul's setting up a dialectical relation between law and gospel, or between letter and spirit. Luther applied this scheme effectively in his Isaiah commentary to break the traditional relegation of the Old Testament to law and the New Testament to gospel. Rather, he demonstrated how the Old Testament could also function according to the Spirit as gospel, whereas the New Testament could be rendered as mere letter and thus fail to grasp the evangelical Word.

Although Irenaeus had spoken of a form of progressive revelation, and Cocceius had struggled to describe the forward movement of God's activity in history, it was in the nineteenth century that the term *Heilsgeschichte* appeared as an attempt to relate the two testaments in an organic development moving toward its ultimate goal of messianic salvation of church and world. The heavy philosophical flavor of nineteenth-century German idealism seemed at first to aid in recovering a genuinely biblical theme, but it also led to a dangerous secularization when it was interpreted as a force within a human cultural process — a concept alien to both Old Testament prophets and New Testament evangelists.

A frequent move of the early Church Fathers, later developed with much skill by Calvin, was to distinguish the mode of God's revelation in the Old Testament while at the same time insisting that the substance of the revelation — that is, its content *(res)* — was the same. This move allowed Calvin in his Isaiah commentary to treat in great detail the historical and cultural *realia* of the text *ad litteram,* from which he was able to exploit his theological reflections to address the themes of God's justice, righteous rule, and mercy to a sinful people. Calvin's exegesis appeared to some of his critics as too restrained in his appeal to a Christological referent, yet a closer reading reveals how his trinitarian theology provided the grounds for his theological understanding of the God of Moses and the prophets. It also explains why Calvin did not need an additional level of allegory by which to render the text's spiritual meaning.

Perhaps the most frequently used scheme to relate the two testaments theologically was the approach of prophecy and fulfillment. Other slight variations of this pattern, often lumped together by the Church Fathers, were type and antitype, or shadow and light, which found their strongest support from the book of Hebrews. Already in Justin's dialogue with Trypho over the interpretation of Isaiah, the exact historical correspondence between prophecy and fulfillment became the major apologetic tool. However, the appeal to a philosophical theory of truth as external reference (cf. Hans Frei) introduced a high level of historical rationalism found, for example, in Vitringa, which soon called forth a more sophisticated interpretation of prophecy in terms of divine promise rather than demonstrable historicity grounded in a natural theology.

To summarize the argument so far: the insistence of the Christian exegetical tradition on taking the relation of the two testaments with utmost seriousness is a characteristic that sets it apart from alternative positions throughout its history. A variety of different theological strategies were pursued with varying success. However, the church continued to respond forcefully in repudiating as heresy the option of removing the Old Testament from the Christian canon, whether in the form proposed by the ancient Gnostics, the latter-day Marcionites of the nineteenth century (Harnack), or Hitler's National Socialist supporters. As a result, for most Christians the battle in defense of the Old Testament has been won, and no one will soon argue for eliminating the Old Testament as unworthy of the Christian faith. However, this theological victory does not mean that the church is not faced with another challenge to its understanding of the unity of the Christian Bible, which has recently emerged from the opposite direction of attack.

In the name of modern ecumenicity, both Rolf Rendtorff (*Canon and Theology*, pp. 31-45) and Walter Brueggemann (*Isaiah*, vol. 2, p. 6; *Theology of the Old Testament*, passim) have argued that the church should hear the voice of the Hebrew Bible on its own, independent of the New Testament. They see the traditional Christian attempt to understand the Hebrew Bible as the Old Testament — that is, as a preparation for the New Testament — not only as a distortion of the meaning of the Hebrew Bible, but also as an offense to Jewish readers. Brueggemann suggests that there is nothing intrinsically Christian about the Old Testament. Rather, the corpus of the Hebrew Bible consists of multiple images capable of generating a limitless number of new semantic constructs. The biblical imagery is completely neutral in form and content and can be rendered freely according to the imaginative capacity of Jewish, Christian, or religiously uncommitted secular interpreters. It thus follows that the New Testament's interpretation of the Old is in no sense normative; it is just another example of a creative imaginative construal. In his Isaiah commentary and Old Testament theology Brueggemann makes frequent reference to the New Testament writings, but he makes it fully clear that his interpretation derives from his own imaginative construal. He denies any claims of an organic link between the two testaments, whether in terms of a prophecy/fulfillment pattern, an appeal to a *Heilsgeschichte,* or, least of all, to a common ontological component. The Christian exegetical tradition of joining the Old and New Testaments within the unity of the Christian Bible rests on an unwarranted claim upon the Jewish scriptures and reflects largely the church's search for political power over its rival.

Rendtorff outlines in his essay what he considers some of the appropriate means by which to overcome the failure in traditional Christian exegesis. It is offered in an irenic tone as a first positive step forward. If there is to be an attempt at a common Jewish-Christian reading of the Hebrew Bible, it can only rest on the recognition that "the Hebrew Bible is the Holy Scriptures of the Jews," and that there is "an acceptance of the dignity and independent value of the Jewish religion" on its own terms, by its Christian partners (p. 40).

In response, I would first acknowledge that the issues raised by Brueggemann and Rendtorff are serious ones and not to be dismissed lightly. However, there are a host of troubling problems that must be addressed in these proposals. It is immediately apparent from Rendtorff's language that he has moved from the dimension of theological dialogue to one appropriate for a history-of-religions analysis. He speaks of "the dignity and independent value of the Jewish religion." In today's multicultural context, who could object to his appeal for respect and tolerance? But however worthy his sentiments are within a secular context, they do not address the crucial theological issues at stake.

Rendtorff's language and approach do not necessarily satisfy a conservative Jewish perspective. In his 1999 address "How Judaism Reads the Bible," Jacob Neusner directs his attack head-on against the widespread description of Jewish faith in the secular terminology of the academy as being an unacceptable compromise with liberal Protestant Christianity. Accordingly, Jews do not *read the Bible,* but affirm and practice Torah study. Judaism is a useless term for the synagogue because of its lack of serious content. It does not occur in any of the normative writings of the sages. Rather, the true recipients of Moses' commands are those people of God who accept his teachings in obedient response. In sum, although Neusner might possibly accept Rendtorff's proposal as a useful political strategy in some contexts, it does not begin to reach to the heart of the Jewish faith. It remains on the plane of an allegedly objective history-of-religions analysis, distant from the worship and practice of faithful Jews.

Furthermore, from a Christian perspective, to speak of interpreting the Old Testament apart from the New Testament in the absolute sense Rendtorff suggests strikes at the heart of the Christian faith's understanding of its Bible. As we have seen, such a suggestion has never been a serious option for the church. Even the name Jesus Christ reflects the indissoluble unity within the Christian confession.

Of course, as we have also seen, the church struggled hard and continues to struggle with the question of how to do justice to the relationship between the two canonical portions of its scripture. Throughout its history, serious Christian theologians have argued against "Christianizing" the Old Testament, by which is meant failing to hear the Old Testament's own voice and drowning out the message of its lawgivers, prophets, and sages. The very fact that the church received the Jewish scriptures without serious editorial revision testifies to their enduring role as the source of divine revelation in their own right. Clearly the Old Testament is not to be fused with the New, but they are also not to be separated.

Often the secular literary critic characterizes the New Testament's reading of the Old as the imposition of an alien message on an ancient religious text. Christian theology assesses it differently. Although there is a substantive distinction between promise and fulfillment and between the old and the new covenant, Christians see in the Old Testament a genuine continuity with the New, integral to its textual meaning, whether expressed in a pattern of sacred history or of an ontological unity undergirding the two testaments. To shift the analogy: in order properly to appreciate a musical symphony, it may help provisionally to isolate the individual instruments by focusing, say, only on the stringed instruments, but ultimately unless we hear the composition as a complete entity, we do not understand its true impact.

Although I sincerely share Rendtorff's passion for reconciliation between Jews and Christians by means of further study together of the Bible, I think that little serious progress can be made by pursuing a history-of-religions approach that remains often theologically sterile and largely uninteresting to both faithful Jews and Christians alike. The proposal for Jews and

Christians to engage in dialogue from a position established by a lowest common denominator can never be compatible with a serious and heart-searching encounter, even with the best of intentions.

4. The Divine and Human Authorship of Scripture

a. The Relation between the Two

The Christian church has always confessed that God was the author of scripture. God's is the voice addressing the people in divine speech (Exod. 20:1ff.; 34:1ff.). Yet at the same time human beings were designated as authors communicating the teachings of God: Moses, David, evangelists, and apostles. What then is the relationship between the divine and the human?

Clearly theologians of the church were already aware of the problem during the period of the Church Fathers. Jerome's great care in translating the biblical texts by employing all the tools of historical, literary, and philological analysis rested on his conviction that the Bible was the inspired vehicle of the divine mysteries. However, it was Thomas who first addressed the problem of the divine and human authorship of the Bible with the greatest clarity (*Summa* 1.1.10). God is the author of scripture, yet human authors are used as vehicles as the "instrumental cause." Thus for Thomas there was no great tension between the two. The literal sense is what the human authors intended in their writings, but because God, the ultimate author of scripture, comprehends everything all at once in his understanding, a multiplicity of senses can also be derived from the one divine intention.

By the time of Calvin, the urgency of the question of relating the divine and the human author had greatly intensified. Calvin's humanistic training made him fully aware of the interpreter's need to deal precisely with the author's literary style, his metaphorical imagery, and the grammatical characteristics of each Old Testament prophet. Yet Calvin's approach could baffle modern interpreters by his announcing at the same time that the scriptures contained no human reasoning, but were the oracles of God revealed by the Holy Spirit. Moreover, Calvin himself did not appear to sense any serious tension between the divine and the human, and when rejecting an interpretation he could assert that "the Holy Spirit has a different intention here." His use of a theory of accommodation also provided a rational hermeneutical transition from the divine to the human. It is therefore apparent that Calvin's view of the "plain sense" of the scriptures had a very different range and inner dynamic from the usual meaning assigned to the terminology of the literal sense.

Unfortunately, in the centuries following Calvin the coherence once reflected in Thomas and the Reformers began to fall apart. Under pressure from the English deists, orthodox apologists sought to defend the divine authorship of the Bible by developing new strategies for defending its inerrancy. However, these attempts were overwhelmed in the nineteenth century, when the debate shifted from rational evidences to human experience as the key to the discovery of biblical truths.

Still, it is highly significant to note that even after the historical-critical approach to scriptural interpretation had won the day in the modern period, vestiges of the church's distant memory were not fully lost. Much of the credit goes to the role of liturgy. The traditional call to the congregation, "hear the Word of the Lord," before a biblical passage was read continued to remind its listeners that words of a fully human author, often poorly read by a stumbling cleric, could nevertheless evoke a startling sense of the divine presence. Although many modern Christians had little understanding of the church's confession in the ancient creed of believing in the Holy Spirit, the experience of life-renewing power sustaining and quickening the believer often emerged in the hymns and liturgy as confirmation of scripture's divine author still actively at work.

b. The Unity of Scripture in Its Diverse Transmission

There is another important hermeneutical question of biblical interpretation related to the issue of the divine and human authorship of scripture. It arises from the theological assumption of the unity of the biblical message of the Old and New Testaments, each having its own integrity as a source of divine revelation. Nevertheless, as I sought to demonstrate in the first chapter regarding the earliest reception of the Hebrew Bible, the Christian church received the Jewish scriptures largely through Greek translations. Although there are many indications within the New Testament that knowledge of the Hebrew and Aramaic (targumic) traditions was often discernible, it is overwhelmingly the case that the New Testament has been indelibly shaped by the Septuagint. Moreover, it shortly became fully evident that the early church was not committed to the orthodox rabbinical dogma that sacred scripture required Hebrew as its authoritative form.

The hermeneutical problem arose when it was perceived by Origen, if not before, that the Hebrew text and the Greek Septuagint did not always agree. This assertion is not to suggest an intentional distortion, but arises from the nature of language itself. The linguistic filter provided by a translation can never exactly reproduce the original. Even when a translation strives for a literal rendering, the semantic nuances that always influence the sense of a passage can often differ. Added to this difficulty was the recognition that at times Hebrew passages were obscure due to textual corruption or grammatical enigmas, and thus called for a degree of speculation by the Greek translators. The problems inherent in the Septuagint were further exacerbated by the freedom used by the New Testament writers in interpreting the Old Testament, especially the Apostle Paul. It is now generally understood that Origen's major goal in providing a Hexapla was to equip Christians for debates with Jews by identifying the additions and omissions of the Greek translations in relation to the Hebrew. However, the larger hermeneutical problems of the New Testament's use of the Septuagint remained unresolved.

Over the succeeding years, various hermeneutical attempts have been offered by which to address the issue:

1. The early church resorted to allegory, and interpreted differences in the Greek translation from the Hebrew as the intended means of presenting a figurative meaning to the text (Jerome).

2. Or again, the tension was resolved with various forms of harmonization. Accordingly, the two testaments differed in verbal form, but not in substance. Or the New Testament's variations from the Old Testament arose from a fresh application of the biblical text while preserving the same general sense as the Old (Calvin).

3. Another option was in finding in the New Testament's interpretation of the Old a warrant for the hermeneutical theory that the Old Testament was authoritative for the Christian church only to the extent of its reinterpretation by the New (cf. H. Hübner: "Vetus Testamentum in novo receptum," not "Vetus Testamentum *per se*").

4. With the rise of the history-of-religions approach, the tension between the Masoretic text and the Septuagint was no longer addressed as a hermeneutical or theological problem. Rather, it was taken for granted that both texts were fully time-conditioned literary entities shaped by historical and cultural forces. The task of critical exegesis lay in determining the impact of the Jewish-Hellenistic milieu in the rendering by the New Testament writers of an inherited Hebrew legacy. The theological problem of the coherence or lack thereof between two authoritative canonical texts was no longer deemed significant, nor was it seriously addressed.

5. Finally, there have been recent postmodern attempts to respond to the largely negative effect of the historical-critical approach. Walter Brueggemann and Fredrick Holmgren have argued that the New Testament's freedom over against the Old Testament serves as a warrant for modern interpreters also to employ a similar form of creative imagination. The assumption is that

the New Testament provides a rhetorical strategy without any claims of finding substantive continuity. Thus, every new generation of interpreters has the challenge to follow the New Testament's example and to seek a new "Spirit-filled" reinterpretation of the Old Testament.

In response I would argue that because sacred scripture has always been conceived of in relation to its two parts, it is from this sense of canon that the church's theological reflection has been concerned with scripture's coherence. Indeed, its continuing attention to the hermeneutical problem reflects an important component of family resemblance within Christian exegesis. It is clear from the history of interpretation just how hard the church has struggled for a resolution. Often its attempts have been influenced by the changing nature of the challenge. By the time of the Reformation, the patristic appeal to allegory as a solution had become increasingly problematic. By the nineteenth century the harmonistic solutions of the Reformed and Anglican theologians were no longer regarded as adequate in the light of the new historical-critical challenges.

Although it would be unwise to suggest that the hermeneutical problem of scripture's diverse transmission has been resolved according to one particular strategy, at least it has become clearer that the heart of the issue derives from the church's continued commitment to the canonical coherence of scripture's twofold witness. Each of the two testaments retains its own integrity. Neither testament is subordinated in principle to the other, but each has its particular function within the one divine economy, such as prophecy and fulfillment. The Christian church awarded a privileged status to both the Old and New Testament, to the Old Testament prophets and to the New Testament evangelists. For this reason it is a fundamental theological error for postmodernists to seek an analogy between the New Testament's use of the Old Testament and a modern so-called "imaginative construal" of the Bible. We are neither prophets nor evangelists, but rather our witness is built upon theirs. The function of the Christian canon was to separate the apostolic witness from the ongoing tradition of the church, whose truth was continually in need of being tested by the apostolic faith. Certainly the church awaits the work of the Holy Spirit to quicken fresh understanding of the teachings of Christ, but the witness of the promised Counselor is joined to, and not independent of, that of the apostles (John 14:26; 15:26; 16:13-15).

The New Testament's witness to the gospel has been made by means of a transformed Old Testament. Each of the four evangelists has made his witness to Jesus Christ in different ways from the Old Testament. The exegetical task of seeking coherence between the testaments does not lie in "Christianizing" the Old Testament, that is, in substituting a New Testament understanding for the Old. Rather, on the assumption of the divine authority of both testaments, the church reflects theologically in a struggle for understanding, often amid tension. The church confesses that the criterion of truth for both the Old Testament and the New Testament is Jesus Christ, the divine reality that undergirds the joint witness of its scriptures. It is this reality of Jesus Christ that measures both testaments, and not the New Testament over against the Old. Moreover, the hermeneutical problem raised by the textual tension between the Hebrew and Greek is a powerful reminder of the time-conditionality of all of sacred scripture. In spite of the differing cultural contexts of the two testaments — ancient Near Eastern and Jewish Hellenistic — the church has received its scripture in human form as the vehicle for bearing truthful witness to the gospel. The New Testament used the witness of the Old Testament both to confess the continuity of the gospel with the Hebrew scriptures, and also to testify to the radical newness of the gospel that transformed the old covenant into a new covenant — a theology articulated often in the language of the Septuagint.

5. The Christological Content of the Christian Bible

Is there a determinate meaning within the biblical texts of the Christian Bible? Traditional Christian exegesis took it for granted that the biblical witness was directed toward a specific reference. Its testimony provided access to the mysteries of divine reality. At times the reality perceived was earthly, bound in time and space. At other times it was a transcendent reality related directly or indirectly to sense perception, but requiring divine inspiration for its full comprehension. Accordingly, scripture contains multiple meanings, but all joined in some manner to a referent. The derogatory dismissal of myths and fables in the New Testament (1 Tim. 1:4; 4:7; 2 Tim. 4:4; 2 Peter 1:16) was set in contrast to a proclamation based on what "we have heard, . . . seen with our eyes, . . . looked upon and touched with our hands" (1 John 1:1).

This traditional hermeneutical position underwent different kinds of attacks over the years. On the one hand, the historical-critical approach arising from the Enlightenment assumed in a variety of ways that the Bible had a determinate reference according to its literal/historical sense, which could be rationally determined if critically scrutinized by means of a proper interpretive method. During much of the nineteenth century, in spite of an assault on the church's traditional interpretations, many believed that the critic could overcome the distortions of historical events by critical acumen (e.g., Julius Wellhausen, F. C. Baur). The key was to be found in the search for the correct historical reference, in which endeavor allegory was rejected from the outset as pious mystification.

On the other hand, a powerful assault against the assumptions of the historical-critical method has recently been launched by postmodernists, who challenge the uncritical self-confidence of the historical modernists as ignoring their own time-conditionality. For postmodernists the search for literary meaning was now seen as an illusive process, and not related to an objective reference to be "excavated." Rather, meaning only emerged as an interaction between reader, text, and context. No meaning was absolute or fixed, but part of an ever-changing activity shaped by shifting cultural forces effecting both text and reader. These postmodernists frequently stressed the tendentious component of all readings, as they described interpretation as a struggle for power rather than truth.

In the light of these two hermeneutical options, the church finds its exegetical tradition challenged on two fronts. Christian theologians have argued that the biblical text must have a definite reference of meaning because their faith has rested upon an apostolic witness. Thus, Irenaeus objected to the Gnostic interpretation of the gospel, which bore no resemblance in its elaborate symbolism to the faith in Jesus Christ preserved in the church's collective historical memory. The subsequent struggle to define the scope of its scriptures during the next centuries was driven by several concerns. First, the function of establishing a canon was to preserve the truth of the apostolic witness upon which the faith was grounded. Second, the canon served to preserve the catholicity of the faith by establishing a parameter inside of which the church's theological diversity was acknowledged (John, Paul, Peter), yet outside of which heresy threatened. The implication of the privileged status of scripture was that its witness was not primarily formulated in terms of a single doctrinal formula, but rather as a prescribed circle designating the accepted range of confessions transmitted in the worship of historic Christian congregations (Jerusalem, Rome, Antioch, etc.).

Above all, the formation of the Christian canon was not initially a formal device by which to order the structure of the church, but a means by which to confess the Christological content of the entire Christian Bible. Its meaning was not in the form of a static deposit to be preserved in an archive; it was a gospel to be proclaimed and a text to be used. The ability of the scriptures continually to evoke new and fresh understandings was commensurate with the promised Spirit of the resurrected Christ to illuminate and guide the church through the Word. Scripture thus has a voice that exerts coercion on its readers. Indeed, a common characteristic of the Christian exegetical tradition through its long history has been the acknowledgement that faithful in-

314

terpretation involves a response to this theocentric force. Thus the challenge of "wrestling with Scripture" lies in the struggle to acquire the capacity to receive its message.

Within recent years a debate has arisen largely in reaction to a powerful new hermeneutical proposal of Walter Brueggemann. In his many books, not least in his Isaiah commentary and Old Testament theology, he has suggested that the crucial requirement of biblical interpretation lies in an "imaginative construal." Using the terminology of postmodernism, Brueggemann objects not only to the terminology of "coercion," but he judges the appeal to a rule of faith to be an unacceptable attempt to restrict and control the "unruly" quality of many parts of the Christian Bible. One of his persistent points when attacking an appeal to a rule of faith is that every interpretation involves an imaginative construal, and that there is no interpretive "given" within the biblical text. A text is a neutral, passive entity that must be rendered into a meaningful sense by the human endeavor of the interpreter (cf. "The Bible as Scripture," pp. 22-26).

My response to this position is as follows:

1. Brueggemann argues that every interpretation, by necessity, involves an imaginative construal. Therefore, the appeal to a rule of faith is just as much a construal as his postmodernist reading. In one sense, Brueggemann's point is correct. Literary interpretation always requires a human activity. Yet Brueggemann mounts his case in the language of a secular, history-of-religions analysis. In contrast, the appeal to a rule of faith rests on a theological argument and works from a very different context. One can best observe it as a recurrent theme throughout the history of Christian exegesis. For example, no one would deny that Calvin's exegesis was a highly sophisticated rational exercise of a disciplined, well-trained mind. Yet Calvin himself subordinated completely these characteristics of his exegesis when he was addressing the source of his interpretation. In this context he appealed fully to a theocentric force of the Holy Spirit at work in revealing the meaning of the biblical text in which human activity was a passive vehicle. Likewise, Augustine emphasized the role of prayer in seeking from God a correct disposition of the interpreter to perceive God's voice. Thus, the biblical text was never understood within traditional Christian theology as a neutral, inert object waiting for human initiative to receive a coherent meaning (cf. Christopher Seitz's brilliant analysis of the shift from theological confession to the philosophical categories of religion, *Figured Out*, pp. 13-33).

2. Brueggemann argues that a so-called canonical reading is misleading when it suggests that such a reading is a "given" in the text itself. His attack is built upon a widespread assumption of postmodern literary studies that

meaning is never a fixed property of a text, but a process of interpretation involving an interaction between text, reader, and context. The acquiring of meaning is therefore not a search for a stable given, but a fluid exchange within an ongoing activity. This postmodern hermeneutical hypothesis is not to be easily dismissed; indeed, it expresses much that is true. Certainly such a postmodern analysis was highly effective in undercutting the linguistic assumptions of much historical-critical exegesis. Yet once again, the analysis fails to understand either the language or the context of the theological argument for a rule of faith.

3. The appeal to a rule of faith rests on a conviction shared by the tradents of the biblical tradition, both Jewish and Christian, that the shaping of the biblical material was not as a haphazard collection, but was the product of theological reflection that the tradents ascribed to divine inspiration. The effect of this canonical shaping was that a framework was given — later called a rule of faith — within which the material was interpreted. For example, the Torah of Moses preceded the prophetic books, with the book of Deuteronomy functioning as Torah's conclusion. Likewise, the four Gospels have been bound together, each with a designated evangelist, but these witnesses are linked as belonging to the one gospel of Jesus Christ. In other words, the biblical material in its larger structure has been rendered in a particular fashion. Often this redaction has been termed "canonical," "kerygmatic," or "confessional." In contrast to an objective, history-of-religions perspective, it arises from a practiced and confessed stance of faith. In this sense, there is a semantic "given" designated by its role as sacred scripture. Thus, when Brueggemann in his Old Testament theology rearranges the Old Testament material into two conflicting interpretations of God's commands, testimony and counter-testimony, he is running against the grain of the canonical shaping and dismissing its given rule of faith.

4. There is another crucial distinction that has to be made between the overall canonical (confessional) shaping of the material and the exegetical task of relating the individual parts, which are often open to multiple meanings and interpretations. Biblical theologians frequently address this hermeneutical distinction between meaning as effected by the canonical shape and meaning as an ongoing exegetical endeavor. The former has an "objective meaning" provided by the larger theological structure, the latter a "subjective meaning" constitutive of the exegetical enterprise. For example, the canonical framework of the Gospels identifies the common genre of the evangelical writings as gospel, bearing testimony to Jesus Christ, but nowhere is an exact historical, literary, or theological relationship among the fourfold collection fixed canonically in its detail. This interpretive activity is assigned to the task

of exegesis, a wrestling with the text in order to hear the nuances of their witnesses. The canonical shape provides the larger framework of scripture — a rule of faith — within which the interpretive function of exegesis is guided. The canonical framework thus serves the interpreter as both positive and negative criteria in assessing those interpretations that fall outside the theological restraints provided for its faithful reading.

These hermeneutical distinctions can be illustrated from the history of interpretation of the book of Isaiah, whose basic canonical structure has long been recognized, even when frequently disregarded. The superscription assigns to the prophet a "vision," a revelation from God. The addressee is named: Judah and Jerusalem, and the timeframe spans the period from Uzziah to Hezekiah. There then follows the speech of YHWH. According to its final form, the Isaianic material has been rendered into a prophetic corpus. However, just what this entails must be discerned by close exegesis. The fact that the dating of Isaiah's prophetic role is concluded with the reign of Hezekiah has important hermeneutical implications for the interpretation of chapters 40–66. Regardless of the critical signs of post-Isaianic dating, the superscription functions canonically to date the historical setting of the prophecy of Isaiah to the pre-exilic period, and thus shapes the interpretation of the latter part of the corpus as well. Chapter 40 provides the link between the first and second parts: the Word of YHWH delivered to the prophet continues (40:8). However, what this linking of these sections means must be interpreted exegetically. Again, the context of chapters 40–55 identifies the servant of YHWH with Israel, but precisely how this identification is to be understood remains an exegetical problem. Throughout the reader is pressured by the canonical structure to reflect on the nature of this prophetic corpus. How is one to understand the designation of the authorship of this collection to Isaiah when the prophet himself does not ever appear after chapter 39? In sum, the canonical shaping of the prophetic corpus functions as a rule of faith, both negatively to exclude certain critical options, and positively to establish an authoritative context for the whole (cf. my commentary on Isaiah, 2001).

6. The Dialectical Nature of History

An intense interest in the nature of history has been an enduring characteristic of the Christian interpretation of the Bible from its inception. This evaluation is hardly surprising when one considers the central role of historical events in both biblical testaments.

I have chosen the term "dialectical" in its non-technical sense in order to describe some of the essential features of the Christian understanding of history. The term refers to distinctions made between various types of historical occurrences. Often a tension has been expressed between ordinary and divine events, between an inner and outer dimension, or between a confessional and secular perception. Even when these formulations remained somewhat imprecise according to modern standards, as for example in the case of Irenaeus, his understanding of an ordered historical process of unfolding public events that spanned both testaments, culminating in the incarnation, implied a special and unique divine purpose at work in the events of the world.

The warrant for this great attention to history evidenced already by the Church Fathers was provided by the Bible itself, especially the Old Testament. Not only were Israel's prophets attentive to the exact chronology of their history; most of the prophets included a lengthy section on the history of the nations as well. Moreover, it is crucial to observe how the two spheres of the earthly and the divine continually interact. The prophet Isaiah begins in chapter 6 with a visit to the temple of Jerusalem, but quite abruptly the imagery shifts to a heavenly temple and a divine monarch upon a throne with seraphic attendants. Or again, in chapter 18 the prophet first describes the political machinations between the Ethiopians and Judah's royal house before suddenly turning his view to God's quietly observing these human activities from above before intervening with his divine judgment. According to the prophet, God has a universal plan (14:26), mysterious yet fully rational, like a farmer's agricultural schedule, that will frustrate the arrogant pretensions of the Assyrians (19:5-12) and other tyrants.

In the early church and extending well up to the period of the Enlightenment, Christian theologians often attempted to describe the special quality of biblical history by an appeal to the supernatural. Yet the concept was not biblical and increasingly needed philosophical buttressing. In contrast, when the Bible spoke of the miraculous, it described surprising and unexpected activity of God, and often part of the natural world.

Among the Reformers Luther's use of a dialectical pattern between letter and spirit, and law and gospel, lent itself to his contrasting a prophetic sense of history with that of merely factual chronology. He sharply contrasted human efforts to control the course of history with the entrance of God's spiritual kingdom. The divine signs within history could both reveal and conceal, as in Isaiah 7. Still, Luther did not develop an elaborate form of *Heilsgeschichte,* but continued a straightforward and plain manner of interpretation that did not sacrifice the concrete quality of historical events through abstraction. In a sense, Luther remained thoroughly "pre-critical" in assuming a direct correspondence between historical events and the biblical account. Still, his sophisticated handling of biblical narrative served him well in preserving a powerful existential dimension to the divine intervention in the daily affairs of life. In contrast, Calvin did not appeal to a dialectical tension in his view of history. Rather, the one divine will gave meaning and direction to every event as the story of Israel and the church shared the same trajectory. Calvin's appeal to typology allowed him to see figurative patterns unfolding in the divine sequence of events. His application of a theology of divine accommodation served somewhat to modify the assumption of direct historical referentiality.

The debate over the nature of biblical history was greatly exacerbated by the Enlightenment. The newer critical approaches were already adumbrated in Grotius's exegesis, when he sought to identify the fulfillment of traditional messianic passages with various temporal events within the Jewish nation. The orthodox Lutheran response defended by Calov flatly rejected any fulfillment other than the Christological interpretations of the New Testament. However, by the time of Vitringa a compromise had been reached when he recognized as legitimate various partial fulfillments within Israel's national history, which were then later fully completed by an ultimate fulfillment in Christ. More significant in this period was the exegesis of Cocceius, who resisted his own student's solution. Cocceius sought to recover the radical eschatological nature of God's action in history. This was not an extension of human events; it was qualitatively different. Cocceius's approach was to interpret biblical prophecy largely in apocalyptic terms as a discontinuity between the old and new ages. In spite of his excesses, Cocceius did succeed in breaking the rigid hold of seventeenth-century Reformed orthodoxy, as he sought to recover an existential quality of history somewhat akin to that of Luther.

By the end of the eighteenth century a widespread historical rationalism within Britain and Europe had deracinated biblical history by assigning its events to rational, immanental causes. However, by the early nineteenth century the heirs of Deism were in full retreat before the powerful forces of Romanticism. Hegel and Schelling focused new attention on developing a philosophy of history as a dialectical process moving in stages toward an abstracted ideal of religion.

Within this larger context, a new and important formulation of history emerged with a concept of *Heilsgeschichte*. Its leading exponent was J. C. K. von Hofmann, who sought to establish a distinction between a history of divine action resulting in the salvation of the world and ordinary secular events into which the divine had entered. Hofmann was again fighting a battle on two fronts. On the one hand, his dynamic understanding of revelation not as isolated prophecies but as an entire organic historical process opposed

Hengstenberg's older, static view of prophecy. On the other hand, he fought against the idealistic abstraction of Hegel in trying to retain the concrete features of the biblical events that culminated in a historical incarnation. In retrospect, one can see the extent to which Hofmann's concept of *Heilsgeschichte* was unduly influenced by features of idealistic Hegelian philosophy.

Hofmann's organic, harmonious unfolding in a unified history of growth suffered a major setback when Wellhausen offered a critical reconstruction of the Old Testament's "real history" by means of source criticism, which radically reordered the historical sequence of Israel's religious development. Indeed, by the end of the nineteenth century the critical methodology of a history-of-religions approach to both Old and New Testaments seemed to have replaced the church's traditional theological concerns to distinguish, in some fashion, divine salvific events from the ordinary secular forces at work in human affairs. Yet once again by the turn of the twentieth century, the emergence of a new, more critical, and theologically profounder formulation of *Heilsgeschichte* in the works of Martin Kähler, Adolf Schlatter, and Gerhard von Rad demonstrated an enduring feature of a family resemblance within Christian exegetical tradition. God's unique action in history cannot be fused with empirical history, nor can it be separated. It is not an esoteric mystery accessible only to the initiated. Rather, within these parameters, the church struggles to discern the ways of God that are revealed to the faithful whose lives of worship and service bear testimony to the promised presence of God's Spirit in the realm of human affairs.

7. History and the Final Form of the Text

There is one final issue to discuss related to the subject of history. Much of the present confusion surrounding the debate over the so-called final, canonical form of the biblical text ultimately stems from the problem of history and its dialectical nature. In a recent monograph *(The Pentateuch in the Twentieth Century)*, Ernest Nicholson expresses his criticism of my emphasis on the final form of the canonical books by citing this sentence from von Rad's Genesis commentary: "For no stage in this work's long period of growth is really obsolete; something of each phase has been conserved and passed on as enduring until the Hexateuch attained its final form" (p. 27). Nicholson uses von Rad's understanding of compositional growth to contrast it with what he considers to be my understanding of biblical history: "Childs regards all stages prior to the final text as irrelevant. . . . To concentrate on the final stage is to foreshadow what was a long process of reflection, debate, and . . . controversy" (p. 267). In my opinion, this characterization of final form versus historical process rests on a basic misunderstanding of my position. Unfortunately this misconstrual, first articulated by James Barr (*Holy Scripture,* 1983), then picked up by John Barton (*Reading the Old Testament,* 1984), has now been continued by Nicholson, along with a host of others (cf. Julio Trebolle Barrera, *The Jewish Bible and the Christian Bible,* pp. 416-21).

The truth is that I agree with von Rad's position that no stage in the Old Testament's long history of growth is obsolete, and that something of each phase has been conserved until its final form. The confusion arises from a disagreement on the nature of the exegetical task being undertaken. It is one thing to attempt to understand the Old Testament as the sacred scriptures of the church. It is quite another to understand the study of the Bible in history-of-religions categories. Both tasks are legitimate, but they are different in goal and procedure. The hermeneutical issue at stake does not lie in an alleged contrast between historical process and scripture's final form. To understand the Bible as scripture means to reflect on the *witnesses* of the text transmitted through the testimony of the prophets and apostles. It involves an understanding of biblical history as the activity of God testified to in scripture. In contrast, a history-of-religions approach attempts to reconstruct a history according to the widely accepted categories of the Enlightenment, as a scientifically objective analysis according to the rules of critical research prescribed by common human experience.

Space is too limited in this project to pursue in detail the hermeneutical attempts to relate these two different approaches. I would only argue that the two approaches are different in goals, assumptions, and results. Yet the complexity is manifest in that the two are to be neither fused nor separated from each other. There is a subtle interrelationship that must be maintained. As we have seen in this study of Isaiah, the church has wrestled hard to understand the historical nature of its confessional stance toward its scriptures.

The confusion respecting the final form of the canonical text arises because of the failure to recognize that two different approaches to exegesis are involved that do not share a common understanding of history. To speak of the privileged state of the canonical form is not to disregard Israel's past history. However, it refuses to fuse the canonical process of the shaping of the *witness* of the prophets and apostles with an allegedly objective scientific reconstruction that uses a critical filter to eliminate those very features that constitute its witness, namely, the presence of God in the history of Israel and the church.

III. Summary of the Hermeneutical Conclusion

I have tried to identify those features of the Christian exegetical tradition that, in my judgment, constitute its family resemblance. The scope of my historical research has been by necessity highly selective by its concentration on the exegesis of the book of Isaiah under the overarching rubric of the church's struggle to understand Isaiah as Christian scripture. I have sought to identify some basic and constitutive features of this hermeneutical endeavor: the authority of scripture, its literal and spiritual senses, scripture's two testaments, its divine and human authorship, its Christological content, and the dialectical nature of history.

I have sought in this project of tracing the interpretation of one biblical book from a theological and hermeneutical perspective to demonstrate the nature of its coherence and diversity. In spite of radical historical and cultural discontinuities continually at work during the church's long history, I have mounted a case for seeing some basic features of enduring theological concerns shaping its exegesis. The conclusion I propose is that an investigation of this history of interpretation that focuses its analysis on the assumption that various cultural forces (historical, sociological, philosophical) are the controlling factors at work misconstrues the most central components of the church's theological reflections.

I have sought to show that the family resemblance does not lie in a single creedal formulation, or in a fixed formula for resolving such difficult issues as biblical authority, the multiple senses of scripture, and the Bible's Christological content. Rather, there has been almost from the beginning, both in oral and written form, an understanding of the parameters of acceptable Christian interpretation expressed in terms of a rule of faith. Increasingly the rule has functioned as a negative measure in challenging theological positions that appear to fall outside the boundaries established by the apostolic tradition. Yet even here, the application of such restraints often necessitated a long process of assembling a consensus, and of confession and repentance for prior failures in its witness to both church and world.

One often hears that there are no rules for interpreting the Bible, that each interpreter offers his or her own imaginative construal. One of the conclusions of this study is that there has always been a family resemblance within the church in regard to understanding its sacred scripture. Of course there have been long periods of deep disagreement and bitter strife. Yet the power of the scriptures continued to break open new vistas in times of greatest cultural flux. There is a continuing need for flexibility and generosity of spirit. Yet there are theological parameters preserving the church that are continually being shaped by the Spirit's quickening in the understanding of its scriptures toward a faithful witness to Jesus Christ. By reviewing the history of the church's biblical interpretation, we can derive new confidence in confessing with the creed: I believe in the one holy catholic and apostolic church.

Bibliography of Hermeneutical Conclusions

Barrera, J. Trebolle. *The Jewish Bible and the Christian Bible.* Leiden: Brill, 1998.

Barton, J. "Canon and Meaning." In *The Spirit and the Letter,* pp. 131-56. London: SPCK, 1997.

Blowers, P. M. "The *Regula Fidei* and the Character of Early Christian Faith." *Pro Ecclesia* 6 (1997): 199-228.

Brueggemann, W. *Theology of the Old Testament: Testimony, Dispute, Advocacy.* Minneapolis: Augsburg Fortress, 1997.

———. *Isaiah* (Westminster Bible Companion). 2 vols. Louisville: Westminster/ John Knox, 1998.

———. "The Bible as Scripture: Canon Fire." *The Christian Century,* vol. 118, no. 33 (December 5, 2001), pp. 22-26.

Childs, B. S. *Isaiah.* Louisville: Westminster/John Knox, 2001.

Ebeling, G. *Die Geschichtlichkeit der Kirche.* Tübingen: Mohr Siebeck, 1954.

Felber, S. *Wilhelm Vischer als Ausleger der Heiligen schrift.* Göttingen: Vandenhoeck & Ruprecht, 1999.

Frei, H. *The Eclipse of Biblical Narrative.* New Haven: Yale University Press, 1974.

Holmgren, F. C. *The Old Testament and the Significance of Jesus.* Grand Rapids: Eerdmans, 1999.

Hübner, H. "Vetus Testamentum und Vetus Testamentum in Novo receptum: Die Frage nach dem Kanon des Alter Testaments aus neutestamentlicher Sicht." *Jahrbuch für biblische Theologie* 3 (1998): 147-62.

Kähler, M. *The So-called Historical Jesus and the Historic Biblical Christ of Faith.* Philadelphia: Fortress, 1964.

Kugel, J. L., and R. A. Greer. *Early Biblical Interpretation,* pp. 126-54. Philadelphia: Westminster, 1986.

Louth, A. *Discerning the Mystery,* pp. 96-131. Oxford: Clarendon, 1983.

Lubac, H. de. *Scripture in the Tradition.* New York: Crossroad, 2000.

Minear, Paul S. *The Bible and the Historian.* Nashville: Abingdon, 2003.

Neusner, J. *How Judaism Reads the Bible.* Baltimore: Chizuk Amuno Congregation, 1999.

Nicholson, E. *The Pentateuch in the Twentieth Century.* Oxford: Oxford University Press, 1998.

Rad, G. von. *Theology of the Old Testament.* 2 vols. New York: Harper & Row, 1962.

Rendtorff, R. "Toward a Common Jewish-Christian Reading of the Hebrew Bible." In *Canon and Theology*, pp. 31-45. Philadelphia: Fortress, 1993.

Seitz, C. *Word without End: The Old Testament as Abiding Theological Witness.* Grand Rapids: Eerdmans, 1998.

————. *Figured Out: Typology and Providence in Christian Scripture.* Louisville: Westminster John Knox, 2001.

Williamson, P. S. *Catholic Principles for Interpreting Scripture: A Study of the Pontifical Biblical Commission. The Interpretation of the Bible in the Church.* Rome: Pontifical Biblical Institute, 2001.

Yeago, D. S. "The Spirit, the Church, and the Scriptures: Biblical Inspiration and Interpretation Revisited." In *Knowing the Triune God: The Work of the Spirit in the Practice of the Church,* edited by James J. Buckley and D. S. Yeago, pp. 49-93. Grand Rapids: Eerdmans, 2001.

Index of Authors

Abarbanel, 241, 252
Abel, F. M., 96, 102, 120, 128
Adam, A. K. M., 291, 296
Aichele, G., 291, 297
Albertz, R., 27
Alexander, J. A., 266-68, 281, 288
Ambrose, Saint, 182
Antin, P., 102
Appold, K. G., 261
Aquinas, Saint Thomas, 148-66, 303
Arnold, Matthew, 283
Ashby, G. W., 145, 146
Attridge, H., 88
Augustine, Saint, 19-20, 94, 101, 144, 182
Aune, D. E., 43
Auvray, P., 102

Bachmann, J., 288
Baker, D. L., 24
Baker, J. A., 72
Bammel, C. P. H., 72
Bardenhewer, O., 128
Bardy, G., 43, 72, 103, 108, 128, 134, 146
Barnabas, Saint, 48, 87
Barnard, L. W., 43
Barnes, T. D., 75, 88
Barr, James, 65-66, 73, 321
Barrera, J. Trebolle, 21, 30, 321, 323
Barrett, C. K., 24, 28
Barth, Karl, 208, 227

Barthélemy, D., 21
Barton, John, 321, 323
Battles, F. L., 214, 227
Bauer, K., 204
Bauer, Walter, 12
Baur, C., 109
Baur, F. C., 313
Bayer, O., 204
Beale, D. H., 24, 30
Bellinger, W. H., 30
Bengel, J. A., 262
Benoit, A., 54
Berger, S., 228
Bernard, Saint, 182
Beutel, A., 204
Bigg, C., 73
Bizer, E., 204, 262
Blanchard, Y.-M., 54
Blowers, P. M., 323
Bluhm, H., 204
Bock, D. L., 27
Bohatec, J., 228
Bokser, B. Z., 43
Bornkamm, H., 181, 204
Bouthillier, D., 164
Bouwsma, W. J., 228
Braveman, J., 103
Breen, Q., 228
Brooke, A. E., 1, 21
Brooke, G. J., 21

Index of Subjects

P